Memory and Emotion

(don't forget)

New Perspectives in Cognitive Psychology

New Perspectives in Cognitive Psychology is a series of works that explore the latest research, current issues, and hot topics in cognitive psychology. With a balance of research, applications, and theoretical interpretations, each book will educate and ignite research and ideas on important topics.

Memory and Emotion: Interdisciplinary Perspectives
Edited by Bob Uttl, Nobuo Ohta, and Amy L. Siegenthaler

Involuntary Memory: New Perspectives in Memory Research
Edited by John Mace

MEMORY
AND EMOTION
INTERDISCIPLINARY PERSPECTIVES

EDITED BY **Bob Uttl, Nobuo Ohta, and Amy L. Siegenthaler**

Blackwell
Publishing

© 2006 by Blackwell Publishing Ltd

BLACKWELL PUBLISHING
350 Main Street, Malden, MA 02148-5020, USA
9600 Garsington Road, Oxford OX4 2DQ, UK
550 Swanston Street, Carlton, Victoria 3053, Australia

The right of Bob Uttl, Nobuo Ohta, and Amy L. Siegenthaler to be identified as the Authors of the Editorial Material in this Work has been asserted in accordance with the UK Copyright, Designs, and Patents Act 1988.

First published 2006 by Blackwell Publishing Ltd

1   2006

Library of Congress Cataloging-in-Publication Data

Memory and emotion : interdisciplinary perspectives / edited by Bob Uttl, Nobuo Ohta, and Amy L. Siegenthaler.
    p. cm. – (New perspectives in cognitive psychology)
    Includes bibliographical references and indexes.
    ISBN-13: 978-1-4051-3981-6 (hardcover : alk. paper)
    ISBN-10: 1-4051-3981-1 (hardcover : alk. paper)
    ISBN-13: 978-1-4051-3982-3 (pbk. : alk. paper)
    ISBN-10: 1-4051-3982-X (pbk. : alk. paper)   1. Memory.   2. Emotions.
3. Memory–Physiological aspects.   4. Emotions–Physiological aspects.
5. Psychology, Pathological.   I. Uttl, Bob.   II. Ohta, Nobuo.
III. Siegenthaler, Amy L.   IV. Series.

    BF371.M4478 2006
    153.1′2–dc22

                                                              2005032608

A catalogue record for this title is available from the British Library.

Set in 10/12.5pt Baskerville
by Graphicraft Limited, Hong Kong
Printed and bound in Singapore
by COS Printers Pte Ltd

The publisher's policy is to use permanent paper from mills that operate a sustainable forestry policy, and which has been manufactured from pulp processed using acid-free and elementary chlorine-free practices. Furthermore, the publisher ensures that the text paper and cover board used have met acceptable environmental accreditation standards.

For further information on
Blackwell Publishing, visit our website:
www.blackwellpublishing.com

CONTENTS

FIGURES

CONTRIBUTORS

Roberto Cabeza is Associate Professor in Psychological and Brain Sciences at Duke University, where he is core faculty at the Center for Cognitive Neuroscience and senior fellow at the Center for the Study of Aging and Human Development. He co-edited the *Handbook of Functional Neuroimaging of Cognition* (2001), the *Special Issue of Functional Neuroimaging of Memory* (2003), and the book *Cognitive Neuroscience of Aging* (2004). In 2003 he was awarded the Young Investigator Award of the Cognitive Neuroscience Society. Dr. Cabeza investigates the neural correlates of memory in young and older adults using functional neuroimaging techniques, such as functional MRI.

Sven Å. Christianson is Professor of Psychology at Stockholm University. He edited the *Handbook of Emotion and Memory* (1992) and is the author/co-author of several books regarding crime, trauma, and memory, including *Traumatic Memories* (2002) and *Crime and Memory* (1996). The objectives of his current research program are to gain an understanding of the relationship between emotion and memory, with a current research focus on victims', bystander witnesses', and offenders' memories of violent and sexual crimes.

Florin Dolcos is a Post-Doctoral Fellow at Duke University's Brain Imaging and Analysis Center. He recently finished his PhD studies and is interested in the neural correlates of affective-cognitive interactions. His research interests include the neural mechanisms underlying the beneficial effect of emotion on episodic memory in young, healthy participants, the elderly, and clinical populations (e.g., depressed patients), as well as the neural mechanisms underlying the detrimental effect of emotion on cognitive functions, with an emphasis on working memory.

Elisabeth Engelberg is a researcher at the Stockholm School of Economics. She is involved in research in the investigation and development of performance-based measures of emotional intelligence in relation to psychological theory that pertains to work environment, attitude to money, and other economic beliefs; she is also interested in the application of theories of emotion and communication in explaining visually mediated risk perception.

Gail S. Goodman is Professor of Psychology at the University of California, Davis, and Professor of Forensic Psychology at the University of Oslo. She has won numerous awards for her research and writing, including the 2005 American Psychological Association Award for Distinguished Contributions to Research on Public Policy. She has also served as President of two Divisions (American Psychology-Law Society; Child, Youth, and Family Services) and one Section (Section on Child Maltreatment) of the American Psychological Association. Her research concerns trauma and memory, memory development, and child maltreatment.

Peter Graf is Professor of Psychology at the University of British Columbia in Vancouver. He served as an associate editor for *Memory and Cognition*, and has co-edited *Implicit Memory: New Directions in Cognition, Development, and Neuropsychology* (1993) and *Lifespan Development of Human Memory* (2002). His research focuses on episodic retrospective and prospective memory, its development across the adult lifespan, and its breakdown in dementia and other disorders.

John F. Kihlstrom is Professor of Psychology at the University of California, Berkeley, where he is also a member of both the Institute of Cognitive and Brain Sciences and the Institute of Personality and Social Research. Perhaps best known for his hypnosis research, his 1987 *Science* paper on "The Cognitive Unconscious" helped spark renewed interest in unconscious mental life. Dr. Kihlstrom has recently begun a new project on the Human Ecology of Memory (www.socrates.berkeley.edu/~kihlstrm/mnemosyne.htm), intended to employ memory as a theme to link cognitive and social psychology, and psychology with the other social sciences, the arts, and the humanities.

Asher Koriat is Professor of Psychology at the University of Haifa. He is head of the Institute of Information Processing and Decision Making (IIPDM), University of Haifa, and Director of the Max Wertheimer Minerva Center for Cognitive Processes and Human Performance (University of Haifa and Technion-Israel Institute of Technology). His research concerns memory and metamemory; specifically, the processes underlying metacognitive monitoring and metacognitive control during learning and remembering, memory accuracy and distortion, information organization and transformation, and memory for action.

Kevin S. LaBar is Assistant Professor of Psychological and Brain Sciences at Duke University. He is also core faculty in the Center for Cognitive Neuroscience and holds an appointment in Psychiatry and Behavioral

Science. He investigates emotional influences on memory and attention using functional brain imaging, psychophysiology, and patient-based research. He serves as Consulting Editor for *Behavioral Neuroscience*. Dr. LaBar has received Young Investigator Awards from the Cognitive Neuroscience Society, Oak Ridge Associated Universities, the National Science Foundation, and the National Alliance for Research on Schizophrenia and Depression.

Linda J. Levine is Associate Professor in the Department of Psychology and Social Behavior at the University of California, Irvine. Her research examines the cognitive processes that lead to the experience of specific emotions such as happiness, sadness, anger, and fear; the effects of these emotions on subsequent reasoning and memory; sources of bias in memory for past emotions; and the relations between children's cognitive and emotional development.

Mara Mather is Associate Professor of Psychology at the University of California, Santa Cruz. She is on the editorial boards of *Psychology and Aging* and the *Journal of Gerontology: Psychological Science*. Her research investigates emotional memory and aging, focusing on how changes in emotional goals and executive function influence emotional memory across the adult lifespan.

Andrew Mathews is a Senior Scientist at the Medical Research Council's Cognition and Brain Sciences Unit in Cambridge, and Visiting Professor at the Institute of Psychiatry, University of London. He was previously Associate Editor of the journal *Cognition and Emotion*, and has co-authored five books, including *Cognitive Psychology and Emotional Disorders* (2nd edition, 1997). He received the British Psychological Society's President's Award in 1993, and a Distinguished Scientist Award by the American Psychological Association in 1995. His research has focused on the experimental study of the interaction between cognitive and emotional processes, and the role of selective cognitive processing biases in the genesis and maintenance of emotional disorders.

Nobuo Ohta is Professor of Psychology at Tokyo University of Social Welfare. He is President of the Japanese Society for Cognitive Psychology, and convener of the Tsukuba International Conference on Memory. He is co-editor of several books, including *Lifespan Development of Human Memory* (2002) and *Dynamic Cognitive Processes* (2005). His research interests are in the areas of memory, cognition, and learning, especially in implicit memory. Topics of his ongoing work include lifespan memory development, false memory, and hypermnesia.

Pedro M. Paz-Alonso received his PhD from the Department of Psychology at the University of the Basque Country in Spain. He is currently a postdoctoral fellow at the University of California, Davis. His research has focused on emotion and eyewitness memory in children and adults. His publications include a chapter in the upcoming *Handbook of Forensic Psychology*.

David A. Pizarro is Assistant Professor of Psychology at Cornell University. His research concerns how emotions influence judgment; moral reasoning and moral intuition; and what factors influence how we attribute moral responsibility to the actions of others.

Daniel Reisberg is Professor of Psychology at Reed College in Portland, Oregon. He is the co-editor (with Paula Hertel) of *Memory and Emotion* (2004) and the author of several other books, including *Cognition: Exploring the Science of the Mind* (2001). He is on the editorial boards of several journals, including *Psychological Science* and *Applied Cognitive Psychology*, and recently finished his term as Associate Editor of *Psychological Bulletin*. His research (with Friderike Heuer) has examined how people remember emotional events, and also how emotional memories can shape (and sometimes distort) eyewitness recollection.

Amy L. Siegenthaler is a Japan Society for Promotion of Science (JSPS) Post-Doctoral Fellow at Tokyo University of Social Welfare. She received her PhD from the University of Toronto. Her research interests are based in cognitive and clinical neuropsychology, with current emphases on the priming and perception of faces and objects, and changes in cognitive processes with age.

Jefferson A. Singer is Professor of Psychology at Connecticut College. He is the author of *In Defense of the Person: Foundations of a Person-based Psychology and Psychotherapy* (2005), as well as *The Remembered Self: Emotion and Memory in Personality* (1993, with Peter Salovey) and *Message in a Bottle: Stories of Men and Addiction* (1997). He is an Associate Editor of the *Journal of Personality* and was a 2003 recipient of a Fulbright Distinguished Scholar Award, which sponsored his research on autobiographical memory with Martin Conway at Durham University. The objective of his current research program is to explore the role of self-defining memories and narrative identity in personality and psychotherapy.

Bob Uttl is Center of Excellence Professor at the Brain Science Research Center, Tamagawa University, Tokyo. He served as co-editor of *Dynamic Cognitive Processes* with Nobuo Ohta and Colin M. MacLeod (2005). His research interests are broadly focused on cognition and cognitive aging. Topics of current and recent work include the relation between perception, processing resources, and memory; changes in perception, processing resources, memory, and intelligence due to normal and pathological aging; and measurement and research methods in psychology.

PREFACE

This volume was inspired by discussions at the Sixth Tsukuba International Conference on Memory held in March 2005 in Tsukuba, Japan. The theme of the conference was *Memory and Emotion* and we were fortunate to attract a stellar line-up of international experts in this field from a variety of disciplines, including cognition, neuroimaging, aging, and psychopathology.

This relatively new field is currently one of the fastest-growing areas of research in psychology and related disciplines. This book includes original articles that cover cutting-edge research in memory and emotion, providing the reader with what is up and coming with respect to research findings, methodological techniques, and theoretical advances. Many of the current "hot" topics in the field are covered, including the effects of stress, arousal, anxiety, and depression on memory; the influence of discrete emotions on memory; dissociative amnesia and post-traumatic stress disorder; false, recovered, and traumatic memories; flashbulb memories; the use of emotional memories in therapy; the influence of emotion on autobiographical memory; emotion–memory interactions across the adult lifespan; as well as the neural correlates of these and other phenomena. The field is ripe for expansion and we hope that many new, as well as current, researchers will be inspired by the ideas in this book to conduct studies paving the way for the next great theories and advances.

We are deeply grateful to the contributors to this book for their hard work in writing timely original chapters that reflect the current and upcoming thinking on emotion and memory. Further, we appreciate having had the opportunity to explore and expand upon ideas presented at the Sixth Tsukuba International Conference on Memory and thank the Japan Society for the Promotion of Science, the University of Tsukuba, the Tsukuba International Congress Center, and all attendees and staff for their contributions toward making the conference a tremendous success. Lastly, we thank Blackwell Publishing for publishing this book.

Bob Uttl
Nobuo Ohta
Amy L. Siegenthaler

Memory and Emotion from Interdisciplinary Perspectives

Bob Uttl, Amy L. Siegenthaler, and Nobuo Ohta

Abstract

Links between emotion and memory have been recognized since the late 1800s; in the past two decades, however, interest has grown at an exponential rate. In this chapter, we identify some of the possible factors responsible for this rapid increase in interest, and provide an introductory overview of the chapters in this book. The chapters are grouped into three general themes: cognition, neuroscience and aging, and psychopathology. The sections complement each other well and we highlight some of the common themes weaving through them.

An impression may be so exciting emotionally as almost to leave a scar upon the cerebral tissues.

William James (1890, p. 670)

▉ MEMORY AND EMOTION

Why memory and emotion? The view that emotion and memory interact was adopted by some of the earliest writers in psychology. While James (1890) seems to argue that emotions tend to make experiences so memorable as "to leave a scar upon the cerebral tissues," Janet (1889) argued that traumatic experiences interfere with the formation of memory, while Freud (1915) suggested that strong unpleasant emotions might be actively suppressed and inaccessible to consciousness. Despite these early claims about the impact of emotion on memory, the radical behaviorism movement delegated emotion to the fringe of scientific inquiry and a number of prominent writers argued that emotion was an unnecessary concept (Lazarus, 1991a). Meyer (1933, quoted in Lazarus, 1991a) predicted:

> Why introduce into science an unneeded term, such as emotion, when there are already scientific terms for everything we have to describe? . . . I predict: the

"will" has virtually passed out of our scientific psychology today; the "emotion" is bound to do the same. In 1950 American psychologists will smile at both these terms as curiosities of the past. (p. 300)

Although anyone who today refers to *American Psychologist* (the journal rather than the person) realizes that, far from passing out of our vocabulary, emotion has increasingly become one of the most discussed and debated topics in contemporary psychology (for some sample commentaries, see Bower, 1981; Davidson, 2000; Frijda, 1988; Lang, 1995; Lazarus, 1981, 1984, 1991b; Reisenzein & Schonpflug, 1992; Staats, 1988; Zajonc, 1981, 1984; Zuk, 1994; though this is by no means an exhaustive list).

To determine just how prevalent the topics of emotion and memory have become in modern psychology, we conducted a "scientific inquiry" by performing keyword searches in the PSYCInfo database to see how many articles have focused on emotion within the past four decades, relative to articles that have focused on the venerable and uncontroversial area of memory, and more importantly, we examined the extent to which researchers became interested in the interactions between emotion and memory. The results of our search can be seen in Figure 1.1. For each year from 1970 to 2004, we searched for (1) articles containing the keyword "emotion" and its derivatives such as "emotional" (using "emotion*" as a keyword); (2) articles containing the keyword "memory"; and (3) articles containing both of these keywords ("emotion" and "memory"). To facilitate comparisons among the trends, we standardized the number of articles to a common starting point by dividing the number of articles containing "memory" by 22 and by dividing the number of articles containing "emotion*" by 40. It is clear that the interest in emotion has not been waning at all; indeed, in 1970, articles on emotion outnumbered articles on memory almost two to one (1,200 versus 700). More importantly, however, the number of articles concerned with the topics of both emotion and memory has been increasing at an exponential rate from about the mid-1980s, and much faster than the number of research articles concerned with either topic alone. While one may argue that our keyword search is not comprehensive, insofar as it did not search for alternative keywords such as "learning" or "depression", even this rather basic measure allows us to conclude that emotion and emotion and memory as objects of scientific inquiry are well with us, and contrary to Meyer's prediction, there is no indication that interest in this topic is about to disappear any time soon.

What could account for this increasing interest in the interactions between memory and emotions? We identified several trends that may have been contributing factors. First, the radical behaviorism movement was replaced by the cognitive revolution emphasizing the influence of thought on behavior (Neisser,

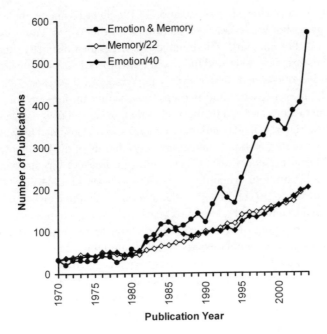

Figure 1.1 Number of articles pertaining to emotion, memory, and emotion and memory by year of publication, as revealed by a keyword search of the PSYCInfo database. The number of articles is standardized to a common starting point by dividing the number of articles containing the keyword "memory" by 22 and by dividing the number of articles containing "emotion" by 40.

1967). Whereas early information processing models of cognition, frequently called box models, were rigid, static, and mechanistic, the newer class of models were flexible, emphasizing how information was processed, rather than how information moved from box to box (e.g., the levels of processing framework; Craik & Lockhart, 1972). Two more theoretical developments – the encoding specificity principle (Tulving & Thomson, 1973) and the idea of transfer appropriate processing (Morris, Bransford, & Franks, 1977) – emphasized context effects on memory and strengthened the notion that memory is dependent on the degree of overlap between study and test processing. From here, it was only a small step to the idea that mood could influence both the encoding and retrieval of information (e.g., Bower, 1981, 1992; Eich, 1980, 1989).

Second, in 1977, Brown and Kulik published their seminal paper on "flash-bulb memory," a term referring to the almost iconic memory that results after experiencing or hearing about a surprising, important, and emotionally arousing event (such as the assassination of President Kennedy, the explosion of the space shuttle *Challenger*, or the attack on the World Trade Center in New York). The hallmark of flashbulb memories is their distinctive and highly detailed nature; they were said to be well remembered and accurate, but later research has questioned these claims (e.g., Winograd & Neisser, 1992).

Third, an even greater and perhaps most significant impetus for research on the interactions between memory and emotion came a few years later when the United States, Canada, and other countries were consumed by widespread accusations of satanic ritual child abuse cases. In one of the best known cases, the McMartin Preschool case, Peggy McMartin Buckey, Virginia McMartin, Ray Buckey, and four school teachers were indicted in 1984 on 208 counts of abuse involving 40 children (Ramsland, n.d.). In all, this case was the longest US criminal trial in history, lasting six years and costing $16 million, yet resulting in no convictions. The entire case was built on the witness testimony of children, who never spontaneously recalled any abuse, but who were led to believe that they had been abused by repeated suggestive questioning in the hands of counselors, interrogators, and examiners. The widespread media attention and mass hysteria that followed sparked copycat cases across the United States and Canada and hundreds of innocent people were accused and some convicted of child abuse.

The outrageous abuse allegations combined with the absence of any physical or corroborative evidence fueled research on the reliability and malleability of child eyewitness testimony and on the possibility that questionable interrogatory practices can "implant" memories (Goodman, 1984; Goodman & Lloyd, 1988; Loftus, 1979; Loftus & Ketcham, 1991). Additionally, a huge field became devoted to investigating the closely related topic of adults who began "recovering" memories during therapy of their own abuse from childhood, a topic which became a virtual industry and which quickly permeated popular culture and society (e.g., books by Bass & Davis, 1988, and Freyd, 1996). Fortunately, the "recovered memory" debate has since been largely settled in favor of scientific evidence debunking the authenticity of such claims; unfortunately, however, this provides little solace for the patients and families traumatized by false allegations.

Fourth, in 1980, spurred in part by the massive numbers of returning Vietnam war veterans suffering from longstanding and debilitating neuroses, the American Psychiatric Association added a new controversial diagnosis – Post Traumatic Stress Disorder (PTSD) – to the third edition of the *Diagnostic and Statistical Manual of Mental Disorders* (DSM-III). Although the concept of disorders such as combat fatigue and war neurosis had been recognized since the mid-1800s, until this time it had not been widely accepted that such "neurosis" could develop from an exogenous etiological event rather than from an inherent psychological weakness alone (Figley, 1978, 1985; Grinker & Spiegel, 1945).

Accordingly, a key criterion for the diagnosis is that an individual be exposed to a catastrophic external "stressor" outside the range of normal experience, such as war, torture, rape, natural disasters, and human-caused disasters. This distinguishes PTSD from the diagnosis of Adjustment Disorder, which is characterized by adverse psychological responses due to "ordinary" stressors such as divorce, loss of a job, death of a loved one, etc. One of the consequences of such extreme traumatic events – and one of the diagnostic criteria – is intrusive recollection of the event evoking intensive emotional responses, including panic, terror, dread, and grief.

Fifth, beginning in the mid-1980s, the increasing accessibility of brain imaging techniques, especially Positron Emission Tomography (PET) and functional Magnetic Resonance Imaging (fMRI), added yet another area of burgeoning research aimed at elucidating the neural correlates of emotion and the interrelations between emotion and memory, with a particular emphasis on the role of the amygdala (Aggleton, 1992; LeDoux, 1996; McGaugh, 2003). Since the mid-1950s, there had been evidence that the limbic system and amygdala had some role in emotional processes, based primarily on lesion data in both animals and humans (e.g., Kluver-Bucy syndrome; Gol, Kellaway, Shapiro, & Hurst, 1963; Marlowe, Mancall, & Thomas, 1975). In the last ten years, however, with the first neuroimaging evidence of the role of the amygdala in processing emotion (e.g., Morris et al., 1996), research in this area has increased rapidly to the point that the words "amygdala" and "emotion" are practically synonymous to most psychology undergraduate students.

This brief overview of some potential catalysts for the rapid increase in the number of research studies investigating the links between memory and emotion suggests that this is one area of scientific inquiry that has been motivated to a large degree not only by scientific curiosity but also by real-life controversies and widespread public interest. In the next section, we provide a brief overview of the chapters contained in this volume, highlighting the current topics and debates in this rapidly expanding field.

■ OVERVIEW OF CHAPTERS

The chapters in this book are organized into three general themes. The first section, Memory, Emotion, and Cognition, consists of four chapters discussing basic research in the field, primarily from the laboratory but also from real-life events. The second section, Memory, Emotion, Aging and the Brain, consists of three chapters presenting research that has extended these basic research findings to the elderly population, as well as a discussion of the current neuroimaging literature investigating emotion and memory. The last section, Memory, Emotion, and Psychopathology, consists of four chapters investigating the application of research techniques to special populations, such as individuals with anxiety, individuals and couples in therapy, and victims of childhood sexual abuse and other traumatic experiences.

The first section begins with a chapter by Reisberg, who draws a distinction between arousal-based and cognitively-based hypotheses of emotion. Although the contribution of arousal to the production of emotion has been recognized since the time of the James-Lange and Cannon-Bard theories of emotion, the importance of cognitive processes was not given true credence until the advent of the Schachter and Singer (1962) Two-Factor theory. Reisberg argues that the arousal-based model is still too influential in guiding the questions asked by emotion researchers and that more attention ought to be devoted to understanding the cognitive contributions. The arousal-based model is too simple, he argues, to explain the diverse effects of emotion on memory, such as improved memory for an event's center or gist and worsened memory for the peripheral details of an event. While biological arousal may be a necessary condition for the enhancement of memory consolidation, it is not on its own sufficient. Cognitive factors, such as attention, rehearsal, personal relevance, and meaning, also play a very important role and deserve a more prominent place in research studies. This idea is also picked up and discussed in the chapters by Levine and Pizarro, by Mathews, and by Goodman and Paz-Alonso. Reisberg argues that researchers have neglected to focus on some crucial questions by letting arousal-based models guide their thinking.

That the arousal-based model of emotion is too limited is also emphasized by Levine and Pizarro in the next chapter. Drawing on research inspired by appraisal theories of emotion, they argue that the particular emotion (e.g., happy, fearful, angry, sad) that one is experiencing will have a large influence on what kind of information is deemed of central importance, and thus subject to further cognitive influence. For example, they argue, positive and negative emotions have very different effects on cognitive processes, even when they evoke similar levels of arousal. Positive emotions tend to promote heuristic, creative, and flexible modes of information processing, while negative emotions tend to promote a more analytic, data-driven mode of information processing. Drawing on appraisal theory, Levine and Pizarro argue that discrete emotions provide "an elegant general-purpose solution to the problem of monitoring information relevant to an individual's many current goals".

In the next chapter, Christianson and Engelberg investigate how research from both laboratory studies and real-life events can be applied to forensic situations in order to develop a better understanding of factors affecting the reliability of memory among bystanders, victims, and perpetrators. While most investigations have focused on how emotion affects memory, Christianson and Engelberg look at the flip side: memory for specific emotions. They argue that recalling the particular emotion experienced during a stressful event can serve as a powerful cue in retrieving information from episodic memory. The ultimate goal of this line of research is to develop effective interviewing techniques to aid both forensic and clinical psychologists in eliciting accurate information from their witnesses, victims, and patients. Factors influencing the recall of traumatic memories are discussed further in the chapters by Goodman and Paz-Alonso and by Kihlstrom.

In the last chapter of this section, Koriat addresses one of the oldest questions in the emotion literature, first posed by William James: do feelings drive behavior or is it behavior that causes feelings? Koriat examines the cause-and-effect relation between subjective emotional feelings and behavior from the modern viewpoint of metacognitive research. This body of research indicates substantial support for both points of view, that monitoring (feelings) affects control (behavior) and that control affects monitoring. Thus, although drawing on a quite different body of literature, Koriat reaches conclusions similar to those of Reisberg and Levine and Pizarro, namely, that biological and cognitive contributions to emotion and memory are far from mutually exclusive, and that equal consideration must be given to both domains in order to understand the relation between emotion and memory more completely.

The next section puts the contribution of biological factors front and center as we turn to neuroimaging studies of emotion and memory and how emotion and memory processes change with the aging brain. First, a chapter by Dolcos, LaBar, and Cabeza begins by providing an excellent tutorial overview of the methodology employed in neuroimaging studies and what can be learned about cognition from employing such techniques – information that is critical in evaluating the neuroimaging studies discussed in later chapters by Mather and Mathews. Next they discuss the extant neuroimaging studies of emotion and memory, most of which support the modulation hypothesis that emotional events are remembered better because the amygdala enhances the function of medial temporal lobe structures such as the hippocampus. Further studies also suggest an important role for the prefrontal cortex in emotional memory, possibly mediated through the enhancement of strategic encoding processes. Dolcos et al. conclude by highlighting a number of issues in emotion and memory research in which neuroimaging has just begun to scratch the surface, such as the role of emotional valence, the mechanism of emotional memory in people with affective disorders (e.g., depression, anxiety, PTSD) and in healthy and pathological aging, as well as mechanisms through which trauma may impair memory, themes which are discussed in the other chapters of this book.

The next two chapters deal with the influence of aging on emotion and memory. Mather describes a wide body of literature suggesting that older adults may show a bias to enhance positive information and diminish the impact of negative information, a finding known as the positivity effect. Similar to Levine and Pizarro's argument that discrete emotions may have evolved to aid in goal-regulation mechanisms, Mather also contends that the positivity effect in older adults may be the result of goal-directed processes used to regulate emotion; she suggests that older adults, compared to their younger counterparts, have a chronically active goal to regulate emotion. Mather puts forth a model to explain the positivity effect; she argues the effect depends on the following preconditions: (1) emotional goals must be activated; (2) cognitive control processes regulating emotions must be available; and (3) individuals must be free to engage in strategic processing of their own choice and allocate their available resources accordingly. She argues that the positivity effect observed in older adults cannot be accounted for by mood-congruent memory effects or by declines in physiological arousal or integrity of the amygdala.

In the memory literature, researchers frequently place more emphasis on retrieval processes than on encoding processes. In the next chapter, however, Uttl and Graf examine not only age differences in retrieval, but also age differences in the encoding of emotional versus non-emotional information. They find that much of the difference in what older versus younger adults remember about pictures of complex scenes can be explained by what they encode initially. While Uttl and Graf did not code for positive versus negative emotions specifically, they found no decline in encoding and retrieval of emotional information with age. Whether the positivity effect is a true phenomenon or a "rose-colored glasses" view of aging, however, is yet unclear. Employing meta-analytic methods, Uttl and Graf review in detail much of the same literature reviewed by Mather and conclude that the present experimental evidence for the positivity of older adults' memories is not entirely convincing one way or the other. Thus, it is important to maintain a healthy skepticism about reported findings and to evaluate the underlying research methods as stringently as the proposed theories.

The last section of the book focuses on the interaction between emotion and memory in special populations, such as people with anxiety, individuals and couples in therapy, and victims of childhood sexual abuse and other traumatic experiences. Mathews examines some of the traditional findings in the emotion and memory literature from the perspective of individual differences. While acknowledging the important roles of arousal and rehearsal in emotional memory, he argues for a special role of selective attention in emotional memory. Specifically, he suggests that anxiety-prone individuals are more likely to selectively attend to and thus remember emotionally threatening stimuli. Further highlighting a theme throughout this book that both biological and cognitive factors are necessary, Mathews also presents evidence that while emotional differences (e.g., anxiety) can influence encoding, it is equally true that different types of encoding may influence emotion. He presents evidence from a neuroimaging study that fear-related activations in the brain, often thought to be automatic, can in fact be modulated by cognitive control processes, and further that these activations are associated with individual differences in fearfulness and attentional control. Importantly, for clinical applications, Mathews and his colleagues have also shown that control over emotional encoding can be learned through behavioral training techniques.

In the next chapter, Singer describes in detail how he has been able to do just that, namely, aid patients in acquiring control over their emotional memories and reactions, through the use of self-defining memories in his clinical practice. Emotional memories are ubiquitous in psychotherapy practice, but Singer, through careful research, argues that a certain kind of autobiographical memory, the self-defining memory, has an important role to play in therapeutic healing by virtue of being a vivid, emotional, familiar, and well-networked memory which is connected to enduring goals and conflicts in one's life. He suggests that therapists can use positive self-defining memories to aid clients in extracting lessons and meaning relevant to goal conflicts in their lives, while at the same time teaching strategies to avoid excessive rumination on negative memories. Here, again, the function of goals as an important aspect of self-regulation of emotion is highlighted, as in earlier chapters by Levine and Pizarro and by Mather.

In the last two chapters of this book, we turn to a discussion of the most extreme form of emotional memories, traumatic memory. A serious scientific discussion of this topic is important as it touches on some of the topics most familiar, yet most misunderstood, in popular psychology books and magazines, such as recovered and false memories of abuse, dissociative amnesia, and post-traumatic stress disorder.

In forging a connection between the laboratory and the real world, Goodman and Paz-Alonso present an overview of how basic research on memory processes can explain memory for stressful events. While traumatic events are typically retained better than ordinary memories, they are also susceptible to forgetting, interference, and distortion; they argue, that, like ordinary memories, traumatic memories are also affected by factors such as time delay, distinctiveness, personal involvement, rehearsal, and arousal. Turning to a discussion of childhood sexual abuse, however, they conclude that while normal memory processes can explain the majority of traumatic memory phenomena, there does seem to be an additional need to appeal to "special" memory mechanisms such as dissociation, especially when the trauma is chronic and experienced during the vulnerable childhood years.

The book closes with an intriguing chapter by Kihlstrom that provides a historical overview and discussion of the relationship between trauma and memory. He notes that the idea that trauma can cause amnesia has been present in psychological literature for over a century, since the time of Freud and Janet, who first suggested the mechanisms of repression and dissociation. In the modern literature, we encounter terminology such as memory suppression and "hot" and "cool" memory systems. Despite the popularity of the idea that trauma can cause amnesia, however, Kihlstrom argues quite convincingly that there is little to no evidence for this claim. Indeed, consistent with the ideas presented in the other chapters of this book, it would seem that the emotion associated with trauma serves to increase, rather than decrease, the saliency of and memory for such events. If this is the case, then it would seem that researchers, the popular press, and the public in general have devoted an incredible amount of time for naught in attempting to explain, portray, and understand a phenomenon that does not exist.

■ CONCLUSIONS

As separate fields of inquiry, emotion and memory each have a long and well-established history. In the last two decades, however, interest in the interactions between emotion and memory has increased at a rate far exceeding the rate of increase in either topic alone. While part of this increased interest may be attributable to changing emphases in the scientific field of psychology itself, it is more likely that this increase was inspired by real-world events and controversies, and increasing public awareness and interest in these topics. The chapters of this book provide a snapshot of the current debates and state of research from diverse areas of psychology in this rapidly growing field. It is our hope that researchers will be inspired by the ideas presented in this book to go out and gather the necessary evidence to advance both scientific and public understanding of the interactions between emotion and memory.

AUTHOR NOTE

Correspondence concerning this chapter should be addressed to Bob Uttl, Brain Science Research Center, University of Tamagawa, Machida, Tokyo, Japan. Email: uttlbob@gmail.com.

REFERENCES

Aggleton, J. P. (Ed.) (1992). *The amygdala: Neurobiological aspects of emotion, memory, and mental dysfunction.* New York: Wiley.

American Psychiatric Association (1980). *Diagnostic and statistical manual of mental disorders* (3rd ed.). Washington, DC: Author.

Bass, E. & Davis, L. W. (1988). *The courage to heal: A guide for women survivors of child sexual abuse.* New York: Harper & Row.

Bower, G. H. (1981). Mood and memory. *American Psychologist, 36,* 129–148.

Bower, G. H. (1992). How might emotions affect learning? In S.-Å. Christianson (Ed.), *Handbook of emotion and memory* (pp. 3–31). Hillsdale, NJ: Erlbaum.

Brown, R. & Kulik, J. (1977). Flashbulb memories. *Cognition, 5,* 73–99.

Craik, F. I. M. & Lockhart, R. S. (1972). Levels of processing: A framework for memory research. *Journal of Verbal Learning and Verbal Behavior, 11,* 671–684.

Davidson, R. J. (2000). Affective style, psychopathology, and resilience: Brain mechanisms and plasticity. *American Psychologist, 55,* 1193–1196.

Eich, E. (1980). The cue-dependent nature of state-dependent retrieval. *Memory & Cognition, 8,* 157–173.

Eich, E. (1989). Theoretical issues in state-dependent memory. In H. L. Roediger, III, & F. I. M. Craik (Eds.), *Varieties of memory and consciousness: Essays in honour of Endel Tulving* (pp. 331–354). Hillsdale, NJ: Erlbaum.

Figley, C. R. (Ed.) (1978). *Stress disorders among Vietnam veterans.* New York: Brunner/Mazel.

Figley, C. R. (Ed.) (1985). *Trauma and its wake.* New York: Brunner/Mazel.

Freud, S. (1915/1957). Repression. In J. Strachey (Ed.), *The standard edition of the complete psychological works of Sigmund Freud* (Vol. 14, pp. 146–158). London: Hogarth.

Freyd, J. (1996). *Betrayal trauma: The logic of forgetting childhood abuse.* Cambridge, MA: Harvard University Press.

Frijda, N. H. (1988). The laws of emotion. *American Psychologist, 43,* 349–358.

Gol, A., Kellaway, P., Shapiro, M., & Hurst, C. M. (1963). Studies of hippocampectomy in the monkey, baboon, and cat. *Neurology, 13,* 1031–1041.

Goodman, G. S. (1984). Children's testimony in historical perspective. *Journal of Social Issues, 40,* 9–31.

Goodman, G. S. & Lloyd, D. W. (1988). The child witness: Evaluation and preparation. In D. C. Bross, R. D. Krugman, M. R. Lenherr, D. A. Rosenberg, & B. D. Schmitt (Eds.), *The new child protection team handbook: Garland reference library of social science* (pp. 414–441). New York: Garland.

Grinker, R. & Spiegel, J. (1945). *War neuroses.* Philadelphia: Blakiston.

James, W. (1890/1980). *Principles of psychology.* Cambridge, MA: Harvard University Press.

Janet, P. (1889). *L'Automatisme psychologique; essai de psychologie expérimentale sur les formes inférieures de l'activité humaine [Psychological automatisms].* Paris: Alcan.

Lang, P. J. (1995). The emotion probe: Studies of motivation and attention. *American Psychologist, 50,* 372–385.

Lazarus, R. S. (1981). A cognitivist's reply to Zajonc on emotion and cognition. *American Psychologist, 36,* 222–223.

Lazarus, R. S. (1984). On the primacy of cognition. *American Psychologist, 39,* 124–129.

Lazarus, R. S. (1991a). *Emotion and adaptation.* New York: Oxford University Press.

Lazarus, R. S. (1991b). Cognition and motivation in emotion. *American Psychologist, 46,* 352–367.

LeDoux, J. (1996). *The emotional brain.* New York: Simon & Schuster.

Loftus, E. F. (1979). *Eyewitness testimony.* Cambridge, MA: Harvard University Press.

Loftus, E. F. & Ketcham, K. (1991). *Witnesses for the defense: The accused, the eyewitness, and the expert who puts memory on trial.* New York: St. Martin's Press.

McGaugh, J. L. (2003). *Memory and emotion: The making of lasting memories.* London: Weidenfeld & Nicolson.

Marlowe, W. B., Mancall, E. L., & Thomas, J. J. (1975). Complete Kluver-Bucy syndrome in man. *Cortex, 11,* 53–59.

Morris, C. D., Bransford, J. D., & Franks, J. J. (1977). Levels of processing versus transfer appropriate processing. *Journal of Verbal Learning and Verbal Behavior, 16,* 519–533.

Morris, J. S., Frith, C. D., Perrett, D. I., Rowland, D., Young, A. W., Calder, A. J., & Dolan, R. J. (1996). A differential neural response in the human amygdala to fearful and happy facial expressions. *Nature, 383,* 812–815.

Neisser, U. (1967). *Cognitive psychology.* New York: Appleton-Century-Crofts.

Ramsland, K. (n.d.). *The McMartin nightmare and the hysteria puppeteers.* Retrieved June 28, 2005 from www.crimelibrary.com/criminal_mind/psychology/mcmartin_daycare/1.html.

Reisenzein, R. & Schonpflug, W. (1992). Stumpf's cognitive-evaluative theory of emotion. *American Psychologist, 47,* 34–45.

Schachter, S. & Singer, J. (1962). Cognitive, social, and physiological determinants of emotional state. *Psychological Review, 69,* 379–399.

Staats, A. W. (1988). Skinner's theory and the emotion-behavior relationship: Incipient change with major implications. *American Psychologist, 43,* 747–748.

Tulving, E. & Thomson, D. M. (1973). Encoding specificity and retrieval processes in episodic memory. *Psychological Review, 80,* 359–380.

Winograd, E. & Neisser, U. (Eds.) (1992). *Affect and accuracy in recall: Studies of "flashbulb" memories: Emory symposia in cognition* (Vol. 4). New York: Cambridge University Press.

Zajonc, R. B. (1981). A one-factor mind about mind and emotion. *American Psychologist, 36,* 102–103.

Zajonc, R. B. (1984). On the primacy of affect. *American Psychologist, 39,* 117–123.

Zuk, G. H. (1994). Mixed emotions about Richard Lazarus' theory of emotion. *American Psychologist, 49,* 76.

PART I

MEMORY, EMOTION, AND COGNITION

2

Memory for Emotional Episodes: The Strengths and Limits of Arousal-Based Accounts

Daniel Reisberg

Abstract

Emotion typically improves memory for an event's gist, but undermines memory for more peripheral elements within the event. These effects are often understood in terms of biological arousal, with the suggestion that arousal promotes memory consolidation and also causes a narrowing of attention. However, this arousal-based view cannot explain the full pattern of the data. Among other concerns, it turns out that the narrowing of memory is not caused by the emotion itself, but instead by the presence of salient, attention-grabbing stimuli within the emotional event. For this and other reasons, it seems important to emphasize cognitive influences on emotional memory as well as arousal-based influences, and the chapter considers some of the research topics demanded by this shift in emphasis.

Many of the episodes we encounter in life are emotional for us – they bring us joy, or sadness, or perhaps anger or fear. We experience episodes that make us proud, and episodes that inspire regret. How do these emotions influence our memory for these episodes? Is the form or content of the memories different from that of memories for *un*emotional episodes? How accurate and how complete are these emotional memories?

There are, of course, several reasons for us to care deeply about these questions. The study of emotional memories provides a fabulous opportunity to explore the biological basis for memory formation, building both on what we already know about the biological processes relevant to memory, and on what we know about the biological concomitants of emotion. The study of emotional memories also is crucial if we are going to understand autobiographical memory in general, for the reason that the *consequential* events in our lives, the events that make us who we are, usually are emotional in one fashion or another.

Therefore, if we seek to understand how people think about themselves, their lives, and their personal past, we must understand emotional memories. Finally, the study of emotional memories is important for another reason. Psychologists have become increasingly interested in the problem of how eyewitnesses to crimes remember what they have seen. This is obviously an issue of both theoretical and practical importance, and, since eyewitnesses are typically angry or afraid during the crime, here too we find a reason to scrutinize emotional memories.

In this chapter, I will survey some of what we know about memory for emotional events. As we will see, a number of studies indicate that emotion has at least two separate effects on memory. On the one hand, emotion improves memory for an episode's *center*, including the gist of the episode and also incidental details that happen to be associated with that gist. On the other hand, emotion seems to undermine memory for an episode's *periphery*, and, specifically, for details that are both irrelevant to the episode's gist and also separated (spatially or temporally) from that gist.

How should we think about these effects? As one option, we might cast our hypotheses in terms of how people pay attention to, and think about, emotional events. Alternatively, we might develop hypotheses that focus on the biological effects that accompany emotion. I will refer to this latter sort of hypothesis as "arousal-based" and, in truth, there can be no question that arousal-based mechanisms do play a role in emotional memory. But these two broad classes of hypotheses – cognitively-based and arousal-based – are not mutually exclusive, and so the question remains: How do cognitive influences, like attention and meaning and rehearsal, influence emotional memory?

I will argue that the arousal-based model is important, but also, on its own, inadequate as a conception of how emotion shapes memory, and that we must therefore give full weight to the cognitive influences. This claim, framed in these general terms, is surely uncontroversial, but, even so, I shall argue that the cognitive influences on emotional memory have been under-researched. Thus, by virtue of their choice of research topics, most investigators seem to have implicitly committed themselves to an arousal-based model, and I shall outline some of the gaps this has produced in the research literature.

As it turns out, the conclusions I will reach, based on these arguments, are similar to those offered by Levine and Pizarro (2004) in what they term a "grumpy overview" of the state of the art. It is striking, though, that Levine and Pizarro reach their conclusions based largely on a consideration of current theorizing about emotion, and in particular current appraisal theories of emotion. With that, much of their evidence comes from a social psychological perspective on emotion and memory. In the present chapter, I shall draw similar conclusions from a cognitive psychological perspective, and studies that focus directly on the interaction between memory and emotion. This convergence of claims, based on differing frameworks and bodies of evidence, is a powerful argument that these claims must be taken seriously.

HOW ARE EMOTIONAL EVENTS REMEMBERED?

There is no question that emotional events tend to be well remembered. This is clear, for example, if we simply consider how vivid these memories seem, subjectively, when they are recalled, and, broadly put, the stronger the emotion associated with an event, the greater the vividness in the recollection (e.g., Pillemer, Goldsmith, Panter, & White, 1988; Porter & Birt, 2001; Reisberg, Heuer, McLean, & O'shaugnessy, 1988; Rubin & Kozin, 1984; Walker, Vogl, & Thompson, 1997).

Emotional memories also seem to be long lasting. More specifically, evidence suggests that emotion slows the process of forgetting, so that emotional episodes are eventually forgotten, but the rate of forgetting is slower than that for neutral episodes. As a result, the memory advantages associated with emotion can be observed even with short retention intervals, but become larger and larger as the retention interval grows (e.g., Burke, Heuer, & Reisberg, 1992; Peace & Porter, 2004).

In addition, and crucially for many purposes, emotional memories also tend to be accurate, in comparison to memories for events that were unemotional but otherwise similar to the emotional events. To be sure, errors do arise in people's recollection of emotional events (e.g., Neisser & Harsch, 1992), but, even so, studies of how people remember real-life emotional events indicate impressive (and in some cases extraordinary) levels of accuracy (e.g., Conway et al., 1994).

These studies of real-life events have been corroborated by a number of studies in the laboratory, and, in the lab, emotional memories seem more complete, longer-lasting, and more accurate, just as they are in field studies. This pattern has been documented in people's memory for emotional pictures (e.g., Canli et al., 2000), emotion-laden word lists (e.g., Dietrich et al., 2001; Jones, O'Gorman, & Byrne, 1987), and in their memory for humor (e.g., Schmidt & Williams, 2001).

The laboratory studies also document a further aspect of emotional remembering, and this returns us to the broad summary of the data that I mentioned early on. In a number of studies, participants have witnessed an event presented via a series of slides, depicting successive moments within a story, with an accompanying (tape-recorded) narrative telling the emotional tale.

In a smaller number of cases, the to-be-remembered event has been presented as a video clip (or, in just a few studies, an animation). An even smaller number of studies have employed live events, witnessed by the study's participants. In all cases, though, the studies compare participants' memory for an emotional version of the event with other participants' memory for an emotionally neutral but otherwise matched event. These studies yield two findings. First, participants who viewed the emotional event have better memory for the emotional story's gist and also details associated with that gist. Second, participants who viewed the emotional event tend to have worse memory for peripheral aspects of the story, in comparison to participants who viewed the neutral materials. Overall, we can think of this pattern as revealing *improved* but *narrowed* memories, created by emotional events (e.g., Burke, Heuer, & Reisberg, 1992; Christianson & Loftus, 1987, 1991; Wessel & Merckelbach, 1997; see Reisberg & Heuer, 2004, for a recent review).

■ STUDIES OF MEMORY NARROWING

The claim of "memory narrowing" obviously depends on the proper definitions of central and peripheral materials. If emotion does indeed have opposite effects on these two types of material, then we will detect this only if we categorize the to-be-remembered materials correctly. How, therefore, should "central" and "peripheral" materials be defined? One option is to appeal to the *meaning* of an event, so that materials are considered "central" if they somehow define the event, and if changing these materials would alter the nature of the event (cf. Heuer & Reisberg, 1990). A different option is to employ a spatial (or perceptual) criterion, so that materials are considered "central" if they are literally in the center of the witness's visual field (cf. Christianson & Loftus, 1987, 1991). It turns out that both of these options capture part of the truth.

Burke, Heuer, and Reisberg (1992) presented half of their participants with an emotional story and half with a neutral story, and then, after a delay, probed participants' memory for the stories. The memory data were then subjected to a fine-grained analysis, examining precisely what it was that participants could or could not remember. Specifically, Burke et al. first distinguished between those items relevant to how the story unfolded and those items that were not relevant to the story's plot. The plot-relevant items were then subdivided into "gist" items, items that essentially defined the story, and "basic level visual information," items that, in the broadest terms, described what each of the slides in the sequence showed. Likewise, the plot-irrelevant items were also subdivided into those irrelevant details that happened to be spatially associated with plot-relevant actors or objects, and those that were truly in the background. Finally, all of these categories were subdivided once again

		Phase	
	1	*2*	*3*
Gist	Weakly helps	Emotion **helps** memory	Weakly helps
Basic-level visual information	Weakly helps	Emotion **helps** memory	Weakly helps
Spatially central details	No effect observed	Emotion **helps** memory	Weakly hurts
Spatially peripheral details	Weakly hurts	Emotion **HURTS** memory	Weakly hurts

Figure 2.1 Summary of the Burke et al. (1992) study. Burke et al. analyzed their participants' memory in a fine-grained fashion. First, they distinguished memory for plot-relevant materials (top two rows) from memory for plot-irrelevant materials (bottom two rows). Each of these categories was then subdivided as shown. All categories were then subdivided temporally (into phases 1, 2, and 3), to distinguish materials presented before, during, and after the emotional aspects of the story. Shown within the figure is a summary of the contrast between participants remembering an emotional story and those remembering a neutral story.

temporally, with questions divided according to whether they probed memory for materials that happened before, during, or after the parts of the story that were, in fact, arousing.

Figure 2.1 depicts the Burke et al. categorization scheme, and, in rough fashion, describes their results. As can be seen, the difference between plot-relevant and plot-irrelevant materials does matter, inasmuch as the pattern in the top half of the figure is different from the pattern in the bottom half. Likewise, the spatial/perceptual distinction also matters; this is evident in the contrast between the figure's third and fourth rows. Finally, the temporal dimension also matters, as can be seen in the contrast between the table's middle column and its two outer columns. (For related data, showing a similar effect of the temporal dimension, see, for example, Bornstein, Liebel, & Scarberry, 1998.)

These data confirm what we earlier labeled a "memory narrowing" pattern, a pattern in which emotion improves memory for materials that are more central to the event, but impairs memory for materials that are more peripheral.

However, the definition of the event's "center" is complex – with materials favored by emotion if they are in any fashion tied to the "action" in the story, either conceptually or spatiotemporally.

Other studies have confirmed this pattern, although not at the same level of detail. Safer, Christianson, Autry, and Österlund (1998), for example, showed participants a sequence in which either a woman was shown gathering flowers in a park (neutral version) or was stabbed in the throat and shown lying on the ground, bleeding (emotional version). The participants' memory was then tested with various photographs differing only in how "zoomed-in" they were; participants were asked to select exactly the photo they had seen in the earlier sequence. We know from other studies (e.g., Intraub & Richardson, 1989) that people often remember photographs as being less zoomed-in than they actually were, and correspondingly remember the photo as including more of the background than it actually did, a pattern known as *boundary extension* (see also Mathews, this volume). Safer et al., however, found precisely the opposite pattern, with the emotional photos remembered as *more* zoomed-in. Apparently, the participants' memories excluded the peripheral information, and also excluded the fact that there even was peripheral information.

Similarly, Wessel and Merckelbach (1997, 1998) invited people with spider phobia to the laboratory and in one procedure showed them a large, live spider (in a glass jar) and in another procedure showed them pictures of spiders. In both cases, these were particularly arousing stimuli for these participants, but not for control subjects. In a subsequent memory test, the more aroused (phobic) participants showed the expected pattern of narrowing, with relatively accurate memory for the event's center (the spider) but impaired memory for the event's periphery, in comparison to control participants.

It should be acknowledged that not all studies confirm this broad picture (see, for example, Libkuman et al., 1999; Wessel, van der Kooy, & Merckelbach, 2000). Even so, the memory-narrowing pattern associated with emotional events has been replicated often enough to be regarded as well established.

 ## BIOLOGICAL MECHANISMS FOR EMOTION'S EFFECT ON MEMORY

The data described so far have been in the literature for several years, and provide us with a well-documented description of how emotional events are remembered. The question we need to ask, however, is *why* emotional events are remembered in this way. As indicated at the start, there are two broad categories of explanation available to us. First, we might seek to explain these data in cognitive terms. Emotional events are usually important to us, virtually guaranteeing that we will pay close *attention* as the event unfolds, and close attention contributes to more accurate and more complete remembering. Emotional events are also emotional precisely because they are related to issues we care about and may have thought about in other contexts; this fosters the sort of memory *connections* that we know promote retention and recall. Finally, we tend to mull over emotional events in the minutes (or hours) following the event, and this is tantamount to *memory rehearsal*, which, again, has a positive effect on memory.

Second, we can also try to explain the data described so far in terms of the biological effects associated with emotion. Of course, the psychological mechanisms described in the previous paragraph (paying attention, promoting memory connections, rehearsing) all have biological analogues. But other biological mechanisms, arguably crucial for emotion's effects, may involve processes that are, in essence, "psychologically invisible." Specifically, consider the process of *memory consolidation*. This process is crucial for memory acquisition, but is unconscious and seemingly uninfluenced by someone's strategies, attention, expectations, or intentions (e.g., Dudai, 2004; McGaugh, 2000). The proposal to be considered, then, is that emotion (and, specifically, its biological aspects) promotes consolidation, and hence emotion's memory effects need to be understood in terms of the relevant biology.

A number of studies do indicate a role for consolidation and, more broadly, biological mechanisms, in mediating emotion's effect on memory. In particular, the data suggest a crucial role for the amygdala; for example, there is a relatively clear relationship between amygdala activation, while viewing an emotional event, and accuracy of subsequent memory (e.g., Canli et al., 2000; Hamann et al., 1999; see also Dolcos, LaBar, & Cabeza, this volume). Likewise, damage to the amygdala seems to disrupt the memory benefits typically associated with emotion (Adolphs et al., 1997).

Crucially, though, amygdala damage does not seem to interfere with the understanding of or immediate emotional reaction to emotional stimuli. Thus, patients with amygdala damage still find emotional slides to be arousing. This suggests that the amygdala does not play its role in governing how people pay attention to or think about emotional materials; instead, the amygdala (and related structures) seems to contribute to the process of consolidating emotional memories (cf. Cahill & McGaugh, 1998; McGaugh, 2003, 2004).

Related evidence comes from a study by Cahill et al. (1994). They showed an emotional stimulus sequence to participants, but, prior to the presentation, injected half of the participants with propanolol, a beta-adrenergic blocker chosen to diminish emotion's bodily (arousal) effects; the remaining participants were injected with a placebo. The beta-blockers presumably would not influence how participants pay attention to the emotional stimulus, or how they think about the stimulus. But the beta-blockers would interfere with the mechanisms promoting consolidation, and, consistent with other findings, did in fact reduce the memory differences between the emotional stimulus and a neutral control stimulus.

■ LIMITS OF AN AROUSAL-BASED MODEL

It seems clear, then, that we can understand some of emotion's memory effects in biological terms and specifically in terms of consolidation. Roughly speaking, the proposal is that neural circuits centered on the amygdala register the presence of an emotional event; this has a number of effects, including an increase in blood levels of norepinephrine, which in turn has a number of effects, including an increase in levels of serum glucose, which is what promotes consolidation. (For evidence for these claims, see among others Buchanan & Adolphs, 2004; McGaugh, 2003; McNay & Gold, 2002; Ochsner & Schacter, 2003; Payne et al., 2004.)

However, while these biological mechanisms may be *necessary* for emotion's memory effects, they are certainly not *sufficient* for emotion's effects. Some of the evidence for the claim of necessity has already been mentioned. When the relevant biological mechanisms are disrupted (by brain damage or drug administration), emotion seems to have little effect on memory. But, at the same time, other results make it clear that bodily arousal, by itself, is not enough to produce the memory effects we have described.

For example, Christianson and his colleagues (Christianson & Mjörndal, 1985; Christianson et al., 1986) found clear differences between how participants injected with a stimulant remembered a neutral picture and how participants injected with a placebo remembered an emotional picture. Likewise, Libkuman et al. (1999) showed half of their participants a sequence of slides depicting an arousing story and half a sequence depicting a neutral story. Within each group, half of the participants viewed the slides after a minute of sitting quietly, and half viewed the slides after spending a minute energetically running in place, to produce a baseline of elevated arousal. The results showed little or no effect of exercise-produced arousal on memory. Another study replicated this finding with the exercise maintained *during* the slide presentation (participants pedaled on an exercise bicycle while viewing the slides).

Clearly, then, the effects of emotion on memory are not the result of arousal per se. When we arouse participants (through exercise or drugs) without emotion, the memory effects are weaker, and, in some data sets, absent altogether. Apparently, there is more to emotion's impact than arousal alone.

In addition, it is surely worth mentioning that the notion of arousal itself may be in need of clarification. As one concern, there has been debate over whether arousal is a unified construct, or whether we need instead to consider individually the various aspects of arousal (the heart rate change, the change in blood chemistry, the change in activation state of various brain areas, etc.; for classic statements of this issue, see Anderson, 1990; Neiss, 1990). Second, it may be crucial, in understanding arousal's effects on memory, to distinguish different *types* of arousal. Specifically, Deffenbacher et al. (2004) distinguish between a type of arousal that is involved in emotional events that are not stressful, and which causes someone to orient toward the stimulus, and a type involved in stressful events, and which produces a defensive response. Moreover, they argue that the latter sort of (defensive) arousal *impairs* memory, whereas the former (orienting) sort *promotes* memory. (For discussion of this proposal and, in particular, of how it might be reconciled with other findings in the research literature, see Reisberg & Heuer, 2005.) Clearly, these issues must be resolved before strong claims about arousal's memory effects can be sustained.

◼ THE SOURCE OF MEMORY NARROWING

It seems, then, that we need theory that goes beyond the simple claim that biological arousal promotes consolidation and thus improves memory. In fact, even without the complications just mentioned, this simple claim is not sufficient to explain the data described earlier in this chapter.

As we have seen, emotion seems to *impair* memory for an event's periphery, and this is the opposite of what one would expect purely on the claim that arousal promotes consolidation. What, therefore, is the source of the memory narrowing? One proposal again assigns a crucial role to arousal, so that, in effect, we would end up arguing that arousal (and, especially, the sort of arousal that Deffenbacher et al. associate with an "orienting" response) has two separate effects on memory. First, as already suggested, this arousal might promote memory consolidation. Second, the arousal might shape and guide attention, and, more precisely, might draw attention away from items that are peripheral in the event and toward more central aspects. This two-part proposal would fit with the data reviewed so far, but, in truth, this proposal turns out to be mistaken.

The claim that arousal shapes attention is typically termed the *Easterbrook hypothesis*, based on Easterbrook's (1959) suggestion that an aroused organism becomes less sensitive to information at the periphery of an event. As a consequence, the organism is likely to become more sensitive to information at the center of the event, perhaps because of diminished distraction from the periphery, or perhaps because the organism's attentional resources are more concentrated on the event's center.

Easterbrook's own data came from studies of animal learning. Arousal was manipulated by means of food deprivation (on the assumption that hunger would arouse the animal). Sensitivity to peripheral cues was literally measured by the organism's sensitivity to cues in its immediate environment. Obviously, then, we need some extrapolation to draw from these findings a claim about how *emotion* influences *event memory*, but, nonetheless, many authors have appealed to the Easterbrook hypothesis as an account of the data described earlier – data showing, of course, that emotion improves memory for central materials, but undermines memory for peripheral materials, just as the hypothesis predicts.

However, there is another way to think about the memory-narrowing pattern, and it is suggested by research focused on eyewitness testimony. The key phenomenon here is known as *weapon focus*, a term that refers to the fact that witnesses to crimes often seem to "lock" their attention onto the criminal's weapon, and seem oblivious to much else in the scene. As a result of this attentional pattern, later on the witness will remember the perpetrator's gun or knife with great clarity, but may remember little else about the crime, including such crucial details as what the perpetrator looked like.

Weapon focus has often been alleged by those in law enforcement, and has also been documented in a variety of laboratory studies (e.g., Loftus, Loftus, & Messo, 1987; Stanny & Johnson, 2000; Steblay, 1992) and in a field study of actual police procedures (Tollestrup, Turtle, & Yuille, 1994). In obvious ways, these findings parallel the pattern observed by Easterbrook. The crime itself is presumably a source of arousal because the crime witness will likely experience fear or anger. The arousal, in turn, will (according to Easterbrook) cause a narrowing of attention, and this fits with the data – good memory for items at the center of the crime (the weapon), but poor memory for items at the periphery.

A number of investigators, though, have suggested an alternative way to think about the weapon-focus pattern. Perhaps eyewitnesses focus on the weapon, not because they are aroused, but because the weapon is by far the most interesting aspect of the visual input. After all, what could be more important to a crime victim than to know whether he or she is in immediate danger and, to this end, nothing in the scene is more important than knowing whether the weapon is cocked and pointed at him or her. On this logic, even an entirely calm witness might still show the weapon-focus pattern, zooming in on the weapon simply because looking toward the weapon provides crucial information.

As it turns out, evidence suggests that both of these mechanisms – one hinging on arousal, and one hinging on the weapon's visual importance – play a role in producing weapon focus. In several studies, weapon focus has been observed even in the absence of emotional arousal, indicating the weapon's potency as an "attention magnet" (Kramer, Buckhout, & Eugenio, 1990; Loftus, Loftus, & Messo, 1987; Maass & Köhnken, 1989). Other studies indicate that it may be the *unusualness* of the weapon, and not the threat, that produces weapon focus (Pickel, 1998). Still other studies, though, suggest that the strength of the weapon focus effect increases as arousal increases, indicating that arousal also plays a role (e.g., Peters, 1988; Steblay, 1992).

These points raise a new question for us. We have already noted that, in situations involving emotion (but no weapon), people show a pattern of memory narrowing, and we have so far suggested that this narrowing is produced by the emotional arousal itself; this is, of course, the Easterbrook proposal. However, studies of weapon focus remind us that there is another possibility, namely, that memory narrowing is observed because emotional situations often provide a specific stimulus that demands the witness's attention, and it is this "attention magnet" (i.e., a stimulus that the witness deems to be well worth focusing on), and not the emotion per se, that produces the narrowing.

◼ VISUAL VS. THEMATIC AROUSAL

In evaluating the hypothesis just sketched, it is important to consider how exactly emotional remembering has usually been studied. Investigators must grapple with the fact that research participants (typically, university undergraduates) are difficult to arouse in the laboratory, and many seemingly emotional stimuli have little effect on them. This fact has led most investigators to rely on a particular type of stimulus that does have a consistent effect on undergraduate participants: the sight of some gruesome or shocking visual input. In our own studies, we have shown participants pictures of a child whose legs had been severed in a car accident, and pictures of surgery with the patient's viscera in plain view. Other studies have shown pictures of a boy who has been shot and is now bleeding from his eyeball, a picture of a woman whose throat has been slit, and so on.

This catalog of grisly stimuli surely raises questions about the generalizability of the available evidence. Have investigators examined how people remember emotional events in general, or have they merely examined how people remember *gruesome* events? In addition, the nature of these stimuli highlights the ambiguity discussed in the previous section. If emotional events studied in the lab are remembered in a narrowed fashion, this might be because emotion itself produces the narrowing, or it might be because the particular stimuli employed in these studies contain salient, attention-demanding objects. Independent of emotional arousal, participants may focus on these attention magnets and so remember them well, but at the cost of remembering less about other aspects of the scene.

To explore this issue, we conducted a pair of experiments concerned with how people remember emotional stories that do not contain shocking, gory, or horrifying material. If the pattern of memory narrowing observed in prior studies is truly a product of emotion (and the arousal that accompanies it), then we would still expect narrowing with these new stimulus materials. If, on the other hand, the narrowing has been produced by the presence of attention magnets within the stimuli, then these new materials, containing no such magnets, will not produce memory narrowing.

In these new studies (Laney et al., 2005), participants viewed a series of slides depicting a story, with an accompanying audio narrative. The slides contained no gory or shocking elements, and so the emotionality of the materials was not in any way evoked by visual inputs. Instead, the emotionality was evoked by means of the narrative, and, in particular, by means of *empathy* with the characters in the stories. We call this sort of emotion *thematically induced*, in contrast to the *visually-induced emotion* present in virtually all prior lab studies of emotional memory.

In one study, the stimulus sequence told about a woman and man having their first date. In the neutral version of the story, participants heard that the woman was relaxed and happy about the date, and the man was polite and friendly. In the emotional version, participants heard that the woman was growing apprehensive as the date progressed, and her fears turn out to be well-founded, as the man attacks her late in the sequence and has to be pushed away. (We emphasize, though, that this attack was described in the auditory narrative, and not depicted in the visual stimuli.)

In a second study, participants viewed a story about a college student named Megan. In the emotional version, subjects learned early on that Megan is doing badly in her classes and may lose the financial support she's been getting from her parents. In addition, Megan's boyfriend just left her, on her birthday. As the story unfolds, Megan discusses the possibility of suicide, and gets quite specific about it – contemplating the combination of pills and alcohol that is, in fact, one of the most common paths to suicide among college students. Once again, though, this upsetting information was conveyed only in the narrative that accompanied the slides; there was nothing in the visuals that was at all upsetting. Indeed, neutral subjects in this study saw the exact same visuals and heard a story with it that was parallel to the emotional story, but with some essential differences. They heard that Megan was doing well in her classes and that she and her boyfriend were getting along fine. They also heard about Megan reaching for a pill bottle, but this time in response to a hangover caused by the celebration of her birthday.

Despite numerous procedural differences, the data from these two studies were essentially identical. In both cases, participants' self-reports made it clear that we had succeeded in creating stimuli that told a plausible, coherent, and emotional story. In both cases, this claim of emotionality was bolstered by trends in the expected direction in the heart-rate data. In both cases, the emotional story was better remembered, overall, than the neutral story, confirming that the memory benefits of emotion can be documented with thematically induced emotion, just as they can be with visually induced emotion. Crucially, though, neither study showed any indication of memory narrowing. That is, thematically induced emotion seemed to benefit memory for *all* aspects of the scene, and not just central aspects. This strongly suggests, therefore, that the memory-narrowing pattern observed in prior studies is not produced by emotional arousal. Instead, the pattern is produced by the presence of specific attention magnets within a scene, stimuli that seize the viewer's attention during the event, and dominate memory afterwards.

None of this takes any importance away from the arousal-based mechanisms (nor from the distinction between arousal types described by Deffenbacher et al.). Nor does it take any importance away from the memory-narrowing phenomenon, for the simple reason that many emotional events – including events of forensic importance – do contain salient visual stimuli. Hence, we must understand memory narrowing if we are to understand how emotional events of various sorts are remembered.

Other data, however, suggest that most real-world emotional experiences are thematically induced, not visually, and so the memory narrowing phenomenon will not be observed in most cases of emotional remembering. In a pair of interview studies (Laney, Heuer, & Reisberg, 2003), we asked participants simply to list a number of their emotional memories, and then we questioned them to find out if the emotion in these memories was visually or thematically induced. The two interview studies differed in numerous ways, including the participant population and the way the memories were elicited. In one study, the categorization of memories as visually or thematically induced was done by a panel of judges; in the other study, we included interview questions that allowed the participants themselves to tell us whether the event had a visual focus for the emotion. Despite all of these differences, the data from the two studies were virtually identical, with the vast majority of the memories being thematically induced (82 percent in a study with undergraduates, 71 percent in a study with an older and more diverse participant group). It seems, then, as we said in our initial report of these data, that emotional memory is not like a blockbuster movie with great special effects; it is instead like a docudrama with complex characters and an emotionally engaging plot. As a consequence, most emotional remembering outside of the laboratory is not the right sort to produce memory narrowing, and the narrowing pattern, well-documented in the lab, may apply only to a narrow subset of real-life emotional memories.

◼ THE *MEANING* OF EMOTIONAL EVENTS

Where does all of this leave us? Emotion, we have seen, generally improves memory for an event's center, and this fact can be understood in part in terms of emotion's effects on memory consolidation. However, this arousal-based account is surely incomplete. As one concern, we have mentioned evidence suggesting that biological arousal may be necessary for emotion's memory benefits, but is not sufficient, and so plainly other mechanisms are involved. As a separate concern, there are probably different types of arousal, each with its own effects on memory, and any full account of arousal's memory effects will have to address this variety. Most important, though, it seems undeniable that other mechanisms (mechanisms best understood in psychological, not biological, terms) are also relevant to emotion's impact on memory. We mentioned earlier the fact that people probably attend more carefully to emotional events, probably mull over these events afterwards, and can easily find connections between the emotional event and other issues or events they care about; these points certainly contribute to how the emotional event is remembered.

In addition, we have reviewed the evidence suggesting that many emotional events are remembered in a narrowed fashion, and this observation, too, is also often attributed to arousal; this is, in short, the Easterbrook claim. Once again, though, this arousal-based account is incomplete, and potentially wrong altogether. This is the message of the Laney et al. (2005) data, showing that emotion does not produce memory narrowing in the absence of salient stimuli that can serve as attention magnets.

All of this, therefore, is plainly driving us toward a hypothesis that has an obvious commonsense appeal: biological arousal matters for emotion's memory effects, presumably because of its effects on consolidation, but psychological factors matter as well. Emotion influences how people interpret, think about, and pay attention to an event, and this has a powerful impact on how people remember the emotional event later on.

Of course, there is really nothing new in this hypothesis, and obviously my colleagues have not forgotten about the importance of memory rehearsal, or the linkage between what one pays attention to and what one remembers (see Uttl & Graf, this volume). Even so, I believe the research community has undervalued this hypothesis, and this is reflected in the fact that the available research neglects some crucial questions that one might ask if one places an emphasis on these cognitive factors, rather than being guided by an arousal-based model.

For example, we know that emotional events are well-rehearsed and often discussed with others, and that this rehearsal and discussion promote memory. This is reflected in the literature on flashbulb memories, which show that the vividness and longevity of these memories is in part due to the rehearsal the memories receive (e.g., Bohannon, 1988; Hornstein, Brown, & Mulligan, 2003; Otani et al., 2005). But what aspects of the event are rehearsed? Does the rehearsal faithfully reflect some aspects of the event, but distort others? And how does the selectivity, content, or frequency of rehearsal interact with emotion? These are surely crucial questions to ask if we are to understand how rehearsal influences the recollection of emotional events, but they are questions that have been largely neglected by researchers. (Although, for a glimpse of how people talk about emotional events, a topic directly relevant to the point at issue here, see Bohanek, Fivush, & Walker, 2005.)

Likewise, both the rehearsal and the sharing of emotional memories could easily introduce systematic errors into these memories, and this invites an inquiry into how emotional events are sometimes *mis*remembered, and how this pattern is influenced by rehearsal or other mechanisms. However, we know little about this issue, because most studies in this domain evaluate memory only through a broad percent-correct measure; few studies assess the actual errors that participants make. In one of the few exceptions to this pattern, we asked, in an early study (Heuer & Reisberg, 1990), what sorts of intrusion errors people make in their recollection of emotional events. We found that the *number* of errors was the same for emotional and neutral events, but the *type* of error was different. Participants who had viewed a neutral stimulus often recalled plot elements that, in fact, had not been mentioned. Participants who had viewed an emotional stimulus, in contrast, tended to recall "psychological elements," including (for example) descriptions of the motives or feelings of the people who appeared in the stimulus, even though these motives and feelings were not mentioned in the original presentation.

We hesitate to draw strong conclusions from this single finding, based on a single stimulus sequence, and using a relatively coarse categorization of memory errors. Nonetheless, this early finding encourages me to believe that a closer scrutiny of how emotional events are misremembered would be quite fruitful. The fact that this topic is largely unexplored, though, provides further indication that investigators have been too much guided by an arousal-based view (which would not lead to the error analysis just described), and correspondingly insensitive to the sorts of questions one might ask if focused instead on the cognitive factors influencing emotional memory.

In the same vein, I have discussed a pair of interview studies by Laney, Heuer, and Reisberg (2003) and also a pair of memory studies by Laney et al. (2005), all hinging on the contrast between visually induced and thematically induced emotion. These studies remind us of a point that surely should have been obvious all along: there is considerable diversity inside the broad category of emotional events, and no reason to assume that different sorts of emotional events will be remembered in the same fashion. In fact, the opposite assumption seems far more plausible. A person's goals in an emotional situation, and also what aspects of the situation that they think are important, will surely be shaped by the nature of the emotion in play. This in turn will certainly influence what the person will pay attention to, and think about, during an emotional event (see Levine & Pizarro, this volume). And this should, of course, have an impact on memory.

This topic too, I believe, is under-researched, although, on this point, the research emphasis seems to be shifting. A number of studies have examined memory for events that specifically caused *anxiety* in the participants, and a comparison between their findings and the findings from experiments that did *not* induce anxiety can tell us a lot about the memory effects of anxiety and stress (cf. Deffenbacher et al., 2004). In addition, a much smaller number of studies have tried, within a single experiment, to compare the memory effects of different emotions. A handful of studies, for example, have compared how people remember emotionally positive and emotionally negative *pictures*, and generally show a memory advantage associated with positive affect (e.g., Bradley et al., 1992; Canli et al., 1999; Hamann et al., 1999). The data suggest that emotionally negative pictures may produce more accurate and more complete memories than emotionally positive pictures (see also Walker, Vogl, & Thompson, 1997), but this claim must be tentative, both because the data are uneven, and because it is not clear that studies have matched the emotional intensity of the two valences.

Intriguingly, Canli et al.'s (1999) data suggest that the pattern of brain activation that is predictive of subsequent memory is different for emotionally positive and emotionally negative pictures. This invites the suggestion that the two valences are not remembered in the same fashion, and, in fact, this suggestion is echoed in another study. Levine and Bluck (2004) examined people's recollection of the event in which the verdict was announced in the criminal trial of O. J. Simpson. Crucially, they contrasted the recollection of people who were *pleased* with the verdict and those who were *upset*. Their results showed that people who were happy about the trial's outcome used a more liberal criterion in judging whether elements had occurred as part of the outcome or not. As a result, those who were happy about the outcome correctly recognized more of the test items that had, in fact, occurred, but also incorrectly recognized more of the foils on the test – items that had not been part of the original event.

These (and other) data suggest that there are some differences in how people remember emotionally positive and emotionally negative events, and Levine and Bluck explain this contrast in terms of the goals created by the two valences. We should not lose sight, though, of the fact that there are also commonalities in how people remember positive and negative events. In my laboratory, for example, we have begun to compare how people remember happy events and sad events, but, once again, these studies must grapple with the fact that it is difficult to evoke an emotional response in undergraduate research participants. We have resorted, therefore, to a type of stimulus that we knew in advance was of interest to the participants. Specifically, we used *anime* presentations – a style of Japanese animation that is immensely popular with many college students.

In a study by Moyer and Reisberg (2002), participants viewed excerpts from three commercially available animes, one depicting an emotionally neutral story, one depicting an emotionally negative story, and one a positive story. The emotionality of the stimuli was confirmed by pilot testing, as was the comparability of the stimuli on several other dimensions (e.g., complexity, duration, number of scene changes).

In remembering the positive anime, the participants remembered 65 percent of the central details, compared to 51 percent in the emotionally neutral stimulus. Thus, once again, we see the broad advantage for emotional materials, relative to neutral ones. In addition, participants remembered 34 percent of the details considered peripheral by a panel of judges, compared to 46 percent for the neutral stimulus. These data therefore replicate the memory-narrowing pattern (with improved memory in the emotional condition for central materials, but impaired memory for peripheral materials), but show this effect for the first time, as far as we know, with an emotionally positive stimulus.

What about the negative anime? Although Moyer and Reisberg did not intend this, the negative anime lacks any specific visual target that can be construed as a focus for viewers' attention. Instead, the affect in this anime involves an overarching feeling of sadness concerned with two children surviving a bombing raid on their city and then losing their mother. Therefore, inadvertently, this stimulus is akin to the thematically arousing stimuli used by Laney et al. (2005), and this is reflected in the data. Once again, the emotion improved memory, with 65 percent of the central details remembered for this negative stimulus, in comparison to 51 percent for the neutral stimulus. However, in keeping with Laney et al.'s results, this (thematically arousing) anime showed no evidence of memory narrowing; that is, no evidence of an emotion-produced impairment for peripheral materials. Concretely, participants remembered 48 percent of the peripheral details of this affectively negative anime, in comparison to 46 percent for the neutral stimulus.

This study suggests an important similarity in how people remember positive and negative events. Both may show the pattern of narrowing if the event contains a suitable attention magnet, capturing the participants' attention. However, we hasten to add that the *nature* of these attention magnets may be influenced by the specific affect associated with an event. More specifically, Levine and Burgess (1997; see also Levine & Pizarro, 2004) have argued that emotions enhance memory for information that is "functionally relevant" to the emotional state, and what information that is will vary from one emotion to another. Thus, a broad categorization of an episode's elements as "central" and "peripheral" may be too crude, because information central for one emotional state may be less so for another state.

To explore this claim, Levine and Burgess (1997) manipulated participants' initial mood by telling them they had received either an "A" or a "D" on a surprise quiz. Participants then took part in what they believed to be an unrelated study during which they heard a narrative that they subsequently had to recall. The results from this memory test were complex, with the content of participants' recall influenced (as predicted) by the participants' exact emotional state. Thus, for example, participants who were *angry* tended to have better recall for information that concerned *goals* of the individuals described in the narrative; there was no relation between degree of anger and recall of other types of information. Sadness, on the other hand, was associated with enhanced recall of information about *outcomes* for individuals described in the narrative, but not with other aspects of recall. (For related data, suggesting differences in how people *report* on negative and positive events, independent of memory accuracy, see Bohanek, Fivush, & Walker, 2005.)

The Levine and Burgess study asks crucial questions, although it is not yet clear whether the details of their proposal (with regard to "goals" and "outcomes" and so on) are warranted by the data. It is also worrisome that the emotion at stake in their experiment was produced by a source external to the to-be-remembered event. (That is, it was the report of a grade that produced the emotion, but this grade had nothing to do with the narrative the participants subsequently had to recall.) This seems ironic, given that the focus of their study was on the nature of (and meaning of) the emotional event and how this influences memory. In any case, this seems an important line of research for investigators to pursue.

■ CONCLUSIONS

It has always been clear that there are two broad ways in which we might think about emotion's memory effects. One way emphasizes the arousal aspect of emotion, and, with that, emphasizes the biological mechanisms through which emotion might influence memory consolidation and attention. The second way emphasizes the cognitive, interpretive aspect of emotion, and revolves around how people pay attention to and think about emotional events. The arousal-based approach has much to recommend it, and must be part of our overall theorizing. But the arousal-based approach is plainly limited in what it can explain, and so, not surprisingly, we must also consider a more cognitive approach. Whether surprising or not, though, a shift to a more cognitive perspective leads to a research agenda somewhat different from that pursued by most investigators in this area (including, for many years, the author of this chapter). The implication, then, is that either investigators have not been considering this more cognitive perspective, or have not fully considered the implications of this perspective. In either case, it would appear that the time is ripe for a shift in how investigators approach emotion's memory effects, and, with that, the way is clear for a number of crucial new lines of work.

AUTHOR NOTE

Correspondence concerning this chapter should be addressed to Daniel Reisberg, Psychology Department, Reed College, Portland OR 97202 USA. Email: reisberg@reed.edu.

REFERENCES

Adolphs, R., Cahill, L., Schul, R., & Babinsky, R. (1997). Impaired declarative memory for emotional material following bilateral amygdala damage in humans. *Learning & Memory, 4,* 291–300.

Anderson, K. J. (1990). Arousal and the inverted-U hypothesis: A critique of Neiss's "Reconceptualizing arousal." *Psychological Bulletin, 107,* 96–100.

Bohanek, J. G., Fivush, R., & Walker, E. (2005). Memories of positive and negative emotional events. *Applied Cognitive Psychology, 19,* 51–66.

Bohannon, J. N. (1988). Flashbulb memories for the space shuttle disaster: A tale of two theories. *Cognition, 29,* 179–196.

Bornstein, B. H., Liebel, L. M., & Scarberry, N. C. (1998). Repeated testing in eyewitness memory: A means to improve recall of a negative emotional event. *Applied Cognitive Psychology, 12,* 119–132.

Bradley, M. M., Greenwald, M. K., Petry, M. C., & Lang, P. J. (1992). Remembering pictures: Pleasure and arousal in memory. *Journal of Experimental Psychology: Learning, Memory, & Cognition, 18,* 379–390.

Buchanan, T. W. & Adolphs, R. (2004). The neuroanatomy of emotional memory in humans. In D. Reisberg & P. Hertel (Eds.), *Memory and emotion* (pp. 42–75). New York: Oxford University Press.

Burke, A., Heuer, F., & Reisberg, D. (1992). Remembering emotional events. *Memory & Cognition, 20,* 277–290.

Cahill, L. & McGaugh, J. (1998). Mechanisms of emotional arousal and lasting declarative memory. *Trends in Neurosciences, 21,* 294–299.

Cahill, L., Prins, B., Weber, M., & McGaugh, J. (1994). ß-Adrenergic activation and memory for emotional events. *Nature, 371,* 702–704.

Canli, T., Zhao, Z., Desmond, J. E., Glover, G., & Gabrieli, J. D. E. (1999). fMRI identifies a network of structures correlated with retention of positive and negative emotional memory. *Psychobiology, 27,* 441–452.

Canli, T., Zhao, Z., Brewer, J., Gabrieli, J. D. E., & Cahill, L. (2000). Event-related activation in the human amygdala associates with later memory for individual emotional response. *Journal of Neuroscience, 20,* 99–103.

Christianson, S.-Å. & Loftus, E. F. (1987). Memory for traumatic events. *Applied Cognitive Psychology, l,* 225–239.

Christianson, S.-Å. & Loftus, E. (1991). Remembering emotional events: The fate of detailed information. *Cognition & Emotion, 5*, 81–108.

Christianson, S.-Å. & Mjörndal, T. (1985). Adrenalin, emotional arousal, and memory. *Scandinavian Journal of Psychology, 26*, 237–248.

Christianson, S.-Å., Nilsson, L.-G., Mjörndal, T., Perris, C., & Tjellden, G. (1986). Psychological versus physiological determinants of emotional arousal and its relation to laboratory induced amnesia. *Scandinavian Journal of Psychology, 27*, 300–310.

Conway, M., Anderson, S., Larsen, S., Donnelly, C., McDaniel, M., McClelland, A. G. R., Rawles, R., & Logie, R. (1994). The formation of flashbulb memories. *Memory & Cognition, 22*, 326–343.

Deffenbacher, K., Bornstein, B. H., Penrod, S. D., & McGorty, E. K. (2004). A meta-analytic review of the effects of high stress on eyewitness memory. *Law and Human Behavior, 28*, 687–706.

Dietrich, D. E., Waller, C., Johannes, S., Wieringa, B. M., Emrich, H. M., & Muente, T. F. (2001). Differential effects of emotional content on event-related potentials in word recognition memory. *Neuropsychobiology, 43*, 96–101.

Dudai, Y. (2004). The neurobiology of consolidation, or, how stable is the engram? *Annual Review of Psychology, 55*, 51–86.

Easterbrook, J. A. (1959). The effect of emotion on cue utilization and the organization of behavior. *Psychological Review, 66*, 183–201.

Hamann, S. B., Ely, T. D., Grafton, S. T., & Kilts, C. D. (1999). Amygdala activity related to enhanced memory for pleasant and aversive stimuli. *Nature Neuroscience, 2*, 289–293.

Heuer, F. & Reisberg, D. (1990). Vivid memories of emotional events: The accuracy of remembered minutiae. *Memory & Cognition, 18*, 496–506.

Hornstein, S., Brown, A. S., & Mulligan, N. W. (2003). Long-term flashbulb memory for learning of Princess Diana's death. *Memory, 11*, 293–306.

Intraub, H. & Richardson, M. (1989). Wide-angle memories of close-up scenes. *Journal of Experimental Psychology: Learning, Memory and Cognition, 15*, 179–187.

Jones, E. B., O'Gorman, J. G., & Byrne, B. (1987). Forgetting of word associates as a function of recall interval. *British Journal of Psychology, 78*, 79–89.

Kramer, T., Buckhout, R., & Eugenio, P. (1990). Weapon focus, arousal and eyewitness memory: Attention must be paid. *Law and Human Behavior, 14*, 167–184.

Laney, C., Campbell, H., Heuer, F., & Reisberg, D. (2005). Memory for thematically-arousing events. *Memory & Cognition, 32*, 1149–1159.

Laney, C., Heuer, F., & Reisberg, D. (2003). Thematically-induced arousal in naturally-occurring emotional memories. *Applied Cognitive Psychology, 17*, 995–1004.

Levine, L. J. & Bluck, S. (2004). Painting with broad strokes: Happiness and the malleability of event memory. *Cognition and Emotion, 18*, 559–574.

Levine, L. J. & Burgess, S. L. (1997). Beyond general arousal: Effects of specific emotions on memory. *Social Cognition, 15*, 157–181.

Levine, L. J. & Pizarro, D. A. (2004). Emotion and memory research: A grumpy overview. *Social Cognition, 22*, 530–554.

Libkuman, T. M., Nichols-Whitenead, P., Griffith, J., & Thomas, R. (1999). Source of arousal and memory for detail. *Memory & Cognition, 27*, 166–190.

Loftus, E., Loftus, G., & Messo, J. (1987). Some facts about "weapon focus." *Law and Human Behavior, 11*, 55–62.

Maass, A. & Köhnken, G. (1989). Eyewitness identification. *Law and Human Behavior, 13*, 397–408.

McGaugh, J. L. (2000). Memory – a century of consolidation. *Science, 287*, 248–251.

McGaugh, J. L. (2003). *Memory and emotion: The making of lasting memories.* New York: Columbia University Press.

McGaugh, J. L. (2004). The amygdala modulates the consolidation of memories of emotionally arousing experiences. *Annual Review of Neuroscience, 27*, 1–28.

McNay, E. C. & Gold, P. E. (2002). Food for thought: fluctuations in brain extracellular glucose provide insight into the mechanisms of memory modulation. *Behavioral and Cognitive Neuroscience Reviews, 1*, 264–280.

Moyer, M. & Reisberg, D. (2002). *Pollyanna revisited: Do we remember equally the good and the bad?* Unpublished BA thesis, Reed College, Portland, Oregon.

Neiss, R. (1990). Ending arousal's reign of error: A reply to Anderson. *Psychological Bulletin, 107*, 101–105.

Neisser, U. & Harsch, N. (1992). Phantom flashbulbs: False recollections of hearing the news about *Challenger*. In E. Winograd & U. Neisser (Eds.), *Affect and accuracy in recall: Studies of "flashbulb" memories* (pp. 9–31). Cambridge: Cambridge University Press.

Ochsner, K. N. & Schacter, D. L. (2003). Remembering emotional events: A social cognitive neuroscience approach. In R. J. Davidson, H. Goldsmith, & K. R. Scherer (Eds.), *Handbook of the affective sciences* (pp. 343–360). New York: Oxford University Press.

Otani, H., Kusumi, T., Kao, K., Matsuda, K., Kern, R. P., Widner, R., Jr., & Ohta, N. (2005). Remembering a nuclear accident in Japan: Did it trigger flashbulb memories? *Memory, 13*, 6–20.

Payne, J. D., Nadel, L., Britton, W. B., & Jacobs, W. J. (2004). The biopsychology of trauma and memory. In D. Reisberg & P. Hertel (Eds.), *Memory and emotion* (pp. 76–128). New York: Oxford University Press.

Peace, K. A. & Porter, S. (2004). A longitudinal investigation of the reliability of memories for trauma and other emotional experiences. *Applied Cognitive Psychology, 18*, 1143–1159.

Peters, D. (1988). Eyewitness memory and arousal in a natural setting. In M. Gruneberg, P. Morris, & R. Sykes (Eds.), *Practical aspects of memory: Current research and issues* (pp. 89–94). New York: John Wiley & Sons.

Pickel, K. L. (1998). Unusualness and threat as possible causes of "weapon focus." *Memory, 6*, 277–295.

Pillemer, D., Goldsmith, L., Panter, A., & White, S. (1988). Very long-term memories of the first year in college. *Journal of Experimental Psychology: Learning, Memory & Cognition, 14*, 709–715.

Porter, S. & Birt, A. (2001). Is traumatic memory special? A comparison of traumatic memory characteristics with memory for other emotional life experiences. *Applied Cognitive Psychology, 15*, S101–S117.

Reisberg, D. & Heuer, F. (2004). Memory for emotional events. In D. Reisberg & P. Hertel (Eds.), *Memory and emotion* (pp. 3–41). New York: Oxford University Press.

Reisberg, D. & Heuer, F. (2005). The influence of emotion on memory in forensic settings. In M. P. Toglia, J. D. Read, D. F. Ross, & R. C. L. Lindsay (Eds.), *Handbook of eyewitness psychology, Vol. 1: Memory for events*. Hillsdale, NJ: Erlbaum.

Reisberg, D., Heuer, F., McLean, J., & O'shaughnessy, M. (1988). The quantity, not the quality, of affect predicts memory vividness. *Bulletin of the Psychonomic Society, 26*, 100–103.

Rubin, D. C. & Kozin, M. (1984). Vivid memories. *Cognition, 16*, 81–95.

Safer, M. A., Christianson, S. Å., Autry, M. W., & Österlund, K. (1998). Tunnel memory for traumatic events. *Applied Cognitive Psychology, 12*, 99–118.

Schmidt, S. R. & Williams, A. R. (2001). Memory for humorous cartoons. *Memory & Cognition, 29*, 305–311.

Stanny, C. J. & Johnson, T. C. (2000). Effects of stress induced by a simulated shooting on recall by police and citizen witnesses. *American Journal of Psychology, 113*, 359–386.

Steblay, N. J. (1992). A meta-analytic review of the weapon focus effect. *Law and Human Behavior, 16*, 413–424.

Tollestrup, P. A., Turtle, J. W., & Yuille, J. C. (1994). Actual victims and witnesses to robbery and fraud: An archival analysis. In D. F. Ross, J. D. Read, & M. P. Toglia (Eds.), *Adult eyewitness testimony: Current trends and developments* (pp. 144–160). New York: Cambridge University Press.

Walker, W. R., Vogl, R. J., & Thompson, C. P. (1997). Autobiographical memory: Unpleasantness fades faster than pleasantness. *Applied Cognitive Psychology, 11*, 399–414.

Wessel, I. & Merckelbach, H. (1997). The impact of anxiety on memory for details in spider phobics. *Applied Cognitive Psychology, 11*, 223–232.

Wessel, I. & Merckelbach, H. (1998). Memory for threat-relevant and threat-irrelevant cues in spider phobics. *Cognition & Emotion, 12*, 93–104.

Wessel, I., van der Kooy, P., & Merckelbach, H. (2000). Differential recall of central and peripheral details of emotional slides is not a stable phenomenon. *Memory, 8*, 95–109.

3

Emotional Valence, Discrete Emotions, and Memory

Linda J. Levine and David A. Pizarro

Abstract

Recently, considerable progress has been made toward understanding whether and how emotion enhances memory, but much of the research on this issue has been limited by its treatment of emotion as merely "arousal." Drawing on appraisal theories of emotion, we argue that a more complete understanding of the effects of emotion on memory will depend on taking into account the motivations and problem-solving strategies associated with discrete emotions. Given their distinct functions, the types of information that are of central importance, and hence well remembered, should differ depending on the specific emotion being experienced. In support of this view, we present research showing that people process and remember information differently depending on whether they are feeling happy, fearful, angry, or sad.

In scientific explanation, parsimony is a good thing. But the appeal to simplicity at the heart of the principle of parsimony can at times lead to oversimplification. Scientists must sometimes ask themselves, how simple is too simple? Take, for instance, the case of emotion and memory. Memory researchers have often conceptualized emotion as "arousal" – a variable that can be measured on a single scale ranging from relaxed to very excited or agitated. While research on memory stemming from an arousal-based model of emotion has led to fundamental advances, we will argue that this account nevertheless errs on the side of simplicity, leaving us with an incomplete picture of the effects of emotion on memory (see Reisberg, this volume, for a similar perspective). Recent findings suggest that a more complete understanding of the effects of emotion on memory will depend on taking into account the differing motivations and problem-solving strategies associated with discrete emotions such as happiness, fear, anger, and sadness.

Our claim that these specific emotions should have unique effects on memory is based on three sources of evidence. First, arousal-based models of emotion are unable to explain some recent findings within the emotion and memory literature. Recent research has shown, for instance, that positive and negative emotions that are similar in terms of the intensity of arousal have very different effects on how information is processed and remembered (e.g., Bless et al., 1996; Bodenhausen, Kramer, & Susser, 1994; Fiedler, Asbeck, & Nickle, 1991; Forgas, 1998; Levine & Bluck, 2004; Park & Banaji, 2000). Second, appraisal theories of emotion provide a strong theoretical and empirical tradition that distinguishes the causes and consequences of discrete emotions (e.g., Ellsworth & Scherer, 2003; Frijda, 1987; Oatley & Johnson-Laird, 1987; Roseman, Wiest, & Swartz, 1994; Scherer, 1984, 1998; Smith & Lazarus, 1993; Stein & Levine, 1987; Stein, Trabasso, & Liwag, 2000; Weiner, 1985). According to this view, emotions such as happiness, fear, anger, and sadness serve important functions because of the different influences they have on thought and behavior. Third, there is now substantial research demonstrating that these specific emotions have differential effects on judgment, and a growing body of research showing that the same may be true for memory (e.g., Bodenhausen, Shepard, & Kramer, 1994; DeSteno et al., 2000; Lench & Levine, 2005; Lerner & Keltner, 2001; Levine & Burgess, 1997; Mathews & Klug, 1993; Small et al., 2005; Tiedens & Linton, 2001).

Accordingly, we first review research on emotion and memory stemming from an arousal-based approach and demonstrate why it may be incomplete. We then describe evidence that positive and negative emotions are associated with different information processing strategies that, in turn, affect memory. This is followed by a discussion of theory and research concerning the functions of discrete emotions and the appraisal processes that elicit them. Finally, we review the effects of these discrete emotions on judgment and memory.

■ EMOTIONAL AROUSAL AND MEMORY

It is clear that emotional arousal has a powerful effect on memory. Converging evidence from autobiographical memory studies, animal and human laboratory studies, and brain imaging studies shows that emotionally arousing events are, by and large, remembered better than non-emotional events. For example, when people are asked to recall autobiographical events that they had previously recorded in diaries, greater emotional intensity is associated with greater memory vividness – even after controlling for event novelty, importance, and the amount of rehearsal (e.g., Conway, 1995; Thompson et al., 1996).

Laboratory studies with animals and humans have provided a compelling neurobiological explanation for this finding. Researchers have shown that stress hormones, such as epinephrine, are released when events evoke strong emotions. These peripheral stress hormones in turn activate noradrenergic systems in the amygdala, and amygdala activation mediates consolidation of long-term memory in other brain regions (e.g., Cahill et al., 1994; for a review, see McGaugh & Cahill, 2003). The causal role of the amygdala in strengthening emotional memories is well documented. For instance, infusing stress hormones directly into the amygdala enhances memory for emotional information, while inactivating this region through the use of lesions or drugs attenuates the enhancing effects of stress hormones on memory (McGaugh, 2000).

Brain imaging studies provide further evidence that the amygdala plays an important role in the consolidation or strengthening of memory for emotionally arousing events (Dolcos, LaBar, & Cabeza, this volume; Ochsner & Schacter, 2003). For example, Canli et al. (2000) conducted an fMRI study in which participants saw negative and neutral pictures. An fMRI response was recorded in the amygdala as participants rated each picture for emotional intensity. Participants were later given a surprise recognition test for the pictures they had rated. The results showed that the more emotionally intense participants found the pictures, the more bilateral activation was found in the amygdala. Pictures that had been rated as the most emotionally intense were remembered better, on average, than pictures rated as less intense. Moreover, the greater the left amygdala activation, the more likely participants were to remember emotionally intense pictures (also see Cahill et al., 1996).

Relative to affectively neutral events, then, emotionally arousing events tend to produce memories that are vivid, detailed, and lasting (LeDoux, 2000). Indeed, some have argued that highly emotional memories are retained with close to photographic accuracy (Brown & Kulik, 1977), or (in the case of conditioned fear) are indelible (Fanselow & Gale, 2003; LeDoux, 1992, 1996). It is increasingly evident, however, that emotional memories are far from perfectly accurate or permanent. Recent research shows that, like memory for neutral information, emotional memories are subject to fading over time and to biases in the direction of current goals and experiences (e.g., Levine, Whalen, Jamner, & Henker, 2005; for reviews, see Levine & Pizarro, 2004; Levine, Safer, & Lench, in press). Thus, characterizing emotional memory as akin to flashbulb photography or indelible ink may be too strong. A more appropriate characterization may be that emotion acts as a mental "highlighter," increasing the salience of information from the environment and from memory much as a hand-held highlighter increases the salience of text.

Over the last couple of decades we have also learned a great deal about the type of information that emotion highlights. Information that is central to the emotional event is typically well retained, but peripheral details can get short shrift (e.g., Christianson & Loftus, 1991). For instance, in one study, participants were presented with one of two matched slide sequences depicting either an emotional event (a boy hit by a car) or a neutral event (a boy walking beside a car). All participants wrote down the central feature of each slide.

Participants who viewed the emotional slide sequence were better able to recall the central features than participants who viewed the neutral sequence, but they were less able to recognize the particular slides they had seen (Christianson & Loftus, 1987). Following Easterbrook (1959), researchers have hypothesized that as arousal increases, the focus of attention narrows to highlight the most relevant aspects of an emotional event; since attention is a limited resource, peripheral details are less likely to be remembered (see also Mathews, this volume; Reisberg, this volume).

Overall, the finding of enhanced memory for central aspects of emotional events has been well supported (e.g., Adolphs, Denburg, & Tranel, 2001; Berntsen, 2002; Burke, Heuer, & Reisberg, 1992; Safer et al., 1998; for a review, see Reisberg & Heuer, 2004). Moreover, some studies have shown better memory for emotionally arousing stimuli, independent of their emotional valence (e.g., Bradley et al., 1992; Hamann et al., 1999). So why look beyond general arousal? A growing body of findings concerning the effects of emotion on judgment and memory cannot be explained in terms of a simple arousal-based model of emotion. We turn first to evidence that positive and negative emotions, even at similar levels of arousal, have very different effects on cognitive processes.

 ## EFFECTS OF EMOTIONAL VALENCE ON JUDGMENT AND MEMORY

Emotional valence and judgment

At least since Aristotle in the fourth century BCE, it has been observed that emotions color the way we think about the world (Aristotle 1991). Advertisers, salespeople, and politicians have long relied on this fact in crafting emotionally based appeals to sell their products and programs. But recently, psychologists have made further strides toward understanding *how* emotions change the way we think. Research on emotion and judgment has demonstrated differences between judgments made while people are experiencing positively and negatively valenced emotions (usually mild happiness or sadness). Across a wide variety of studies, it has been shown that positive and negative emotions are associated with different information processing strategies which affect judgment.

When happy people evaluate arguments or make social judgments, they tend to rely more on prior knowledge, stereotypes, or heuristics than do people in a neutral or negative mood (e.g., Fiedler, 2000; Forgas, 1998, 2003; Higgins, 2001). They also tend to be creative and flexible when solving reasoning problems or generating semantic associates of words (Fredrickson, 2001; Isen, Daubman, & Nowicki, 1987). This may be because people experiencing positive and negative emotions have different motivations. According to Schwarz and Clore (1983), people experience happiness when goals have been attained and no immediate problem demands to be solved. Having appraised circumstances as favorable or benign, happiness appears to promote a schema-based, top-down information processing strategy in which people draw freely and flexibly on prior knowledge (i.e., pre-existing ideas, attitudes, and expectations); often referred to as "heuristic processing." In contrast, people experience negative emotions when goals have failed and there is a problem to solve. When people are feeling negative emotions, they tend to process information in an analytic, data-driven manner, and are more conservative in their judgments; often referred to as "systematic processing." For instance, researchers have demonstrated that experiencing sadness leads people to rely less on stereotypes and to perform better on certain deductive reasoning tasks (for a review, see Bless & Schwarz, 1999).

Emotional valence and memory

The differing information processing strategies associated with positive and negative emotion affect not only judgment, but memory as well. For instance, Bless et al. (1996) induced a happy or sad mood in participants, and then presented them with information about common activities (e.g., eating at a restaurant). Some of the information was consistent with general knowledge or schemas (e.g., "the hostess placed the menus on the table") and some was not consistent (e.g., "he put away his tennis racket"). Later, participants were given a surprise recognition test with both old and new information. The results showed that happy people were more likely than sad people to "recognize" information consistent with general knowledge – independent of whether that information had actually been presented. In contrast, sad people tended to be more conservative and more accurate in their recognition judgments. Similarly, Park and Banaji (2000) found that happy participants showed a bias toward greater leniency in recognizing ethnic names as members of stereotypical categories, leading to many instances of false recognition. In contrast, participants in a negative mood used a more stringent criterion when making recognition judgments. Thus laboratory studies have shown that positive emotion leads to greater reliance on general knowledge or stereotypes, and to intrusion errors in memory, whereas negative emotion leads to more conservative recognition judgments.

Distinguishing between the information processing strategies associated with positive and negative emotion helps explain otherwise puzzling findings in the literature on autobiographical memory. For example, Berntsen (2002) had independent judges code the content of people's most negative and positive autobiographical memories for central and peripheral information. Negative memories focused primarily on central information, as would be predicted by arousal-based models, but positive memories did not. Instead, positive memories tended to include a wide range of information. In addition, positive and negative autobiographical memories often differ in both subjective clarity and objective accuracy. When asked about the subjective clarity or vividness of autobiographical memories that they have previously recorded in diaries, people tend to rate positive life events as better remembered than negative life events (e.g., Matlin & Stang, 1978; Rubin & Berntsen, 2003; Thompson et al., 1996; Walker, Vogl, & Thompson, 1997). Paradoxically, though, when researchers look at the objective accuracy of people's accounts, they typically find no valence effect (e.g., Holmes, 1970) or superior memory for negative events (e.g., Banaji & Hardin, 1994; Bluck & Li, 2001; Kreitler & Kreitler, 1968). Thus people seem to believe that they remember happy events better than they actually do.

One explanation for these findings is that people experiencing positive and negative emotions (that are similar in terms of level of arousal) process information differently. Levine and Bluck (2004) hypothesized that, when recalling events that made them happy, people may "paint with broad strokes," drawing on information encoded when events first occurred but also drawing freely on their general knowledge about what is plausible to fill in gaps in their representations. If so, happy memories should be associated with greater subjective memory clarity, but also with more intrusion errors, than negative memories. To test this hypothesis, they assessed participants' emotions and memories concerning the televised announcement of the verdict in the murder trial of O. J. Simpson. In the memory assessment, half of the events presented had actually occurred; for example, "O. J. Simpson mouthed the words 'thank you' to the jury." Half were plausible but hadn't occurred, for example, "O. J. Simpson gave the 'thumbs up' sign to his lawyer, Robert Shapiro." (These events were pretested with a separate group of participants who had not seen the verdict announcement on TV. The pretest showed that the true and false events did not differ significantly in plausibility.) After two months, participants rated how clearly they recalled the events. After 14 months, they completed a surprise recognition test.

The results showed that, after two months, participants whose initial emotional reaction to the verdict announcement was positive recalled events with greater clarity than participants whose initial reaction was negative or neutral. Similarly, after more than a year, participants whose initial reaction was positive recognized more events than participants whose initial reaction was negative. This does not mean that participants who felt happy about the verdict were more accurate, however – they were not. Happy participants recalled events with greater clarity, and recognized more events, independent of whether or not the events had actually occurred. Participants whose reaction

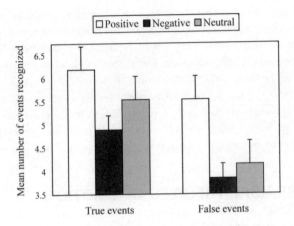

Figure 3.1 Mean number of true and false events recognized after 14 months by participants whose emotional response to O. J. Simpson's acquittal was positive, negative, or neutral (Levine & Bluck, 2004).

to the verdict was negative were more likely to err in a conservative fashion by rejecting events. Figure 3.1 shows participants' recognition judgments. Signal detection analyses confirmed that the threshold for judging events as having occurred was lower for people who were happy about the verdict than for people whose reaction was negative.

These findings demonstrated that the association between happiness and reconstructive memory errors, previously found in brief laboratory studies, extends to memory for real-world events and over prolonged retention intervals. Memories become sketchy over time. When remembering events that made them happy (i.e., events that are consistent with their goals), people seem to draw flexibly on general knowledge, sometimes confusing plausible and actual events. Incorporating plausible or schema-congruent information from general knowledge when remembering events that evoked happiness would result in representations that are *experienced* as more complete. This may explain why people often rate positive events as better remembered than negative events (e.g., Thompson et al., 1996), even though studies with objective measures tend to show no differences or even superior memory for negative events (e.g., Banaji & Hardin, 1994; Bluck & Li, 2001). When remembering events that evoked negative emotion (i.e., events that conflict with their goals), people were more conservative in their memory judgments. People may adopt a more conservative, data-driven strategy when remembering negative events in the service of repairing past negative outcomes or avoiding future ones (see also Mather, this volume, for a similar argument regarding memory retrieval in older adults).

The broader point is that these findings cannot be explained in terms of general emotional arousal. People experiencing positive and negative emotions have different motivations. They process information differently as a result, and these differences affect memory. The emotional life of an individual consists of more than positive and negative moods, however. People make judgments and store, retrieve, and act on information when they are experiencing a variety of specific emotions such as fear, anger, and sadness. These emotions may each have their own influences on what people think and remember. Thus, we turn next to theory and research on discrete emotions.

■ APPRAISAL THEORIES OF EMOTION

Appraisal theories of emotion grew out of a long tradition in emotion research that recognized that emotions come in a variety of basic types, each with its own causes, consequences, and functions. The evolutionary approach characterizes specific emotions as solutions to the general problem of survival (e.g., Darwin, 1965). For example, fear motivates animals to avoid danger, allowing them to live long enough to pass along their genes. Like fear, other discrete emotions are thought to have evolved to solve particular types of problems. Appraisal theories extended this broad evolutionary approach to address the cognitive elicitors of emotion. That is, if a rapidly approaching figure engenders fear in an individual, it is because it is recognized as a threat to an important goal. The process of appraisal that leads to fear would instead lead to happiness if the approaching figure were recognized, not as a predator, but as a loved one. Although appraisal theories developed independently from research on emotion and memory, we believe that they provide a useful framework for addressing some of the limitations of arousal-based models. Thus, we first take a closer look at the assumptions underlying appraisal theories and then discuss how they may elucidate the effects of emotions on judgment and memory.

Beginning with the work of Magda Arnold (1960) and Richard Lazarus (1968), and influenced by the approach of Herbert Simon (1967), appraisal theories have focused on identifying the functions that specific emotions fulfill within the cognitive system. In his 1967 paper "Motivational and Emotional Controls of Cognition," Simon noted that models of human information processing typically neglect the interaction of cognition with emotion. He argued that the cognitive system simply could not function without processes that do what emotions do. Unlike computers, human beings are constrained in a number of ways: we have multiple and ever-shifting goals, limited cognitive resources, and an environment that is in constant flux. Given these constraints, people need a way to keep track of information that is important. Thus, to ensure survival, a certain amount of continuous background processing (not necessarily conscious) is necessary to monitor the environment for information that an important goal has been threatened, especially given that the goal in question may not be within current attentional focus. When information relevant to the status of a goal is detected, it must be possible to interrupt ongoing processing and behavior, reprioritize goals, and direct cognitive resources to the affected goal. Simon argued that emotion fulfills this function by acting as an "interrupt mechanism" that signals the presence of information relevant to a goal.

To illustrate how emotions might serve this interrupting function, consider another set of subjective feeling states that is critical for survival: hunger, thirst, and fatigue. In the absence of such feelings, people would have to actively monitor how long it had been since they had last eaten, drunk, or slept, a task that would require considerable cognitive resources. Undifferentiated arousal alone (i.e., signaling that "some essential goal" is affected) would not provide enough information about the type of behavior needed to respond to the situation. Because people have discrete subjective states associated with the needs for food, liquid, and rest, though, no one is in danger of lying down to take a nap when the body needs food. Given their importance for survival, it is not surprising that these subjective states influence subsequent cognitions in a goal-consistent manner. For example, hungry people rate high calorie snacks as more desirable than people who have just eaten (Gilbert, Driver-Linn, & Wilson, 2002; Read & van Leeuwen, 1998). Thirsty people rate water as more important to hikers in the wilderness than those who are not thirsty (Van Boven & Loewenstein, 2003). Thus, for a small set of physiological goals that must be maintained to ensure survival, each goal is associated with a unique subjective feeling state that interrupts ongoing thought and behavior, reprioritizes goals, and directs cognitive resources toward information relevant to fulfilling those goals.

Human beings have thousands of goals, however, ranging from keeping family relations intact, to finishing an article, to stopping at the market to buy milk before it runs out. Indeed, human beings have far too many goals for it to be feasible to have a distinct subjective feeling that monitors the status of each one, especially since these goals are constantly changing. This is where discrete emotions enter the picture. Discrete emotions provide an elegant general-purpose solution to the problem of monitoring information relevant to an individual's many current goals. This is because, unlike drive states such as hunger and thirst, each of which are tied to the status of one specific goal, discrete emotions such as happiness, fear, anger, and sadness are sensitive to a wide variety of goals. According to cognitive appraisal theories, people experience emotions when events are appraised as relevant to the status of *some* goal, and a response is required – typically, revising goals and beliefs and constructing new plans. Discrete emotions are thought to have evolved so that organisms could respond adaptively to different types of changes in the status of their goals. Once evoked, discrete emotions direct attention to information that is functional – that is, useful for responding to the type of situation that typically evokes the emotion (e.g., Frijda, 1987; Oatley & Johnson-Laird, 1987; Ortony, Clore, & Collins, 1988; Scherer, 2003; Stein & Levine, 1987, 1990).

Several models have been proposed describing the different goal-related appraisals, motivations, and problem-solving strategies associated with discrete emotions. Researchers have provided evidence for these models using a variety of methods, including analyses of accounts of autobiographical events, responses to vignettes in which appraisal dimensions have been varied, and experimental manipulations of emotions (e.g., Ellsworth & Scherer, 2003; Frijda, 1987; Levine, 1995, 1996; Oatley & Johnson-Laird, 1987; Ortony, Clore & Collins, 1988; Roseman, 1991; Roseman, Wiest, & Swartz, 1994; Scherer, 1984, 1998; Smith & Lazarus, 1993; Stein & Levine, 1989; Weiner, 1985). We have chosen to focus on the emotions happiness, fear, anger, and sadness because, even among researchers who question the notion that certain emotions are basic and universal (e.g., Ortony & Turner, 1990), there is significant agreement that these four states are associated with unique and coherent patterns of eliciting appraisals, facial expressions, subjective feeling states, motivations, and action tendencies.

While appraisal theories differ in details, the results support the following general rules concerning the patterns of appraisal that elicit basic emotions. *Happiness* is evoked when people perceive events as conducive to goal attainment. That is, people feel happy when they attain something they value or avoid something they find unpleasant. Conversely, people feel negative emotions such as fear, anger, and sadness when they fail to attain or maintain something they value or fail to avoid something unpleasant. *Fear* is evoked when goal failure is threatened but has not yet occurred. *Anger* is evoked when goals are obstructed and people believe that something can be done to reinstate the goal (Levine, 1995; Stein & Levine 1989) or that they have power or control over the situation (Roseman, 1991; Scherer, 1984). In contrast, *sadness* is evoked when people believe that a goal has failed irrevocably and cannot be reinstated, leaving them with little power or control over the loss (Izard, 1977; Levine 1995; Roseman, 1991; Scherer, 1984; Smith & Lazarus, 1993; Stein & Levine, 1989).

Because these emotions depend on people's appraisals of a situation, the same events can elicit anger or sadness, depending on people's beliefs about their ability to cope with goal failure, and their beliefs about whether the failure was caused by an intentional agent or by an uncontrollable force. Intentional harm may come to evoke anger because people realize that events that are under a person's control can often be changed or prevented from recurring. When harm is caused accidentally or by forces outside human control, there are fewer options for reversing the situation, leading more often to the experience of sadness (Levine, 1995).

The appraisals associated with discrete emotions are not a sophisticated adult overlay on more primitive emotional processes. Developmental psychologists have shown that in the first year of life infants display facial expressions of happiness in response to success at instrumental attempts to attain a goal, anger when goals are obstructed, fear when danger is threatened (e.g., fear of heights), and sadness at losses (Alessandri, Sullivan, & Lewis, 1990; Campos, Bertenthal, & Kermoian, 1992; Lewis et al., 1992; Sroufe & Waters, 1976; Stenberg, Campos, & Emde, 1983; for reviews, see Lewis, 2000; Witherington, Campos, & Hertenstein, 2001). Children as young as three explain emotions in terms of whether goals have been attained or obstructed (Stein & Levine, 1989), and by the age of five, distinguish anger from sadness based in part on whether they believe that goal reinstatement is possible or impossible (Levine, 1995).

Once elicited, how might discrete emotions affect subsequent cognitive processes? According to appraisal theories, by reprioritizing goals, emotions serve as a powerful organizing force, not just for behavior, but for perception, judgment, and memory as well (Dalgleish, 2004; Frijda, 1987; Lerner & Keltner, 2000; Oatley & Johnson-Laird, 1987; Roseman, Wiest, & Swartz, 1994; Stein & Levine, 1987). In the service of responding to the types of circumstances that lead to their elicitation, discrete emotions should cause people to become attuned to, and to search for, information that is relevant to their emotional state. Thus, the types of information that are of central importance, as opposed to being peripheral details, would be expected to differ depending upon a person's specific emotional state (Levine & Pizarro, 2004). Because the activation of one goal can automatically inhibit the accessibility of alternative goals (Shah, Friedman, & Kruglanski, 2002), information peripheral to the motivational state of the emotion being experienced may become less accessible.

Appraisal theories allow one to make predictions about the types of information that should be most relevant or central in specific emotional states. Happiness has been found to exert a variety of cognitive and behavioral effects that Frederickson (1998) has characterized as "broaden-and-build" tendencies. It promotes expansive thoughts and actions such as affiliation, play, exploration, creative thinking, and the use of broader sources of information when making decisions. Fear is elicited by the perception of a threat of goal failure and motivates thoughts and behaviors directed toward avoiding the threat. Thus, when frightened, people would be expected to selectively attend to, encode, and retrieve information concerning threats and means of avoiding them. Anger is elicited when goals are obstructed; it motivates thoughts and behaviors directed toward removing the obstruction. Thus, angry people should selectively encode and retrieve information concerning goals and the agents or causes responsible for obstructing the goal. This focus on goals and the causes of failure would serve an important function. People are most likely to construct effective plans to reinstate their goals if they understand who or what caused the situation that they are trying to change. In contrast, sadness is elicited when people appraise goal failure as irrevocable. For the sad person, information concerning the risks and causes of failure (central information for the frightened or angry person, respectively) would be irrelevant or peripheral. When a goal fails and cannot be reinstated, its failure affects all of the goals, beliefs, and plans that are associated with it. Thus, when sad, understanding the outcomes and consequences of failure becomes centrally important. Sadness may ultimately be followed by plans to substitute more attainable goals. In the midst of the emotional episode, however, the withdrawal and passivity commonly associated with sadness may reflect the difficult mental work of coming to terms with the need to revise prior goals and expectations (Levine, 1996).

Based on appraisal theories, then, emotions should differ in their effects on subsequent cognition. A growing body of research supports this view, but much of it has focused on the effects of specific emotions on judgment. We review these findings below and then turn to the sparse but intriguing findings suggesting that discrete emotions also affect the content of memories.

 ## EFFECTS OF DISCRETE EMOTIONS ON JUDGMENT AND MEMORY

Discrete emotions and judgment

Researchers have shown differing effects of discrete emotions on judgment in domains as disparate as risk and probability, stereotyping, economic decision-making, public policy, and moral judgment. These effects have been demonstrated even when the emotions were elicited by events unrelated to the judgment at hand (e.g., Bodenhausen, Sheppard, & Kramer, 1994; DeSteno et al., 2000; Forgas, 1998; Lerner & Keltner, 2001; Park & Banaji, 2000; Small et al., 2005). So while anger may certainly affect the way you think about the neighbor who just crashed into your car, that same anger also affects the way you think about your spouse when you later walk in the door. In a series of studies, Lerner and her colleagues assessed the effects of anger and fear on judgments concerning risk. They found that inducing fear caused people to be very sensitive to the possibility of risk, and to inflate the probability that something bad might happen. Inducing anger, on the other hand, caused people to minimize the risk associated with acting (Lerner & Keltner, 2001; Small et al., 2005). Lench and Levine (2005) found that inducing fear reduced people's unrealistic optimism that negative outcomes were more likely to happen to others than to themselves.

Researchers have also contrasted the effects of anger and sadness on judgments in a variety of domains. The results are consistent with the view that anger increases the salience of the causes or agents responsible for goal obstruction, whereas sadness increases the salience of irrevocable losses. For example, DeSteno et al. (2000) found that inducing anger in participants led to greater estimates of the likelihood of events in which others intentionally caused harm (e.g., being knowingly sold a "lemon" by a dishonest car dealer), whereas inducing sadness led to greater estimates of the likelihood of losses (e.g., a best friend moving away). Bodenhausen, Sheppard, & Kramer (1994) found that participants made to feel angry relied more on stereotypes when making judgments concerning blame than participants made to feel sad; for example, judging a person with an ethnic (i.e., Latino) name as more legally culpable for an alleged incident of misconduct than a person with a traditional English name. In another study, inducing anger led to more spontaneous judgments of causality and blame about the September 11 terrorist attacks than inducing sadness (Small et al., 2005).

Thus, a growing body of evidence indicates that discrete emotions differ in their effects on judgment. Researchers studying social judgment initially assumed that emotions act by influencing the processing of information in one of two ways – by encouraging slow and careful "systematic" processing or by encouraging quick-and-dirty "heuristic" processing. For instance, Tiedens and Linton (2001) elegantly demonstrated that discrete emotions associated with appraisals of *certainty* (such as happiness, anger, and disgust) encourage more heuristic processing, such as relying on the expertise of a source of communication when evaluating arguments. Emotions associated with *uncertainty* (such as sadness and fear), on the other hand, promoted more careful, systematic styles of thinking. The findings above, however, point to a more complex picture of how emotions affect judgment. Rather than simply affecting the *type* of processing, discrete emotions appear to influence the *content* of information processing. Thus, while anger and fear might both lead to the use of heuristics, the information that an angry person draws on from prior knowledge may be very different from the information accessed while afraid. Further research is needed to examine whether anger leads to heuristic processing about blame, sadness to heuristic processing about loss, and fear to heuristic processing about risk. The conditions under which discrete emotions promote heuristic versus systematic processing also remain to be specified.

Discrete emotions and memory

Research on memory and discrete emotions, albeit limited, reveals a pattern of findings similar to the literature on discrete emotions and judgment. Fearful people display enhanced memory for threat-related information and poorer memory for threat-irrelevant details. For example, Wessel and Merckelbach (1998) investigated the effects of fear on memory in a sample of spider phobics. Phobic and low-fear control participants were shown a bulletin board to which central (pictures of spiders) and peripheral (pictures of babies and pens) stimuli were attached. As expected, spider phobics displayed an increase in physiological markers of fear when viewing the display. Later, when asked to recall the display, spider phobics showed enhanced memory for the central, threatening information and impaired memory for peripheral, non-threatening information. The association between fear and enhanced memory for threatening stimuli also has been noted by investigators assessing the accuracy and completeness of eyewitness testimony. For instance, "weapon focus" refers to witnesses' tendency to focus on and remember the weapon used to commit a crime, often at the expense of memory for other information such as the perpetrator's face (e.g., Kramer, Buckhout, & Eugenio, 1990; Loftus, Loftus, & Messo, 1987; Steblay, 1992; see also Reisberg, this volume).

Clinically anxious people also exhibit attentional and memory biases characterized by hypersensitivity to threat. These biases are found most reliably when researchers assess attention to, and encoding of, threat-related information rather than retrieval (MacLeod & Mathews, 2004; see also Mathews, this volume). For example, Mathews and Klug (1993) used an emotional Stroop paradigm to assess color-naming latencies (a sign of greater attention) for positive and negative threat-related words, positive and negative non-threat-related words, and neutral words. Participants were patients with a variety of anxiety disorders and controls. They found that anxious patients took longer to name the colors of both positive and negative threat-related words (but not positive or negative words unrelated to threat) than to name the colors of neutral words. Selective retrieval of threatening information has also been found (though less consistently) in studies using implicit memory measures (for reviews, see MacLeod & Mathews, 2004; Minetka, Rafaeli, & Yovel, 2003). For example, Mathews, Richards, and Eysenck (1989) had clinically anxious people and controls listen to and write down homophones (words that sound alike but have two meanings and spellings). Each of the homophones had a threatening meaning and a neutral meaning (e.g., *die* and *dye*). They found that anxious participants were more likely than controls to write down the threatening meaning when they heard the sound of the word, suggesting that threatening information may be more accessible in memory for these people.

One explanation for these findings is that they have little to do with discrete emotions but are simply further evidence for the memory-enhancing effects of emotional arousal. But appraisal theory makes very different predictions about memory across specific emotional states that may be similar in terms of levels of arousal. Preliminary support for these predictions comes from research showing that people experiencing different emotions seem to display enhanced memory for different types of information. People in a depressed mood who are asked to recall autobiographical events tend to focus, not on sources of threat, but on negative outcomes such as personal losses and defeats. For instance, Lyubomirsky, Caldwell, and Nolen-Hoeksema (1998) found that moderately sad or depressed people recalled more negative autobiographical events associated with loss (e.g., failing a test, losing a girlfriend, their parents' divorce) than did non-depressed people. Moreover, although depression and post-traumatic stress disorder (PTSD) are both characterized by the presence of intrusive memories, the content of the intrusive information for these two disorders differs. Consistent with the differing motivations associated with sadness and fear, depression is characterized by rumination on past negative outcomes and their consequences for the self, whereas PTSD is characterized by intrusive memories related to past threats to safety (e.g., Lyubomirsky, Caldwell, & Nolen-Hoeksema, 1998; Reynolds & Brewin, 1999; Watkins & Teasdale, 2001).

In an attempt at a more direct test of the predictions made by appraisal theory, Levine and Burgess (1997) conducted a study contrasting discrete emotions in the same study, to see if each emotion would lead to enhanced memory for particular kinds of information. Specifically, they assessed the effects of happiness, anger, and sadness on the encoding of information in a narrative. Emotions were evoked in undergraduates by randomly assigning grades of "A" or "D" on a surprise quiz. Immediately afterwards, students participated in what they believed to be an unrelated study. During the study they heard and later recalled a narrative about a student's first term in college. Finally, they rated how happy, angry, and sad they had felt when they received their quiz grade. In contrast to happy participants, who demonstrated enhanced memory for the narrative as a whole, participants who reported feeling primarily sad or primarily angry tended to recall specific types of information. As predicted, sad participants recalled significantly more information concerning event outcomes than did angry participants (e.g., "They receive a bad grade on the speech"). Angry participants showed a non-significant tendency to recall more information about the protagonist's goals than did sad participants (e.g., "Mary wants her speech to be really good"). In addition, a significant positive correlation was found between the intensity of anger reported and the amount of information that participants recalled about goals.

Further research is needed to identify the mechanisms underlying the effects of discrete emotions on memory, but the findings reported above lend support to the view that discrete emotions evoke "appraisal tendencies" (Lerner & Keltner, 2000) as well as "action tendencies" (Frijda, 1987), influencing the processing, encoding, and retrieval of information in ways consistent with their differing functions.

■ CONCLUSION

A great deal of research on emotion and memory has been based on the assumption that emotion can be characterized as general arousal. This model has been fruitful. Fundamental advances have been made toward identifying the mechanisms underlying the memory-enhancing effects of emotional arousal, including the roles played by stress hormones and by the amygdala. So, why should researchers studying emotion and memory be interested in valence and discrete emotions? Assumptions about the characteristics of emotion determine the very questions researchers ask. While illuminating certain phenomena, favored assumptions may leave others in the dark (Campos, Campos, & Barrett, 1989). We have argued that a more complete understanding of how emotion affects memory will necessitate taking into account properties of emotion that are just as fundamental as arousal. Namely, discrete emotions such as happiness, fear, anger, and sadness are responses to very different types of changes in the status of goals, and they motivate cognitions as well as behaviors directed toward maintaining, preventing, or coping with those changes.

Further research on discrete emotions and memory is needed to confirm this claim, but three sources of evidence provide reason to take this approach to emotion seriously. First, positive and negative memories differ in ways that cannot be explained using a solely arousal-based model of emotion. It is well documented that positive and negative emotion can lead to conceptually driven and data-driven processing, respectively. A growing body of evidence shows that these information-processing strategies affect memory. Second, research based on appraisal theories has provided evidence that discrete emotions are elicited by different interpretations of events and promote dissimilar problem-solving strategies. Third, although research comparing the effects of discrete emotions on memory is sparse, a few studies have shown that information relevant to the functions of discrete emotions appears to be particularly salient in memory.

We began by comparing emotional arousal to a highlighter that enhances the salience of central information. Drawing on recent research on the effects of emotional valence and discrete emotions on memory, this illustration can now be extended. Rather than a single highlighter, emotions appear to be akin to a set of highlighters with differing properties. Whereas happiness acts as a broad, inclusive highlighter that increases the salience of a wide swath of information, negative emotions seem to work like fine-tip highlighters, increasing the salience of a narrow range of information in the service of either preventing (fear), fixing (anger), or adjusting to (sadness) goal failure. By conceptualizing emotions not as general arousal but as a group of related responses, each with its own functions, causes, and consequences, we hope to encourage further advances toward understanding the information processing strategies evoked by particular emotions and the types of information that are of central importance, and hence well remembered, in specific emotional states.

AUTHOR NOTE

Correspondence concerning this chapter should be addressed to Linda J. Levine, Department of Psychology and Social Behavior, University of California, Irvine, 3340 Social Ecology Building II, Irvine, CA 92697-7085 USA. Email: llevine@uci.edu.

REFERENCES

Adolphs, R., Denburg, N. L., & Tranel, D. (2001). The amygdala's role in long-term declarative memory for gist and detail. *Behavioral Neuroscience, 115*, 983–992.

Alessandri, S. M., Sullivan, M. W., & Lewis, M. (1990). Violation of expectancy and frustration in early infancy. *Developmental Psychology, 26*, 738–744.

Aristotle (1991). *The art of rhetoric*. (H. C. Lawson-Tranced, Trans.) Oxford: Penguin Books.

Arnold, M. (1960). *Emotion and personality: Vol 1. Psychological aspects*. New York: Columbia University Press.

Banaji, M. R. & Hardin, C. (1994). Affect and memory in retrospective reports. In N. Schwarz & S. Sudman (Eds.), *Autobiographical memory and the validity of retrospective reports* (pp. 71–86). New York: Springer-Verlag.

Berntsen, D. (2002). Tunnel memories for autobiographical events: Central details are remembered more frequently from shocking than from happy experiences. *Memory and Cognition, 30*, 1010–1020.

Bless, H., Clore, G. L., Schwarz, N., Golisano, V., Rabe, C., & Wölk, M. (1996). Mood and the use of scripts: Does a happy mood really lead to mindlessness? *Journal of Personality and Social Psychology, 71*, 665–679.

Bless, H. & Schwarz, N. (1999). Sufficient and necessary conditions in dual process models: The case of mood and information processing. In S. Chaiken & Y. Trope (Eds.), *Dual process theories in social psychology* (pp. 423–440). New York: Guilford Press.

Bluck, S. & Li, K. Z. H. (2001). Predicting memory completeness and accuracy: Emotion and exposure in repeated autobiographical recall. *Applied Cognitive Psychology, 15*, 145–158.

Bodenhausen, G. V., Kramer, G. P., & Susser, K. (1994). Happiness and stereotypic thinking in social judgment. *Journal of Personality & Social Psychology, 66*, 621–632.

Bodenhausen, G. V., Sheppard, L. A., & Kramer, G. P. (1994). Negative affect and social judgment: The differential impact of anger and sadness. *European Journal of Social Psychology, 24*, 45–62.

Bradley, M. M., Greenwald, M. K., Petry, C., & Lang, P. J. (1992). Remembering pictures: Pleasure and arousal in memory. *Journal of Experimental Psychology: Learning, Memory, & Cognition, 18*, 379–390.

Brown, R. & Kulik, J. (1977). Flashbulb memories. *Cognition, 5*, 73–99.

Burke, A., Heuer, F., & Reisberg, D. (1992). Remembering emotional events. *Memory & Cognition, 20,* 277–290.

Cahill, L., Haier, R., Fallon, J., Alkire, M., Tang, C., Keater, D., Wu, J., & McGaugh, J. L. (1996). Amygdala activity at encoding correlated with long-term, free recall of emotional information. *Proceedings of the National Academy of Sciences, USA, 93,* 8016–8021.

Cahill, L., Prins, B., Weber, M., & McGaugh, J. L. (1994). Adrenergic activation and memory for emotional events. *Nature, 371,* 702–704.

Campos, J. J., Bertenthal, B. I., & Kermoian, R. (1992). Early experience and emotional development: The emergence of wariness of heights. *Psychological Science, 3,* 61–64.

Campos, J., Campos, R., & Barrett, K. (1989). Emergent themes in the study of emotional development and emotion regulation. *Developmental Psychology, 25,* 394–402.

Canli, T., Zhao, Z., Brewer, J., Gabrieli, J. D. E., & Cahill, L. (2000). Event-related activation in the human amygdala associates with later memory for individual emotional response. *Journal of Neuroscience, 20,* RC99.

Christianson, S. Å. & Loftus, E. F. (1987). Memory for traumatic events. *Applied Cognitive Psychology, 1,* 225–239.

Christianson, S. Å. & Loftus, E. F. (1991). Remembering emotional events: The fate of detailed information. *Cognition & Emotion, 5,* 81–108.

Conway, M. A. (1995). *Flashbulb memories.* Hillsdale, NJ: Erlbaum.

Dalgleish, T. (2004). Cognitive approaches to post-traumatic stress disorder: The evolution of multirepresentational theorizing. *Psychological Bulletin, 130,* 228–260.

Darwin, C. (1965). *The expression of the emotions in man and animals.* Chicago: University of Chicago Press.

DeSteno, D., Petty, R. E., Wegener, D. T., & Rucker, D. D. (2000). Beyond valence in the perception of likelihood: The role of emotion specificity. *Journal of Personality and Social Psychology, 78,* 397–416.

Easterbrook, J. A. (1959). The effects of emotion on cue utilization and the organization of behavior. *Psychological Review, 66,* 183–201.

Ellsworth, P. C. & Scherer, K. R. (2003). Appraisal processes in emotion. In R. J. Davidson, K. R. Scherer, & H. H. Goldsmith (Eds.), *Handbook of Affective Sciences* (pp. 572–595). New York: Oxford University Press.

Fanselow, M. S. & Gale, G. D. (2003). The amygdala, fear, and memory. *Annals of the New York Academy of Sciences, 985,* 125–134.

Fiedler, K. (2000). Toward an integrative account of affect and cognition phenomena using the BIAS computer algorithm. In J. P. Forgas (Ed.), *Feelings and thinking: The role of affect in social cognition* (pp. 223–252). Cambridge: Cambridge University Press.

Fiedler, K., Asbeck, J., & Nickel, S. (1991). Mood and reconstructive memory effects on social judgment. *Cognition & Emotion, 5,* 363–378.

Forgas, J. P. (1998). On being happy and mistaken: Mood effects on the fundamental attribution error. *Journal of Personality and Social Psychology, 75,* 318–331.

Forgas, J. P. (2003). Affective influences on attitudes and judgments. In R. J. Davidson, K. R. Scherer, & H. H. Goldsmith (Eds.), *Handbook of affective sciences* (pp. 596–218). New York: Oxford University Press.

Fredrickson, B. L. (1998). What good are positive emotions? *Review of General Psychology*, *2*, 300–319.

Fredrickson, B. L. (2001). The role of positive emotions in positive psychology: The broaden-and-build theory of positive emotions. *American Psychologist*, *56*, 218–226.

Frijda, N. H. (1987). Emotion, cognitive structure, and action tendency. *Cognition and Emotion*, *1*, 115–143.

Gilbert, D. T., Driver-Linn, E., & Wilson, T. D. (2002). The trouble with Vronsky: Impact bias in the forecasting of future affective states. In L. F. Barrett & P. Salovey (Eds.), *The wisdom in feeling: Psychological processes in emotional intelligence* (pp. 114–143). New York: Guilford Press.

Hamann, S. B., Ely, T. D., Grafton, S. T., & Kilts, C. D. (1999). Amygdala activity related to enhanced memory for pleasant and aversive stimuli. *Nature Neuroscience*, *2*, 289–293.

Higgins, E. T. (2001). Promotion and prevention experiences: Relating emotions to nonemotional motivational states. In J. P. Forgas (Ed.), *Handbook of affect and social cognition* (pp. 186–211). Hillsdale, NJ: Erlbaum.

Holmes, D. S. (1970). Differential change in affective intensity and the forgetting of unpleasant experiences. *Journal of Personality and Social Psychology*, *3*, 234–239.

Isen, A. M., Daubman, K. A., & Nowicki, G. P. (1987). Positive affect facilitates creative problem solving. *Journal of Personality and Social Psychology*, *52*, 1122–1131.

Izard, C. E. (1977). *Human emotions*. New York: Plenum.

Kramer, T. H., Buckhout, R., & Eugenio, P. (1990). Weapon focus, arousal, and eye-witness memory: Attention must be paid. *Law and Human Behavior*, *14*, 167–184.

Kreitler, H. & Kreitler, S. (1968). Unhappy memories of "the happy past": Studies in cognitive dissonance. *British Journal of Psychology*, *59*, 157–166.

Lazarus, R. S. (1968). Emotions and adaptation: Conceptual and empirical relations. In W. J. Arnold (Ed.), *Nebraska symposium on motivation*. Lincoln: University of Nebraska Press.

LeDoux, J. E. (1992). Emotion as memory: Anatomical systems underlying indelible neural traces. In S. Å. Christianson (Ed.), *The handbook of emotion and memory: Research and theory* (pp. 269–288). Hillsdale, NJ: Erlbaum.

LeDoux, J. E. (1996). *The emotional brain*. New York: Touchstone.

LeDoux, J. E. (2000). Emotion circuits in the brain. *Annual Review of Neuroscience*, *23*, 155–184.

Lench, H. C. & Levine, L. J. (2005). Effects of fear on risk and control judgments and memory: Implications for health promotion messages. *Cognition and Emotion*, *19*, 1049–1069.

Lerner, J. S. & Keltner, D. (2000). Beyond valence: Toward a model of emotion-specific influences on judgment and choice. *Cognition and Emotion*, *14*, 473–493.

Lerner, J. S. & Keltner, D. (2001). Fear, anger, and risk. *Journal of Personality and Social Psychology*, *81*, 146–159.

Levine, L. J. (1995). Young children's understanding of the causes of anger and sadness. *Child Development*, *66*, 697–709.

Levine, L. J. (1996). The anatomy of disappointment: A naturalistic test of appraisal models of sadness, anger, and hope. *Cognition and Emotion*, *10*, 337–359.

Levine, L. J. & Bluck, S. (2004). Painting with broad strokes: Happiness and the malleability of event memory. *Cognition and Emotion, 18*, 559–574.

Levine, L. J. & Burgess, S. L. (1997). Beyond general arousal: Effects of specific emotions on memory. *Social Cognition, 15*, 157–181.

Levine, L. J. & Pizarro, D. A. (2004). Emotion and memory research: A grumpy overview. *Social Cognition, 22*, 530–554.

Levine, L. J., Safer, M. A., & Lench, H. C. (in press). Remembering and misremembering emotions. In L. J. Sanna & E. C. Chang (Eds.), *Judgments over time: The interplay of thoughts, feelings, and behaviors.* New York: Oxford University Press.

Levine, L. J., Whalen, C. K., Jamner, L. D., & Henker, B. (2005). Looking back on September 11, 2001: Appraised impact and memory for emotions in adolescents and adults. *Journal of Adolescent Research, 20*, 497–523.

Lewis, M. (2000). The emergence of human emotions. In M. Lewis & J. M. Haviland-Jones (Eds.), *Handbook of emotions* (2nd ed., pp. 265–280). New York: Guilford Press.

Lewis, M., Sullivan, M. W., Ramsay, D. S., & Alessandri, S. M. (1992). Individual differences in anger and sad expressions during extinction: Antecedents and consequences. *Infant Behavior & Development, 15*, 443–452.

Loftus, E. F., Loftus, G. R., & Messo, J. (1987). Some facts about "weapon focus." *Law & Human Behavior, 11*, 55–62.

Lyubomirsky, S., Caldwell, N. D., & Nolen-Hoeksema, S. (1998). Effects of ruminative and distracting responses to depressed mood on retrieval of autobiographical memories. *Journal of Personality and Social Psychology, 75*, 166–177.

McGaugh, J. L. (2000). Memory: A century of consolidation. *Science, 287*, 248–251.

McGaugh, J. L. & Cahill, L. (2003). Emotion and memory: Central and peripheral contributions. In R. J. Davidson, K. R. Scherer, & H. H. Goldsmith (Eds.), *Handbook of affective sciences* (pp. 93–116). New York: Oxford University Press.

MacLeod, C. & Mathews, A. (2004). Selective memory effects in anxiety disorders: An overview of research findings and their implications. In D. Reisberg, & P. Hertel (Eds.), *Memory and emotion* (pp. 155–185). Oxford: Oxford University Press.

Mathews, A. & Klug, F. (1993). Emotionality and interference with color-naming in anxiety. *Behaviour Research and Therapy, 31*, 57–62.

Mathews, A., Richards, A., & Eysenck, M. (1989). Interpretation of homophones related to threat in anxiety states. *Journal of Abnormal Psychology, 98*, 31–34.

Matlin, M. W. & Stang, D. J. (1978). *The Pollyanna principle: Selectivity in language, memory, and thought.* Cambridge, MA: Schenkman Publishing.

Minetka, S., Rafaeli, E., & Yovel, I. (2003). Cognitive biases in emotional disorders: Information processing and social-cognitive perspectives. In R. J. Davidson, K. R. Scherer, & H. H. Goldsmith (Eds.), *Handbook of affective sciences* (pp. 976–1009). New York: Oxford University Press.

Oatley, K. & Johnson-Laird, P. N. (1987). Toward a cognitive theory of emotions. *Cognition and Emotion, 1*, 29–50.

Ochsner, K. N. & Schacter, D. L. (2003). Remembering emotional events: A social cognitive neuroscience approach. In R. J. Davidson, K. R. Scherer, & H. H. Goldsmith (Eds.), *Handbook of affective sciences* (pp. 643–660). New York: Oxford University Press.

Ortony, A., Clore, G. L., & Collins, A. (1988). *The cognitive structure of emotions.* Cambridge: Cambridge University Press.

Ortony, A. & Turner, T. J. (1990). What's basic about basic emotions? *Psychological Review, 97,* 315–331.

Park, J. & Banaji, M. R. (2000). Mood and heuristics: The influence of happy and sad states on sensitivity and bias in stereotyping. *Journal of Personality and Social Psychology, 78,* 1005–1023.

Read, D. & van Leeuwen, B. (1998). Predicting hunger: The effects of appetite and delay on choice. *Organizational Behavior and Human Decision Processes, 76,* 189–205.

Reisberg, D. & Heuer, F. (2004). Memory for emotional events. In D. Reisberg & P. Hertel (Eds.), *Memory and emotion* (pp. 3–41). New York: Oxford University Press.

Reynolds, M. & Brewin, C. R. (1999). Intrusive memories in depression and post-traumatic stress disorder. *Behaviour Research & Therapy, 37,* 201–215.

Roseman, I. J. (1991). Appraisal determinants of discrete emotions. *Cognition and Emotion, 5,* 161–200.

Roseman, I. J., Wiest, C., & Swartz, T. S. (1994). Phenomenology, behaviors, and goals differentiate discrete emotions. *Journal of Personality and Social Psychology, 67,* 206–221.

Rubin, D. C. & Berntsen, D. (2003). Life scripts help to maintain autobiographical memories of highly positive, but not highly negative, events. *Memory & Cognition, 31,* 1–14.

Safer, M. A., Christianson, S. Å., Autry, M. W., & Osterlund, K. (1998). Tunnel memory for traumatic events. *Applied Cognitive Psychology, 12,* 99–117.

Scherer, K. R. (1984). Emotion as a multicomponent process. In P. Shaver (Ed.), *Review of personality and social psychology* (Vol. 5, pp. 37–63). Beverley Hills, CA: Sage.

Scherer, K. R. (1998). Appraisal theory. In T. Dalgleish & M. Power (Eds.), *Handbook of cognition and emotion* (pp. 637–664). Chichester: Wiley.

Scherer, K. R. (2003). Cognitive components of emotion. In R. J. Davidson, K. R. Scherer, & H. H. Goldsmith (Eds.), *Handbook of the affective sciences* (pp. 563–571). New York: Oxford University Press.

Schwarz, N. & Clore, G. L. (1983). Mood, misattribution, and judgments of well-being: Information and directive function of affective states. *Journal of Personality and Social Psychology, 45,* 513–523.

Shah, J. Y., Friedman, R., & Kruglanski, A. W. (2002). Forgetting all else: On the antecedents and consequences of goal shielding. *Journal of Personality & Social Psychology, 83,* 1261–1280.

Simon, H. (1967). Motivational and emotional controls of cognition. In H. Simon (Ed.), *Models of thought* (pp. 29–38). New Haven, CT: Yale University Press.

Small, D. A., Lerner, J. S., Gonzalez, R. M., & Fischoff, B. (2005). *Emotion priming and attributions for terrorism: Americans' reactions in a national field experiment.* Unpublished manuscript.

Smith, C. A. & Lazarus, R. S. (1993). Appraisal components, core relational themes, and the emotions. *Cognition and Emotion, 7,* 233–269.

Sroufe, L. A. & Waters, E. (1976). The ontogenesis of smiling and laughter: A perspective on the organization of development in infancy. *Psychological Review, 83,* 173–89.

Steblay, N. M. (1992). A meta-analytic review of the weapon focus effect. *Law & Human Behavior, 16,* 413–424.

Stein, N. L. & Levine, L. J. (1987). Thinking about feelings: The development and organization of emotional knowledge. In R. E. Snow & M. Farr (Eds.), *Aptitude, learning, and instruction: Vol. 3. Cognition, conation and affect* (pp. 165–197). Hillsdale, NJ: Erlbaum.

Stein, N. L. & Levine, L. J. (1989). The causal organization of emotional knowledge: A developmental study. *Cognition and Emotion, 3,* 343–378.

Stein, N. L. & Levine, L. J. (1990). Making sense out of emotion: The representation and use of goal-structured knowledge. In N. L. Stein, B. Leventhal, & T. Trabasso (Eds.), *Psychological and biological approaches to emotion* (pp. 45–73). Hillsdale, NJ: Erlbaum.

Stein, N. L., Trabasso, T., & Liwag, M. D. (2000). A goal appraisal theory of emotional understanding: Implications for development and learning. In M. Lewis & J. M. Haviland-Jones (Eds.), *Handbook of emotions* (2nd ed., pp. 436–457). New York: Guilford Press.

Stenberg, C. R., Campos, J. J., & Emde, R. N. (1983). The facial expression of anger in seven-month-old infants. *Child Development, 54,* 178–184.

Thompson, C. P., Skowronski, J. J., Larsen, S. F., & Betz, A. (1996). *Autobiographical memory: Remembering what and remembering when.* Mahwah, NJ: Erlbaum.

Tiedens, L. Z. & Linton, S. (2001). Judgment under emotional certainty and uncertainty: The effects of specific emotions on information processing. *Journal of Personality and Social Psychology, 81,* 973–988.

Van Boven, L. & Loewenstein, G. (2003). Projection of transient drive states. *Personality and Social Psychology Bulletin, 29,* 1159–1168.

Walker, W. R., Vogl, R. J., & Thompson, C. P. (1997). Autobiographical memory: Unpleasantness fades faster than pleasantness over time. *Applied Cognitive Psychology, 11,* 399–413.

Watkins, E. & Teasdale, J. D. (2001). Rumination and overgeneral memory in depression: Effects of self-focus and analytic thinking. *Journal of Abnormal Psychology, 110,* 353–357.

Weiner, B. (1985). An attributional theory of achievement motivation and emotion. *Psychological Review, 92,* 548–573.

Wessel, I. & Merckelbach, H. (1998). Memory for threat-relevant and threat-irrelevant cues in spider phobics. *Cognition and Emotion, 12,* 93–104.

Witherington, D. C., Campos, J. J., & Hertenstein, M. J. (2001). Principles of emotion and its development. In G. Bremner & A. Fogel (Eds.), *Blackwell handbook of infant development* (pp. 427–464). Oxford: Blackwell.

Remembering Emotional Events: The Relevance of Memory for Associated Emotions

4

Sven Å. Christianson and Elisabeth Engelberg

Abstract

The chapter presents a brief review of basic principles uncovered in studies of the relations between emotion and memory. Understanding these principles is crucial when eliciting and evaluating the recall of witnesses to and victims and perpetrators of violent crime. Research shows that traumatic experiences tend to persist in memory, both with respect to the emotional event itself and with respect to the central, critical detail information of the emotion-eliciting event. Such consistent findings make it possible to capitalize on the interconnection that seems to exist between memory for the event as such and associated emotions. We discuss the issue of memory of associated emotions in order to highlight their potential as cues in retrieving information from episodic memory.

During the past two decades there has been a keen interest in the study of emotion and memory for stressful events, and part of the aim of this chapter is to provide a brief overview. There is a need for this line of research in view of the many important forensic applications. It has been revealed that mistaken eyewitness identification is responsible for more wrongful convictions than are all other causes combined (Yarmey, 2001), and the issue has been raised about the risk of both jurors and judges making faulty analyses of eyewitness testimony (Patterson, 2004; Wise & Safer, 2004).

A related field of research is the study of *memory for emotion*, which is a relevant and important issue to pursue. Emotional reactions experienced in response to violence and trauma are usually thought to be elicited by critical details of such events. In other words, memory for emotions seems to be dependent to some degree upon recall of critical details of event memory and vice versa. A better understanding of the interconnection that seems to exist between memory of emotional events, on the one hand, and emotions evoked at that time, on the other, may enable the development of more efficient interviewing techniques.

First, our review covers prior research on memory for emotional events. It mainly consists of a comparison of the relative merits of laboratory experiments and real-life studies in furthering our understanding of the factors that determine the reliability of memories of crime events among bystanders, victims, and perpetrators. Second, research findings are rather consistent in that the recall pattern for emotional events centers on details that are thought to have caused the evoked emotions. Such consistent findings make it possible to capitalize on the interconnection that seems to exist between memory for the event as such and associated emotions. We focus, therefore, on the issue of memory of associated emotions in order to highlight their potential as cues in retrieving information from episodic memory. The ultimate aim of obtaining greater insight into the representation of emotional events in memory is the application of a proper interviewing technique that will enable more comprehensive recall of the emotional event.

Our overall discussion deals primarily with memory for negative emotional events and emotions. This is the result of the forensic psychologist's efforts to obtain information about a crime from a witness or victim and the clinical psychologist's interest in eliciting the memories of traumatized patients.

■ MEMORY FOR EMOTIONAL EVENTS

Current psychological research shows that there is no single effect of emotion and trauma on memory for a traumatic event. Rather, there appear to be a variety of patterns that vary in both amount (from total memory loss, through recall of a few details, to a very detailed account) and accuracy (from a false account, through accuracy concerning the main "gist"/central details, to an almost completely accurate account) (Yuille & Daylen, 1998; see also Goodman & Paz-Alonso, this volume; Kihlstrom, this volume). Which of these recall patterns is exhibited appears to be a function of the type of emotional/traumatic event, the person's emotional involvement, and the memory measurements used.

Findings from both real-life studies and experimental studies suggest that certain characteristics of negative emotional events are perceived and retained in an automatic fashion. In particular, experimental research reveals that there is a superior advantage for the detection and recognition of stimuli indicative of threatening situations (Christianson, 1997). A study by Christianson and colleagues (Christianson et al., 1991) showed that the level of memory performance for subjects presented with emotional stimuli (e.g., involving blood) at very short exposures (180 ms) was almost identical to that found for subjects presented with the same emotional stimuli at longer exposure durations. Another finding is that the level of recognition is higher for unpleasant stimuli (pictures of victims of traffic accidents, war, malady, famine), as compared to neutral scenes (people in everyday situations) and positive stimuli (e.g., sexual pictures of nudes in very sensual summer scenes) (Christianson & Fällman, 1990). Neuropsychological studies suggest that individuals are able to process fear-related visual stimuli in the absence of attention because emotional stimuli activate the amygdala, even when individuals are unaware that the information has been presented (e.g., Vuilleumier et al., 2002).

Perhaps we are predisposed to retain certain characteristics of emotional information that had a survival value in earlier stages of evolution. In line with Öhman (1979, 1991), we argue that when people are exposed to a stressful event, critical stimulus features, such as blood stains, may be extracted and evaluated as emotionally significant and thus activate an orienting response Due to attention-demanding stimulus characteristics and personal involvement, controlled conceptual resources are subsequently allocated for further analysis of the stimulus. In short, critical details will be extracted by pre-attentive mechanisms and controlled processes will subsequently be allocated to the emotionally relevant information. This mode of processing would hypothetically promote memory for central-detail information, but impair memory for peripheral details that are irrelevant and/or spatially peripheral to the emotion-eliciting event. In support of this assumption, there is the main finding, from both laboratory studies and studies of real-life events, that emotions improve memory for central details, or the gist of an event, but at the same time undermine memory for peripheral aspects of the event (e.g., Burke, Heuer, & Reisberg, 1992; Christianson, 1984; Christianson & Loftus, 1987, 1990, 1991; Wessel & Merckelbach, 1997; for reviews, see Christianson, 1992; Reisberg & Heuer, 2004). In an early study by Christianson (1984), participants were presented with a slide sequence depicting an emotional or neutral version of an event. Participants who had been exposed to the emotional version (a boy hit by a car) showed higher memory performance for main features of the event, as compared to participants in the neutral condition (a boy walking beside a car). When they were tested by means of a recognition test, in which the main features of each stimulus slide were held constant and only the peripheral or surrounding details were manipulated, no difference was found between conditions; that is, all subjects remembered equally well.

In a subsequent study by Christianson and Loftus (1991) the memory of background information was specifically controlled for. Participants were shown a thematic series of slides in which the emotional valence of the critical slide was varied by holding the to-be-remembered features, that is the central and peripheral details, constant. In the neutral version, the critical slide showed a woman riding a bicycle. In the emotional version, the same woman was seen lying injured on the street near the bicycle. In both versions, a car was parked in the distant background. A series of experiments using this material showed that the central or critical information associated with the woman was better retained in the emotional condition, whereas the parked car was better retained among participants in the neutral condition.

Real-life events

Is it possible to generalize laboratory findings to real-life traumatic events? The advantage of laboratory studies over studies of real-life situations is that, in the laboratory, normative data may be collected to assist in the definition of centrality of detail. It must be that "centrality" as well as associated information, such as information preceding and succeeding events, is defined by a continuum and not by absolute categories. Nonetheless, the approach of studying both laboratory findings and case studies is essential. There are unique benefits of studying the effects of emotion on memory by analyzing traumatic events as they have occurred naturally; however, the precise mechanisms underlying such effects may only be delineated in laboratory studies. Yet, in most laboratory studies, emotion has generally been evoked by some salient visual stimulus (e.g., the sight of a child's bleeding eyeball or wounded legs). It may be, then, that these "attention magnets" (see Reisberg, this volume) and not emotional arousal per se have been the cause of the observed narrowing of memory. In examining memory for thematically induced arousal in either laboratory events or in naturally occurring emotional memories, results indicate that emotionality improves memory for all aspects of these events, with no memory narrowing (Laney et al., 2003, 2004). Although caution is appropriate when applying laboratory results to real-life events, there are indications of selective focusing in real-life situations, especially in extreme cases of negative emotional impact, for example shooting situations (Karlsson & Christianson, 2003), rape cases (Christianson & Nilsson, 1989), and in cases of repeated child sexual abuse (Christianson & Lindholm, 1998; Terr, 1990).

One example of real-life situations is flashbulb events. Since Brown and Kulik (1977) introduced the phenomenon of flashbulb memory, a great number of studies have shown a rather impressive concordance in people's memories of the circumstances they were in when they received the news of nationally shocking events (e.g., Bohannon & Symons, 1992; McCloskey, Wible, & Cohen, 1988; Pillemer, 1984; Warren & Swartwood, 1992). Many of these studies, however, have not included a control event for comparison. In a study on the flashbulb memory of the murder of Swedish Prime Minister Olof Palme, respondents were asked to recount a personal event they had experienced during the weekend prior to the murder (Christianson, 1989). When comparing the memory data collected one year later, it was found that respondents showed better recall for the circumstances surrounding the news of the flashbulb event than for the personal event. Only 22 percent of the respondents were able to recall anything at all about the control event. In contrast, 80–90 percent of the respondents reported roughly the same information in response to the canonical flashbulb questions that they had provided a year earlier. A more stringent analysis of the data revealed, however, that memory for some details had markedly deteriorated, such as the exact time at which they received the news, and the clothing worn. Several other studies have shown that flashbulb memories may very well contain some erroneous information and that the "flashbulb" or "video camera" metaphors are misleading (e.g., Greenberg, 2004; McCloskey et al., 1988; Neisser, 1982; Neisser & Harsch, 1992).

In order to investigate whether consistent memory for event details was linked to accurate memory for associated emotions, we included measures of emotional reactions that were evoked in response to yet another nationally shocking event. Our study was based on the flashbulb memory of the news about the Estonia ferry disaster on the Baltic Sea in 1994 (Christianson & Engelberg, 1999). After 14 months, participants' recollections of the circumstances surrounding the news were well retained; however, less than a third of the participants could accurately recall their emotions. When analyzing data broken down with respect to under- and over-estimators, results revealed that approximately two thirds of the sample showed inconsistency in their recall of emotional reactions (see also Levine & Pizarro, this volume). This result is likely explained by the fact that the participants did not have relatives or friends on board the ferry. Although respondents assigned a high degree of national importance to the disaster, the event did not have any foreseeable repercussions that would affect their day-to-day life (see also Goodman & Paz-Alonso, this volume). Another finding from the literature on flashbulb events similarly implies that there is no given relation between emotions and the perception of consequentiality. For instance, the investigation of people's recollections of the football tragedy at the Hillsborough stadium in 1989 showed that men considered it to be more important than did women, but men also thought it was less emotional (Wright, Gaskell, & Muirchaertaigh, 1998).

With regard to forensic situations, however, research on so-called flashbulb memories may not fully apply. Rather, studying police reports and interviewing victims and witnesses of actual crimes, such as murders or bank robberies, may be of greater personal relevance for the people affected due to their direct involvement in these types of events. In a study by Yuille and Cutshall (1986), 13 witnesses to a murder were interviewed within two days after the crime and again four to five months later. The results showed a high degree of accuracy of memory and little decline over time. Furthermore, subjects who reported the highest amount of stress showed a mean accuracy of 93 percent in the initial police interview and a mean accuracy of 88 percent four to five months later. On the basis of the results from this study and similar studies using the same approach (Fisher, Geiselman, & Amandor, 1989; Yuille & Cutshall, 1989, Yuille & Tollestrup, 1992), we may conclude that a high stress level at the time of a traumatic event does not appear to negatively affect memory for actions and details. Christianson and Hübinette (1993) asked 110 witnesses of 22 bank robberies to fill out a questionnaire four to fifteen months after the crime event. The data showed that witnesses remembered details related to the crime event itself, such as how it was initiated as well as the weapon and the robber's clothing. They showed poorer memory for details peripheral to the crime event, such as the time of day and the number of customers present in the bank. When comparing the data from the survey with the memory of the staff that had been directly threatened by the robbers, it was found that the staff showed better memory for details of the crime event. This difference in event memory may be explained by the relative difference in the emotional reactions elicited among witnesses as compared to the staff.

A variation of the witness interview approach is to simply ask people about their memories for emotional events. In a survey of college students' positive and negative childhood event memories, Butler and Wolfner (2000) found that negative and positive memories were similar with respect to recall, vividness, and number of central as well as peripheral details. However, negative memories were found to be associated with less present emotion than were positive memories and with more instances of a highly memorable detail. Peace and Porter (2004) examined the consistency and characteristics of memories for traumatic and other non-traumatic emotional experiences over time. Results indicated that traumatic experiences tended to persist in memory, whereas positive memories were subject to considerable distortion. In a diary study of traumatized persons' involuntary memories, Berntsen (2001) found that trauma memories were extraordinarily persistent. Moreover, when asking people about their autobiographical memories, Reisberg et al. (1988) found that the more intense the emotional event, the more confident one was of the memory. In a similar interview study by Christianson and Loftus (1990), over 400 subjects were asked to report their "most traumatic memory" and to answer questions about their chosen memory. A major finding was a significant relationship between rated degree of emotion and the number of "central" details, but not "peripheral" details, the subjects believed they remembered. This result contradicts to some extent the results of Butler and Wolfner (2000), but as argued by Christianson and Lindholm (1998), much of the difference across studies concerning memories for traumatic events is caused by differences in what detail information is studied.

Taken together, according to most laboratory studies and survey studies of emotional/traumatic events, and interviewing victims and witnesses of violent crimes, there seems to be a strong correlation between affect strength and rated memory vividness, at least for the central and critical details of the emotional events. However, there are exceptions to these patterns. For example, victims of rape, torture, sexual abuse, and war, who have experienced extreme states of negative emotions, may sometimes initially show episodes of partial or complete amnesia (Christianson & Engelberg, 1997; Terr, 1990; van der Kolk, 1988; Williams, 1994; see also Goodman & Paz-Alonso, this volume; Kihlstrom, this volume). Furthermore, in forensic psychology, the vast majority of existing research on memory and emotion has focused on bystander witnesses and victims of crime. In recent years, however, researchers have shown increasing interest in offenders, and in the way offenders remember their crimes. An often-reported finding is that claims of amnesia regularly occur in murder cases, sexual crime cases, and domestic violence cases (for a review, see Christianson & Merckelbach, 2004). The next section will address memory loss in crime victims and the effects of trauma on the recall of *offenders*, or more specifically, crime-related amnesia.

Memory loss in crime victims and offenders

In some cases of violent crime, the emotional impact may lead to memory loss. Nonetheless, central details tend to constitute critical retrieval cues, as illustrated by the case study of CM (Christianson & Nilsson, 1989). The young woman was jogging on a trail in a wooded area where she was attacked and beaten. She made ferocious attempts to escape the assailant, but was overpowered and dragged out into a meadow where she was raped. When later found by another jogger, she was unable to recall what had happened to her. Her memory loss was diagnosed as a dissociative amnesia[1] (see also Kihlstrom, this volume). It was several months later that she recovered her memory. It was during her first jogging occasion following the assault that fragments of the traumatic event flashed before her eyes. After slowly being able to retrieve a more coherent memory of the rape event, she realized that the trail she had just been running on was partially covered with crushed brick. It was similar to the brick that was spread out over the trail in the area where the rape had occurred. She remembered the pieces of red brick in visual focus during her panicked attempt to escape the rapist. During the time of her memory loss, she had been brought back to the area by the police and had spontaneously uttered "the brick and the path." When brought onto the actual path, she began to perspire profusely and showed intense distress.

Central details of the crime event were seemingly retained and stored separately from episodic memory of the event as such (cf., Brewin, Dalgliesh, & Joseph, 1996). Sensory information, especially of the visuospatial kind, may be accessed automatically upon exposure to relevant cues and may be spontaneously re-experienced in the form of detailed visual images, affective responses, and emotion-laden flashbacks corresponding to moments of intense arousal during the trauma. In the particular case of CM, there was a narrow focus on the pieces of bricks that were spread along the path that she used as her escape route. Although she did not specifically recognize relevant places in the area of the crime, she revealed indirect or implicit memory of associated details through her mentioning of the bricks and the path, as well as her intense distress at the sight of these. The isolated memory fragments could be considered as corresponding to critical details in the sequence of events and to have the strongest cue validity in relation to the traumatic event. In some accordance with this conjecture, there is the suggestion that trauma memories in which perceptual details are poorly integrated into the overall representation are more easily accessed by a match between those details and corresponding retrieval cues encountered after the trauma (Conway & Pleydell-Pearce, 2000).

In line with theory on the relationship between memory and post-traumatic stress disorder, it is possible that disturbances at encoding produce fragmented memory representations (Foa & Hearst-Ikeda, 1996). This suggestion is probable in view of the limited capacity of working memory to maintain and manipulate information. Research using working memory tasks with negative and neutral stimuli has shown that emotional salience can, in some instances, impede working memory performance. For instance, it has been found that latency in responses to emotional faces was longer when they followed another emotional stimulus (Kensinger & Corkin, 2003). In the context of trauma, it is possible that an overload of emotion-laden stimuli leads to disorganized memory due to superficial processing of the eliciting event.

There are, however, several other theoretical assumptions that apply to the case of CM and the way in which traumatic memories are encoded in the brain. Horowitz (1978) argued that unassimilated traumatic experiences are stored in a special kind of "active memory," which has an intrinsic tendency to repeat the representation of contents. Only when the victim develops a new mental "schema" for understanding what has happened is the trauma resolved. Other researchers claim that traumatic memories lack verbal narrative and context and that they are encoded in the form of vivid sensations and images. For example, neuroimaging studies of trauma patients have shown that Broca's area, responsible for translating personal experiences into communicable language, is inactivated (Rauch et al., 1996). Furthermore, van der Kolk (1988) argued that, in states of high sympathetic nervous system arousal, the linguistic encoding of memory is inactivated, and the central nervous system reverts to the sensory and iconic forms of memory that predominate in early life. That is, in a predominance of imagery and bodily sensations, and in an absence of verbal narrative, traumatic memories resemble the memories of young children. Moreover, Payne et al. (2004) argued that traumatic stress impairs the function of the hippocampus and the formation of memories. This causes stressful events to be recorded in a "fragmented" manner. According to Payne et al. (2004), emotion (via the amygdala) at the same time promotes memory for the gist of an event, leading to well-encoded memories for the thematic content of an emotional event. Along similar lines, Buchanan and Adolphs (2004) emphasized the role of the amygdala in the enhancement of memory for emotional events, during the period of memory consolidation as well as during retrieval of emotional memories.

Not only the victims, but also the perpetrators of violent crimes may display difficulties in remembering emotion-laden events (Christianson & Merckelbach, 2004; Schacter, 1986; Taylor & Kopelman, 1984), and the large majority of these claims are circumscribed to the crime itself (Bradford & Smith, 1979). People, in general, have the tendency to remove stressful thoughts, feelings, and memories from their conscious awareness. The perpetrator, however, has even stronger motivation to engage in cognitive avoidance. It is common among sexual and homicide offenders, as well as among victims of repeated sexual and physical abuse, to develop strategies to avoid thinking about the event. Many homicide offenders have developed, from an early age, avoidance skills that involve distortion, displacement, and stop-thinking activity. Over time, strategies of this kind, which underlie active avoidance, may cause links and associations to specific event details to become less robust (e.g., Wegner, Quillian, & Houston, 1996). This circumstance, in turn, will limit access to detailed information.

In order to investigate memory for crime among homicide offenders, Christianson and von Vogelsang (2003) collected data from 88 homicide cases. Of these, 34 were coded as instrumental and 54 as reactive. A distinction is made between instrumental/proactive and reactive/expressive homicide offenders. A homicide is purely instrumental when the murder is clearly goal directed, for example, perpetrated to fulfill a sexual or material need or simply to obtain a thrill, with no evidence of an immediate emotional or situational provocation. By contrast, a purely reactive homicide is an immediate, rapid, and powerful affective response. The offender experiences a high level of angry arousal at the time of the violent event, but there is no apparent goal other than to harm the victim following a provocation or conflict, typically with a spouse or someone well known to the offender.

Twenty-six percent (14 offenders) of the reactive offenders compared with 12 percent (4 offenders) of the instrumental offenders consistently claimed to be amnesic for the act of killing throughout the police investigation. Averaged across the two groups, this percentage is 21 percent, which is highly similar to percentages reported in other studies on amnesia for homicide (e.g., Cima et al., 2004;

Guttmacher, 1955; Leitch, 1948; Parkin, 1987). The question arises whether these rates reflect true proportions of genuine amnesia for homicidal violence.

In comparing the offenders' memory before, during, and after the crime, it was more common to report complete memory loss for what happened during the crime than for information immediately before and after the crime. Is it possible that negative emotions are sufficiently intense and overwhelming to trigger amnesic mechanisms in these cases? In comparing the experience of negative emotions as reported by the offenders, their answers were consistent with the type of crime committed. Sexual and thrill themes were the most common motives among instrumental offenders, and 59 percent experienced negative emotional arousal during the crime, and 44 percent after the crime. Among reactive offenders, rage and relational themes were the two most common crime motives, and all reactive offenders reported negative emotions at the time of the crime and 91 percent reported such emotions for the period after the crime.

The perpetrator, thus, has to deal with feelings associated with his or her crime and to confront them. Perhaps the experience of negative emotions provides a motivation to avoid emotion-laden memories of the crime. The far-reaching impact of such memories is illustrated by the fact that some perpetrators who are fully aware of what they have done sometimes develop post-traumatic stress disorder (see Pollock, 1999). It has also been shown that a motive to avoid working through and dealing with the factors underlying the homicidal behavior is particularly expressed by recidivists (Cima et al., 2004).

The issue of motivation to remember violent crimes was studied in an experiment by Christianson and Bylin (1999). Subjects were presented a case vignette of a murder and were then instructed to identify themselves with the offender. Next, one group of subjects was told to play the role of an amnesic offender during a task that consisted of a series of questions about the case. The control group was encouraged to perform as well as they could on this task. After a week, subjects returned to the lab and, again, answered questions about the case. This time, all subjects were instructed to perform as well as they could. During the first session, subjects who played an amnesic role gave fewer correct answers than did control subjects, which is not remarkable. It only shows that the "amnesic" subjects took their role seriously. However, at the one-week follow-up test, the former "amnesic" subjects were still performing below the level of control subjects. This is remarkable because it shows that simulating amnesia or being motivated not to think about the homicidal details has memory-undermining effects.

The memory-undermining effect of simulating amnesia seems to be a robust phenomenon (Van Oorsouw & Merckelbach, 2004), for which there are several explanations. One plausible explanation concerns rehearsal of crime details. For example, the first test occasion in the Christianson and Bylin experiment may serve as an act of repetition from which control subjects, but not simulators, benefit. Another possibility is that simulators think of a new version that better fits their wish to be less responsible for the crime. This type of processing implies that subjects who feign amnesia confuse their own version with the original event and subsequently have difficulties understanding how their own memory has changed. This may result in source monitoring errors (Johnson, Hashtroudi, & Lindsay, 1991).

Taken together, research shows that people are more likely to remember emotion-arousing events than neutral, everyday events. Indeed, they may even claim near-perfect memories for the circumstances surrounding unique emotion-laden events. Nonetheless, there are cases where emotional events, especially highly arousing and traumatic ones, are poorly retained. For example, victims of sexual crimes, as well as perpetrators of such crimes, may show a temporary inability to remember a traumatic event. Various studies also indicate that the accuracy of recollection of emotional events depends on the type of detail information asked for, the amount of retrieval information provided, and the time of retrieval. Thus, although it is clear that emotional events are remembered differently than neutral or ordinary events, there is no simple relationship between emotion and memory, such that emotion or stress impairs memory, or the opposite, that emotion leads to generally detailed, accurate, and persistent memory. In fact, research in this field, independent of the approach used, shows that the way in which emotion and memory interact is a rather complex matter. Additionally, there are examples in the literature suggesting the existence of an interconnection between event memory and associated emotional information.

▊ MEMORY FOR ASSOCIATED EMOTIONS

The review so far makes it clear that affective reactions in response to an emotional or traumatic event seem to be inextricably linked to event memory. An understanding of memory for emotional events may therefore not be as extensive or meaningful without a discussion on memory for the emotions aroused at the time of the event. More importantly, we may be able to capitalize on the natural correspondence that seems to exist between a person's feelings and the emotion-eliciting information in emotionally arousing situations. By activating such links, it should be possible to enhance availability of information stored in memory about the event to be recalled. Thus, interviewing techniques aimed at recreating feelings or emotions experienced at the time of the event may facilitate retrieval of more detailed information. As a result, the retrieval process may then take place by increasing the number of links in memory associated with the representation of the specific event.

The effects of activating event memory by cueing associated emotions were investigated among preschool children between the ages of 2.5 and 6.5 years (Liwag & Stein, 1995). Parents were interviewed about a recent event that had made their child happy, sad, angry, or afraid. Each child was interviewed about the event in one of four conditions. In the first condition, the child was only asked to tell the experimenter about the event that she or he had experienced. In the second condition, the child was also asked "what did you think?", "what did you do?", and "what did you feel?" In the third condition, an instruction was added to make a face corresponding to the emotion that the child had experienced at the time of the event. To the fourth condition, yet another instruction was added. The child was also asked to act out the scene and to show, using his/her whole body, how he/she had felt at the time. Results showed that children in the fourth condition provided the most nonverbal cues and remembered significantly more about the event than did children in any of the other conditions. Furthermore, children in the fourth condition not only recalled more details that were directly related to the specific event, but they also mentioned other related types of incidents. For instance, a boy who was interviewed about his visit to the dentist also recalled the time when his brother had been taken to the hospital.

The principle of using emotions to increase links in memory is also seen in some studies of adults' memory for emotional events. Engelberg and Christianson (2000) assessed adults' recall using memory-enhancing principles of the Cognitive Interview (CI) technique (Fisher & Geiselman, 1992). Specifically, two groups of participants were shown a 10-minute unpleasant and violent film clip and were then asked to rate their emotional reactions. At recall six weeks later, various instructions encouraged participants in one of the groups to recount what they recalled of the film session by describing auditory and visual stimuli, internal physiological sensations, but also environmental details and to some extent thoughts associated with the emotional experience. When compared to the other group of participants who did not receive these instructions at free recall, these instructions were shown to generate more detailed descriptions of the event to be recalled. Instructions were also shown to enhance consistency in the recall of emotional reactions. In spite of these differences in overall memory between the two conditions, participants in both recall conditions reported remembering and attributing the elicitation of their emotional reaction to the same detail in the film plot. In other words, they remembered the critical detail information that was associated with the gist of the emotional experience (cf., Christianson, 1984; Christianson & Loftus, 1991).

The emotional content of stimuli is likely to capture attention and gain prioritized processing, and the subsequent elaboration of emotional information increases the likelihood of strengthening associative ties at different levels of memory. Additional dimensions, such as the individual's emotional state and arousal, may provide additional distinctiveness at encoding, or additional features to be used later as retrieval cues. This line of reasoning is in accordance with the view of recall as drawing on associative relations of a perceptual, semantic, and other contextual kind as bound together by episodic memory, which is the term for the storage of specific events and personal experiences in memory (e.g., Schacter, 1994). In probing less accessible, associative ties, emotional information may be made more available, particularly as several studies show that autobiographical events are high in judged visual detail, sound, smell, and taste (e.g., Johnson et al., 1988; see also Brewer, 1986). Thus, event memory may be regarded as organized at multiple levels, and various types of information contained in those levels may be differently accessible depending on the retrieval cues.

Moreover, the empirical findings on the effects of memory-enhancing principles are in accordance with the proposition made by Izard (1993). His main argument is that emotion has a significant role in evolution and adaptation, and cognitive processes can therefore not be the sole, primary mechanism for generating emotions. In addition to cognitive processes, emotions can be aroused neurologically through direct stimulation of the brain (activating certain neurotransmittors, neural circuits, or networks of structures), through certain expressions and motor actions (e.g., contracting facial muscles, vocal expressions, body postures), and through motivation such as pain. For example, pain brings about certain feeling states, certain facial and postural expressions, and it is possible that pain elicits emotions directly via subcortical mechanisms without cognitive mediation. Thus, it may presumably be that memories for emotion differ as a function of the mode of arousal, and that memories of cognitively aroused emotions are more likely to be recalled than other types of emotional memories (see also Levine & Pizarro, this volume).

Obviously, gaining a more thorough insight into the representation of emotional events in memory may help us in our use of alternative strategies for retrieving information about an event. Importantly, a greater understanding in this regard may enable an interviewer or interrogator to assist a person in retrieving such information more effectively and with greater care.

 THE REPRESENTATION OF EMOTIONAL EVENTS IN MEMORY

Some psychologists have argued for a unique memory for emotions, separate from a memory for the emotion-arousing event. The turn-of-the-century French psychologist Ribot not only claimed separate distinguishable memories for emotions, but also that emotional memories had their own unique affective logic, which was different from cognitive memories (Ross, 1991). Zajonc

(1980) similarly makes a claim for the independence, indeed the primacy, of affective memory over event memory. He put forth the argument that an affective memory is necessary for speedy judgments that allow an organism to survive in a hostile environment.

Both classic and contemporary observations provide some empirical support for these propositions. It has been observed that aspects of past emotion are represented as non-cognitive representations in memory, and that these representations are possible to retrieve in a manner that does not require high-level cognitive processing. The most tangible evidence for this claim is found in observations that some emotional responses are triggered by very idiosyncratic types of perceptual cues (e.g., Janet, 1893). The sight of the doctor, as in the frequently cited example by Claparède (1911/1951), constitutes such a perceptual stimulus. The doctor had once pricked the hand of a severely amnesic patient. From that time on, the patient refused to shake hands with him, even though he was unable to remember having met the doctor before.

Another case study similarly illustrates the role of emotion-laden perceptual stimuli in providing additional contextual support. An elderly man turned up at an emergency ward and claimed that he had no idea of his personal identity. He was fortunate enough to eventually be recognized by a former neighbor. The amnesic man was therefore accompanied to the apartment where somebody else now lived; still the man had no recollection of the apartment or the neighbor. Shortly after the visit to his former apartment, the man suddenly recalled that he had lost his memory following the death of his wife, to whom he had been very attached (Domb & Beaman, 1991). The apartment, which was associated with an emotionally gratifying time in the man's life, may have triggered an affective link that bridged the gap to the episodic memory that was blocked (cf., Erdelyi & Goldberg, 1979).

Empirical research has provided compelling evidence that emotional information may be retrieved by mechanisms at a non-verbal level of consciousness (see Johnson & Multhaup, 1992). Neuropsychological studies, in particular, have shown that subcortical mechanisms ensure automatic and non-conscious retention of distinct emotional information from stressful events. In a study by Christianson, Säisä, & Silfvenius (1995), emotional reactions and memory were studied in patients with unilateral temporal and/or frontal lobe epilepsy, using a sodium amytal testing procedure. The patients were presented with pictures of ordinary faces and accompanying biographical descriptions while either the right or the left cerebral hemisphere was deactivated. When testing the non-speech dominant right hemisphere, results showed superior recognition of faces associated with unpleasant biographies. Although the content of the biographical information could not be recognized, the ratings of the faces associated with the unpleasant biographies were less favorable. Other research has given overall support to different formulations based on the idea that emotional processing takes place in two different systems and, further, that these are hierarchically organized (for an overview, see Gainotti, Caltagirone, & Zoccolotti, 1993).

On the basis of the empirical evidence and many observations suggesting a dual representation of emotional information, different formulations have been made to account for the cognitive complexity that enables non-intentional, non-conscious retrieval of past emotion. Marcia K. Johnson sees such retrieval mechanisms as being mediated by non-verbal, so-called "perceptual subsystems" (Johnson & Multhaup, 1992) as opposed to the later developed "reflective subsystems." Another formulation has been proposed to account specifically for the phenomenon of traumatic memory. At a non-conscious level, "situationally accessible knowledge" is stored to trigger emotional responses as originally conditioned in situations where some aspect is reminiscent of the eliciting event. By contrast, "verbally accessible knowledge" is generic knowledge that enables the individual to appraise the implications of the event and to integrate it with existing schemata of self-image and the world in general (Brewin, Dalgleish, & Joseph, 1996). The different formulations are in many respects reminiscent of the distinctions between implicit and explicit memory (Graf & Schacter, 1985). Implicit memory consists of learned behaviors and responses, does not operate at a conscious level, and is expressed through behaviors and actions. Implicit recall is thus expressed when information is retrieved that was originally encoded at a specific occasion in time without actually retrieving an episodic memory of the event itself. By contrast, explicit memory includes deliberate, conscious recall of events and information.

Yet another formulation is the two-system framework in which a hot emotional system and a cool cognitive system are interconnected (Metcalfe & Mischel, 1999). The former system is largely under stimulus control and is connected to response programs that are reflexive, rapid, and direct. The latter system weaves knowledge about sensations and emotions, thoughts, actions, and context into a coherent, strategic process. In contrast to other formulations, this framework includes a rather elaborate account of how emotional information (in the hot system) is made available by cognitive means. More specifically, thoughts that trigger appropriate locations in the cool network may result in hot activation. An example of the activation of emotional information from a cognitive level is provided by the case study of a woman who, as a child, was caught in an avalanche. As a result, she experienced feelings of intense discomfort at the mere thought of snow and found it unbearable to listen to forecasts about snow on the weather report (Laughlin, 1967).

It should follow that the more specifically past memories are evoked, the more intensely the associated emotion will be felt. A counterintuitive finding is that the memory of emotional intensity is inversely related to the willful activation of a specific personal memory. Recall was compared to ratings for daily events that participants had selected to report at the end of the day in a diary that was kept for a fortnight. The emotional intensities associated with each of the specific events that had occurred at a particular place and time were underestimated, whereas the intensities associated with events of a general or recurring character were remembered with greater consistency (Philippot, Schaefer, & Herbette, 2003). Additional research on events of greater salience, and thus not of an entirely everyday nature, shows that erroneous beliefs about recurring events or situations, in particular, appear to bias retrospective emotion ratings as compared to online ratings.

According to Ross (1989), erroneous beliefs are schematic knowledge structures that include specific conditions likely to maintain stability or to promote change. As one example, studies of mood and the menstrual cycle have revealed disparities between retrospective and concurrent reports of emotion. When comparing actual ratings on daily mood reports and at recall, it was found that women tended to remember more negative affect premenstrually than at other times during the cycle (Slade, 1984). Another example is a study on blood donors, who were found to overestimate the anxiety they experienced before being tapped for blood, as compared to actual ratings. Somewhat surprisingly, the same tendency was found among more experienced participants who regularly donated blood (Breckler, 1994). Dental treatment provides another example of something about which people generally have schematic knowledge. This is illustrated by a study on fearful patients who were asked to rate their expectation of pain and emotional distress one month before a scheduled dental appointment. Three months after the appointment, they remembered having experienced more pain and distress than was indicated in their own ratings during the actual treatment. Although characteristically anxious individuals expect to feel more pain and anxiety during treatment, they do not in fact experience more pain and anxiety than do individuals of low anxiety (Arntz, van Eck, & Heijmans, 1990).

People apparently resort to schematic knowledge at recall, even though the accumulated experience of the affect-laden situation is inconsistent with such beliefs. In spite of disconfirming experiences, it seems quite difficult to adjust schematic beliefs. Some scholars argue that people actually form beliefs about themselves that become dissociated from their experiences in everyday life (e.g., Markus, 1983). Memory for emotions is similarly reconstructed on the basis of stereotypes. As one example, there are gender stereotypes of emotion that people tend to share. Generally speaking, women are thought to display more emotion than men do and to feel emotion more intensely (for an overview, see Brody & Hall, 1993). Although it has been shown that gender stereotypes parallel self-reported gender differences, this phenomenon has been observed only under certain conditions. That is, gender differences in emotion are more likely when people make retrospective judgments than when they make online reports about their emotions in specific situations (Shields, 1991). Presumably, people are less likely to use gender-stereotypic information as a heuristic for inferring emotional intensity when they have an available and readily accessible, recent experience on which to base their judgments. The implication is that people rely on gender stereotypes when remembering past emotions and, as a result, that there is a biasing effect on recall.

However, the major obstacle to recall of events of an unpleasant or traumatic nature is that willful retrieval of such personal memories seems to be related to processes strategically aimed at inhibiting the reactivation of associated emotion (Philippot, Schaefer, & Herbette, 2003). The finding is consistent with the notion of mood maintenance, as well as the phenomenon of overgenerality (Williams et al., 2000). By remaining at a general or abstract level of information, individuals attempt to avoid the reactivation of acute and painful emotions felt in specific experiences of personal relevance. The general tendency to avoid reactivation of unpleasant memories and emotions may nonetheless be overcome with the application of memory-enhancing principles of the Cognitive Interview when assisting a person in information retrieval. Care is taken to allow sufficient time for an individual to recall all unique characteristics of a particular event before trying to retrieve details that are not immediately accessible. In applying the principles of the CI, plenty of time is allowed to recreate the circumstances surrounding an event, including time to recreate the emotional feelings associated with the event. As the interviewee is allowed to take the time he or she feels is necessary, the information is retrieved successively at a pace that is tolerable to the individual being assisted. Further, as has been suggested earlier in this chapter, nonverbal information pertaining to body movements and sensory perception (sights, colors, sounds, olfactory and gustatory details) may not only take time to access in memory in their own right, but may be particularly imbued with salient emotions. The reactivation of such details may therefore be especially strenuous and painful. Many clinicians, therefore, let the person talk about his or her experience in the third person, that is, as if it had happened to someone else, and as if he or she had merely been an observer. This procedure does not always yield a detailed description, but it is a suitable first attempt at recall, for example, when working with victims of rape or sexual abuse, for whom shock, shame, and violated integrity bar any sharing of the most intimate details of their traumata.

■ CONCLUDING REMARKS

The present chapter has presented a review of some basic principles uncovered in studies of the relations between emotion and memory. Understanding these principles is crucial when eliciting and evaluating the recall of witnesses to and victims and perpetrators of violent crime. Current psychological research, including laboratory studies and survey studies of emotional/traumatic events and interviews with victims of and witnesses to violent crimes, shows a strong correlation between affect strength and rated memory vividness. Research also shows that traumatic experiences tend to persist in memory, both with respect to the emotional event itself and with respect to the central, critical detail information of the emotion-eliciting event; that is, the information that elicits the emotional reaction. However, current psychological research also shows that there is no single effect of trauma on memory for a traumatic event. Rather, there appear to be a variety of patterns that vary in both amount (from total memory loss, through recall of a few details, to a very detailed account) and accuracy (from a false account, through accuracy concerning the main "gist"/central details, to an almost completely accurate account). For example, while the general pattern among victims and bystander witnesses is that negative emotional events are retained well, victims who have sustained sexual abuse or perpetrators of violent and sexual crimes often retain or report emotional/traumatic events poorly.

Furthermore, most research has examined the influence of emotions on the content that is recalled, thus ignoring how well emotions per se can be recalled. A more comprehensive insight into the representation of emotion may enable the use of additional access routes to support retrieval from episodic memory. We argue that retrieval from memory tends to be richer in amount and detail when instructions to remember are geared toward emotion-laden perceptions associated with the event. Thus, greater insight may enable the development of alternative interviewing techniques based on the strategy of asking questions about details that evoked emotions. That kind of event information usually consists of the critical or central details and tends to be readily available to recall, possibly unlike peripheral details, which may involve more cueing.

AUTHOR NOTE

Correspondence concerning this chapter should be addressed to Sven Å Christianson, Department of Psychology, Stockholm University, S-106 91 Stockholm, Sweden. E-mail: scn@psychology.su.se.

NOTE

1 In spite of the diagnosis of dissociative amnesia made at the hospital where she was brought after being found, it cannot be ruled out that blows to her head may have partly caused her condition.

REFERENCES

Arntz, A., van Eck, M., & Heijmans, M. (1990). Predictions of dental pain: The fear of any expected evil is worse than the evil itself. *Behavior Research and Therapy, 28,* 29–41.

Berntsen, D. (2001). Involuntary memories of emotional events: Do memories of traumas and extremely happy events differ? *Applied Cognitive Psychology, 15,* 135–158.

Bohannon, J. N. & Symons, V. L. (1992). Flashbulb memories: Confidence, consistency, and quantity. In E. Winograd & U. Neisser (Eds.), *Affect and accuracy in recall: Studies of "flashbulb" memories* (pp. 65–91). New York: Cambridge University Press.

Bradford, J. W. & Smith, S. M. (1979). Amnesia and homicide: The Padola case and a study of thirty cases. *Bulletin of the American Academy of Psychiatry and Law, 7,* 219–231.

Breckler, S. (1994). Memory for the experience of donating blood: Just how bad was it? *Basic and Applied Social Psychology, 15,* 467–488.

Brewer, W. F. (1986). What is autobiographical memory? In D. C. Rubin (Ed.), *Autobiographical memory* (pp. 25–49). Cambridge: Cambridge University Press.

Brewin, C. R., Dalgleish, T., & Joseph, S. (1996). A dual representation theory of post-traumatic stress disorder. *Psychological Review, 103,* 670–686.

Brody, L. R. & Hall, J. R. (1993). Gender and emotion. In M. Lewis & J. M. Haviland (Eds.), *Handbook of emotions* (pp. 447–460). New York: Guilford Press.

Brown, R. & Kulik, J. (1977). Flashbulb memories. *Cognition, 5,* 73–99.

Buchanan, T. W. & Adolphs, R. (2004). The neuroanatomy of emotional memory in humans. In D. Reisberg & P. Hertel (Eds.). *Memory and emotion: Series in affective science* (pp. 42–75). Oxford: Oxford University Press.

Burke, A., Heuer, F., & Reisberg, D. (1992). Remembering emotional events. *Memory & Cognition, 20,* 277–290.

Butler, L. & Wolfner, A. L. (2000). Some characteristics of positive and negative ("most traumatic") event memories in a college sample. *Journal of Trauma & Dissociation, 1,* 45–68.

Christianson, S.-Å. (1984). The relationship between induced emotional arousal and amnesia. *Scandinavian Journal of Psychology, 25,* 147–160.

Christianson, S.-Å. (1989). Flashbulb memories: Special, but not so special. *Memory and Cognition, 17,* 435–443.

Christianson, S.-Å. (1992). Emotional stress and eyewitness memory: A critical review. *Psychological Bulletin, 112,* 284–309.

Christianson, S.-Å. (1997). On emotional stress and memory: We need to recognize threatening situations and we need to "forget" unpleasant experiences. In D. G. Payne & F. G. Conrad (Eds.), *Intersections in basic and applied memory research* (pp. 133–156). Hillsdale, NJ: Erlbaum.

Christianson, S.-Å. & Bylin, S. (1999). Does simulating amnesia mediate genuine forgetting for a crime event? *Applied Cognitive Psychology, 13,* 495–511.

Christianson, S.-Å. & Engelberg, E. (1997). Remembering and forgetting traumatic experiences: A matter of survival. In M. A. Conway (Ed.), *Recovered memories and false memories* (pp. 231–250). Oxford: Oxford University Press.

Christianson, S.-Å. & Engelberg, E. (1999). Memory and emotional consistency: The *MS Estonia* ferry disaster. *Memory, 7,* 471–482.

Christianson, S.-Å. & Fällman, L. (1990). The role of age on reactivity and memory for emotional pictures. *Scandinavian Journal of Psychology, 31,* 291–301.

Christianson, S.-Å. & Hübinette, B. (1993). Hands up! A study of witnesses' emotional reactions and memories associated with bank robberies. *Applied Cognitive Psychology, 7,* 365–379.

Christianson, S.-Å. & Lindholm, T. (1998). On the fate of traumatic memories in childhood and adulthood. *Development and Psychopathology, 10,* 761–780.

Christianson, S.-Å. & Loftus, E. F. (1987). Memory for traumatic events. *Applied Cognitive Psychology, 1,* 225–239.

Christianson, S.-Å. & Loftus, E. F. (1990). Some characteristics of people's traumatic memories. *Bulletin of the Psychonomic Society, 28,* 195–198.

Christianson, S.-Å. & Loftus, E. F. (1991). Remembering emotional events: The fate of detailed information. *Cognition and Emotion, 5,* 81–108.

Christianson, S.-Å., Loftus, E. F., Hoffman, H., & Loftus, G. R. (1991). Eye fixations and memory for emotional events. *Journal of Experimental Psychology: Learning, Memory, and Cognition, 17,* 693–701.

Christianson, S.-Å. & Merckelbach, H. (2004). Are homicide offenders who claim amnesia liars? In P. A. Granhag & L. A. Strömvall (Eds.), *The detection of deception in forensic contexts.* Cambridge: Cambridge University Press.

Christianson, S.-Å. & Nilsson, L.-G. (1989). Hysterical amnesia: A case of aversively motivated isolation of memory. In T. Archer, & L.-G. Nilsson (Eds.), *Aversion, avoidance, and anxiety: Perspectives on aversively motivated behavior* (pp. 289–310). Hillsdale, NJ: Erlbaum.

Christianson, S.-Å., Säisä, J., & Silfvenius, H. (1995). The right hemisphere recognizes the bad guys. *Cognition and Emotion, 9,* 309–324.

Christianson, S.-Å. & von Vogelsang, X. (2003). Homicide offenders who claim amnesia for their crime. Unpublished manuscript.

Cima, M., Nijman, H., Merckelbach, H., Kremer, K., & Hollnack, S. (2004). Claims of crime-related amnesia in forensic patients. *International Journal of Law and Psychiatry, 27,* 215–221.

Claparède, E. (1911/1951). Recognition and "me" ness. In D. Rapaport (Ed.), *Organization and pathology of thought* (pp. 58–75). New York: Columbia University Press.

Conway, M. A. & Pleydell-Pearce, C. W. (2000). The construction of autobiographical memories in the self-memory system. *Psychological Review, 107,* 261–288.

Domb, Y. & Beaman, K. (1991). Mr. X – A case of amnesia. *British Journal of Psychiatry, 158,* 423–425.

Engelberg, E. & Christianson, S.-Å. (2000). Recall of unpleasant emotion using memory-enhancing principles. *Psychology, Crime, and Law, 6,* 99–112.

Erdelyi, M. H. & Goldberg, B. (1979). Let's not sweep repression under the rug: Toward a cognitive psychology of repression. In J. F. Kihlstrom & F. J. Evans (Eds.), *Functional disorders of memory* (pp. 355–402). Hillsdale, NJ: Erlbaum.

Fisher, R. P. & Geiselman, R. E. (1992). *Memory-enhancing techniques for investigative interviewing.* Springfield, IL: Charles C. Thomas.

Fisher, R. P., Geiselman, R. E., & Amandor, M. (1989). Field test of the cognitive interview: Enhancing the recollection of actual victims and witnesses of crime. *Journal of Applied Psychology, 74*, 722–727.

Foa, E. B. & Hearst-Ikeda, D. (1996). Emotional dissociation in response to trauma: An information processing approach. In L. K. Michelson & W. J. Ray (Eds.), *Handbook of dissociation: Theoretical, empirical, and clinical perspectives* (pp. 207–224). New York: Plenum Press.

Gainotti, G., Caltagirone, C., & Zoccolotti, P. (1993). Left/right and cortical/subcortical dichotomies in the neuropsychological study of human emotions. *Cognition and Emotion, 7*, 71–93.

Graf, P. & Schacter, D. L. (1985). Implicit and explicit memory for novel associations in normal and amnesic subjects. *Journal of Experimental Psychology: Learning, Memory, and Cognition, 11*, 501–518.

Greenberg, D. L. (2004). President Bush's false "flashbulb" memory of 9/11/01. *Applied Cognitive Psychology, 18*, 363–370.

Guttmacher, M. S. (1955). *Psychiatry and the law*. New York: Grune & Stratton.

Horowitz, M. (1978). *Stress response syndromes* (2nd ed.). New York: Jason Aronson.

Izard, C. E. (1993). Four systems for emotion activation: Cognitive and non-cognitive processes. *Psychological Review, 100*, 68–90.

Janet, P. (1893). Continuous amnesia. *Revue Generale des Sciences, 4*, 167–179.

Johnson, M. K., Foley, M. A., Suengas, A. G., & Raye, C. L. (1988). Phenomenal characteristics of memories for perceived and imagined autiobiographical events. *Journal of Experimental Psychology: General, 117*, 371–376.

Johnson, M. K. & Multhaup, K. S. (1992). Emotion and MEM. In S.-Å. Christianson (Ed.), *The handbook of emotion and memory: Research and theory* (pp. 33–66). Hillsdale, NJ: Erlbaum.

Johnson, M. K., Hashtroudi, S., & Lindsey, D. S. (1991). Source monitoring. *Psychological Bulletin, 114*, 3–28.

Karlsson, I. & Christianson, S.-Å. (2003). The phenomenology of traumatic experiences in police work. *Policing: An International Journal of Police Strategies & Management, 3*, 419–438.

Kensinger, E. A. & Corkin, S. (2003). Effect of negative emotional content on working memory and long-term memory. *Emotion, 3*, 378–393.

Laney, C., Campbell, H. V., Heuer, F., & Reisberg, D. (2004). Memory for thematically arousing events. *Memory & Cognition, 32*, 1149–1159.

Laney, C., Heuer, F., & Reisberg, D. (2003). Thematically induced arousal in naturally occuring emotional memories. *Applied Cognitive Psychology, 17*, 995–1004.

Laughlin, H. P. (1967). *The neuroses*. Washington, DC: Butterworth.

Leitch, A. (1948). Notes on amnesia in crime for the general practitioner. *The Medical Press, 26*, 459–463.

Liwag, M. & Stein, N. (1995). Children's memory for emotional events: The importance of emotion-related cues. *Journal of Experimental Child Psychology, 60*, 2–31.

McCloskey, M., Wible, C. G., & Cohen, N. J. (1988). Is there a special flashbulb-memory mechanism? *Journal of Experimental Psychology: General, 117*, 171–181.

Markus, H. (1983). Self-knowledge: An expanded view. *Journal of Personality, 51*, 543–565.

Metcalfe, J. & Mischel, W. (1999). A hot/cool-system analysis of delay of gratification: Dynamics of willpower. *Psychological Review, 106,* 3–19.

Neisser, U. (1982). Snapshots or benchmarks? In U. Neisser (Ed.), *Memory observed* (pp. 43–48). San Francisco: W. H. Freeman.

Neisser, U. & Harsch, N. (1992). Phantom flashbulbs: False recollections of hearing the news about *Challenger.* In E. Winograd & U. Neisser (Eds.), *Affect and accuracy in recall: Studies of "flashbulb memories"* (pp. 9–31). New York: Cambridge University Press.

Öhman, A. (1979). The orienting response, attention, and learning: An information processing perspective. In H. D. Kimmel, E. H. van Olst, & J. F. Orlebeke (Eds.), *The orienting reflex in humans* (pp. 443–472). Hillsdale, NJ: Erlbaum.

Öhman, A. (1991). Orienting and attention: Preferred preattentive processing of potentially phobic stimuli. In B. A. Campell, R. Richardson, & H. Hayne (Eds.), *Attention and information processing in infants and adults: Perspectives from human and animal research* (pp. 263–295). Hillsdale, NJ: Erlbaum.

Parkin, A. J. (1987). *Memory and amnesia.* Oxford: Blackwell.

Patterson, B. W. (2004). The "tyranny of eyewitness." *Law and Psychology Review, 28,* 195–203.

Payne, J. D., Nadel, L., Britton, W. B., & Jacobs, W. J. (2004). The biopsychology of trauma and memory. In D. Reisberg & P. Hertel (Eds.), *Memory and emotion: Series in affective science* (pp. 76–128). Oxford: Oxford University Press.

Peace, K. A. & Porter, S. (2004) A longitudinal investigation of the reliability of memories for trauma and other emotional experiences. *Applied Cognitive Psychology, 18,* 1143–1159.

Philippot, P., Schaefer, A., & Herbette, G. (2003). Consequences of specific processing of emotional information: Impact of general versus specific autobiographical memory priming on emotion elicitation. *Emotion, 3,* 270–283.

Pillemer, D. B. (1984). Flashbulb memories of the assassination attempt on President Reagan. *Cognition, 16,* 63–80.

Pollock, P. H. (1999). When the killer suffers: Post-traumatic stress reactions following homicide. *Legal and Criminological Psychology, 4,* 185–202.

Rauch, S., van der Kolk, B. A., Fisler, R., Alpert, N. M., Orr, S. P., Savage, C. R., Fischman, A. J., Jenike, M. A., & Pitman, R. K. (1996). A symptom provocation study of post-traumatic stress disorder using positron emission tomography and script-driven imagery. *Archives of General Psychiatry, 53,* 380–387.

Reisberg, D. & Heuer, F. (2004). Memory for emotional events. In D. Reisberg & P. Hertel (Eds.), *Memory and emotion: Series in affective science* (pp. 3–41). Oxford: Oxford University Press.

Reisberg, D., Heuer, F., McLean, J., & O'Shaughnessy, M. (1988). The quantity, not the quality, of affect predicts memory vividness. *Bulletin of the Psychonomic Society, 26,* 100–103.

Ross, B. M. (1989). Relation of implicit theories to the construction of personal histories. *Psychological Review, 96,* 341–357.

Ross, B. M. (1991). *Remembering the personal past.* New York: Oxford University Press.

Schacter, D. L. (1986). Amnesia and crime: How much do we really know? *American Psychologist, 41,* 286–295.

Schacter, D. L. (1994). Priming and multiple memory systems: Perceptual mechanisms of implicit memory. In D. L. Schacter & E. Tulving (Eds.), *Memory systems 1994* (pp. 33–68). Hong Kong: MIT Press.

Shedler, J., Mayman, M., & Manis, M. (1993). The illusion of mental health. *American Psychologist, 48*, 1117–1131.

Shields, S. A. (1991). Gender in the psychology of emotion: A selective research review. In K. T. Strongman (Ed.), *International review of studies on emotion* (Vol. 1, pp. 212–232). Thousand Oaks, CA: Sage.

Slade, P. (1984). Premenstrual emotional changes in normal women: Fact or fiction? *Journal of Psychosomatic Research, 28*, 1–7.

Taylor, P. J. & Kopelman, M. D. (1984). Amnesia for criminal offences. *Psychological Medicine, 14*, 581–588.

Terr, L. (1990). *Unchained memories: True stories of traumatic memories, lost and found.* New York: Basic Books.

van der Kolk, B. A. (1988). The trauma spectrum: The interaction of biological and social events in the genesis of the trauma response. *Journal of Traumatic Stress, 1*, 273–290.

Van Oorsouw, K. & Merckelbach, H. (2004). Feigning amnesia undermines memory for a mock crime. *Applied Cognitive Psychology, 18*, 505–518.

Vuilleumier, P., Armony, J. L., Clarke, K., Husain, M., Driver, J., & Dolan, R. J. (2002). Neural response to emotional faces with and without awareness: Event-related fMRI in a parietal patient with visual extinction and spatial neglect. *Neuropsychologia, 40*, 2156–2166.

Warren, A. R. & Swartwood, J. N. (1992). Developmental issues in flashbulb memory research: Children recall the *Challenger* event. In E. Winograd & U. Neisser (Eds.), *Affect and accuracy in recall: Studies on flashbulb memories* (pp. 95–120). New York: Cambridge University Press.

Wegner, D. M., Quillian, F., & Houston, C. E. (1996). Memories out of order: Thought suppression and the disturbance of sequence memory. *Journal of Personality and Social Psychology, 71*, 680–691.

Wessel, I. & Merckelbach, H. (1997). The impact of anxiety on memory for details in spider phobics. *Applied Cognitive Psychology, 11*, 223–231.

Williams, J. M. G., Teasdale, J. D., Segal, Z. V., & Soulsby, J. (2000). Mindfulness-based cognitive therapy reduces overgeneral autobiographical memory in formerly depressed patients. *Journal of Abnormal Psychology, 109*, 150–155.

Williams, L. M. (1994). Recall of childhood trauma: A prospective study of women's memories of child sexual abuse. *Journal of Consulting and Clinical Psychology, 62*, 1167–1176.

Wise, R. A. & Safer, M. A. (2004). What US judges know and believe about eye-witness testimony. *Applied Cognitive Psychology, 18*, 427–443.

Wright, D. B., Gaskell, G. D., & Muirchaertaigh, C. A. (1998). Flashbulb memory assumptions: Using national surveys to explore cognitive phenomena. *British Journal of Psychology, 89*, 103–121.

Yarmey, A. D. (2001). Expert testimony: Does eyewitness memory research have probative value for the courts? *Canadian Psychology, 42*, 92–100.

Yuille, J. C. & Cutshall, J. L. (1986). A case study of eyewitness memory of a crime. *Journal of Applied Psychology, 71*, 291–301.

Yuille, J. C. & Cutshall, J. L. (1989). Analysis of the statements of victims, witnesses and suspects. In J. C. Yuille (Ed.), *Credibility assessment* (pp. 175–191). Dordrecht: Kluwer.

Yuille, J. C. & Daylen, K. J. (1998). The impact of traumatic events on eyewitness memory. In C. Thompson, D. Hermann, D. Read, D. Payne, & M. Toglia (Eds.), *Eyewitness memory: Theoretical and applied perspectives.* Hillsdale, NJ: Erlbaum.

Yuille, J. C. & Tollestrup, P. A. (1992). A model of the diverse effects of emotion on eyewitness memory. In S.-Å Christianson (Ed.), *The handbook of emotion and memory: Reserach and theory* (pp. 201–215). Hillsdale, NJ: Erlbaum.

Zajonc, R. B. (1980). Feeling and thinking: Preferences need no inferences. *American Psychologist, 35,* 151–175.

Are We Frightened Because We Run Away? Some Evidence from Metacognitive Feelings

5

Asher Koriat

Abstract

William James asked whether we run away because we are frightened or we are frightened because we run away. This issue is addressed here with regard to the relationship between metacognitive monitoring and metacognitive control. While discussions of metacognition generally assume that feelings of knowing drive controlled action, other discussions imply that such feelings are based on feedback from controlled action, and thus follow rather than precede behavior. Recent evidence is reported suggesting that when the investment of effort is goal driven, greater effort enhances metacognitive feelings, consistent with the "feelings-affect-behavior" hypothesis. When effort is data driven, however, metacognitive feelings decrease with increasing effort, suggesting that such feelings are based on feedback from behavior. Both types of causal effects can occur simultaneously.

A long-lasting issue in theories of emotion concerns the cause-and-effect relation between subjective emotional feelings and bodily reactions. This issue is part of the general issue of the cause-and-effect relationship between subjective experience and behavior, which has attracted a heated philosophical debate. Within psychology, the dominant view has been that conscious awareness exerts a causal effect on controlled, voluntary action (Posner & Snyder, 1975; Schacter, 1989). This view has been reinforced by observations about the behavioral deficits of brain-damaged patients who suffer from different forms of loss of consciousness. With regard to emotional feelings, the layman's naive theory is that feelings drive behavior. William James (1884), however, challenged this view, proposing that subjective feelings rather than driving behavior are themselves caused by these behaviors. In his words:

> Common sense says, we lose our fortune, are sorry and weep; we meet a bear, are frightened and run; we are insulted by a rival, and angry and strike. The

hypothesis here to be defended says that this order of sequence is incorrect . . . and that the more rational statement is that we feel sorry because we cry, angry because we strike, afraid because we tremble. Without the bodily states follow-ing on the perception, the latter would be purely cognitive in form, pale, colourless, destitute of emotional warmth. We might then see the bear, and judge it best to run, receive the insult and deem it right to strike, but we could not actually *feel* afraid or angry. (p. 190)

This quote assumes that bodily reactions are not simply "manifestations" or "expressions" of subjective feelings. Rather, subjective emotional feelings emerge as feedback from the bodily reactions. James' quote also antecedes the current distinction between experience-based and information-based judgments (Koriat & Levy-Sadot, 1999; Strack, 1992), as discussed below. We may then distinguish between two models of the cause-and-effect relation between emotional experi-ence and behavior. In the first, emotional feelings are the *cause* of behavior: we run away because we are frightened. In the second, favored by William James, emotional feelings are the *effect*: they follow rather than precede behavior.

In what follows I shall examine the issue raised by William James in the context of metacognition. The question to be addressed is whether meta-cognitive feelings drive controlled behavior or are themselves based on the feedback from such behavior. I shall examine evidence that has been seen to sup-port each of these positions and will then discuss how the two positions may be combined within one conceptual framework. Although much of our discussion will concern noetic feelings (or "knowing feelings"; see Clore, 1992), I believe that the proposed conceptual framework applies to feelings in general.

 ## METACOGNITIVE MONITORING AND METACOGNITIVE CONTROL

The study of metacognition concerns the knowledge that people have about their cognition, the online monitoring of their learning and remembering processes and the strategic regulation of these processes in accordance with one's monitoring and with the constraints imposed by the task at hand (see Flavell, 1979; Koriat, 2005).

Metacognitive processes are ubiquitous in everyday life. When we read a text, we monitor our comprehension and when we feel that we do not under-stand the text, we read it again. Thus, the subjective monitoring of our com-prehension seems to drive the decision whether to reread the text and how much attention to pay in reading it. Students preparing for an exam must also monitor the degree of mastery of the material online and decide whether they are ready for the exam or whether they should continue studying. They must also decide how much time to allocate to each section based on their feelings of mastery and competence.

When we have a scheduled appointment, we often need to judge whether we have to write it in our calendar or take some other special precaution not to forget it. Sometimes we do not make a special effort to remember the appointment because we feel that we will remember it anyway, and consequently end up missing that appointment. Even when we do remember to perform a planned action, we have to remember that we already did it in order not to repeat the action once again. Deficiencies in output monitoring, as occur in old age, may result in a person taking a medicine more often than needed or in telling the same story again and again (Koriat, Ben-zur, & Sheffer, 1988).

Monitoring processes also take place during remembering. When we search our memory for a forgotten name, we often experience a *feeling of knowing* (FOK), and can even sense that the name is on the tip of the tongue and is about to emerge into consciousness. When the name does emerge into consciousness, we can generally feel that it is indeed the one for which we have been searching. Of course, when we have a feeling that we know the name, we will try harder to look for it than when we feel that we do not know it. However, feelings of knowing might sometimes deceive us (Koriat, 1998). Monitoring processes also occur in trying to report information from memory. A person on the witness stand, who is expected to tell the whole truth and nothing but the truth, must monitor the correctness of information that comes to mind before deciding whether to volunteer it or withhold it. Thus, subjective feelings of confidence might guide one's reporting behavior (Koriat & Goldsmith, 1996).

These examples illustrate the distinction between *monitoring* and *control* processes. Metacognitive monitoring refers to the subjective assessment of one's own cognitive processes and knowledge. For example, such assessments are reflected in the feelings of mastery, competence, or comprehension that we experience as we encode new material, in the feeling of knowing that we experience as we search our memory for an elusive name, and in the subjective confidence that we feel regarding the correctness of retrieved information. Metacognitive control, in turn, refers to the processes that regulate cognitive processes and behavior. Such processes include, for example, the choice of strategies for studying new material, the allocation of learning resources between these materials, the decision to continue searching for a solicited answer or quit, and the decision whether to volunteer that answer or not when the accuracy of the report is at stake.

As suggested by the above examples, the assumption underlying most of the discussions of metacognition is that metacognitive monitoring drives metacognitive control. This assumption agrees with common sense, like the assumption that we run away because we are afraid. That is, subjective feelings are assumed to exert a causal effect on behavior. As we shall see below, however, some of the current discussions in metacognition also imply a cause-and-effect relation in the opposite direction, from behavior to subjective metacognitive feelings.

In what follows, I first review evidence that has been taken to support the view that monitoring affects control. This evidence comes from studies that have focused on the presumed adaptive *function* of noetic feelings. Although most of that evidence is correlational, some is based on experimental manipulations. I then turn to findings and discussions suggesting that metacognitive feelings in fact follow rather than precede controlled action. Support for this claim comes from studies that have focused on the *bases* of noetic feelings. Thus, I will discuss the distinction between noetic feelings and noetic judgments, and then, focusing on noetic feelings, I will examine theories and findings that would seem to imply that these feelings are actually based on feedback from controlled actions. Finally, I will discuss evidence pertinent to the possibility that both types of cause-and-effect relations exist, and examine the conditions for the occurrence of each of them. The conclusion from this analysis is that the models considered by William James are not mutually exclusive, but actually occur simultaneously or sequentially in the course of information processing and behavior.

THE CAUSAL INFLUENCE OF SUBJECTIVE EXPERIENCE ON BEHAVIOR

The recent upsurge of interest in metacognition derives in part from the conviction that subjective experience is not a mere epiphenomenon, but actually influences and guides information processing and behavior (Koriat, 2000; Nelson, 1996). A commonly held assumption among most researchers of metacognition is that the effective monitoring of one's own knowledge has direct consequences for efficient learning and remembering (Koriat & Goldsmith, 1996; Metcalfe & Kornell, 2003; Nelson & Dunlosky, 1991). Therefore, emphasis has been placed on the need to educate intuitive feelings and alleviate illusions of competence (Bjork, 1999; Hogarth, 2001). Indeed, the growing interest in memory accuracy, memory distortion, and false memory has turned attention to the critical contribution of qualitative aspects of memory experience in assisting source monitoring and reality monitoring (see Kelley & Jacoby, 1998; Koriat, Goldsmith, & Pansky, 2000; Mitchell & Johnson, 2000). A similar emphasis on the role of subjective feelings in guiding judgments and behavior can also be seen in current research in social psychology (Bless & Forgas, 2000; Schwarz & Clore, 2003) and decision-making (Slovic et al., 2002).

The assumption underlying this growing body of research and theorizing is that subjective feelings exert a causal role on behavior. This assumption underlies a great many studies in metacognition that have attempted to demonstrate some of the presumed effects of monitoring on control. What is the evidence for these effects? Studies of monitoring processes during learning have assumed a causal chain: monitoring–control–performance. Consider a little study by Thiede, Anderson, and Therriault (2003) on reading comprehension. They asked participants to generate keywords that captured the essence of several texts. Participants who wrote keywords after a delay exhibited better monitoring accuracy than those who wrote keywords immediately after reading. The superior monitoring of the delay participants resulted in a more effective regulation of study, which in turn produced greater overall test performance (reading comprehension). Thus, the assumption is that the output of monitoring serves to guide the regulation of control processes, which can then affect learning and performance.

Other researchers have also provided evidence suggesting that judgments of learning (JOLs) affect the choice of which items to restudy and how much time to allocate to each item. Indeed, when learners are allowed to control the allocation of study time to different items, they tend to invest more time in items that are judged to be difficult to learn than in those that are judged to be easier to learn (for a review, see Son & Metcalfe, 2000). Dunlosky and Hertzog (1998; see also Thiede & Dunlosky, 1999) proposed a discrepancy-reduction model according to which learners monitor online the increase in encoding strength that occurs as more time is spent studying an item, and cease study when a desired level of strength has been reached. This level is preset according to various motivational factors and according to various constraints. Thus, monitoring is assumed to drive study in the same way that fear may be said to drive running away until a desired feeling of safety has been achieved.

There are conditions, however, in which learners invest more study time in the easier items. This occurs, for example, when learners are presented with an easy goal (e.g., to be able to recall only 10 out of 60 items; see Thiede & Dunlosky, 1999), or when the overall amount of time available for study is severely limited (Son & Metcalfe, 2000). To account for these findings, Thiede and Dunlosky proposed a hierarchy of control levels with a superordinate level that determines whether to concentrate on the easier or on the more difficult items. Once a strategic decision has been reached, the online regulation of study time is then delegated to a subordinate level in which the allocation of study time is dictated by the online monitoring of degree of mastery.

Feeling-of-knowing (FOK) judgments made during recall attempts have been assumed also to affect the effort invested in trying to retrieve a solicited item from memory (e.g., Nelson & Narens, 1990). Consider a person who attempts to retrieve a name or a word from memory. Even when recall fails, he may still experience a feeling of knowing and may even have a tip-of-the-tongue (TOT) experience (see Schwartz, 2002). When FOK judgments are high, or when a person is in a TOT state, he is likely to search longer for a memory target before giving up than when FOK is low (Barnes et al., 1999; Gruneberg, Monk, & Sykes, 1977; Schwartz, 2001). Once again, the assumption is that the feeling that one knows or does not know the answer to a question exerts a causal effect on behavior. Reder (1987), in fact, proposed that preliminary FOK judgments not only affect search time, but also influence the choice of strategy for answering a question. Importantly, when FOK judgments are misled by irrelevant factors they also misguide the choice of strategy.

In a similar manner subjective confidence judgments have been assumed to influence controlled behavior regardless of their accuracy. The more confident people are in the correctness of a certain statement, the more likely they are to commit themselves to it. For example, people are willing to stake money on the correctness of their answer when they are confident in it even when their confidence is entirely unwarranted (Fischhoff, Slovic, & Lichtenstein, 1977).

Koriat and Goldsmith (1994, 1996) proposed that an eyewitness who is sworn to tell the truth and nothing but the truth, must monitor the subjective likelihood that a memory response that comes to mind is correct. On the basis of his confidence in the correctness of a candidate response, he then decides whether to volunteer it or not. Thus, confidence is assumed to affect memory reporting. Indeed, the correlation between confidence and volunteering was found to be almost perfect, suggesting that people take for granted the validity of their subjective intuitive feelings. In fact, rememberers have been found to rely heavily on their subjective confidence even when it was not diagnostic of accuracy (Koriat & Goldsmith, 1996). Confidence judgments also influence the "grain size" of the memory report. When a person is not entirely certain about a piece of information that comes to mind, he might choose to report it at a coarse level rather than at a precise level, thus sacrificing informativeness (degree of precision) for accuracy (Goldsmith, Koriat, & Weinberg-Eliezer, 2002). To the extent that monitoring is accurate, allowing participants freedom to control their memory reporting enhances the accuracy of their reports.

In sum, much of the work on metacognitive control is predicated on the assumption that monitoring drives and guides information processing and behavior. This work, then, implies a causal influence of subjective experience on behavior. The assumption underlying that work is that control processes are goal driven; they capitalize on the general validity of noetic feeling to improve the effectiveness of learning and remembering.

We turn now to evidence that supports the "control affects monitoring" hypothesis. This evidence comes from studies that have focused on the question: how do we know that we know? The studies that have attempted to elucidate the *bases* of the metacognitive feelings underlying JOLs, FOK judgments, and subjective confidence seem to suggest that such feelings are based on the feedback from behavior, as William James suggested for emotional feelings.

EXPERIENCE-BASED AND INFORMATION-BASED JUDGMENTS

In discussing the basis of metacognitive judgments, a distinction must be drawn between two types of processes leading to such judgments. Metacognitive judgments may be based either on information retrieved from memory, or may rely directly on sheer subjective feelings. This distinction follows the general distinction which is currently in vogue between two modes of thought underlying judgments, decisions, and behavior (see Chaiken & Trope, 1999; Epstein & Pacini, 1999; Kahneman, 2003; Strack, 1992). In the context of metacognition, information-based (or theory-based) judgments are based on a deliberate and explicit inferential process, in which the person consults his or her long-term memory for pertinent information, and uses that information as a basis for an analytic deduction. Experience-based (or affect-based) judgments, in contrast, are based on sheer subjective feelings. Koriat and Levy-Sadot (1999) used the term *noetic judgments* (or judgments of knowing) to designate information-based judgments, and *noetic feelings* (or feeling of knowing) to designate the subjective experience that underlies experience-based judgments. Consider, for example, the monitoring of one's knowledge during study. A person may judge that they are ready for the exam on the basis of an explicit inference: "I have read the chapter so many times, I am sure that I will succeed in the exam." However, they may also base their judgment on a sheer noetic feeling – an immediate sense of mastery and competence. Similarly, when learners are asked to make JOLs regarding the likelihood of recalling the studied items at test, they may base their judgments on inferences from beliefs or theories; for example, the belief that one has a bad memory, or that an item that was presented three times is likely to be better recalled than one that was presented only once. However, JOLs may also be based on a sheer feeling of competence (Koriat, 1997; Koriat et al., 2004). In that case, the person uses that feeling as a basis for recall predictions.

In like manner, when a person is required to recall the answer to a general-information question, he may provide a "feeling-of-knowing" judgment based on a deliberate, educated inference about the plausibility that the solicited answer will be subsequently recalled or recognized. Such a noetic judgment would be based on domain-specific memories and beliefs (see Nelson, Gerler, & Narens, 1984), and may sometimes take the form "I *ought* to know the answer," rather than "I feel that I know the answer."

In other cases, FOK judgments may be based on a sheer noetic feeling as occurs, for example, in the TOT state. Here the judgment that one knows the elusive word or name is based on a kind of gut feeling rather than on a deliberate, analytic inference based on retrieved beliefs and memories. The feeling has the phenomenal quality of self-evidence (see Epstein & Pacini, 1999), and the person generally has little access to evidence that may question the validity of that feeling.

■ THE BASIS OF NOETIC FEELINGS

Discussions of the basis of noetic feelings are relevant to the question whether such feelings precede controlled processes or actually follow them. Noetic feelings are immediately given and have the quality of direct perception. This phenomenal quality of noetic feelings has motivated trace-access theories (see Koriat, 1993; Schwartz, 1994), according to which such feelings are based on direct access to memory traces. For example, JOLs elicited during learning have been assumed to reflect the monitoring of the strength of the memory trace that is formed during learning (Cohen, Sandler, & Keglevich, 1991). Thus, in studying a list of words, a learner is assumed to detect directly the increase in encoding strength that occurs as more time is spent studying each word. In fact, he or she can then stop studying when a desired strength has been reached. This direct access model can also explain why JOLs are generally accurate. If JOLs monitor encoding strength, they should be accurate in predicting future recall because recall probability should also increase with increasing memory strength.

In a similar manner, FOK judgments have been assumed to be based on direct access to memory traces. Hart (1965), for example, proposed that FOK judgments are based on accessing a special memory-monitoring module that can directly inspect the information stored in memory to determine whether the solicited target is stored there. Thus, whenever a person is required to recall a target, the monitoring module is activated to make sure that the target is present in store before attempting to retrieve it. This model too can easily explain the accuracy of FOK judgments.

In contrast to the direct access models, recent discussions of the bases of noetic feelings subscribe to a cue-utilization view, according to which such feelings are also based on inferences from a variety of cues (e.g., Begg et al., 1989; Benjamin & Bjork, 1996; Koriat, 1993, 1997). However, the type of cues on which they rely, as well as the nature of the inferential process, differ from those underlying noetic judgments. Thus, noetic feelings are assumed to rely on internal, mnemonic cues that derive from the online processes involved in learning and remembering rather than on the content of beliefs and information retrieved from long-term memory. Indeed, evidence has accumulated suggesting that JOLs are based on the ease with which studied items are processed during encoding (Begg et al., 1989; Koriat, 1997; Matvey, Dunlosky, & Guttentag, 2001), or on the ease with which they are retrieved during study (Koriat & Ma'ayan, 2005; Nelson, Narens, & Dunlosky, 2004). Begg et al. (1989), for example, reported results suggesting that the effects of several attributes of words (e.g., concreteness–abstractness) on JOLs are mediated by their effects on ease of processing. Matvey, Dunlosky, and Guttentag (2001) found that JOLs increased with increasing speed of generating the targets to the cues at study, and Hertzog et al. (2003) also found that JOLs increased with the success and speed of forming an interactive image between the cue and the target. More direct evidence regarding the effects of retrieval fluency on JOLs was reported by Benjamin, Bjork, and Schwartz (1998): the faster it took participants to retrieve an answer to a question, the higher was their estimate that they would be able to recall that answer at a later time, although in reality the opposite was the case. Koriat and Ma'ayan (2005) and Nelson, Narens, and Dunlosky (2004) observed that when learners were required to retrieve the target just before making JOLs, JOLs increased with the probability of recalling the target and decreased with the latency of retrieving it.

In a similar manner, when recall of a solicited target fails, FOK judgments have been shown to rely on the familiarity of the cue that is used to probe memory (Metcalfe, Schwartz, & Joaquim, 1993; Reder & Ritter, 1992; Reder & Schunn, 1996), on the amount of partial information retrieved about the target, and on the ease with which that information comes to mind (Koriat, 1993, 1995). Importantly, according to Koriat's (1993) accessibility model, both correct and incorrect partial clues about the target contribute to the enhancement of FOK judgments.

Confidence judgments in the correctness of one's retrieved information have also been claimed to rely on the ease with which that information is retrieved. Indeed, several researchers have documented an inverse relationship between confidence judgments and the latency of selecting an answer from among distractors or the latency of recalling an item from memory (e.g., Costermans, Lories, & Ansay, 1992; Nelson & Narens, 1990; Robinson, Johnson, & Herndon, 1997). Kelley and Lindsay (1993), who used priming to speed up the emergence of an answer, found confidence judgments to increase accordingly. This was true for both correct and incorrect answers. However, it is generally the case that correct answers are associated with shorter latencies than incorrect answers, so that latency of responding is generally a valid cue for the correctness of the answer.

In sum, like noetic judgments, noetic feelings also have been assumed to be based on an inference. However, an important difference between noetic feelings and noetic judgments is that the latter require consulting the content of beliefs and knowledge stored in long-term memory, a process that generally takes time and effort. The former, in contrast, are based on the quality of information processing in the here and now. Such cues as encoding fluency, familiarity, amount of partial information accessed, and the ease with which information comes to mind, convey information about the quality of information processing, and can be detected online, with little effort, because they are the by-products of the normal processes of learning and remembering.

To illustrate this difference, consider the study of Koriat et al. (2004). That study was based on the assumption that if JOLs monitor the online process-ing of the items during study, they should be indifferent to the expected time of testing, because the processing fluency of an item will be the same whether testing is expected after a week or immediately after study. Indeed, when par-ticipants made JOLs for tests that were expected immediately after study, a day after study, or a week after study, JOLs were entirely indifferent to the expected retention interval, although actual recall exhibited a typical forget-ting function. The result was such that JOLs matched actual recall very closely for immediate testing, whereas for a week's delay, participants predicted over 50 percent recall whereas actual recall was less than 20 percent.

The inference underlying noetic feelings is also assumed to differ in quality from the type of inference underlying noetic judgments. As indicated earlier, noetic judgments entail deliberate, analytic deductions that rely on beliefs and memories. In contrast, noetic feelings are mediated by the implicit applica-tion of nonanalytic heuristics (see Jacoby & Brooks, 1984; Koriat & Levy-Sadot, 1999). These heuristics operate below full consciousness to influence and shape subjective experience itself. Once a noetic feeling has been formed, it can then serve as the immediate basis for metacognitive judgments.

Indeed, the work of Jacoby, Kelley, and their associates on the fluency heur-istic (see Kelley & Jacoby, 1998), as well as that of Whittlesea (2002, 2004), provided ample evidence for the claim that subjective experience can be shaped by unconscious inferential processes. Thus, fluent processing of a stimulus, when it is enhanced by advance priming, may be attributed to the past, result-ing in the feeling of familiarity (Jacoby & Dallas, 1981; Jacoby, Kelley, & Dywan, 1989). Fluent processing may also be attributed to characteristics of the stimulus, resulting in such perceptual experiences as enhanced brightness or clarity (for a review, see Kelley & Rhodes, 2002).

 ## THE CAUSAL INFLUENCE OF BEHAVIOR ON SUBJECTIVE EXPERIENCE

Examination of the mnemonic cues that have been assumed to shape noetic feelings indicates that they all reside in the feedback from control processes, implying that monitoring *follows* control rather than vice versa. Consider, as an example, Koriat's accessibility model of FOK. This model departs from the classical, trace-access model proposed by Hart (1965). As noted earlier, Hart's model assumes that monitoring precedes and guides control (see also Barnes et al., 1999): when a person is asked to recall a memory target, he or she first consults the monitoring mechanism in order to ascertain that the target is indeed available in memory before attempting to retrieve it. The advantage of such a monitoring mechanism, according to Hart, is that it can save the time and effort looking for a target that is not in store.

Koriat's accessibility model, in contrast, actually places control ahead of monitoring. According to that model, it is by attempting to search for a solicited target that one can judge whether the target is "there" and worth continuing to search for. The cues for FOK are assumed to reside in the products of the retrieval process itself. Whenever we search our memory for a name or a word, many clues often come to mind, including fragments of the target, semantic attributes, episodic information, and a variety of activations emanating from other sources. Although such clues may not be articulate enough to support an analytic inference, they can still act in concert to produce the subjective feeling that the target is "there." Indeed, FOK judgments have been found to increase with the amount of partial information retrieved about the target and with the ease with which that information is retrieved (Koriat, 1993, 1995). Such cues, of course, are not available prior to attempted retrieval.

Because monitoring follows retrieval, if retrieval goes wrong, so will monitoring. Thus, retrieval may be fooled by a variety of clues deriving from many sources, such as neighboring targets, priming, misleading postevent information, and so on. In that case monitoring too will go wrong. Indeed, because of the non-analytic nature of the accessibility heuristic, both correct and wrong partial information have been found to enhance FOK judgments. Wrong partial clues can readily lead to faulty intuitions and unwarranted positive FOK (Koriat, 1994).

Consider next the claim that confidence judgments in an answer are based in part on the latency of recalling or selecting that answer or that solution: the more effort and the longer the deliberation needed to reach an answer the lower will be the confidence in that answer (e.g., Barnes et al., 1999; Costermans, Lories, & Ansay, 1992; Kelley & Lindsay, 1993; Nelson & Narens, 1990; Robinson, Johnson, & Herndon, 1997). This claim implies that confidence judgments are based on the feedback from controlled action: When faced with a problem, the person spends as much time and effort as is needed to reach a solution. Once a solution has been produced, confidence is based on a retrospective review of the process that has led to the solution, particularly the amount of effort invested. Thus, again the assumption is that monitoring follows control and is based on the feedback from control processes.

In the same way, the idea that JOLs during learning are based on encoding fluency or retrieval fluency also implies that it is by attempting to commit an item to memory or by attempting to retrieve it that one can appreciate the likelihood of recalling that item in the future. Presumably, the mnemonic cues gained from the learning process help to shape a feeling of competence, and that feeling can then be used as a basis for recall predictions.

In conclusion, examination of the mnemonic cues that have been assumed to shape noetic feelings suggest that these cues reside in the feedback from the control processes engaged in learning and remembering. Reviewing the work on the bases of metacognitive feelings, Koriat and Levy-Sadot (1999) concluded that the cues for noetic feelings lie in structural aspects of the information-processing system. It is as if the cognitive system inspects its own functioning as it attempts to carry out its information-processing chores, and uses the product of that inspection as a basis for metacognitive feelings.

An important implication of this view is that metacognitive judgments are not based on specialized modules that are dedicated to monitoring. Rather, monitoring occurs as a by-product of the normal processes of learning and remembering. People carry out their routine cognitive processes designed to achieve certain goals, and cues stemming from these processes (fluency of processing, effort, ease of access, etc.) are used to shape noetic feelings. Thus, the process underlying noetic feelings can be said to be parasitic on the normal processes of learning and remembering (Koriat, 1993). This idea seems to agree with the spirit of William James' position: fear is simply a by-product of running away from danger.

 ## THE RECIPROCAL EFFECTS BETWEEN SUBJECTIVE EXPERIENCE AND BEHAVIOR

To summarize the foregoing discussion, the work in metacognition reveals ambivalence regarding the cause-and-effect relation between monitoring and control or, more generally, between subjective experience and behavior. When researchers focus on the presumed adaptive *function* of noetic feelings, they tend to endorse the view that monitoring affects control (Nelson & Leonesio, 1988). In contrast, when they focus on the *bases* of noetic feelings, their theorizing would seem to imply that noetic feelings are actually based on the feedback from controlled operations, and thus follow rather than precede behavior.

How can these two meta-theoretical positions be reconciled? A recent study by Koriat, Ma'ayan and Nussinson (2006) attempted to do just that. First, they attempted to specify the conditions under which monitoring can be said to affect control and those in which monitoring would seem to rely on the feedback from control operations; and second, they attempted to examine how the two types of cause-and-effect relations may be combined in the course of information processing and behavior.

The logic underlying Koriat et al.'s investigation can be illustrated with regard to emotional behavior. Consider the question addressed by William James: do we run away because we are frightened or are we frightened because we run away? Because the feeling of fear and the action of running away generally go hand in hand, one way to distinguish cause from effect is to consider the strength of each of the two variables. If it is the feeling of fear that causes one to run away from danger, then the faster one runs away, the less fear one should experience after running. In contrast, if it is running away that produces a feeling of fear, then the faster one runs away the *more* fear one should experience. Thus, the correlation between the speed of running away and the intensity of fear experienced afterwards can disclose the cause-and-effect relation between emotional feelings and behavior.

Applying this logic to metacognition, Koriat et al. (2006) considered the relationship between the amount of effort invested in a task (control) and the noetic feelings experienced after performing that task (monitoring). If monitoring drives control, noetic feelings should *increase* with the effort invested in the task. Thus, for example, the more time and effort invested in studying a certain material, the stronger should be the feeling of competence experienced after study. In contrast, if monitoring is based on the feedback from control operations, then noetic feelings should *decrease* with the effort invested in the task. For example, JOLs following study should decrease with increased study time and effort.

Koriat et al. (2006) proposed that a positive relationship between control effort and noetic feelings should be obtained when the regulation of control effort is *goal driven*, that is, when that regulation is used as a strategic tool for improving performance and achieving certain objectives. For example, a student may place a premium on a particular exam, strategically investing more effort in studying for that exam than he or she would do otherwise. In that case, the added effort would be expected to instill a *stronger* sense of competence. Similarly, when different incentives are awarded to the remembering of different items in a list (e.g., Castel et al., 2002; Dunlosky & Thiede, 1998), we should expect the high-incentive items to draw more study time and in parallel to result in higher JOLs following study.

In contrast, when the regulation of control effort is *data driven*, dictated by the nature of the task itself, we should expect a negative correlation between control effort and noetic feelings. In that case, effortless, fluent processing would serve as a mnemonic cue that instills a sense of competence. Thus, a student who spends more time studying a particular segment of the material because that segment is intrinsically more difficult than others, would be expected to feel *less* confident about the future recall of that segment, in comparison with other segments.

This conceptual framework received support in a number of experiments involving the self-paced study of a list of paired associates. Participants were allowed to control the amount of time spent on each item, and before moving to the next item they made JOLs on a 0–100 percent scale, reflecting the likelihood that they would be able to recall the target word in response to the cue word at test. Consistent with previous findings, participants spent more time studying the more difficult items than the easier items. The standard explanation of this finding is that the differential allocation of study time reflects a strategic attempt to compensate for the greater difficulty of the more difficult items. Thus, according to the discrepancy-reduction model (e.g., Dunlosky & Hertzog, 1998), in self-paced learning learners continuously monitor the online increase in encoding strength that occurs as more time is spent studying an item, and cease study when a desired level of strength has been reached. In this model, the allocation of study time is used as a strategic tool to achieve certain goals, and is guided by the online monitoring of degree of mastery.

The discrepancy-reduction model, however, encounters serious difficulties. Not only was the greater investment of study time found to be useless in terms of enhancing the recall of the difficult items, but participants continued to assign lower JOLs to the difficult items. Thus, when participants studied the same list of paired associates under self-paced conditions, they continued to invest more study time in the more difficult items even in the fourth presentation, and in parallel continued to admit that the difficult items were less likely to be recalled. Why do learners stick to a maladaptive strategy if they are aware of its futility?

Koriat et al. (2005) proposed that in self-paced learning, the differential allocation of study time does not reflect a premeditated policy to invest more study effort in difficult items with the intention either to compensate for their *a priori* difficulty or to achieve a predetermined level of mastery. Rather, the allocation of study time is generally *data driven*: learners spend as much time as is required for a particular item. The amount of time and effort invested in attempting to commit the item to memory is then used as a cue for JOLs under the heuristic that the more time invested in studying an item the less likely it is to be later recalled. Therefore, monitoring can be said to *follow* control rather than precede it. It is by investing a greater amount and effort studying an item that a learner "knows" that the item will be difficult to recall.

If study effort is data driven then a *negative* correlation should be expected between study time and JOLs. Indeed, in several experiments (Koriat et al., 2005) JOLs were found to *decrease* with the amount of study time invested in each item. This negative correlation is analogous to the idea that the faster one runs away from a bear the more fear one should feel. In parallel to the effects of study time on JOLs, recall was also found to *decrease* with study time, supporting the validity of the memorizing effort heuristic. These results are consistent with the idea that monitoring *follows* control or, more generally, that subjective experience is based on the feedback from controlled behavior.

In contrast to the negative correlation between study time and JOLs, a positive correlation is expected when study time is *goal driven*. In fact, students know that their success in a forthcoming exam should increase with the amount of time spent preparing for it. To examine the relationship between JOLs and study time when study time is goal driven, Koriat et al. (2005) manipulated the incentive associated with the recall of different items in the list. Participants were presented with the same learning task as before except that they were instructed that they would win 1 point for recalling some of the items and 3 points for recalling the other items. The incentive associated with each item was announced just prior to its presentation. This differential manipulation of incentive resulted in a *positive* correlation between JOLs and study time. Participants spent more time studying the high-incentive items (5.22 s per item) than the low-incentive items (4.33 s) and, in parallel, assigned higher JOLs to the high-incentive items (61.4 percent) than to the low-incentive items (56.6 percent). This positive correlation is the postulated signature of goal-driven metacognitive regulation: the greater the effort invested, the stronger the ensuing feeling of competence. This is analogous to idea that the faster one runs away the more secure one should feel.

However, the presence of a positive correlation between study time and JOLs did not preclude the occurrence of a negative correlation for each level of incentive. Thus, when the results were analyzed separately for the low-incentive and high-incentive items, JOLs were found to *decrease* with study time. The correlation between study time and JOLs averaged −.45 for the low-incentive items, and −.56 for the high-incentive items, suggesting that the allocation of study time between same-incentive items was data driven.

These results suggest that the two models considered by William James with respect to the cause-and-effect relation between emotional feelings and emotional behavior are not mutually exclusive. In fact, as just noted, evidence for both models was found within the same situation. Whereas the effects of goal-driven regulation are consistent with the feeling-affects-behavior model, the data-driven regulation is consistent with the behavior-affects-feeling model.

The above results suggest that the two models can coexist within the same situation. However, they can also occur sequentially. For example, even if an emotional feeling occurs as feedback from an emotional behavior (behavior-affects-feeling), it can be expected, in turn, to exert its own effects on subsequent behaviors (feeling-affects-behavior). This possibility is suggested by Schachter and Singer's (1962) work. They showed that the arousal produced by injected epinephrine could be experienced either as anger or happiness depending on the person's attributions. Thus, in agreement with the James-Lange theory, emotional feelings are assumed to emerge in response to bodily changes. However, once an emotional feeling has been produced, that feeling can then cause specific actions (see also Carver & Scheier, 1990).

In a similar manner, we may imagine a sequence of events such that monitoring drives control, and feedback from control operations then produces monitoring output, which in turn drives control, and so on. Evidence for such sequencing is provided by Koriat and Levy-Sadot (2001), who suggested that two heuristics, cue familiarity and accessibility, exert their influence on FOK in a cascaded manner: at an early stage of searching for a memory target, FOK judgments are primarily determined by the familiarity of the cue that probes memory. When cue familiarity is high, it can drive the search for the target, and then the accessibility of pertinent clues about the target may contribute further to FOK judgments. Indeed, the effects of accessibility on FOK judgments were found to be stronger when cue familiarity was high than when it was low. This pattern suggests that the familiarity of the cue, perhaps resulting from greater processing fluency, can motivate memory search (i.e., monitoring affects control), and the feedback from that search can then affect later FOK judgments (i.e., control affects monitoring).

▉ CONCLUDING REMARKS

The recent advances in metacognition provide opportunities for scratching the surface of some old standing meta-theoretical issues regarding the role of subjective experience in behavior. One such issue concerns the function of subjective experience (see Koriat, 2000). Another issue touched upon in this chapter concerns the cause-and-effect relation between subjective experience and behavior. The research and theorizing in metacognition discloses ambivalence regarding this issue. This ambivalence, however, may actually suggest that the two options considered by William James in the quote at the beginning of this chapter are not mutually exclusive. We propose that some of the dynamics discussed with regard to noetic feelings also hold true for other types of feelings. To the extent that our running away from a bear is entirely data driven, dictated by the speed (or size) of the bear, then the faster we run away, the more fear we should experience, as would be predicted by William James' model. However, if we make a goal-driven effort that goes beyond that called for by the stimulus situation, then the extra effort invested in running away should contribute towards reducing our feeling of fear.

AUTHOR NOTES

The preparation of this chapter was supported by the Israel Science Foundation (grant No. 928/00) and by a grant from the German Federal Ministry of Education and Research (BMBF) within the framework of German–Israeli Project Cooperation (DIP). I am grateful to Hilit Ma'ayan and Ravit Nussinson (Levy-Sadot) who made significant contributions to the ideas presented in this chapter. Correspondence concerning this chapter should be addressed to Asher Koriat, Department of Psychology, University of Haifa, Haifa, Israel. Email: akoriat@research.haifa.ac.il.

REFERENCES

Barnes, A. E., Nelson, T. O., Dunlosky, J., Mazzoni, G., & Narens, L. (1999). An integrative system of metamemory components involved in retrieval. In D. Gopher & A. Koriat (Eds.), *Attention and performance XVII – Cognitive regulation of performance: Interaction of theory and application* (pp. 287–313). Cambridge, MA: MIT Press.

Begg, I., Duft, S., Lalonde, P., Melnick, R., & Sanvito, J. (1989). Memory predictions are based on ease of processing. *Journal of Memory and Language, 28,* 610–632.

Benjamin, A. S. & Bjork, R. A. (1996). Retrieval fluency as a metacognitive index. In L. Reder (Ed.), *Implicit memory and metacognition* (pp. 309–338). Hillsdale, NJ: Erlbaum.

Benjamin, A. S., Bjork, R. A., & Schwartz, B. L. (1998). The mismeasure of memory: When retrieval fluency is misleading as a metamnemonic index. *Journal of Experimental Psychology: General, 127,* 55–68.

Bjork, R. A. (1999). Assessing our own competence: Heuristics and illusions. In D. Gopher & A. Koriat (Eds.), *Attention and performance XVII – Cognitive regulation of performance: Interaction of theory and application* (pp. 435–459). Cambridge, MA: MIT Press.

Bless, H. & Forgas, J. P. (Eds.) (2000). *The message within: The role of subjective experience in social cognition and behavior.* Philadelphia: Psychology Press.

Carver, C. S. & Scheier, M. F. (1990). Origins and functions of positive and negative affect: A control-process view. *Psychological Review, 97,* 19–35.

Castel, A. D., Benjamin, A. S., Craik, F. I. M., & Watkins, M. J. (2002). The effects of aging on selectivity and control in short-term recall. *Memory & Cognition, 30,* 1078–1085.

Chaiken, S. & Trope, Y. (Eds.) (1999). *Dual-process theories in social psychology:* New York: Guilford Press.

Clore, G. L. (1992). Cognitive phenomenology: Feelings and the construction of judgment. In A. Tesser & L. L. Martin (Eds.), *The construction of social judgments* (pp. 133–163). Hillsdale, NJ: Erlbaum.

Cohen, R. L., Sandler, S. P., & Keglevich, L. (1991). The failure of memory monitoring in a free recall task. *Canadian Journal of Psychology, 45,* 523–538.

Costermans, J., Lories, G., & Ansay, C. (1992). Confidence level and feeling of knowing in question answering: The weight of inferential processes. *Journal of Experimental Psychology: Learning, Memory, and Cognition, 18,* 142–150.

Dunlosky, J. & Hertzog, C. (1998). Training programs to improve learning in later adulthood: Helping older adults educate themselves. In D. J. Hacker (Ed.), *Metacognition in educational theory and practice* (pp. 249–275). Mahwah, NJ: Erlbaum.

Dunlosky, J. & Thiede, K. W. (1998). What makes people study more? An evaluation of factors that affect self-paced study. *Acta Psychologica, 98,* 37–56.

Epstein, S. & Pacini, R. (1999). Some basic issues regarding dual-process theories from the perspective of cognitive–experiential self-theory. In S. Chaiken & Y. Trope (Eds.), *Dual-process theories in social psychology* (pp. 462–482). New York: Guilford Press.

Fischhoff, B., Slovic, P., & Lichtenstein, S. (1977). Knowing with certainty: The appropriateness of extreme confidence. *Journal of Experimental Psychology: Human Perception and Performance, 3,* 552–564.

Flavell, J. H. (1979). Metacognition and cognitive monitoring: A new area of cognitive–developmental inquiry. *American Psychologist, 34,* 906–911.

Goldsmith, M., Koriat, A., & Weinberg-Eliezer, A. (2002). The strategic regulation of grain size in memory reporting. *Journal of Experimental Psychology: General, 131,* 73–95.

Gruneberg, M. M., Monks, J., & Sykes, R. N. (1977). Some methodological problems with feelings of knowing studies. *Acta Psychologica, 41,* 365–371.

Hart, J. T. (1965). Memory and the feeling-of-knowing experience. *Journal of Educational Psychology, 56,* 208–216.

Hertzog, C., Dunlosky, J., Robinson, A. E., & Kidder, D. P. (2003). Encoding fluency is a cue used for judgments about learning. *Journal of Experimental Psychology: Learning, Memory, and Cognition, 29,* 22–34.

Hogarth, R. M. (2001). *Educating intuition.* Chicago: University of Chicago Press.

Jacoby, L. L. & Brooks, L. R. (1984). Nonanalytic cognition: Memory, perception, and concept learning. In G. H. Bower (Ed.), *The psychology of learning and motivation: Advances in research and theory* (Vol. 18, pp. 1–47). San Diego: Academic Press.

Jacoby, L. L. & Dallas, M. (1981). On the relationship between autobiographical memory and perceptual learning. *Journal of Experimental Psychology: General, 110,* 306–340.

Jacoby, L. L., Kelley, C. M., & Dywan, J. (1989). Memory attributions. In H. L. Roediger III & F. I. M. Craik (Eds.), *Varieties of memory and consciousness: Essays in honour of Endel Tulving* (pp. 391–422). Hillsdale, NJ: Erlbaum.

James, W. (1884). What is an emotion? *Mind, 9,* 188–205.

Kahneman, D. (2003). A perspective on judgment and choice: Mapping bounded rationality. *American Psychologist, 58,* 697–720.

Kelley, C. M. & Jacoby, L. L. (1998). Subjective reports and process dissociation: Fluency, knowing, and feeling. *Acta Psychologica, 98,* 127–140.

Kelley, C. M. & Lindsay, D. S. (1993). Remembering mistaken for knowing: Ease of retrieval as a basis for confidence in answers to general knowledge questions. *Journal of Memory and Language, 32,* 1–24.

Kelley, C. M. & Rhodes, M. G. (2002). Making sense and nonsense of experience: Attributions in memory and judgment. In B. H. Ross (Ed.), *Psychology of learning and motivation: Advances in theory and research* (Vol. 41, pp. 293–320). New York: Academic Press.

Koriat, A. (1993). How do we know that we know? The accessibility model of the feeling of knowing. *Psychological Review, 100,* 609–639.

Koriat, A. (1994). Memory's knowledge of its own knowledge: The accessibility account of the feeling of knowing. In J. Metcalfe & A. P. Shimamura (Eds.), *Metacognition: Knowing about knowing* (pp. 115–135). Cambridge, MA: MIT Press.

Koriat, A. (1995). Dissociating knowing and the feeling of knowing: Further evidence for the accessibility model. *Journal of Experimental Psychology: General, 124,* 311–333.

Koriat, A. (1997). Monitoring one's own knowledge during study: A cue-utilization approach to judgments of learning. *Journal of Experimental Psychology: General, 126,* 349–370.

Koriat, A. (1998). Metamemory: The feeling of knowing and its vagaries. In M. Sabourin, F. I. M. Craik, & M. Robert (Eds.), *Advances in psychological science* (Vol. 2, pp. 461–469). Hove, UK: Psychology Press.

Koriat, A. (2000). The feeling of knowing: Some metatheoretical implications for consciousness and control. *Consciousness and Cognition, 9,* 149–171.

Koriat, A. (2005). Metacognition and consciousness. In P. D. Zelazo, M. Moscovitch, & E. Thompson (Eds.), *Cambridge handbook of consciousness.* New York: Cambridge University Press.

Koriat, A., Ben-zur, H., & Sheffer, D. (1988). Telling the same story twice: Output monitoring and age. *Journal of Memory and Language, 27,* 23–39.

Koriat, A., Bjork, R. A., Sheffer, L., & Bar, S. K. (2004). Predicting one's own forgetting: The role of experience-based and theory-based processes. *Journal of Experimental Psychology: General, 133,* 643–656.

Koriat, A. & Goldsmith, M. (1994). Memory in naturalistic and laboratory contexts: Distinguishing the accuracy-oriented and quantity-oriented approaches to memory assessment. *Journal of Experimental Psychology: General, 123,* 297–315.

Koriat, A. & Goldsmith, M. (1996). Monitoring and control processes in the strategic regulation of memory accuracy. *Psychological Review, 103,* 490–517.

Koriat, A., Goldsmith, M., & Pansky, A. (2000). Toward a psychology of memory accuracy. *Annual Review of Psychology, 51,* 481–537.

Koriat, A. & Levy-Sadot, R. (1999). Processes underlying metacognitive judgments: Information-based and experience-based monitoring of one's own knowledge. In S. Chaiken & Y. Trope (Eds.), *Dual process theories in social psychology* (pp. 483–502). New York: Guilford Press.

Koriat, A. & Levy-Sadot, R. (2001). The combined contributions of the cue-familiarity and accessibility heuristics to feelings of knowing. *Journal of Experimental Psychology: Learning, Memory, and Cognition, 27,* 34–53.

Koriat, A. & Ma'ayan, H. (2005). The effects of encoding fluency and retrieval fluency on judgments of learning. *Journal of Memory and Language, 52,* 478–492.

Koriat, A., Ma'ayan, H., & Nussinson, R. (2006). The intricate relationships between monitoring and control in metacognition: Lessons for the cause-and-effect relation between subjective experience and behavior. *Journal of Experimental Psychology: General,* in press.

Matvey, G., Dunlosky, J., & Guttentag, R. (2001). Fluency of retrieval at study affects judgments of learning (JOLs): An analytic or nonanalytic basis for JOLs? *Memory & Cognition, 29,* 222–233.

Metcalfe, J. & Kornell, N. (2003). The dynamics of learning and allocation of study time to a region of proximal learning. *Journal of Experimental Psychology: General, 132,* 530–542.

Metcalfe, J., Schwartz, B. L., & Joaquim, S. G. (1993). The cue-familiarity heuristic in metacognition. *Journal of Experimental Psychology: Learning, Memory, and Cognition, 19,* 851–864.

Mitchell, K. J. & Johnson, M. K. (2000). Source monitoring: Attributing mental experiences. In F. I. M. Craik & E. Tulving (Eds.), *The Oxford handbook of memory* (pp. 179–195). Oxford: Oxford University Press.

Nelson, T. O. (1996). Gamma is a measure of the accuracy of predicting performance on one item relative to another item, not of the absolute performance on an individual item. *Applied Cognitive Psychology, 10,* 257–260.

Nelson, T. O. & Dunlosky, J. (1991). When people's judgments of learning (JOLs) are extremely accurate at predicting subsequent recall: The "delayed-JOL effect." *Psychological Science, 2,* 267–270.

Nelson, T. O., Gerler, D., & Narens, L. (1984). Accuracy of feeling of knowing judgments for predicting perceptual identification and relearning. *Journal of Experimental Psychology: General, 113,* 282–300.

Nelson, T. O. & Leonesio, R. J. (1988). Allocation of self-paced study time and the "labor-in-vain effect." *Journal of Experimental Psychology: Learning, Memory, and Cognition, 14,* 676–686.

Nelson, T. O. & Narens, L. (1990). Metamemory: A theoretical framework and new findings. In G. Bower (Ed.), *The psychology of learning and motivation: Advances in research and theory* (Vol. 26, pp. 123–125). San Diego: Academic Press.

Nelson, T. O., Narens, L., & Dunlosky, J. (2004). A revised methodology for research on metamemory: Pre-judgment recall and monitoring (PRAM). *Psychological Methods, 9,* 53–69.

Posner, M. I. & Snyder, C. R. R. (1975). Attention and cognitive control. In R. L. Solso (Ed.), *Information processing and cognition: The Loyola symposium* (pp. 55–85). Hillsdale, NJ: Erlbaum.

Reder, L. M. (1987). Strategy selection in question answering. *Cognitive Psychology, 19,* 90–138.

Reder, L. M. & Ritter, F. E. (1992). What determines initial feeling of knowing? Familiarity with question terms, not with the answer. *Journal of Experimental Psychology: Learning, Memory, and Cognition, 18,* 435–451.

Reder, L. M. & Schunn, C. D. (1996). Metacognition does not imply awareness: Strategy choice is governed by implicit learning and memory. In L. M. Reder (Ed.), *Implicit memory and metacognition* (pp. 45–77). Mahwah, NJ: Erlbaum.

Robinson, M. D., Johnson, J. T., & Herndon, F. (1997). Reaction time and assessments of cognitive effort as predictors of eyewitness memory accuracy and confidence. *Journal of Applied Psychology, 82,* 416–425.

Schachter, S. & Singer, J. (1962). Cognitive, social, and physiological determinants of emotional state. *Psychological Review, 69,* 379–399.

Schacter, D. L. (1989). On the relations between memory and consciousness: Dissociable interactions and conscious experience. In H. L. Roediger & F. I. M. Craik (Eds.), *Varieties of memory and consciousness: Essays in honour of Endel Tulving* (pp. 355–389). Hillsdale, NJ: Erlbaum.

Schwartz, B. L. (1994). Sources of information in metamemory: Judgments of learning and feelings of knowing. *Psychonomic Bulletin and Review, 1,* 357–375.

Schwartz, B. L. (2001). The relation of tip-of-the-tongue states and retrieval time. *Memory & Cognition, 29,* 117–126.

Schwartz, B. L. (2002). *Tip-of-the-tongue states: Phenomenology, mechanism, and lexical retrieval.* Mahwah, NJ: Erlbaum.

Schwarz, N. & Clore, G. L. (2003). Mood as information: 20 years later. *Psychological Inquiry, 14,* 296–303.

Slovic, P., Finucane, M., Peters, E., & MacGregor, D. G. (2002). The affect heuristic. In T. Gilovich, D. Griffin, & D. Kahneman (Eds.), *Heuristics and biases: The psychology of intuitive judgment* (pp. 397–420). New York: Cambridge University Press.

Son, L. K. & Metcalfe, J. (2000). Metacognitive and control strategies in study-time allocation. *Journal of Experimental Psychology: Learning, Memory, and Cognition, 26,* 204–221.

Strack, F. (1992). The different routes to social judgments: Experiential versus informational strategies. In L. L. Martin & A. Tesser (Eds.), *The construction of social judgments* (pp. 249–275). Hillsdale, NJ: Erlbaum.

Thiede, K. W., Anderson, M. C. M., & Therriault, D. (2003). Accuracy of metacognitive monitoring affects learning of texts. *Journal of Educational Psychology, 95,* 66–73.

Thiede, K. W. & Dunlosky, J. (1999). Toward a general model of self-regulated study: An analysis of selection of items for study and self-paced study time. *Journal of Experimental Psychology: Learning, Memory, and Cognition, 25,* 1024–1037.

Whittlesea, B. W. A. (2002). Two routes to remembering (and another to remembering not). *Journal of Experimental Psychology: General, 131,* 325–348.

Whittlesea, B. W. A. (2004). The perception of integrality: Remembering through the validation of expectation. *Journal of Experimental Psychology: Learning, Memory, and Cognition, 30,* 891–908.

PART II

MEMORY, EMOTION, AGING, AND THE BRAIN

6

The Memory Enhancing Effect of Emotion: Functional Neuroimaging Evidence

Florin Dolcos, Kevin S. LaBar, and Roberto Cabeza

Abstract

Emotional events are usually remembered better than neutral events. The anatomical and functional correlates of this phenomenon have been investigated in both animals and humans, with approaches ranging from neuropsychological and pharmacological to electrophysiological and functional neuroimaging. The present chapter reviews this evidence, focusing in particular on functional neuroimaging studies in humans, which have examined the effects of emotion on memory-related activity during both encoding and retrieval. The available evidence emphasizes the role of the amygdala, the medial temporal lobe memory system, and the prefrontal cortex. The chapter ends with a discussion of open issues and future directions.

Among the multitude of stimuli comprising our environment, at any moment there are some stimuli that are more relevant to us than others, and thus are more likely to engage our processing resources. What is it, though, that makes some stimuli more relevant than others? To some extent, stimuli with virtually identical properties may still be preferentially processed because they better serve our current activities and goals. Nevertheless, some stimuli tend to "capture" our attention regardless of their relevance with respect to our present activity. This latter category comprises emotional stimuli, which as a result of evolution and ontogenesis have gained relevance that transcends that of present activities.

What are the neural mechanisms though that allow for such privileged access to processing resources that can make us both emotionally resonate and behave accordingly by approaching something that is desirable, or avoiding something that is potentially harmful? Also, what are the mechanisms that make possible the transition from the activity-specific to the more general relevance of these stimuli? Particularly, what are the mechanisms underlying our ability to encode, store, and retrieve information about our experiences, which ultimately allow us to distinguish what may be approached from what should be avoided? Finally, how do alterations of these mechanisms contribute to clinical conditions, such as apathy, anxiety, depression, or post-traumatic stress disorders?

These are only a few questions that humans have tried to answer for centuries, and neuroscientists have fervidly engaged in answering particularly during the last few decades. Consequently, a new field has emerged: the *cognitive neuroscience of emotion*. Different approaches ranging from neuropsychological and pharmacological to functional neuroimaging have attempted to define the neural mechanisms underlying the operations associated with different aspects of emotional processing in both humans and animals (reviewed in Damasio, 1994; Davidson & Irwin, 1999; Davis & Whalen, 2001; Lane & Nadel, 2000; LeDoux, 2000; McGaugh, 2004; Phan et al., 2002; Phelps, 2004; Zald, 2003).

This chapter focuses on evidence concerning the neural correlates of the memory-enhancing effect of emotion, as obtained from functional neuroimaging studies of neurologically intact human subjects. In the following sections, we first introduce a few key concepts, and then highlight the role of functional neuroimaging techniques in revealing the neural correlates of the modulatory effect of emotion during encoding and retrieval of episodic memories (i.e., explicit memory for personal events; Tulving, 1983). The chapter ends with a discussion of future directions.

▪ CONCEPTS AND METHODS

Recent developments in the cognitive neuroscience of emotion have led to important progress in identifying the nature of emotional phenomena and their relationship with other psychological processes, as well as in understanding their features and neural correlates. Among the various psychological phenomena involving emotional processing in humans, the modulatory effect of emotion on different stages of memory (e.g., encoding, retrieval) has received substantial attention in the literature. Concerning the main features defining emotional phenomena, a critical distinction in the emotion literature is the one between two orthogonal affective dimensions: *arousal* and *valence* (Lang et al., 1993; Russell, 1980). Arousal refers to a continuum that varies from calm to excitement, whereas valence refers to a continuum that varies from pleasant to unpleasant with neutral as an intermediate value (for methods to assess these dimensions, see Bradley & Lang, 1994). Specific emotions can be positioned within this dimensional space according to the specific arousal and valence levels associated with them. In addition, important progress has also been made regarding the neural mechanisms underlying the operations associated with various aspects of emotional processing. Among the brain regions most typically associated with emotional processing, the amygdala and the prefrontal cortices have been the most thoroughly investigated (e.g., Damasio, 1994; Davidson & Irwin, 1999;

Davis & Whalen, 2001; Lane & Nadel, 2000; LeDoux, 1996; McGaugh, 2000; Phan et al., 2002; Phelps, 2004; Zald, 2003), although the role of other brain regions such as the basal ganglia and insular cortex has also been studied (e.g., Davidson & Irwin, 1999).

A significant contribution to this recent progress has been made by functional neuroimaging methods. Particularly important are non-invasive techniques, such as those involving hemodynamic (e.g., event-related functional magnetic resonance imaging: ER-fMRI) or electrophysiological (e.g., event-related potentials: ERP) measurements, both of which are assumed to be associated with changes in the neural activity underlying various psychological processes. Functional MRI typically involves measurements of blood oxygenation, and is characterized by excellent spatial resolution (at the level of millimeters), whereas ERPs typically involve recording of electrical potentials through electrodes placed on the scalp, and are characterized by excellent temporal resolution (at the level of milliseconds). These two techniques can thus offer complementary information concerning the brain mechanisms and the timing associated with various cognitive operations.

An important advance in understanding the neural correlates of emotional memory has been made by application of event-related designs and the *subsequent memory paradigm*. One important feature of event-related designs is that recording of functional neuroimaging data (e.g., ER-fMRI/ERP) can be time-locked to "events" that occur either in the external environment (e.g., the onset of a stimulus) or in the participants' minds (Picton, Lins, & Scherg, 1995; Rugg, 1995). In contrast to other functional neuroimaging techniques that use "blocked" designs (e.g., blocked fMRI and Positron Emission Tomography – PET), ER-fMRI and ERP data can be analyzed offline on a trial-by-trial basis and selectively sorted and averaged on the basis of subjects' behavior. For instance, one may compare activity for items that are remembered vs. forgotten in a memory test, thereby establishing a direct link between brain activity and successful memory performance in individual participants. Comparing brain activity for remembered vs. forgotten items can be done both during the encoding (learning) phase and during the retrieval (test) phase. During encoding, one can identify regions showing greater activity for items that are subsequently remembered than for items that are subsequently forgotten in a later memory test (*subsequent memory paradigm*). The difference in activity between remembered vs. forgotten items during encoding is known as *difference in memory* or *Dm effect* (e.g., Paller, Kutas, & Mayes, 1987; Paller & Wagner, 2002). Brain regions showing Dm effects are assumed to mediate processes that lead to successful encoding of incoming information. The "remembered-minus-forgotten" difference can be also investigated during retrieval. In this case, the contrast identifies regions showing greater activity for items in which retrieval was successful (hits) than for items in which retrieval failed (misses). The activity difference between remembered vs. forgotten items during retrieval is known as *retrieval success* (Prince, Daselaar, & Cabeza, 2005; Weis et al., 2004).

One of the advantages of Dm and retrieval success analyses is that they can disentangle the effects of emotion on perception-related vs. memory-related activity. The effects of emotion on perception-related activity can be identified by comparing activity for processing emotional vs. non-emotional stimuli (for reviews, see Davidson & Irwin, 1999; Phan et al., 2002; Wager et al., 2003). In contrast, identifying the effects of emotion on memory-related activity requires isolating first activity specifically associated with memory processes, that is, successful encoding activity (Dm effect) and successful retrieval activity. For example, in a study of emotional memory encoding, one can identify the brain regions associated with encoding success, separately for emotional (emotional Dm = remembered emotional stimuli – forgotten emotional stimuli) and neutral stimuli (neutral Dm = remembered neutral stimuli – forgotten neutral stimuli). By contrasting the emotional Dm to the neutral Dm, the effects of emotion on successful memory activity can be identified. Similarly, during retrieval, one can identify the brain regions where successful retrieval activity is greater for emotional than for the neutral stimuli. In combination, these comparisons reveal brain regions that show an interaction between emotion and memory at different stages of memory processing.

In the next sections, we will review evidence from functional neuroimaging studies investigating the neural correlates of the modulatory effect of emotional arousal on episodic memory encoding and retrieval. The emphasis will be on the role of the amygdala and the medial temporal lobe (MTL) memory regions, including the hippocampus and parahippocampal regions (Squire & Zola-Morgan, 1991). In addition, we will emphasize ER-fMRI studies that allow identification of brain regions showing greater encoding/retrieval success activity for emotional than for neutral events.

 # FUNCTIONAL NEUROIMAGING OF EMOTIONAL MEMORY

Neural mechanisms of emotional memory encoding

Role of the amygdala and the MTL memory regions

One influential hypothesis concerning the neural mechanisms underlying the beneficial effect of emotion on memory (Bradley et al., 1992; Christianson, 1992b) is the so-called *modulation hypothesis* (McGaugh, Cahill, & Roozendaal, 1996; McGaugh, McIntyre, & Power, 2002). According to this hypothesis, emotional events are remembered better than neutral events because the amygdala enhances the function of MTL memory structures associated with declarative memory and other brain regions involved in non-declarative memory (McGaugh, 2000). Studies on non-human animals have clearly established that the amygdala, a brain region important in the processing of emotional arousal, is critical for mediating the influences of both neuronal and neurohormonal mechanisms that lead to enhanced memory for emotional events (McGaugh, 2000; McGaugh et al., 1996, 2002). Moreover, these studies also specifically have identified the basolateral nucleus of the amygdala (BLA) as the main site responsible for the modulatory influences of the amygdala on activity in brain regions associated with mnemonic processes. Importantly, at a basic level, the neuronal and neurohormonal mechanisms mentioned above involve activation of the central and peripheral adrenergic systems, which are engaged as a result of experiencing emotionally arousing events, as part of the general response to stressful situations.

Pharmacological, lesion, and functional neuroimaging studies in humans also provide evidence supporting the modulation hypothesis (for reviews, see Cahill & McGaugh, 1998; Hamann, 2001; McGaugh, 2004; Phelps, 2004). Most of these studies have presented participants with visual images (words or pictures) or audiovisual narratives that vary in their emotional content, and assess memory performance as a function of stimulus category. Pharmacological studies have shown that adrenergic agonists given prior to or after a learning episode enhanced memory performance (Soetens et al., 1995), whereas adrenergic antagonists specifically decreased memory performance for emotional information (Cahill et al., 1994). Lesion studies show that patients with amygdalar lesions often do not exhibit a memory advantage for emotionally arousing stimuli (Adolphs et al., 1997; Adolphs, Tranel, & Denburg, 2000; Cahill et al., 1995; LaBar & Phelps, 1998; Phelps et al., 1998). Finally, functional neuroimaging studies have yielded some key findings that provide complementary support for the modulation hypothesis: (1) activity in the amygdala correlates with memory for emotionally arousing stimuli (e.g., Cahill et al., 1996); (2) this effect holds for both pleasant and unpleasant stimuli (Hamann et al., 1999); (3) memory-related activity in the amygdala correlates with the intensity of the emotional response (Canli et al., 2000); (4) increased memory performance for emotional stimuli is associated with successful encoding activity in both the amygdala and the MTL memory regions (Dolcos, LaBar, & Cabeza, 2004b; Kensinger & Corkin, 2004), which is greater for emotional than for neutral stimuli (Dolcos et al., 2004b); and (5) the memory-enhancing effect of emotional arousal is associated with interaction between the amygdala and the MTL memory regions (Dolcos et al., 2004b; Kensinger & Corkin, 2004; Kilpatrick & Cahill, 2003; Richardson, Strange, & Dolan, 2004).

Despite their consistency, most evidence from studies on humans has been rather indirect and/or lacks spatial specificity with respect to the neural mechanisms responsible for the memory-enhancing effect of emotion. Pharmacological studies in neurologically intact humans, for instance, can only indirectly link the modulatory effect of adrenergic agonists/antagonists to activity in the amygdala or other brain regions. As for the evidence from neuropsychological studies, because lesions are typically not restricted to the amygdala proper, it is unclear whether the deficits in memory performance for emotional items reflect a lack of amygdalar modulation or damage of the neighboring MTL regions. Similar spatial limitations also apply to most functional neuroimaging studies. Below, we will review the main limitations of the functional neuroimaging approach, while presenting the chronological development that cumulatively provides strong evidence for the modulation hypothesis in neurologically intact human participants.

The main limitations of the early PET and fMRI studies of emotional memory encoding are related to the nature of blocked-trial designs, which cannot accommodate the subsequent memory paradigm. Early PET studies suggested a link between amygdala activity at encoding and later retrieval of emotionally arousing material (Cahill et al., 1996; Hamann et al., 1999). However, despite their better spatial resolution relative to pharmacological and lesion studies, these studies could not distinguish brain activity for successfully vs. unsuccessfully encoded stimuli within participants, and thus could not directly assess the role of the amygdala in *successful encoding* of emotional stimuli. More recent fMRI studies (e.g., Canli et al., 2000) have used event-related designs to examine emotional memory formation, but they did not employ the subsequent memory paradigm either. Furthermore, these studies have focused mainly on the amygdala, and thus did not provide evidence for the interaction of the amygdala with other memory-related brain regions during the formation of emotional memories.

An ERP study by Dolcos and Cabeza (2002) employed the subsequent memory paradigm with emotional stimuli and reported greater successful encoding activity (Dm) for emotional than for neutral stimuli. Event-related potentials were recorded while subjects rated a randomized series of emotionally arousing (both pleasant and unpleasant) and neutral pictures for pleasantness. Based on memory performance in a subsequent memory task, ERPs were separately averaged for each emotion category and, within each category, for subsequently remembered and forgotten items. The main finding was that enhanced memory performance for emotional pictures was associated with greater successful encoding activity (Dm) for emotional than for neutral items during an early time window (i.e., 400–600 ms). This result suggests that emotional stimuli have privileged access to processing resources, which could be one of the mechanisms responsible for the memory-enhancing effect of emotion. Given the relatively closed-field configuration of amygdalar neurons, which yields little volume conduction (Gloor, 1992), it is unlikely that the amygdala was a direct source of this scalp ERP. It is possible, however, that the amygdala may influence such ERPs measured at the scalp indirectly through its widespread cortical projections. Recent studies have made significant advances by incorporating the subsequent memory paradigm and by considering how the amygdala interfaces with other memory-processing areas of the brain (Dolcos et al., 2004b; Kensinger & Corkin, 2004; Kilpatrick & Cahill, 2003; Richardson et al., 2004). For instance, the study by Kilpatrick and Cahill (2003) involved structural equation modeling with PET data and found that increased memory for subsequently remembered emotional vs. neutral video clips was associated with increased functional connectivity between the amygdala and parahippocampal regions. The study by Richardson and colleagues (2004) involved ER-fMRI recording in patients with amygdala and hippocampal lesions and found evidence for reciprocal dependence between these two brain regions during the encoding of emotional memories: hippocampal activity for subsequently remembered emotional verbal material correlated with the degree of amygdalar pathology, and amygdalar activity for the same items correlated with the degree of hippocampal pathology. Although these studies did not involve the subsequent memory paradigm to compare activity for subsequently remembered vs. forgotten items, they provide support for the idea that the amygdala exerts modulatory influences on encoding activity in memory-related brain regions (see also Hamann et al., 1999). Finally, the ER-fMRI studies by Dolcos et al. (2004b) and Kensinger and Corkin (2004) involved event-related designs and the subsequent memory paradigm and found that the memory-enhancing effect of emotion was associated with greater successful encoding activity for emotional than for neutral stimuli (emotional Dm > neutral Dm) in both the amygdala and the MTL memory regions, as well as with greater amygdala–MTL correlations. In sum, these studies have provided strong evidence supporting the notion that the memory-enhancing effect of emotional arousal involves interactions between the amygdala and the MTL memory structures during the initial encoding of emotionally charged events.

It is important to note that, despite the advances in recent ER-fMRI studies, there are still limitations in the spatial resolution of these studies. Specifically, most of the studies reviewed above have used voxel-wise analyses, which do not provide the most accurate localization of activity coming from neighboring MTL regions because of image smoothing and normalization of individual variation in human anatomy to a standard brain template. This limitation is illustrated in figure 6.1, which shows the results of a voxel-based analysis performed on normalized and smoothed fMRI data comparing activity for remembered emotional and neutral pictures from an event-related fMRI study of emotional memory encoding (Dolcos et al., 2003). As indicated by the

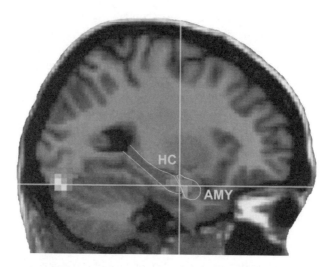

Figure 6.1 Illustration of the difficulty to separate the fMRI signal coming from two MTL neighboring regions (i.e., the amygdala and the hippocampus head), if smoothing and normalization to a standard template is involved. The figure shows a sagittal view of a high-resolution brain image with an activation *t* map superimposed. Although the findings (greater amygdalar-hippocampal activity for remembered-emotional than for remembered-neutral stimuli) are interesting and consistent with the modulation hypothesis, it is difficult to delineate the contribution of the two neighboring regions to the observed effect. Amy = amygdala, HC = hippocampus. The colored lines follow the sagittal borders of the two regions. See color insert after page 116.

color-coded lines delineating the amygdala–hippocampal border, the activation encompasses portions of both regions (i.e., the amygdala and hippocampus head), but due to normalization and smoothing it is difficult to precisely separate activity from these two neighboring areas. In addition, there is individual variation in MR-related susceptibility artifact in the vicinity of the amygdala that can reduce overall activation in voxel-based group-averaged analyses due to susceptibility-related offsets in spatial registration of observed activity (LaBar et al., 2001).

These issues were addressed in a recent ER-fMRI study (Dolcos et al., 2004b) that used the subsequent memory paradigm with emotional and neutral stimuli similar to that used in the ERP study described above (Dolcos & Cabeza, 2002). In this study, data analysis entailed extraction of the fMRI signal from ana-tomically defined regions of interest (ROIs) within adjacent MTL structures that were manually traced on each subject's anatomical scans (figure 6.2A–B). In addition, preprocessing of fMRI data did not involve normalization or

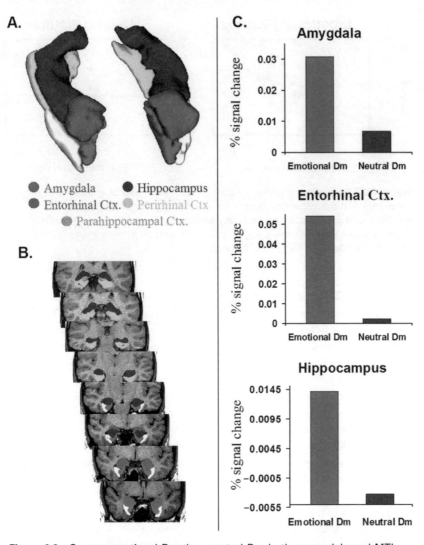

Figure 6.2 Greater emotional Dm than neutral Dm in the amygdala and MTL memory system. (A) Three-dimensional view of the anatomically defined ROIs from one representative subject. (B) Coronal view of eight representative slices showing the location in the brain of the MTL subregions. (C) Bar graphs comparing the percent signal change for emotional and neutral Dms, extracted from the MTL subregions showing greater emotional than neutral Dm. The bar for emotional Dm is based on the fMRI signal averaged across the emotional conditions (pleasant and unpleasant collapsed). Ctx. = Cortex, Dm = Remembered – Forgotten. See color insert after page 116.

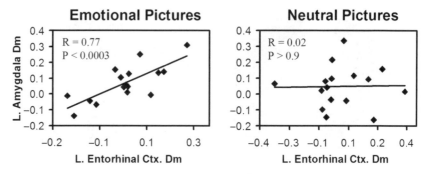

Figure 6.3 Stronger correlations between successful encoding activity in the amygdala and the entorhinal cortex for emotional Dm (left panel) than for neutral Dm (right panel). The plots are based on the emotional and neutral Dms, as extracted from left amygdala and left entorhinal cortex (Ctx.). Dm = Remembered – Forgotten, L = Left.

smoothing. This analysis method enabled a more precise quantification of signal changes arising from subregions of the amygdala, and the MTL memory regions (including the hippocampus and the parahippocampal cortices: entorhinal cortex, perirhinal cortex, and parahippocampal cortex proper). Results showed that memory performance was greater for emotional (both pleasant and unpleasant) than for neutral stimuli. This emotional memory advantage was reflected in greater emotional Dm activity than neutral Dm activity in both the amygdala (especially the BLA) and the MTL memory system (especially entorhinal cortex and the head of the hippocampus; figure 6.2C). Moreover, Dm activity in the amygdala and the MTL memory regions was more strongly correlated with each other for the emotional stimuli than for the neutral stimuli (figure 6.3). These findings reveal interactions between an amygdala-based emotional processing system and other memory-related MTL regions that support successful encoding of emotional stimuli.

Finally, a double dissociation was found along the longitudinal axis of the MTL memory system such that activity in anterior regions predicted memory for emotional items whereas activity in posterior regions predicted memory for neutral items. These anterior portions of the hippocampus and parahippocampal gyrus are directly and reciprocally interconnected with the amygdala (Amaral et al., 1992) and may form a mechanism by which emotion and memory are synergistically enhanced. In sum, these results complement the studies reviewed above to provide key evidence in support of the modulation hypothesis in humans, and they also uncover a functional specialization along the rostrocaudal axis of the MTL regarding the effects of emotion on memory formation.

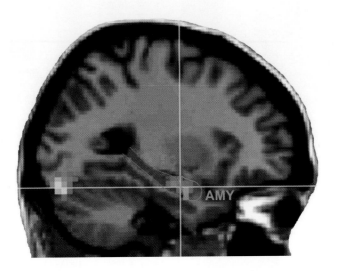

Figure 6.1 Illustration of the difficulty to separate the fMRI signal coming from two MTL neighboring regions (i.e., the amygdala and the hippocampus head), if smoothing and normalization to a standard template is involved. The figure shows a sagittal view of a high-resolution brain image with an activation *t* map superimposed. Although the findings (greater amygdalar-hippocampal activity for remembered-emotional than for remembered-neutral stimuli) are interesting and consistent with the modulation hypothesis, it is difficult to delineate the contribution of the two neighboring regions to the observed effect. Amy = amygdala, HC = hippocampus. The colored lines follow the sagittal borders of the two regions.

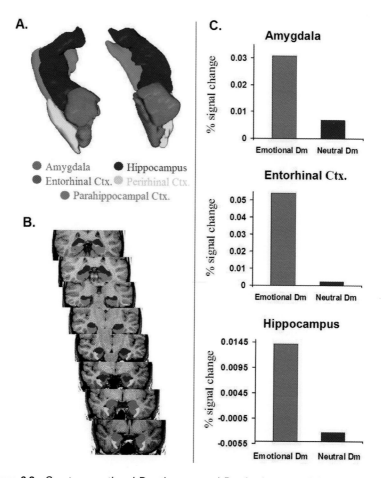

Figure 6.2 Greater emotional Dm than neutral Dm in the amygdala and MTL memory system. (A) Three-dimensional view of the anatomically defined ROIs from one representative subject. (B) Coronal view of eight representative slices showing the location in the brain of the MTL subregions. (C) Bar graphs comparing the percent signal change for emotional and neutral Dms, extracted from the MTL subregions showing greater emotional than neutral Dm. The bar for emotional Dm is based on the fMRI signal averaged across the emotional conditions (pleasant and unpleasant collapsed). Ctx. = Cortex, Dm = Remembered – Forgotten.

Role of the prefrontal cortical regions (PFC)

Although the findings discussed above link the memory-enhancing effect of emotion to an MTL mechanism, as predicted by the modulation hypothesis, they do not exclude the possibility that other brain regions, such as the PFC, also play a major role. Functional neuroimaging studies have consistently shown that PFC regions are as strongly associated with successful encoding operations as are MTL regions (e.g., Brewer et al., 1998; Paller & Wagner, 2002; Wagner et al., 1998). Thus, it is quite likely that the memory-enhancing effect of emotion is also mediated by the PFC.

The role of PFC in memory is diverse, and PFC contributions to strategic, organizational, and semantic aspects of emotional memory may operate in the absence of high arousal (see discussion in Kensinger et al., 2002; LaBar, 2003; Phelps et al., 1998) and can be valence-specific (Dolcos, LaBar, & Cabeza, 2004a; Kensinger & Corkin, 2004). Here we focus on the role of the PFC in arousal-mediated memory effects to complement our discussion of the MTL mechanisms above. Several studies have reported a role of PFC in arousal-mediated memory effects (e.g., Canli et al., 2002; Dolcos et al., 2004a; Kilpatrick & Cahill, 2003; Sergerie, Lepage, & Armony, 2005). For instance, the PET study by Kilpatrick and Cahill (2003) also reported increased functional connectivity between the amygdala and the PFC, specifically in a ventrolateral PFC region (Brodmann area 47), during the encoding of highly arousing negative vs. low arousing neutral video clips. Also, the ER-fMRI study by Canli et al. (2002) reported that encoding activity in a dorsolateral PFC region (BA 6) correlated positively with both greater emotional arousal and better subsequent memory for pictorial material. Moreover, Dolcos et al. (2004a) found that emotional arousal enhanced successful encoding activity (Dm) in two subregions of the left lateral PFC: one ventral (BA 47) and the other dorsal (BA 9/6). In these regions, the Dm effect was greater for highly arousing (both pleasant and unpleasant) items relative to low arousing and neutral ones.

The ventrolateral PFC regions have been consistently associated with encoding success in previous functional neuroimaging studies of episodic memory (e.g., Brewer et al., 1998; Kirchhoff et al., 2000; Paller & Wagner, 2002; Wagner et al., 1998), thus it is not surprising that they were also identified by the above-mentioned studies of emotional memory encoding. Given the role of left ventrolateral PFC regions in semantic processing (Kapur et al., 1996; Poldrack et al., 1999; Shallice et al., 1994) and the role of the dorsolateral PFC regions in working memory operations (D'Esposito, Postle, & Rypma, 2000; Owen et al., 1999; Petrides, 1995), it is possible that arousing events are better remembered in part because they receive deeper semantic processing and attentional maintenance in working memory buffers during encoding (see also Reisberg, this volume).

These results expand the above-mentioned evidence concerning the role of the MTL during emotional memory encoding by showing that the enhancing effect of emotion on memory formation is also mediated by changes in PFC activity. The effects of emotion on MTL and PFC regions, however, may relate to different memory mechanisms. Given the functions typically attributed to these regions (Moscovitch, 1992; Simons & Spiers, 2003), it is reasonable to assume that, in MTL, emotion enhances the storage and consolidation of memory representations whereas, in PFC, it enhances strategic encoding processes. Taken together, these findings suggest that the enhancing effect of emotion on memory formation (1) is largely but not exclusively influenced by arousal; (2) is mediated by changes in both MTL and PFC activity; and (3) may involve an enhancement of storage and consolidation processes in MTL, as well as an amplification of semantic and working memory processes in PFC.

Neural mechanisms of emotional memory retrieval

Effect of emotion on retrieval activity in the amygdala and the MTL memory regions

What about the mechanisms involved during retrieval of emotional memories: are they the same as those identified during encoding? Although it is reasonable to expect that emotional arousal can enhance not only early memory stages (i.e., encoding and early consolidation), but also later stages (e.g., retrieval), very little is known about the neural correlates of emotional memory retrieval. The paucity of functional neuroimaging evidence may reflect the fact that the modulation hypothesis as inspired by early animal research focuses mainly on encoding and consolidation (McGaugh, 2004), and thus the majority of studies on the neural mechanisms of emotional memory have correspondingly focused on encoding (e.g., Cahill et al., 1996; Canli et al., 2000, 2002; Dolcos & Cabeza, 2002; Dolcos et al., 2004b; Hamann et al., 1999; Kensinger & Corkin, 2004; Kilpatrick & Cahill, 2003; Richardson et al., 2004; Sergerie, Lepage, & Armony, 2005). Recent evidence from animal research, however, suggests that the amygdala is also involved in reconsolidation processes initiated upon retrieval of emotional memories (LeDoux, 2000), although the exact nature of its involvement is a matter of current debate (Nadel, 2000; Nader, 2003).

The situation in the functional neuroimaging literature is very similar – some studies do not report amygdala activity during emotional memory retrieval (e.g., Kosslyn et al., 1996; Taylor et al., 1998), and most of the studies that do report activity in the amygdala could not directly link it to retrieval processes per se (e.g., Dolan et al., 2000), and/or to increased memory for emotional items compared to neutral items (e.g., Fossati et al., 2004; Maratos, Allan, & Rugg, 2000; Sharot, Delgado, & Phelps, 2004). One study reported evidence linking activity in the amygdala with retrieval processes and with emotion-mediated enhancement of memory performance (Smith et al., 2004b), but this study focused on identifying the neural correlates of retrieving neutral items encoded in emotional versus neutral contexts (see also Maratos et al., 2001; Smith et al., 2004a), rather than on identifying the neural correlates of retrieving emotional vs. neutral items.

These retrieval studies also share many of the same limitations as the early studies of emotional memory encoding. For instance, most of them either used blocked designs that do not allow assessment of the functional neuroimaging data on a trial-by-trial basis (e.g., Dolan et al., 2000; Kosslyn et al., 1996; Taylor et al., 1998), and/or did not compare activity associated with successfully vs. unsuccessfully retrieved items to distinguish brain activity specifically associated with retrieval success from brain activity generally associated with perceptual processing (e.g., Fossati et al., 2004; Maratos et al., 2000; Sharot et al., 2004). Moreover, as a general limitation, most of these studies have used short retention intervals (e.g., minutes), which could explain why some of them did not find a memory advantage for emotional stimuli. Additionally, the involvement of short retention intervals could not allow a clear separation between early consolidation processes and actual retrieval operations.

We addressed these issues in a recent ER-fMRI study (Dolcos, LaBar, & Cabeza, 2005) by creating an experimental design with the following key features: (1) it allowed identification of transient brain activity on a trial-by-trial basis using an event-related design; (2) it compared activity for successfully (*hits*) vs. unsuccessfully (*misses*) retrieved items for emotional and neutral items to identify the MTL subregions associated with the interaction of emotion and successful memory retrieval; and (3) it assessed retrieval following a retention interval of one year to distinguish retrieval processes from early consolidation processes. Participants encoded highly arousing emotional (pleasant and unpleasant) and low arousing neutral pictures, and one year later they were scanned while distinguishing between the pictures they had seen previously vs. new pictures. These subjects were a subgroup of the participants that were also scanned during encoding (Dolcos et al., 2004a, 2004b). Finally, activity in the amygdala and the MTL memory regions was extracted using a MTL mask, which can localize activity more precisely from various MTL subregions.

We found that, one year after encoding, emotionally arousing stimuli (both pleasant and unpleasant) were remembered better than neutral stimuli, and this behavioral effect was associated with greater retrieval success activity in the amygdala and the MTL memory system for emotional than for neutral items. Importantly, this activation cannot be attributed to general emotional perceptual processes, as it reflected a difference between retrieval activity for emotional pictures correctly classified as old (Emotional Hits) and activity for emotional pictures incorrectly classified (Emotional Misses). Moreover, this difference was also identified when emotional retrieval success activity (Emotional Hits > Emotional Misses) was compared to the neutral retrieval success activity (Neutral Hits > Neutral Misses). Therefore, activity related to perception of emotion was subtracted out, and the observed differences reflect the interaction between emotion and memory. These findings provide strong evidence that successful retrieval of emotional memories involves MTL mechanisms similar to those identified during successful emotional encoding.

Effect of emotion on recollection- vs. familiarity-based retrieval

In addition to the general issue concerning the effect of emotion on the neural correlates underlying memory retrieval, another issue is the specific effect of emotion on the neural mechanisms associated with different types of memory retrieval processes. One such distinction refers to differences between the neural mechanisms associated with *recollection-* vs. *familiarity*-based retrieval operations. Memories for personal events are not always retrieved in the same way; some are fully recollected (for instance, we can *remember* rich details about the time and place that specific events took place), whereas other memories are only familiar to us (we just *know* that certain events took place, but cannot retrieve specific details about their occurrence) (Gardiner, 1988; Jacoby & Dallas, 1981; Mandler, 1980; Tulving, 1985).

The theoretical models proposing such dissociations are not new in the memory literature, but only recently have received support from neuroimaging studies concerning the existence of distinguishable neural mechanisms underlying these two types of retrieval (for a review, see Yonelinas, 2002). Distinguishing recollection from familiarity is critical because there is behavioral evidence that the memory-enhancing effect of emotion specifically modulates recollection rather than familiarity processes (Ochsner, 2000; Talarico, LaBar, & Rubin, 2005). Although several functional neuroimaging studies have identified dissociable neural correlates supporting recollection- vs. familiarity-driven retrieval (Dobbins et al., 2003; Eldridge et al., 2000; Henson et al., 1999), it is not clear how emotion modulates these mechanisms in order to enhance our ability to distinguish between what we *remember* from what we *know*. It is possible that this effect relies on arousal-mediated enhancement of activity in brain regions that distinguish between recollection and familiarity (e.g., hippocampus). However, most of the functional neuroimaging studies investigating the neural correlates of recollection and familiarity (e.g., Dobbins et al., 2003; Eldridge et al., 2000; Henson et al., 1999) have not examined the effect of emotion on these two types of memory retrieval.

Two recent studies have provided evidence concerning the neural correlates of the differential effect of emotion on recollection- vs. familiarity-based retrieval (Dolcos et al., 2005; Sharot et al., 2004). For instance, the study by Sharot et al. (2004) measured brain activity associated with the feeling of remembering during retrieval of emotional and neutral items, using a recognition task that distinguishes between recollection- and familiarity-based responses (Tulving, 1985). Thus, in addition to distinguishing between previously seen (*Old*) and new items, for each item considered as *Old* participants also indicated whether their memory for the item was accompanied by specific details about its occurrence during encoding session ("*Remember-R*" responses), or whether they only knew that the item was old but could not retrieve specific details ("*Know-K*" responses). Sharot et al. found that *remember* judgments for emotional items were enhanced, even though the actual retrieval accuracy did not differ for the emotional and neutral categories, and that this enhanced *feeling* of remembering for emotional items was associated with increased activity in the amygdala.

The study by Dolcos et al. (2005) reviewed above provides further evidence for the effect of emotion on recollection vs. familiarity by identifying the neural mechanisms associated not only with enhanced feeling of recollection but also with enhanced actual recollection of emotional memories. The differential effect of emotion on recollection and familiarity was investigated using the same recognition task (Tulving, 1985) that distinguishes between recollection- and familiarity-based responses. To identify the MTL regions associated with the effect of arousal on recollection vs. familiarity, retrieval success activity (Hits – Misses) for emotional and neutral items was calculated separately for recollection- vs. familiarity-based responses. Further, to investigate whether the amygdala and the MTL memory regions are coactivated during successful retrieval as well as during successful encoding of emotional memories (Dolcos et al., 2004b), correlations between retrieval success activity in the amygdala and the memory-related MTL regions were performed for both R and K responses and compared for emotional and neutral pictures.

Consistent with the predicted differential effect of emotional arousal on recollection and familiarity, the study generated three main findings. First, the memory-enhancing effect of arousal was driven by recollection-based responses (figure 6.4A). This finding extends the behavioral evidence that emotional arousal differentially enhances recollection (Ochsner, 2000) by showing that this effect extends over a period of one year. Second, this differential effect of arousal on recollection was accompanied by greater recollection vs. familiarity-based retrieval success activity in both the amygdala and the hippocampus, but not in other MTL memory regions such as the entorhinal cortex (figure 6.4B). These findings provide clear evidence that activity in the amygdala and hippocampus is associated not only to enhanced *feelings* of

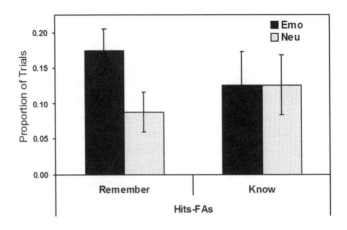

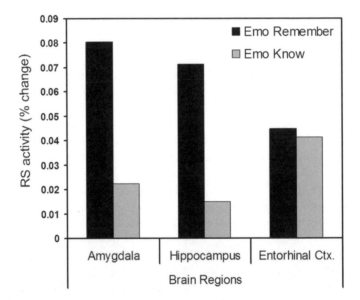

Figure 6.4 Effect of arousal on recollection and familiarity: behavioral and fMRI results. (A) The memory enhancing effect of emotion was driven by recollection. Corrected recognition scores (Hits – False Alarms) for emotional (positive and negative collapsed) and neutral pictures are presented. Emo = Emotional; Neu = Neutral; Remember = Recollection-based responses; Know = Familiarity-based responses; FAs = False alarms. (B) Dissociable effect of emotion on retrieval success (RS) activity in the amygdala and hippocampus vs. entorhinal cortex. In the right amygdala and hippocampus head, RS activity for emotional pictures was greater for recollection than for familiarity, whereas in the entorhinal cortex it was similar for both types of retrieval. RS = Hits – Misses; Remember = Recollection-based RS (Hits-R > Misses); Know = Familiarity-based RS (Hits-K > Misses).

Table 6.1 Correlations (R-scores) between the amygdala and the MTL memory regions. Correlations were calculated between the amygdala and the MTL memory regions showing greater recollection- vs. familiarity-based retrieval success activity for emotional than for neutral pictures. The greatest differences were in the case of recollection-based responses. RS = retrieval success activity (Hits – Misses), rRS = recollection-based RS, kRS = familiarity-based RS.

MTL region/ Hippocampal region	Amygdala			
	Emotional rRS	*Neutral rRS*	*Emotional kRS*	*Neutral kRS*
Head (R)	.94****	.97****	.98****	.86*
Body (L)	.82*	.71	.90***	.74
Tail/PPHG (R)	.87**	.33	.48	.72
Tail/PPHG (L)	.77*	.66	.81*	.76*

* $p < 0.05$; ** $p < 0.01$; *** $p < 0.005$; **** $p < 0.0005$.

recollection for emotional stimuli, but also to enhanced *successful* recollection of emotional stimuli. These results provide the first converging evidence that links findings from behavioural studies showing arousal-mediated enhancement of recollection (Ochsner, 2000) with findings from functional neuroimaging studies associating the amygdala and the hippocampus with emotional arousal (Zald, 2003) and recollection (Yonelinas, 2002), respectively.

Finally, correlation analyses showed that the amygdala and the hippocampus were more systematically coactivated during successful recollection of emotional pictures than during successful recollection of neutral pictures (table 6.1). Therefore, these two regions are part of a synergistic mechanism in which emotion enhances recollection and recollection enhances emotion. Emotion may enhance recollection because reinstating the affective context of the original episode is likely to facilitate the recovery of contextual details, such as where, when, and how the original events happened. Conversely, the recollection of the context surrounding an emotional event is likely to augment the emotional arousal elicited by the event during retrieval.

In sum, the available evidence concerning the effect of emotion during memory retrieval shows that the memory advantage for emotionally arousing stimuli is associated with activity in both the amygdala and the MTL memory structures, and that the differential effect of arousal on recollection is accompanied by both amygdalar and hippocampal involvement but is independent of processing in the entorhinal cortex.

CONCLUDING REMARKS, OPEN ISSUES, AND FUTURE DIRECTIONS

The overarching goal of this chapter was to review the functional neuroimaging evidence concerning the effect of emotional arousal on the neural mechanisms underlying the encoding and retrieval of emotional episodic memory in neurologically intact humans. An important contribution in elucidating these mechanisms was made by the introduction of event-related designs that allow comparisons of brain activity for successfully vs. unsuccessfully encoded/retrieved items (i.e., the subsequent memory paradigm). This paradigm has provided an ideal way of linking the memory-enhancing effect of emotion observed behaviorally to the neural mechanisms underlying this phenomenon.

The available ERP and ER-fMRI studies using this paradigm provide evidence for possible mechanisms of the memory-enhancing effect of emotion. ERP evidence from encoding studies suggests that emotional stimuli have privileged access to processing resources, and this effect may be linked to increased successful encoding activity for emotional stimuli in specific MTL and PFC regions. Evidence from ER-fMRI studies of encoding also shows that the memory-enhancing effect of emotional arousal is associated with the coactivation of two apparently independent MTL systems: an amygdalar system, typically associated with emotional processes, and a hippocampal system, typically associated with mnemonic processes. These findings from neurologically intact humans, along with the findings from animals, provide strong converging evidence for the modulation hypothesis. As for the functional neuroimaging studies of emotional memory retrieval, the available evidence shows that similar MTL mechanisms are also involved during successful retrieval of emotional memories. Finally, studies of retrieval also show that the differential effect of emotional arousal on recollective processes is associated with dissociable patterns of activity in the amygdala and the MTL memory structures.

Although functional neuroimaging studies provide valuable evidence concerning the neural mechanisms underlying the beneficial effect of emotion on memory, a number of issues remain unclear. First, one open issue is the role played by emotional valence in the observed effects. While most of the evidence suggests that arousal is the main factor influencing the memory-enhancing effect of emotion, the neural correlates underlying the contribution of emotional valence have been less specified (e.g., see Levine & Pizarro, this volume; Reisberg, this volume). Of particular interest are differences between the neural mechanisms underlying the effect of positive and negative emotions on memory, as positive and negative emotions have evolved to subserve different functions. Thus, it is reasonable to expect that their contribution to the memory-enhancing effect of emotion may be specifically associated with different neural mechanisms, which work in synchrony with the mechanisms underlying the more general effect of emotional arousal.

Second, another unsolved problem is whether top-down processes can alter activity in the neural networks responsible for the modulatory effect of emotion on memory. Specifically, to date, studies of emotional memory have typically manipulated the emotional content of the to-be-remembered material (bottom-up control), rather than the perceived emotional content (top-down control). Using methods similar to those involved in a recently emerging body of literature investigating the neural correlates of emotion regulation (Jackson et al., 2000; Ochsner et al., 2004) to manipulate the perceived nature of emotions, future studies of emotional memory could better delineate the neural mechanisms underlying the beneficial effect of emotion on memory.

Third, it is uncertain how the emotional memory mechanisms described in this chapter operate in people suffering from affective disorders, such as depression and post-traumatic stress disorder (PTSD). For instance, it is known that depressed patients ruminate on negative or unpleasant memories, and that PTSD patients suffer from intrusive traumatic memories. These problems may reflect a pathology in how the memory system processes emotional stimuli, either during the encoding or retrieval stages. Therefore, findings from normal populations (e.g., from studies using manipulation of the mechanisms involved in emotional regulation, along with studies investigating the mechanisms involved in memory suppression; Anderson et al., 2004, Ochsner & Gross, 2005) could provide hints to future studies investigating neural alterations associated with such clinical populations. Furthermore, corroboration of findings from studies on normal and clinical populations (e.g., Mayberg et al., 1999; Protopopescu et al., 2005; Rauch et al., 1996; Seminowicz et al., 2004) will contribute to a better understanding of clinical conditions associated with augmented processing and experiencing of emotional memories.

Fourth, a very important area that has not received enough attention is how emotional memory mechanisms are affected by healthy and pathological aging. Although emotional processing is generally preserved in healthy older adults, there is evidence that they show a bias towards positive emotions (positivity bias) not seen in younger adults (Mather, this volume; Mather et al., 2004). There is virtually no evidence about whether the age-related positivity bias has an impact on the neural correlates of emotional memory. In contrast with healthy older adults, in patients with Alzheimer's disease (AD) the memory-enhancing effect or emotion is disrupted (Hamann, Monarch, & Goldstein, 2000; Kensinger et al., 2002). One of the earliest signs of AD is the deterioration of anterior MTL regions, such as entorhinal cortex and the amygdala. Thus, the study of emotional memory in AD is also important from a diagnostic point of view.

Fifth, another issue concerns investigation of gender-related differences in the neural mechanisms of emotional memory. For instance, evidence from studies investigating sex-related differences in the neural correlates of emotional memory encoding have identified an interesting hemispheric asymmetry concerning the role of the amygdala, with the left amygdala being more involved during emotional memory encoding in females and right amygdala being more involved during emotional memory encoding in males (Cahill et al., 2004). It is not clear, however, whether a similar pattern of lateralization is also present during retrieval of emotional memories.

Sixth, a more recently emerging issue concerns the dissociation between the neural mechanisms of emotional memories for *content* vs. *context* (Erk, Martin, & Walter, 2005; Maratos et al., 2001; Medford et al., 2005; Smith et al., 2004b). That is, most of the studies of emotional memory have investigated the neural correlates of encoding/retrieval of items with emotional vs. neutral contents. However, it is not clear whether the same mechanisms are responsible for the enhancement of memory for items embedded in emotional vs. neutral contexts. Future studies investigating this issue will contribute to better understanding of the neural correlates distinguishing the enhancing effect of emotional content vs. context on episodic memory.

Seventh, whereas most memory and emotion studies have focused on how emotion *enhances* memory, very little is known regarding the mechanisms of how emotion *impairs* or distorts memory. There is some evidence that experiencing extreme emotions can lead to forgetting of traumatic events experienced in childhood (Williams, 1994, but see Goodman & Paz-Alonso, this volume; Kihlstrom, this volume). In addition, as evidence from the eyewitness testimony literature shows, highly arousing emotions may hinder memory for "peripheral" details of emotional events (Christianson, 1992a; Christianson & Engleberg, this volume; Mathews, this volume). Such studies could contribute to better understanding of the neural correlates of affective-cognitive interactions, in general, and of those underlying the modulatory effect of emotion on memory, in particular.

Finally, critical to further elucidation of the neural correlates of emotional memory is that, in addition to corroborating converging evidence from separate studies investigating various aspects of the processing (e.g., animal vs. human, normal vs. clinical, ERP vs. fMRI; Cahill et al., 1995; McGaugh, 2004; Dolcos et al., 2002; Dolcos et al., 2004b), future studies should also aim at more extensively investigating different aspects within the same studies (e.g., pharmacological and neuroimaging, lesion and neuroimaging, personality and neuroimaging and genotyping, etc.; Richardson et al., 2004; van Stegeren et al., 2005).

In conclusion, research on the neural correlates of the memory-enhancing effect of emotion has contributed substantially to the recent development in the field of cognitive neuroscience of emotion. An important contribution has been from using functional neuroimaging tools that allow investigation of the neurologically intact human brain. Evidence from recent functional neuroimaging studies provides strong evidence for the modulation hypothesis by clearly showing that the memory enhancing effect of emotion is associated with joint activity in both an emotion-based system involving the amygdala and a memory-based system involving the hippocampus and associated MTL memory regions as well as the PFC. Moreover, evidence from recent functional neuroimaging studies of emotional memory retrieval has extended this finding by showing that mechanisms similar to those identified during initial encoding are also involved during successful retrieval of emotional memories. Finally, recent studies of emotional memory retrieval have also revealed the neural mechanisms underlying the differential effect of emotion on recollection- vs. familiarity-based retrieval. Thus, involvement of functional neuroimaging tools in corroboration with other methods will prove essential in future studies investigating the neural mechanisms of affective and mnemonic processes in both normal and clinical populations.

AUTHOR NOTES

Portions of the research reviewed in this chapter were part of Florin Dolcos's doctoral dissertation. Therefore, he would like to reiterate his profound gratitude to all the people who have made it possible. Florin Dolcos's doctoral research was supported by grants from AHFMR and NSERC (Canada) and by grant R01 AG19731 from NIH (USA) to Roberto Cabeza. Kevin S. LaBar was supported by grant R01 DA14094 from NIH, a Young Investigator Award from the National Alliance for Research on Schizophrenia and Depression, and by Career Award 0239614 from the National Science Foundation. During his doctoral studies, Florin Dolcos has been supported by a Chia PhD Scholarship and a Dissertation Fellowship from the University of Alberta (Canada), and by Graduate Research Assistantships from Duke University (USA).

Correspondence concerning this chapter should be addressed to Florin Dolcos, Brain Imaging and Analysis Center, Room 163, Bell Building, Duke University, Durham, NC, 27710, USA. Email: fdolcos@duke.edu or to Roberto Cabeza, Center for Cognitive Neuroscience, Duke University, Room B203, LSRS Building, Durham, NC, 27708, USA. Email: Cabeza@duke.edu.

Figures 6.2 and 6.3 were modified with permission from Dolcos et al., 2004b, and Figure 6.4 and Table 6.1 were modified with permission from Dolcos et al., 2005.

REFERENCES

Adolphs, R., Cahill, L., Schul, R., & Babinsky, R. (1997). Impaired declarative memory for emotional material following bilateral amygdala damage in humans. *Learning & Memory, 4*, 291–300.

Adolphs, R., Tranel, D., & Denburg, N. (2000). Impaired emotional declarative memory following unilateral amygdala damage. *Learning & Memory, 7*, 180–186.

Amaral, D. G., Price, J. L., Pitkanen, A., & Carmichael, S. T. (1992). Anatomical organization of the primate amygdaloid complex. In J. P. Aggleton (Ed.), *The amygdala, neurobiological aspects of emotion, memory and mental dysfunction* (pp. 1–66). New York: Wiley.

Anderson, M. C., Ochsner, K. N., Kuhl, B., Cooper, J., Robertson, E., Gabrieli, S. W., Glover, G. H., & Gabrieli, J. D. E. (2004). Neural systems underlying the suppression of unwanted memories. *Science, 303*, 232–235.

Bradley, M. M., Greenwald, M. K., Petry, M. C., & Lang, P. J. (1992). Remembering pictures: Pleasure and arousal in memory. *Journal of Experimental Psychology: Learning, Memory, & Cognition, 18*, 379–390.

Bradley, M. M. & Lang, P. J. (1994). Measuring emotion: The self-assessment manikin and the semantic differential. *Journal of Behavior Therapy & Experimental Psychiatry, 25*, 49–59.

Brewer, J. B., Zhao, Z., Desmond, J. E., Glover, G. H., & Gabrieli, J. D. E. (1998). Making memories: Brain activity that predicts how well visual experience will be remembered. *Science, 281*, 1185–1187.

Cahill, L., Babinsky, R., Markowitsch, H., & McGaugh, J. L. (1995). The amygdala and emotional memory. *Nature, 377*, 295–296.

Cahill, L., Haier, R. J., Fallon, J., Alkire, M. T., Tang, C., Keator, D., Wu, J., & McGaugh, J. L. (1996). Amygdala activity at encoding correlated with long-term, free recall of emotional information. *Proceedings of the National Academy of Sciences USA, 93*, 8016–8021.

Cahill, L. & McGaugh, J. L. (1998). Mechanisms of emotional arousal and lasting declarative memory. *Trends in Neurosciences, 21*, 294–299.

Cahill, L., Prins, B., Weber, M., & McGaugh, J. L. (1994). Beta-adrenergic activation and memory for emotional events. *Nature, 371*, 702–704.

Cahill, L., Uncapher, M., Kilpatrick, L., Alkire, M. T., & Turner, J. (2004). Sex-related hemispheric lateralization of amygdala function in emotionally influenced memory: An fMRI investigation. *Learning & Memory, 11*, 261–266.

Canli, T., Desmond, J. E., Zhao, Z., & Gabrieli, J. D. E. (2002). Sex differences in the neural basis of emotional memories. *Proceedings of the National Academy of Sciences USA, 99*, 10789–10794.

Canli, T., Zhao, Z., Brewer, J., Gabrieli, J. D. E., & Cahill, L. (2000). Event-related activation in the human amygdala associated with later memory for individual emotional experience. *Journal of Neuroscience, 20*, 1–5.

Christianson, S.-Å. (1992a). Emotional stress and eyewitness memory: A critical review. *Psychological Bulletin, 112*, 284–309.

Christianson, S.-Å. (Ed.) (1992b). *Handbook of emotion and memory: Research and theory.* Hillsdale, NJ: Erlbaum.

D'Esposito, M., Postle, B. R., & Rypma, B. (2000). Prefrontal cortical contributions to working memory: Evidence from event-related fMRI studies. *Experimental Brain Research, 133*, 3–11.

Damasio, A. R. (1994). *Descartes' error*. New York: Putnam.

Davidson, R. J. & Irwin, W. (1999). The functional neuroanatomy of emotion and affective style. *Trends in Cognitive Sciences, 3*, 11–20.

Davis, M. & Whalen, P. J. (2001). The amygdala: Vigilance and emotion. *Molecular Psychiatry, 6*, 13–34.

Dobbins, I. G., Rice, H. J., Wagner, A. D., & Schacter, D. L. (2003). Memory orientation and success: Separable neurocognitive components underlying episodic recognition. *Neuropsychologia, 41*, 318–333.

Dolan, R. J., Lane, R., Chua, P., & Fletcher, P. (2000). Dissociable temporal lobe activations during emotional episodic memory retrieval. *NeuroImage, 11*, 203–209.

Dolcos, F. & Cabeza, R. (2002). Event-related potentials of emotional memory: Encoding pleasant, unpleasant, and neutral pictures. *Cognitive, Affective, & Behavioral Neuroscience, 2*, 252–263.

Dolcos, F., Graham, R., LaBar, K., & Cabeza, R. (2003). Coactivation of the amygdala and hippocampus predicts better recall for emotional than for neutral pictures. *Brain and Cognition, 51*, 221–223.

Dolcos, F., LaBar, K. S., & Cabeza, R. (2004a). Dissociable effects of arousal and valence on prefrontal activity indexing emotional evaluation and subsequent memory: An event-related fMRI study. *NeuroImage, 23*, 64–74.

Dolcos, F., LaBar, K. S., & Cabeza, R. (2004b). Interaction between the amygdala and the medial temporal lobe memory system predicts better memory for emotional events. *Neuron, 42*, 855–863.

Dolcos, F., LaBar, K. S., & Cabeza, R. (2005). Remembering one year later: Role of the amygdala and medial temporal lobe memory system in retrieving emotional memories. *Proceedings of the National Academy of Sciences USA, 102*, 2626–2631.

Eldridge, L. L., Knowlton, B. J., Furmanski, C. S., Bookheimer, S. Y., & Engel, S. A. (2000). Remembering episodes: A selective role for the hippocampus during retrieval. *Nature Neuroscience, 3*, 1149–1152.

Erk, S., Martin, S., & Walter, H. (2005). Emotional context during encoding of neutral items modulates brain activation not only during encoding but also during recognition. *NeuroImage, 26*, 829–838.

Fossati, P., Hevenor, S. J., Lepage, M., Graham, S. J., Grady, C., Keightley, M. L., Craik, F. I., & Mayberg, H. S. (2004). Distributed self in episodic memory: Neural correlates of successful retrieval of self-encoded positive and negative personality traits. *NeuroImage, 22*, 1596–1604.

Gardiner, J. M. (1988). Functional aspects of recollective experience. *Memory & Cognition, 16*, 309–313.

Gloor, P. (1992). Role of the amygdala in temporal lobe epilepsy. In J. P. Aggleton (Ed.), *The amygdala, neurobiological aspects of emotion, memory, and mental dysfunction* (pp. 505–538). New York: Wiley.

Hamann, S. (2001). Cognitive and neural mechanisms of emotional memory. *Trends in Cognitive Sciences, 5*, 394–400.

Hamann, S. B., Ely, T. D., Grafton, S. T., & Kilts, C. D. (1999). Amygdala activity related to enhanced memory for pleasant and aversive stimuli. *Nature Neuroscience, 2,* 289–293.

Hamann, S. B., Monarch, E. S., & Goldstein, F. C. (2000). Memory enhancement for emotional stimuli is impaired in early Alzheimer's disease. *Neuropsychology, 14,* 82–92.

Henson, R. N. A., Rugg, M. D., Shallice, T., Josephs, O., & Dolan, R. J. (1999). Recollection and familiarity in recognition memory: An event-related functional magnetic resonance imaging study. *Journal of Neuroscience, 19,* 3962–3972.

Jackson, D. C., Malmstadt, J. R., Larson, C. L., & Davidson, R. J. (2000). Suppression and enhancement of emotional responses to unpleasant pictures. *Psychophysiology, 37,* 515–522.

Jacoby, L. L. & Dallas, M. (1981). On the relationship between autobiographical memory and perceptual learning. *Journal of Experimental Psychology: General, 110,* 306–340.

Kapur, S., Tulving, E., Cabeza, R., McIntosh, A. R., Houle, S., & Craik, F. I. M. (1996). The neural correlates of intentional learning of verbal materials: A PET study in humans. *Cognitive Brain Research, 4,* 243–249.

Kensinger, E. A., Brierley, B., Medford, N., Growdon, J. H., & Corkin, S. (2002). Effects of normal aging and Alzheimer's disease on emotional memory. *Emotion, 2,* 118–134.

Kensinger, E. A. & Corkin, S. (2004). Two routes to emotional memory: Distinct neural processes for valence and arousal. *Proceedings of the National Academy of Sciences USA, 101,* 3310–3315.

Kilpatrick, L. & Cahill, L. (2003). Amygdala modulation of parahippocampal and frontal regions during emotionally influenced memory storage. *NeuroImage, 20,* 2091–2099.

Kirchhoff, B. A., Wagner, A. D., Maril, A., & Stern, C. E. (2000). Prefrontal-temporal circuitry for episodic encoding and subsequent memory. *Journal of Neuroscience, 20,* 6173–6180.

Kosslyn, S. M., Shin, L. M., Thompson, W. L., McNally, R. J., Rauch, S. L., Pitman, R. K., & Alpert, N. M. (1996). Neural effects of visualizing and perceiving aversive stimuli: A PET investigation. *Neuroreport, 7,* 1569–1576.

LaBar, K. S. (2003). Emotional memory functions of the human amygdala. *Current Neurology and Neuroscience Reports, 3,* 363–364.

LaBar, K. S., Gitelman, D. R., Mesulam, M.-M., & Parrish, T. B. (2001). Impact of signal-to-noise on functional MRI of the human amygdala. *Neuroreport, 12,* 3461–3464.

LaBar, K. S. & Phelps, E. A. (1998). Arousal-mediated memory consolidation: Role of the medial temporal lobe in humans. *Psychological Science, 9,* 490–493.

Lane, D. R. & Nadel, L. (2000). *Cognitive neuroscience of emotion.* New York: Oxford University Press.

Lang, P. J., Greenwald, M. K., Bradley, M. M., & Hamm, A. O. (1993). Looking at pictures: Affective, facial, visceral, and behavioral reactions. *Psychophysiology, 30,* 261–273.

LeDoux, J. E. (1996). *The emotional brain.* New York: Simon & Shuster.

LeDoux, J. E. (2000). Emotion circuits in the brain. *Annual Review of Neuroscience, 23,* 155–184.

McGaugh, J. L. (2000). Memory: A century of consolidation. *Science, 287,* 248–251.

McGaugh, J. L. (2004). The amygdala modulates the consolidation of memories of emotionally arousing experiences. *Annual Review of Neuroscience, 27,* 1–28.

McGaugh, J. L., Cahill, L., & Roozendaal, B. (1996). Involvement of the amygdala in memory storage: Interaction with other brain systems. *Proceedings of the National Academy of Sciences USA, 93,* 13508–13514.

McGaugh, J. L., McIntyre, C. K., & Power, A. E. (2002). Amygdala modulation of memory consolidation: Interaction with other brain systems. *Neurobiology of Learning and Memory, 78,* 539–552.

Mandler, G. (1980). Recognizing: The judgment of previous occurrence. *Psychological Review, 87,* 252–271.

Maratos, E. J., Allan, K., & Rugg, M. D. (2000). Recognition memory for emotionally negative and neutral words: An ERP study. *Neuropsychologia, 38,* 1452–1465.

Maratos, E. J., Dolan, R. J., Morris, J. S., Henson, R. N., & Rugg, M. D. (2001). Neural activity associated with episodic memory for emotional context. *Neuropsychologia, 39,* 910–920.

Mather, M., Canli, T., English, T., Whitfield, S. L., Wais, P., Ochsner, K. N., Gabrieli, J. D. E., & Carstensen, L. L. (2004). Amygdala responses to emotionally valenced stimuli in older and younger adults. *Psychological Science, 15,* 259–263.

Mayberg, H. S., Liotti, M., Brannan, S. K., McGinnis, S., Mahurin, R. K., Jerabek, P. A., Silva, J. A., Tekell, J. L., Martin, C. C., Lancaster, J. L., & Fox, P. T. (1999). Reciprocal limbic-cortical function and negative mood: Converging PET findings in depression and normal sadness. *American Journal of Psychiatry, 156,* 675–682.

Medford, N., Phillips, M. L., Brierley, B., Brammer, M., Bullmore, E. T., & David, A. S. (2005). Emotional memory: Separating content and context. *Psychiatry Research: Neuroimaging, 138,* 247–258.

Moscovitch, M. (1992). Memory and working-with-memory: A component process model based on modules and central systems. *Journal of Cognitive Neuroscience, 4,* 257–267.

Nadel, L. (2000). Memory traces revisited. *Nature Reviews: Neuroscience, 1,* 209–212.

Nader, K. (2003). Memory traces unbound. *Trends in Neurosciences, 26,* 65–72.

Ochsner, K. N. (2000). Are affective events richly recollected or simply familiar? The experience and process of recognizing feelings past. *Journal of Experimental Psychology: General, 129,* 242–261.

Ochsner, K. N. & Gross, J. J. (2005). The cognitive control of emotion. *Trends in Cognitive Sciences, 9,* 242–249.

Ochsner, K. N., Ray, R. D., Cooper, J. K., Robertson, E. R., Chopra, S., Gabrieli, J. D. E., & Gross, J. J. (2004). For better or for worse: Neural systems supporting the cognitive down- and up-regulation of negative emotion. *NeuroImage, 23,* 483–499.

Owen, A. M., Herrod, N. J., Menon, D. K., Clark, J. C., Downey, S. P., Carpenter, T. A., Minhas, P. S., Turkheimer, F. E., Williams, E. J., Robbins, T. W., Sahakian, B. J., Petrides, M., & Pickard, J. D. (1999). Redefining the functional organization of working memory processes within human lateral prefrontal cortex. *European Journal of Neuroscience, 11,* 567–574.

Paller, K. A., Kutas, M., & Mayes, A. R. (1987). Neural correlates of encoding in an incidental learning paradigm. *Electroencephalography and Clinical Neurophysiology, 67,* 360–371.

Paller, K. A. & Wagner, A. D. (2002). Observing the transformation of experience into memory. *Trends in Cognitive Sciences, 6*, 93–102.

Petrides, M. (1995). Functional organization of the human frontal cortex for mnemonic processing. Evidence from neuroimaging studies. *Annals of the New York Academy of Sciences, 769*, 85–96.

Phan, K. L., Wager, T., Taylor, S. F., & Liberzon, I. (2002). Functional neuro-anatomy of emotion: A meta-analysis of emotion activation studies in PET and fMRI. *NeuroImage, 16*, 331–348.

Phelps, E. A. (2004). Human emotion and memory: Interactions of the amygdala and hippocampal complex. *Current Opinion in Neurobiology, 14*, 198–202.

Phelps, E. A., LaBar, K. S., Anderson, A. K., O'Connor, K. J., Fulbright, R. K., & Spencer, D. D. (1998). Specifying the contributions of the human amygdala to emotional memory: A case study. *Neurocase, 4*, 527–540.

Picton, P. W., Lins, O. G., & Scherg, M. (1995). The recording and analysis of event-related potentials. In F. Boller & J. Grafman (Series Eds.) & R. Johnson, Jr. (Vol. Ed.), *Handbook of neuropsychology* (Vol. 10, pp. 2–75). Amsterdam: Elsevier.

Poldrack, R. A., Wagner, A. D., Prull, M. W., Desmond, J. E., Glover, G. H., & Gabrieli, J. D. (1999). Functional specialization for semantic and phonological processing in the left inferior prefrontal cortex. *NeuroImage, 10*, 15–35.

Prince, S. E., Daselaar, S. M., & Cabeza, R. (2005). Neural correlates of relational memory: Successful encoding and retrieval of semantic and perceptual associations. *Journal of Neuroscience, 25*, 1203–1210.

Protopopescu, X., Pan, H., Tuescher, O., Cloitre, M., Goldstein, M., Engelien, W., Epstein, J., Yang, Y., Gorman, J., LeDoux, J., Silbersweig, D., & Stern, E. (2005). Differential time courses and specificity of amygdala activity in post-traumatic stress disorder subjects and normal control subjects. *Biological Psychiatry, 57*, 464–473.

Rauch, S. L., van Der Kolk, B. A., Fisler, R. E., Alpert, N. M., Orr, S. P., Savage, C. R., Fischman, A. J., Jenike, M. A., & Pitman, R. K. (1996). A symptom provocation study of post-traumatic stress dissorder using positron emission tomography and script-driven imagery. *Archives of General Psychiatry, 53*, 380–387.

Richardson, M. P., Strange, B. A., & Dolan, R. J. (2004). Encoding of emotional memories depends on amygdala and hippocampus and their interaction. *Nature Neuroscience, 7*, 278–285.

Rugg, M. D. (1995). ERP studies of memory. In M. G. H. Coles & M. D. Rugg (Eds.), *Electrophysiology of mind: Event-related brain potentials and cognition* (pp. 132–170). Oxford: Oxford University Press.

Russell, J. (1980). A circumplex model of affect. *Journal of Personality and Social Psychology, 39*, 1161–1178.

Seminowicz, D. A., Mayberg, H. S., McIntosh, A. R., Goldapple, K., Kennedy, S., Segal, Z., & Rafi-Tarib, S. (2004). Limbic-frontal circuitry in major depression: A path modeling metanalysis. *NeuroImage, 22*, 409–418.

Sergerie, K., Lepage, M., & Armony, J. L. (2005). A face to remember: Emotional expression modulates prefrontal activity during memory formation. *NeuroImage, 24*, 580–585.

Shallice, T., Fletcher, P., Frith, C. D., Grasby, P., Frackowiak, R. S., & Dolan, R. J. (1994). Brain regions associated with acquisition and retrieval of verbal episodic memory. *Nature, 368*, 633–635.

Sharot, T., Delgado, M. R., & Phelps, E. A. (2004). How emotion enhances the feeling of remembering. *Nature Neuroscience, 7*, 1376–1380.

Simons, J. S. & Spiers, H. J. (2003). Prefrontal and medial temporal lobe interactions in long-term memory. *Nature Reviews: Neuroscience, 4*, 637–648.

Smith, A. P., Henson, R. N. A., Dolan, R. J., & Rugg, M. D. (2004a). Event-related potential correlates of the retrieval of emotional and nonemotional context. *Journal of Cognitive Neuroscience, 16*, 760–775.

Smith, A. P. R., Henson, R. N. A., Dolan, R. J., & Rugg, M. D. (2004b). fMRI correlates of episodic retrieval of emotional contexts. *NeuroImage, 22*, 868–878.

Soetens, E., Casaer, S., D'Hooge, R., & Hueting, J. E. (1995). Effect of amphetamine on long-term retention of verbal material. *Psychopharmacology, 119*, 155–162.

Squire, L. R. & Zola-Morgan, S. (1991). The medial temporal lobe memory system. *Science, 253*, 1380–1386.

Talarico, J. T., LaBar, K. S., & Rubin, D. C. (2005). Emotional intensity predicts autobiographical memory experience. *Memory & Cognition, 32*, 1118–1132.

Taylor, S. F., Liberzon, I., Fig, L. M., Decker, L. R., Minoshima, S., & Koeppe, R. A. (1998). The effect of emotional content on visual recognition memory: A PET activation study. *NeuroImage, 8*, 188–197.

Tulving, E. (1983). *Elements of episodic memory*. Oxford: Oxford University Press.

Tulving, E. (1985). Memory and consciousness. *Canadian Psychologist, 26*, 1–12.

van Stegeren, A. H., Goekoop, R., Everaerd, W., Scheltens, P., Barkhof, F., Kuijer, J. P. A., & Rombouts, S. A. R. B. (2005). Noradrenaline mediates amygdala activation in men and women during encoding of emotional material. *NeuroImage, 24*, 898–909.

Wager, T. D., Phan, K. L., Liberzon, I., & Taylor, S. F. (2003). Valence, gender, and lateralization of functional brain anatomy in emotion: A meta-analysis of findings from neuroimaging. *NeuroImage, 19*, 513–531.

Wagner, A. D., Schacter, D. L., Rotte, M., Koutstaal, W., Maril, A., Dale, A. M., Rosen, B. R., & Buckner, R. L. (1998). Building memories: Remembering and forgetting of verbal experiences as predicted by brain activity. *Science, 281*, 1188–1191.

Weis, S., Klaver, P., Reul, J., Elger, C. E., & Fernandez, G. (2004). Temporal and cerebellar brain regions that support both declarative memory formation and retrieval. *Cerebral Cortex, 14*, 256–267.

Williams, L. M. (1994). Recall of childhood trauma: A prospective study of women's memories of child sexual abuse. *Journal of Consulting and Clinical Psychology, 62*, 1167–1176.

Yonelinas, A. P. (2002). The nature of recollection and familiarity: A review of 30 years of research. *Journal of Memory and Language, 46*, 441–517.

Zald, D. H. (2003). The human amygdala and the emotional evaluation of sensory stimuli. *Brain Research Reviews, 41*, 88–123.

7 Why Memories May Become More Positive as People Age

Mara Mather

Abstract

Recent studies reveal a positivity effect in older adults' memories, in which they show a bias to enhance positive information and diminish negative information. In this chapter, I review findings of the positivity effect in memory for autobiographical events, choices, words, pictures, and faces. The effect does not appear to be the result of mood-congruent memory, age-related decline in physiological arousal mechanisms, or age-related decline in the amygdala. Instead, older adults' positivity effect appears to be the result of goal-directed processes that allocate attention and shape memory in ways that enhance well-being.

Because of their influence on emotions, memories have a utility that goes beyond the information they convey. Depending on their content, memories can either depress or enhance mood, and people often use memory in strategic ways to help them regulate emotion. For instance, when in a negative mood, people sometimes retrieve positive memories for mood repair and this memory retrieval strategy seems to help ward off depression (Josephson, Singer, & Salovey, 1996; Joormann & Siemer, 2004; Singer, this volume). The self-enhancing bias seen in autobiographical memory may benefit mental health (Taylor, 1991). People work hard at creating and maintaining happy memories, sometimes even at the cost of current experience (for example, bringing an attention-demanding videocamera on vacation).

Older adults are one population that is particularly effective at emotion regulation, and memory seems to play a role in this success (Carstensen, Mikels, & Mather, 2006; Mather, 2004). In this chapter I review evidence that older adults show a positivity effect in memory, favoring information that is emotionally gratifying in their memories and forgetting information that might increase negative affect. I also examine whether this positivity effect is simply the fortuitous by-product of age-related decline in emotional memory systems or whether it is the result of older adults' greater focus on regulating emotion.

Many studies suggest that motivations change with age and that, in particular, emotional goals become more salient as people approach the end of life. Carstensen's socioemotional selectivity theory posits that people's sense of the time they have left in life affects their goals and motivations (Carstensen, Isaacowitz, & Charles, 1999). Early in adulthood, an expansive future leads people to focus on knowledge seeking, whereas as time becomes more limited, goals related to emotional meaning and well-being gain precedence. One way that these shifts in goals have been examined is in studies giving people a hypothetical choice to spend time with a close friend or family member or meet someone new such as a famous author (Fung, Carstensen, & Lutz, 1999; Fung, Lai, & Ng, 2001). Older adults are more likely to select the emotionally close social partner whereas younger adults are more likely to select the social partner who may provide new information. Importantly, asking older adults to imagine that their lifespan has been expanded by new advances in medicine makes their preferences resemble those of younger adults, whereas asking younger adults to imagine they are about to move away from their current hometown, giving them a more limited time perspective, makes their preferences resemble those of older adults. Compared with younger adults, older adults are also more likely to emphasize emotional dimensions than other personal dimensions when categorizing people (Fredrickson & Carstensen, 1990), a pattern also seen among younger adults with a terminal illness (Carstensen & Fredrickson, 1998). Thus, the shift with age to give emotional goals greater priority seems to be linked to people's time perspective.

Prioritizing emotional goals should help everyday well-being. Indeed, older adults do seem to be more effective at maintaining positive affect and avoiding negative affect. An experience sampling study in which participants carried pagers that went off at random intervals throughout a week, signaling them to fill out an emotion rating scale based on their current affect, revealed that when older adults experience negative affect, it ends sooner than it does for younger adults (Carstensen et al., 2000). In addition, the study found that older adults are less likely than younger adults to experience negative affect. A longitudinal study revealed that negative affect decreases over time for individuals (Charles, Reynolds, & Gatz, 2001), ruling out the possibility that older adults' enhanced emotional experience is simply due to cohort effects. In addition, on questionnaire studies, older adults are more likely to report being good at regulating their emotions or focusing more on emotional control (Diehl, Coyle, & Labouvie-Vief, 1996; Gross et al., 1997; Lawton et al., 1992).

This increased focus on emotion regulation seems likely to have an impact on the way that controlled processes are deployed when people encounter emotional events. If the desire to optimize affect is chronically active among older adults, they may recruit cognitive control mechanisms in order to enhance emotionally gratifying information and diminish negative information in attention and memory.

POSITIVITY EFFECTS IN MEMORY FOR VARIOUS TYPES OF INFORMATION

There are a number of studies across a wide variety of domains that reveal more emotionally gratifying memories among older adults than younger adults. The following overview describes findings from studies of memory for autobiographical information, choices, words, pictures, and faces.

Memory for autobiographical information

Autobiographical memories are powerful emotion elicitors. Indeed, one method that emotion researchers use to put people into positive or negative moods is to ask them to recall a happy or sad memory. Despite the greater weight given to negative than positive information in attention, impression formation, and judgment (Baumeister et al., 2001; Rozin & Royzman, 2001), negative autobiographical memories do not show an advantage in memory. In fact, if anything, people tend to be more likely to remember positive events (e.g., Matlin & Stang, 1978) and the intensity of the affect associated with an event fades faster when negative than positive (for a review, see Walker, Skowronski, & Thompson, 2003). This asymmetry in autobiographical memory may reflect healthy coping processes, in which people attempt to minimize the impact of negative events on their well-being (Taylor, 1991). Indeed, dysphoric undergraduates do not show the same fading in memory over time in the intensity of negative affect as non-dysphoric undergraduates do (Walker et al., 2003).

Various findings suggest that older adults are more likely than younger adults to forget negative autobiographical events and to underestimate the intensity of their past negative emotions. As time passes, mothers are more likely to recall their children as having had desirable traits when young, such as being cooperative and popular with peers (Yarrow, Campbell, & Burton, 1970). Moreover, as people get older, they rate their childhood as happier (Field, 1981). Of course, because as people get older their childhoods (or their children's childhoods) also becomes more distant, the increasingly rosy picture of childhood may be the result of fading memories over time rather than the age of the person remembering. But the link between positivity and age is supported by research showing that negative memories are more likely to fade for older adults than for younger adults. For younger adults, highly negative events seem to be accessible for a longer time than highly positive events (Berntsen, 2001, 2002), but by age 60, the pattern reverses and memories for negative events seem to be accessible for a shorter time than for positive events (Berntsen & Rubin, 2002). Participants in these studies were asked to describe a memory for an extremely happy event or for an extremely sad or traumatic event and then asked when the event happened. For younger adults, the negative events tended to have happened a longer time ago than the positive events, whereas the opposite was the case for the older adults, suggesting an age difference in whether positive or negative memories tend to be more long lasting. Another study that had participants recall positive, negative, and neutral autobiographical memories suggests that older adults are more likely than younger adults to reappraise negative events in ways that make them seem more positive (Comblain, D'Argembeau, & Van der Linden, 2005). The study revealed that negative memories were associated with a less complex storyline and more intense positive feelings for older adults than for younger adults.

A study examining memory for reactions to a political event also provides evidence for greater fading of negative affect in memory for older adults than for younger adults (Levine & Bluck, 1997). In 1992, Ross Perot abruptly withdrew from the presidential race. Both his younger and older supporters expressed sadness at the withdrawal at the time. A few months later, among Perot's supporters who still wished he had been elected, memories of their negative reactions had faded more for older adults than for younger adults. In contrast, among people who had previously supported Perot but no longer wished he had been elected, there were no age differences – both younger and older adults underestimated how sad they had been. This study suggests that older adults who were still enthusiastic about Perot may have forgotten just how much they were saddened by his withdrawal from the race in order to help them avoid re-experiencing those emotions. Greater forgetting of negative events among older adults has also been seen in memory for traumatic events. Among a group of survivors of a World War II Nazi concentration camp who testified both shortly after the war and a couple of decades later, the oldest survivors were those who showed the most forgetting (Wagenaar & Groeneweg, 1990). Unfortunately, there was no control positive event in this study to test whether the older adults simply had worse memory overall.

When asked to remember their past selves, people often paint a picture of their past actions and characteristics that is more favorable than accurate (Greenwald, 1980; Ross & Wilson, 2003). For example, college students asked to recall their high school grades remember more A's than were actually on their transcripts (Bahrick, Hall, & Berger, 1996). Current goals also influence which personal experiences or characteristics are most likely to be remembered (Sanitioso, Kunda, & Fong, 1990).

A study with several hundred nuns examining the impact of emotional goals and age on autobiographical memory revealed that age and emotional focus are associated with more positive biases in autobiographical memory (Kennedy, Mather, & Carstensen, 2004). Fourteen years after completing a questionnaire about their demographic background, health practices, physical and mental illnesses, and family medical history, the nuns completed a retrospective version of the questionnaire and were randomly assigned to one of three focus conditions. In the emotion-focused condition, participants were told that it was very important that they focus on their feelings while answering the questions. In addition, after every few questions, they rated the extent to which they were currently feeling each of five emotions. In the accuracy-focused condition, participants were told that it was very important that they answer the questions as accurately as they could. These participants periodically rated the extent to which they used each of five memory strategies in recalling information in the questionnaire. In the control condition, participants did not receive any focusing instructions. In all three conditions, participants were asked to think back 14 years and answer the questions as they thought they answered them then.

A general index of participants' overall direction of memory bias across all dependent variables revealed that the oldest controls were more likely than the youngest controls to have a positive memory bias (for example, remembering having fewer headaches 14 years ago than indicated on the original survey). In addition, regardless of age, emotion-focused participants were likely to show a positive memory bias and accuracy-focused participants were likely to show a negative memory bias. No differences were found across age or condition for baseline levels of positive or negative mood. Nevertheless, mood ratings completed after the retrospective questionnaire revealed that the oldest controls experienced more positive emotion than the youngest controls after remembering themselves 14 years earlier. In addition, mood improved after the retrospective questionnaire for the emotion-focused participants but not the accuracy-focused participants. This suggests that positive memory biases exhibited by the oldest controls and the emotion-focused participants helped them regulate emotion.

Thus, in summary, studies looking at autobiographical memory reveal that older adults are more likely to distort their memories in a positive direction, more likely to forget how negative events were, and more likely to have long-lasting positive memories than long-lasting negative memories.

Memory for choices

Memories of chosen as well as forgone alternatives can be a powerful influence on well-being. Studies with younger adults reveal that they tend to remember their choices as being better than they actually were (Mather, Shafir, & Johnson, 2000, 2003). These younger participants were asked to make memory attributions about features from previously considered options (e.g., was "easily discouraged" associated with the first job candidate, the second job candidate, or is it a new feature?). They attributed more positive features to the option they had chosen and more negative features to the option they had rejected. A study in which participants were misinformed about which option they chose indicates that beliefs at the time of retrieval about which option was chosen are a key factor in generating these choice-supportive biases (Henkel & Mather, in preparation). In this study, participants made a series of choices and then returned a week later and were given a surprise memory test. For each choice scenario, the experimenters reminded the participants about which option they had selected. However, a randomly selected half of the reminders were false and half were correct (manipulation checks confirmed that most of the participants believed the reminders – those who did not were not included in the analyses). Participants showed strong choice-supportive biases both for the options they actually had chosen and for the options the experimenter told them they had chosen (but that they had actually rejected), with no differences in the magnitude of the biases. Thus, the biases seem to reflect the belief that "I chose this option and therefore it must be the better option."

It is the contrast between a chosen option and the forgone alternatives that often leads to the sharpest pangs of regret or the most pleasure at having made the right choice (e.g., Kahneman & Miller, 1986). Choice-supportive memory distortion may help maintain positive affect and reduce negative affect. If so, older adults should be more likely to show choice-supportive biases in memory. In a study designed to address this question (Mather & Johnson, 2000) both older and younger adults made several hypothetical two-option choices. Each of the options was described by a list that included both positive and negative features. For example, "lots of sunlight" was a positive feature associated with one of the houses and "has a roach problem" was a negative feature. If older adults focus more on emotion regulation, they should engage in more choice-supportive memory distortion than younger adults. However, younger adults should be as choice-supportive as older adults if they focus on the emotional implications of making choices. To test this, a focus manipulation was included in the study. After making all four choices, one group of participants was asked to review how they felt about the options from each choice and another group was asked to review the features of the options. A third group was not asked to review the choices at all, and instead was asked to do an unrelated task. Participants completed source identification memory tests two days after making their choices. Overall, older adults were more choice-supportive in their memory attributions than younger adults. However, in the affective review condition, younger participants were as choice-supportive as older adults. Asking younger adults to focus on how they felt about the choices made them more choice-supportive than asking them to review the features of the choice options or not to review the choices at all. In contrast, the review condition did not have a significant impact on older adults' choice-supportiveness.

One possibility is that the age-related biases were simply a result of poorer memory. But another group of older participants who were tested after 30 minutes were just as choice-supportive as the older adults in the 2-day delay group – despite the fact that they had significantly more accurate memory than the 2-day older group and were as accurate as the 2-day younger group. Thus older adults' greater degree of choice-supportive bias was not just a result of lower overall memory accuracy. Instead, they seemed to be more motivated than younger adults to avoid negative affect when remembering past choices.

A subsequent study replicated this finding of greater choice-supportiveness in older adults' source attributions for choice option features than younger adults' choice attributions (Mather & Carstensen, 2004). In addition, it revealed that compared with younger adults, older adults' recall, recognition, and ratings of choice option features were also more positive. More of a positivity bias in older adults' recognition memory for choice option features was also seen in another study looking at memory for choices (Mather, Knight, & McCaffrey, 2005).

Memory for words

Although words are not the most emotionally evocative type of stimuli, a couple of studies have found age differences in memory for positive versus negative words. A study comparing the effects of a sad mood induction on various memory tests for older and younger adults revealed two significant positivity effects in the neutral mood control condition (Knight, Maines, & Robinson, 2002). Older adults remembered a higher proportion of positive words and a lower proportion of negative words than younger adults on both immediate and delayed tests. In addition, older adults were less likely to spell the negatively valenced version of homophones than younger adults. The two other memory tasks (autobiographical recall and prose recall) did not reveal significant age differences by valence in the control condition.[1]

Another study that looked at age differences in memory for emotional words had participants rate the valence of 27 positive, negative, and neutral words (Leigland, Schulz, & Janowsky, 2004). There were no age differences in the valence of the words recalled on an immediate or 30-minute delayed recall test. However, the authors reported a trend on a recognition test for the older adults to recognize more positive than negative words whereas the younger

adults showed no difference by valence on the recognition test. A similar procedure was used in another study, in which older and younger adults rated
the valence of 27 positive, negative, and neutral words (Kensinger et al., 2002).
This study included only an immediate recall test and there were no significant age differences by valence. Thus, age differences in whether positive or
negative words are more likely to be remembered are not always found, but
when they are, they reveal a positivity effect for older adults' memories.

Memory for pictures

Several studies have used emotional pictures from the International Affective
Picture System (IAPS: Lang, Bradley, & Cuthbert, 1995). This widely used
picture set consists of photographs of people, animals, objects, and scenes that
have been normed for the emotional valence and arousal they convey. In two
experiments (Charles, Mather, & Carstensen, 2003) participants were asked to
watch a slide show with positive, negative, and neutral pictures. Participants
were given recall or recognition tests after a 15-minute delay. In both experiments, there were equal numbers of European Americans in each age group
and equal numbers of African Americans in each group, with gender and socioeconomic status stratified within each of these groups. Relative to other types
of items, the number of negative items recalled decreased with age. Older adults'
recognition accuracy for negative pictures was also diminished relative to their
recognition accuracy for the other pictures. Including gender, ethnicity, and
socioeconomic status revealed that these age-related positivity effects were not
driven by any one group in particular but instead were seen broadly across
the different categories of participants.

   These findings have been replicated by some studies, whereas others have
found no age differences in terms of the valence of memories. A study with
younger adults and older adults (Kensinger et al., 2002) found no age by valence
interaction when participants were asked to recall pictures that they had just
rated for valence (older adults viewed the pictures twice, while younger adults
viewed the pictures once). A study with younger, middle-aged, and older adults
showed participants a slide show of pictures, each with a caption read by the
experimenter. Participants were asked to try to feel the emotion that was being
depicted (Denburg et al., 2003). Memory was tested in a variety of ways. For
the first test, a 24-hour free recall test, there was a marginally significant age
by valence interaction ($p = .08$), with younger adults showing a larger advantage in memory for the negative pictures than the other two age groups. The
next test, a cued-recall test, showed no significant age by valence interaction,
but the authors reported that while the younger adults remembered both
neutral and negative pictures significantly better than the older adults, the

difference was not significant for the positive pictures. No significant age by valence effects were seen on a subsequent forced-choice recognition test or a long-term follow-up eight months later (however, the older adults were at floor in terms of their recall eight months later).

Mather and Knight (2005) replicated the positivity effect in three separate experiments. In the first experiment, younger and older adults viewed pictures and then were asked to recall as many of them as they could both 20 minutes and 48 hours later or were only asked to recall the pictures 48 hours later. Participants rated the valence of the pictures at the end of the experiment. The positivity effect for older adults increased with repeated testing, but did not increase with the passage of time if there was no intervening test. In both of the two subsequent experiments, participants recalled the pictures 20 minutes after viewing them. All three experiments revealed significant age by valence interactions that were stronger when participants' own valence ratings were used to categorize the pictures. As in Charles et al. (2003), in this series of experiments participants were simply asked to view a slide show of pictures, without any specific encoding task. In contrast, in studies showing weaker or no positivity effects (Comblain et al., 2004; Denburg et al., 2003; Kensinger et al., 2002), participants were given specific encoding tasks, such as rating the valence of the pictures (see Mathews, this volume). These encoding tasks may have reduced the likelihood that emotion regulation goals could affect the way in which the pictures were processed.

Memory for faces

Older adults also tend to have relatively worse memory for negative faces than for positive faces. Older adults asked to rate the valence of a series of emotional and neutral faces recognized fewer of the negative faces 30 minutes later than younger adults completing the same task, but showed no difference for neutral or positive faces (Leigland et al., 2004). In another study that examined memory for faces, the participants' task was to indicate whether a dot appeared on the left or right side of the screen (Mather & Carstensen, 2003). Before each dot appeared, two faces were shown, one on either side of the screen, for one second. Participants did not have to respond to the faces, but analyses of the reaction times revealed that older adults were faster to respond to dots that appeared "behind" positive faces than their neutral face pair and slower to respond to dots that appeared "behind" negative faces than their neutral face pair. Both recognition and forced-choice memory tests revealed that older adults remembered those faces that had appeared with positive expressions better than those that had appeared with negative expressions, whereas younger adults did not show this positivity bias.

POSSIBLE MECHANISMS OF THE POSITIVITY EFFECT

Mood-congruent memory

Being in a certain mood can enhance the encoding or retrieval of memories that share the same valence (Blaney, 1986). It is possible that, when compared with younger adults, older adults show a bias against negative information in memory because they are less likely to be in negative moods than younger adults. However, age differences in the positivity of memories remains significant when current mood ratings or depression scale scores are used as covariates (Charles, Mather, & Carstensen, 2003; Kennedy et al., 2004; Mather & Carstensen, 2003; Mather & Knight, 2005). Thus, the effects do not appear to be the result of mood-congruent memory.

Arousal and the amygdala

Much of the enhancement seen in memory for emotional information can be attributed to the amygdala, a region of the brain that is closely connected to regions of the brain required for encoding new information, such as the hippocampus (see Dolcos, LaBar, & Cabeza, this volume). Patients with lesions in both amygdalae show no impairment in remembering neutral information, but do not show the typical enhancement for emotionally arousing information (Bechara et al., 1995; Phelps et al., 1998). Neuroimaging studies have also shown that amygdala activation at the time of encoding emotional information is correlated with its long-term recall (Cahill et al., 1996; Canli et al., 1999, 2000). The amygdala seems especially attuned to emotionally arousing (or emotionally intense) information and, when arousal levels have been equated, does not show differential activity for positive relative to negative stimuli (Anderson et al., 2003; Cunningham, Raye, & Johnson, in press; Kensinger, 2004; Kensinger & Corkin, 2004; see also Dolcos, LaBar, & Cabeza, this volume).

In general, negative stimuli tend to be more intense and emotionally arousing than positive stimuli (Baumeister et al., 2001; Bradley et al., 2001; Rozin & Royzman, 2001). If arousal is less likely to lead to memory enhancement for older adults and the most arousing stimuli tend to be negative, this could lead to a pattern in which the biggest declines in older adults' memory would be for negative stimuli.

Is it the case that arousal-based memory enhancements are less likely for older adults? The physiological arousal induced by emotional stimuli can be measured by changes in both cardiovascular and electrodermal responses. Several studies have found that cardiovascular responses to emotionally arousing information decrease with age (Levenson, Carstensen, & Gottman, 1994; Levenson et al., 1991; Tsai, Levenson, & Carstensen, 2000), although this age-related decrease is not always seen (Kunzmann, Kupperbusch, & Levenson, 2005). This decrease in the responsiveness to emotional stimuli may have implications for memory; however, the cardiovascular system declines more generally with age (Cacioppo et al., 1998) and so it may be that older adults experience as much arousal but show fewer cardiovascular signs of that arousal. Indeed, despite the age differences in cardiovascular responses to emotional events, there were no age differences in the subjective ratings of those events (Levenson et al., 1991; Tsai, Levenson, & Carstensen, 2000). In addition, there typically are no age differences in electrodermal responses (as measured by skin conductance) while viewing emotionally arousing stimuli (Denburg et al., 2003; Levenson et al., 1991, 1994; Tsai, Levenson, & Carstensen, 2000). Among younger adults, skin conductance level during exposure to stimuli frequently predicts better memory for the stimuli later (Revelle & Loftus, 1992), but there is less information on whether cardiovascular responses are associated with later memory enhancement. Thus, the lack of age differences in skin conductance responses to emotional stimuli may be more important for the relationship between arousal and memory than the age differences seen in cardiovascular reactivity.

Indeed, behavioral studies that control for the arousal level of positive and negative pictures find that older and younger adults' memories benefit equally from arousal (Charles, Mather, & Carstensen, 2003; Denburg et al., 2003; Mather & Knight, 2005; see also Levine & Pizarro, this volume; Reisberg, this volume). In addition, neuroanatomical studies find relatively little decline in the amygdala compared with other brain regions (for a review, see Mather, 2004).

In one functional magnetic resonance imaging (fMRI) study, younger and older participants viewed emotional facial expressions consisting of mostly negative expressions and made judgments about the age or the emotional expression of the face (Gunning-Dixon et al., 2003). The most striking age difference was that younger adults showed amygdala activation when making emotion judgments, whereas the older adults did not. In contrast, the older adults showed anterior cingulate activation whereas the younger adults did not. The authors argued that the findings indicate "both structural and functional age-related changes on a cellular level" (p. 292). However, it is also possible that the age differences reflect differences in the cognitive strategies used when viewing the mostly negative faces (Knight & Mather, in press). The anterior cingulate is one region that plays an important role in emotion regulation (Ochsner & Gross, 2004; Ochsner et al., 2004). Older adults may have been attempting to down-regulate their emotional reactions to the negative faces, and in so doing may have shown greater anterior cingulate activation and less amygdala activation than younger adults. Younger adults instructed to up-regulate or down-regulate their emotions when viewing aversive scenes showed amygdala activation that was modulated up or down in concordance with their regulatory goal (Ochsner et al., 2004).

In another fMRI study, younger and older participants saw pairs of faces and had to indicate which one was male or which one was female (Iidaka et al., 2002). In one block of trials, all the faces were negative, in another they were all positive, and in a third they were all neutral. Younger adults showed more activation than older adults in the amygdala during the negative face block, but not during the other two blocks. As in the Gunning-Dixon et al. (2003) study, older adults showed significant anterior cingulate activation while viewing the negative faces, whereas younger adults did not.

Another fMRI study examined age differences in amygdala activation in response to emotional pictures (Mather et al., 2004). Younger adults showed greater amygdala activation in response to both positive and negative pictures compared with neutral pictures, replicating a number of previous studies showing amygdala sensitivity to emotional stimuli in younger adults (for a review, see Phan et al., 2002). Older adults also showed an amygdala response that was greater for emotional pictures than for neutral pictures, but in contrast with the younger adults, they also showed greater amygdala activation for positive than for negative pictures. This study indicates that the amygdala still functions among older adults, but that the type of affective stimuli it is most responsive to changes.

Goal-directed selective processing

Older adults' positivity effects do not appear to be the result of mood-congruent processing, declines in the effects of physiological arousal, or deterioration in the amygdala. Socioemotional selectivity theory (Carstensen, Isaacowitz, & Charles, 1999) provides an explanation for this pattern of emotionally gratifying memory in its tenet that regulating emotion is a more central goal for older adults than for younger adults. Thus older adults should engage in more goal-directed processing in order to diminish the emotional impact of negative information. Strategies for regulating negative emotion include selecting situations based on their predicted emotional impact, changing existing situations to modify their emotional impact, directing attention to cues that should support desired emotions and ignoring cues that might support undesired emotions, reappraising a situation to decrease its emotional impact, and suppressing the outward signs of emotion (Gross, 2001). These strategies (especially the attention deployment and reappraisal strategies) are likely to require cognitive control mechanisms supported by prefrontal brain regions (Ochsner & Gross, 2004). Consistent with this link between emotion regulation and resource-demanding cognitive processes are studies indicating that dividing attention or otherwise limiting cognitive resources reduces the ability to regulate emotion (Muraven, Tice, & Baumeister, 1998; Wegner, Erber, & Zanakos, 1993).

The idea that older adults use cognitive control processes to help them forget negative information may seem unlikely because many studies have shown that older adults are worse than younger adults at tasks requiring cognitive control (Hedden & Gabrieli, 2004; Johnson & Raye, 2000; Knight & Mather, in press; Zacks, Hasher, & Li, 2000). But even with less effective cognitive control processes, older adults may be more successful in regulating emotion if they devote a larger proportion of their resources to such goals. Findings that a larger proportion of what older adults remember is emotional information (Carstensen & Turk-Charles, 1994; Hashtroudi, Johnson, & Chrosniak, 1990), that the vividness of their memories depends on the strength of their emotional reactions more than it does for younger adults (Comblain et al., 2004), and that their source monitoring is more effective when it is framed in emotional terms (Rahhal, May, & Hasher, 2002) are consistent with the idea that older adults devote more cognitive resources to processing emotional information than to neutral information.

To test the idea that older adults recruit cognitive control processes to help them regulate emotions when encountering emotional stimuli, Mather & Knight (2005) had younger and older participants both watch a slide show of emotional pictures with a recall test 20 minutes later and complete a set of tasks requiring cognitive control. These tasks involved ignoring peripheral information (Fan et al., 2002), refreshing recently activated information (Johnson et al., 2002), and keeping information in mind while performing another task (Baddeley et al., 1985). Performance on the cognitive control tasks did not predict the valence of younger adults' memories, but did predict older adults' positivity effect. Older adults who performed highly on the cognitive control tasks were more likely to show a positivity effect than those who performed poorly.

As a further test of the role of cognitive resources in older adults' encoding of emotional information, a subsequent experiment (Mather & Knight, 2005) included a group of participants who performed a concurrent task (listening to rhythmic sounds and indicating how often they changed) while watching the picture slide show. Comparing the younger and older adults in the control condition replicated the age by valence interaction seen in previous studies (e.g., Charles, Mather, & Carstensen, 2003; Mather & Carstensen, 2003; Mather, Knight, & McCaffrey, 2005). Comparisons of participants in the divided attention group and the full attention control group revealed that, as expected, dividing attention reduced how many pictures people could recall later. Nevertheless, for younger adults, dividing attention did not affect the relative proportion of positive versus negative pictures recalled, consistent with the hypothesis that younger adults do not have chronic emotion-regulation goals; thus, it doesn't matter whether younger adults have the cognitive resources to implement emotion regulation strategies. However, a striking reversal was seen in the divided attention condition for older adults. In contrast with the control condition, where they remembered more positive than negative pictures, in the divided attention condition the majority of what they remembered consisted of negative pictures. Thus, when older adults' cognitive resources are limited, they are no longer able to enhance positive and diminish negative information as effectively during encoding.

The fact that negative pictures had such a large advantage under divided attention is intriguing. One possibility is that older adults were experiencing an effect Wegner (1994) called the ironic process of mental control. Wegner argued that attempting to control the contents of one's thoughts involves both an effortful operating process that attempts to create the desired mental state and an automatic ironic process that searches the contents of thought for evidence of failure of mental control. The effortful operating process can be very successful, but it requires cognitive resources. If those resources are temporarily devoted elsewhere, the ironic process will continue to search for the undesired thoughts, leading to rebound of suppressed thoughts. Older adults' emotion regulation processes may involve both effortful processes that focus on information that should enhance mood and an automatic process that searches for information that might worsen mood in order to initiate regulation processes to diminish the impact of that information. Thus, under conditions of divided attention, older adults might be especially aware of negative information.

 PUTTING THE PIECES TOGETHER: CRITERIA REQUIRED FOR POSITIVITY EFFECT

Figure 7.1 outlines a model of the conditions necessary to generate the positivity effect. The first criterion is whether emotion regulation goals are activated. Older adults report focusing more on regulating emotion (Diehl, Coyle, & Labouvie-Vief, 1996; Gross et al., 1997; Lawton et al., 1992). The fact that older adults' positivity biases occur even without any explicit reminder of their emotional goals suggests that older adults' emotional goals are automatically activated. As such, they fall into the category of "chronic" goals that can influence information processing at unconscious as well as conscious levels (Bargh, Gollwitzer et al., 2001; Fitzsimons & Bargh, 2004; Higgins, 1996). Thus, for older adults, the answer to the first question in figure 7.1 ("Are emotion regulation goals activated?") is most likely to be "yes." In contrast, for younger adults, emotion regulation is not a chronically active goal and so they are most likely to fall into the "no" category for the first criterion, leading them not to

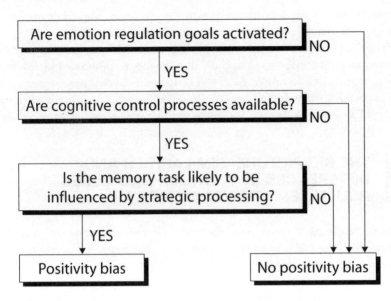

Figure 7.1 Conditions necessary to generate the positivity effect.

show positivity effects in memory. However, if asked to focus on their own feelings, younger adults can be reminded of the desire to regulate emotion and show memory biases that are just as emotionally gratifying as those of older adults in control conditions (Kennedy, Mather, & Carstensen, 2004; Mather & Johnson, 2000).

The second criterion is the availability of cognitive control processes. Executive or strategic processes are necessary to enhance goal-consistent information and diminish goal-inconsistent information. Thus, older adults with decline in executive processes or anyone whose cognitive resources are consumed by another task will be unlikely to be able to implement emotion regulation goals (e.g., Mather & Knight, 2005). The integral role of cognitive control in enhancing positive and diminishing negative information in this model distinguishes it from Labouvie-Vief and Medler's (2002) proposal that the type of affect optimization that increases across the life span is based on automatic processing that is "relatively effortless and efficient, making it ideal for rapid action in emergency situations" (p. 573). The need for cognitive control to regulate emotion may also help explain findings that older adults with cerebrovascular risk factors are prone to late-life onset of depression with a different symptom profile than those with nonvascular depression (Kales, Maixner, & Mellow, 2005). Cerebrovascular risk factors are often associated with undetected strokes, and a key factor linking them with depression seems to be whether strokes have occurred in frontal regions of the brain, impairing executive processes (Firbank et al., 2004; Mast et al., 2004; Thomas et al., 2002).

The final criterion is whether the memory task is likely to be influenced by cognitive control processes. The more that the task is constrained by external circumstances, the less room there will be for goal-directed processes to have an impact. For example, positivity effects should be less likely to occur when the focus of attention or thought is constrained by rating tasks during encoding.

 ## THE BIG PICTURE: SIMILARITIES AND DIFFERENCES IN YOUNGER AND OLDER ADULTS' EMOTIONAL MEMORY

When comparing younger and older adults' emotional memories, a useful organizing principle may be that of automatic and controlled processes (e.g., Jennings & Jacoby, 1993).

Automatic and controlled processes in emotional memory

Both automatic and controlled processes can lead to enhancement of emotional events in memory. First, consider the role of controlled processes – in other words, self-initiated, strategic processing that requires cognitive control. Because emotional events are quite often of special interest and importance, they are more likely to be attended to, told to others, and thought about frequently. Emotional events are also more likely to elicit elaborative processing, as people think about their meaning and relationship to other events and themselves (see Reisberg, this volume). Personal goals and motivations help direct controlled processes and can lead to biases in memory (Levine & Safer, 2000; Ross & Wilson, 2000; Walker, Skowronski, & Thompson, 2003). These goal-directed cognitive control processes that can enhance (or diminish) memory for emotional events are likely to be implemented in the same prefrontal brain regions that support cognitive control more generally.

Automatic processes also play a role in enhancing memories for emotional events. Threatening stimuli tend to pop out and get noticed automatically (MacLeod, Mathews, & Tata, 1986; Mather & Knight, 2006; Öhman, Flykt, & Esteves, 2001). Even when attention is divided when seeing pictures, people later show an advantage in memory for the most emotionally arousing pictures (Kensinger & Corkin, 2004). Even when not attended to at encoding and showing no advantage on an immediate test, emotional stimuli end up being those most likely to survive the longer-term consolidation process (Sharot &

Phelps, 2004). These automatic advantages for emotional stimuli seem primarily due to the amygdala and its interactions with the hippocampus (Dolcos, LaBar, and Cabeza, this volume; McGaugh, 2000; Phelps, 2004). For instance, although under conditions of limited attention normal people are more likely to perceive aversive words than neutral words, a patient with bilateral amygdala damage showed no enhanced perception for the aversive words (Anderson & Phelps, 2001). Moreover, another case study revealed that bilateral damage to the amygdala eliminated the memory benefits seen for arousal, but not those seen for valence (Phelps et al., 1998). The authors suggest that the enhancement in memory for valenced words may be the result of cognitive processes such as schemas and categories that do not require the amygdala.

Automatic and controlled processes in aging and emotional memory

Generally, age differences are most pronounced when the memory task requires self-initiated, controlled processing that could be characterized as involving strategic processes (Balota, Dolan, & Duchek, 2000; Craik & Byrd, 1982; Zacks, Hasher, & Li, 2000). Strategic memory processes rely on prefrontal regions of the brain, which are disproportionately affected with aging (e.g., Johnson & Raye, 2000; Stuss, Alexander, & Benson, 1997). However, there are significant individual differences in how much decline is seen in strategic processes (e.g., Park & Gutchess, 2005). Thus, as seen in Mather and Knight's (2005) study, older adults' ability to implement their emotional goals will depend in part on whether their cognitive control processes have declined significantly or not. In contrast, older adults show little decline in automatic processes of memory. For example, Jacoby (2001) exposed younger and older adults to pairs of associatively related words in a training phase (e.g., knee bend might appear multiple times) and then gave them short lists of to-be-remembered pairs (e.g., knee bone) followed by a cued-recall test for the pairs (e.g., knee b_n_). When the correct response from the study list and the more accessible response from the previous training were placed in opposition, older adults were less likely to recollect the correct response, but showed no decrease in accessibility of the more automatic response.

This pattern of age differences for controlled but not automatic processes of memory also seems to hold true for emotional memory, but for somewhat different reasons. Age differences in emotional memory should be most pronounced when the process of encoding and retrieval permits the influence of goal-directed processing, because it is then that older adults' chronically activated emotional goals can influence what will be remembered. In contrast, automatic processes of emotional memory should show little change, because there is relatively little decline in the amygdala with age (Mather, 2004) and emotional goals should have little influence on automatic processes.

■ OVERVIEW

Older adults tend to remember in ways that help them regulate affect. These positivity effects show up in memory for a variety of types of information and cannot be accounted for by age differences in mood or arousal. Instead, they seem to be the result of goal-directed processes and provide an example of an age-related change where it is critical to take into account the interaction of motivation and cognition. Neither one alone can account for the pattern of findings, as it is those older adults who have the best cognitive ability to implement their goals that show the biggest effects of motivated remembering.

AUTHOR NOTES

Work on this chapter was supported by a grant from the National Institute on Aging (AG025340). Correspondence concerning this chapter should be addressed to Mara Mather, Department of Psychology, UC Santa Cruz, Santa Cruz, CA 95064, USA. Email: mather@ucsc.edu.

NOTE

1 The results from the sad mood induction are also of interest, but they were mixed and therefore hard to interpret, with older adults showing significantly less of a mood induction effect than younger adults for one measure and more of a mood induction effect for another two measures.

REFERENCES

Anderson, A. K., Christoff, K., Stappen, I., Panitz, D., Ghahremani, D. G., Glover, G., Gabrieli, J. D. E., & Sobel, N. (2003). Dissociated neural representations of intensity and valence in human olfaction. *Nature Neuroscience, 6,* 196–202.

Anderson, A. K. & Phelps, E. A. (2001). Lesions of the human amygdala impair enhanced perception of emotionally salient events. *Nature, 411,* 305–309.

Baddeley, A., Logie, R., Nimmosmith, I., & Brereton, N. (1985). Components of fluent reading. *Journal of Memory and Language, 24,* 119–131.

Bahrick, H. P., Hall, L. K., & Berger, S. A. (1996). Accuracy and distortion in memory for high school grades. *Psychological Science, 7,* 265–271.

Balota, D. A., Dolan, P. O., & Duchek, J. M. (2000). Memory changes in healthy older adults. In E. Tulving & F. I. M. Craik (Eds.), *Oxford handbook of memory* (pp. 395–410). Oxford: Oxford University Press.

Bargh, J. A., Gollwitzer, P. M., Lee-Chai, A., Barndollar, K., & Trotschel, R. (2001). The automated will: Nonconscious activation and pursuit of behavioral goals. *Journal of Personality and Social Psychology, 81*, 1014–1027.

Baumeister, R. F., Bratslavsky, E., Fickenauer, C., & Vohs, K. D. (2001). Bad is stronger than good. *Review of General Psychology, 5*, 323–370.

Bechara, A., Tranel, D., Damasio, H., Adolphs, R., Rockland, C., & Damasio, A. R. (1995). Double dissociation of conditioning and declarative knowledge relative to the amygdala and hippocampus in humans. *Science, 269*, 1115–1118.

Berntsen, D. (2001). Involuntary memories of emotional events: Do memories of traumas and extremely happy events differ? *Applied Cognitive Psychology, 15*, 135–158.

Berntsen, D. (2002). Tunnel memories for autobiographical events: Central details are remembered more frequently from shocking than from happy experiences. *Memory & Cognition, 30*, 1010–1020.

Berntsen, D. & Rubin, D. C. (2002). Emotionally charged autobiographical memories across the life span: The recall of happy, sad, traumatic, and involuntary memories. *Psychology and Aging, 17*, 636–652.

Blaney, P. H. (1986). Affect and memory: A review. *Psychological Bulletin, 99*, 229–246.

Bradley, M. M., Codispoti, M., Cuthbert, B. N., & Lang, P. J. (2001). Emotion and motivation I: Defensive and appetitive reactions in picture processing. *Emotion, 1*, 276–298.

Cacioppo, J. T., Berntsen, G. B., Klein, D. J., & Poehlmann, K. M. (1998). Psychophysiology of emotion across the life span. In K. W. Schaie & M. P. Lawton (Eds.), *Annual review of gerontology and geriatrics: Focus on emotion and adult development* (Vol. 17, pp. 27–74). New York: Springer.

Cahill, L., Haier, R. J., Fallon, J., Alkire, M. T., Tang, C., Keator, D., Wu, J., & McGaugh, J. L. (1996). Amygdala activity at encoding correlated with long-term, free recall of emotional information. *Proceedings of the National Academy of Sciences of the United States of America, 93*, 8016–8021.

Canli, T., Zhao, Z., Brewer, J. B., Gabrieli, J. D. E., & Cahill, L. (2000). Event-related activation in the human amygdala associates with later memory for individual emotional response. *Journal of Neuroscience, 20*, RC99.

Canli, T., Zhao, Z., Desmond, J. E., Glover, G. H., & Gabrieli, J. D. E. (1999). fMRI identifies a network of structures correlated with retention of positive and negative emotional memory. *Psychobiology, 27*, 441–452.

Carstensen, L. L. & Fredrickson, B. L. (1998). Influence of HIV status and age on cognitive representations of others. *Health Psychology, 17*, 494–503.

Carstensen, L. L., Isaacowitz, D. M., & Charles, S. T. (1999). Taking time seriously: A theory of socioemotional selectivity. *American Psychologist, 54*, 165–181.

Carstensen, L. L., Mikels, J. A., & Mather, M. (2005). Aging and the intersection of cognition, motivation and emotion. In J. E. Birren & K. W. Schaie (Eds.), *Handbook of the psychology of aging* (6th ed.). San Diego: Academic Press, 343–362.

Carstensen, L. L., Pasupathi, M., Mayr, U., & Nesselroade, J. R. (2000). Emotional experience in everyday life across the adult life span. *Journal of Personality and Social Psychology, 79*, 644–655.

Carstensen, L. L. & Turk-Charles, S. (1994). The salience of emotion across the adult life course. *Psychology and Aging, 9*, 259–264.

Charles, S. T., Mather, M., & Carstensen, L. L. (2003). Aging and emotional memory: The forgettable nature of negative images for older adults. *Journal of Experimental Psychology: General, 132,* 310–324.

Charles, S. T., Reynolds, C. A., & Gatz, M. (2001). Age-related differences and change in positive and negative affect over 23 years. *Journal of Personality and Social Psychology, 80,* 136–151.

Comblain, C., D'Argembeau, A., & Van der Linden, M. (2005). Phenomenal characteristics of autobiographical memories for emotional and neutral events in older and younger adults. *Experimental Aging Research, 31,* 173–189.

Comblain, C., D'Argembeau, A., Van der Linden, M., & Aldenhoff, L. (2004). Impact of ageing on the recollection of emotional and neutral pictures. *Memory, 12,* 673–684.

Craik, F. I. M. & Byrd, M. (1982). Aging and cognitive deficits: The role of attentional resources. In F. I. M. Craik & S. E. Treehub (Eds.), *Aging and cognitive processes* (pp. 191–211). New York: Plenum Press.

Cunningham, W. A., Raye, C. L., & Johnson, M. K. (in press). Implicit and explicit evaluation: fMRI correlates of valence, emotional intensity, and control in the processing of attitudes. *Journal of Cognitive Neuroscience.*

Denburg, N. L., Buchanan, D., Tranel, D., & Adolphs, R. (2003). Evidence for preserved emotional memory in normal elderly persons. *Emotion, 3,* 239–254.

Diehl, M., Coyle, N., & Labouvie-Vief, G. (1996). Age and sex differences in strategies of coping and defense across the life span. *Psychology and Aging, 11,* 127–139.

Eich, E. & Macaulay, D. (2000). Are real moods required to reveal mood-congruent and mood-dependent memory? *Psychological Science, 11,* 244–248.

Fan, J., McCandliss, B. D., Sommer, T., Raz, A., & Posner, M. I. (2002). Testing the efficiency and independence of attentional networks. *Journal of Cognitive Neuroscience, 14,* 340–347.

Field, D. (1981). Retrospective reports by healthy intelligent elderly people of personal events of their adult lives. *International Journal of Behavioral Development, 4,* 77–97.

Firbank, M. J., Lloyd, A. J., Ferrier, N., & O'Brien, J. T. (2004). A volumetric study of MRI signal hyperintensities in late-life depression. *American Journal of Geriatric Psychiatry, 12,* 606–612.

Fitzsimons, G. M. & Bargh, J. A. (2004). Automatic self-regulation. In R. F. Baumeister & K. D. Vohs (Eds.), *Handbook of self-regulation: Research, theory, and applications* (pp. 151–170). New York: Guilford Press.

Fleischman, D. A., Wilson, R. S., Gabrieli, J. D. E., Bienias, J. L., & Bennett, D. A. (2004). A longitudinal study of implicit and explicit memory in old persons. *Psychology and Aging, 19,* 617–625.

Fredrickson, B. L. & Carstensen, L. L. (1990). Choosing social partners: How old age and anticipated endings make people more selective. *Psychology and Aging, 5,* 335–347.

Fung, H. H., Carstensen, L. L., & Lutz, A. M. (1999). Influence of time on social preferences: Implications for life-span development. *Psychology and Aging, 14,* 595–604.

Fung, H. H., Lai, P., & Ng, R. (2001). Age differences in social preferences among Taiwanese and mainland Chinese: The role of perceived time. *Psychology and Aging, 16,* 351–356.

Greenwald, A. G. (1980). The totalitarian ego: Fabrication and revision of personal history. *American Psychologist*, *35*, 603–618.

Gross, J. J. (2001). Emotion regulation in adulthood: Timing is everything. *Current Directions in Psychological Science*, *10*, 214–219.

Gross, J. J., Carstensen, L. L., Pasupathi, M., Tsai, J., Skorpen, C. G., & Hsu, A. Y. C. (1997). Emotion and aging: Experience, expression, and control. *Psychology and Aging*, *12*, 590–599.

Gunning-Dixon, F. M., Gur, R. C., Perkins, A. C., Schroeder, L., Turner, T., Turetsky, B. I., et al. (2003). Age-related differences in brain activation during emotional face processing. *Neurobiology of Aging*, *24*, 285–295.

Hashtroudi, S., Johnson, M. K., & Chrosniak, L. D. (1990). Aging and qualitative characteristics of memories for perceived and imagined complex events. *Psychology and Aging*, *5*, 119–126.

Hedden, T. & Gabrieli, J. D. E. (2004). Insights into the ageing mind: A view from cognitive neuroscience. *Nature Reviews Neuroscience*, *5*, 87–U12.

Higgins, E. T. (1996). Knowledge activation: Accessibility, applicability, and salience. In E. T. Higgins & A. W. Kruglanksi (Eds.), *Social psychology: Handbook of basic principles* (pp. 133–168). New York: Guilford Press.

Iidaka, T., Okada, T., Murata, T., Omori, M., Kosaka, H., Sadato, N., & Yonekura, Y. (2002). Age-related differences in the medial temporal lobe responses to emotional faces as revealed by fMRI. *Hippocampus*, *12*, 352–362.

Jacoby, L. L. (2001). Proactive interference, accessibility bias, and process dissociations: Valid subjective reports of memory. *Journal of Experimental Psychology: Learning, Memory, and Cognition*, *27*, 686–700.

Jennings, J. M. & Jacoby, L. L. (1993). Automatic versus intentional uses of memory: Aging, attention, and control, *Psychology and Aging*, *8*, 283–293.

Johnson, M. K. & Raye, C. L. (2000). Cognitive and brain mechanisms of false memories and beliefs. In D. L. Schacter & E. Scarry (Eds.), *Memory, brain, and belief* (pp. 25–86). Cambridge, MA: Harvard University Press.

Johnson, M. K., Reeder, J. A., Raye, C. L., & Mitchell, K. J. (2002). Second thoughts versus second looks: An age-related deficit in reflectively refreshing just-activated information. *Psychological Science*, *13*, 64–67.

Joormann, J. & Siemer, M. (2004). Memory accessibility, mood regulation, and dysphoria: Difficulties in repairing sad mood with happy memories? *Journal of Abnormal Psychology*, *113*, 179–188.

Josephson, B. R., Singer, J. A., & Salovey, P. (1996). Mood regulation and memory: Repairing sad moods with happy memories. *Cognition & Emotion*, *10*, 437–444.

Kahneman, D. & Miller, D. T. (1986). Norm theory: Comparing reality to its alternatives. *Psychological Review*, *93*, 136–153.

Kales, H. C., Maixner, D. F., & Mellow, A. M. (2005). Cerebrovascular disease and late-life depression. *American Journal of Geriatric Psychiatry*, *13*, 88–98.

Kennedy, Q., Mather, M., & Carstensen, L. L. (2004). The role of motivation in the age-related positivity effect in autobiographical memory. *Psychological Science*, *15*, 208–214.

Kensinger, E. A. (2004). Remembering emotional experiences: The contribution of valence and arousal. *Reviews in the Neurosciences*, *15*, 241–251.

Kensinger, E. A., Brierley, B., Medford, N., Growdon, J. H., & Corkin, S. (2002). Effects of normal aging and Alzheimer's disease on emotional memory. *Emotion, 2*, 118–134.

Kensinger, E. A. & Corkin, S. (2004). Two routes to emotional memory: Distinct neural processes for valence and arousal. *Proceedings of the National Academy of Sciences of the United States of America, 101*, 3310–3315.

Knight, B. G., Maines, M. L., & Robinson, G. S. (2002). The effects of sad mood on memory in older adults: A test of the mood congruence effect. *Psychology and Aging, 17*, 653–661.

Knight, M. & Mather, M. (in press). The affective neuroscience of aging and its implications for cognition. In T. Canli (Ed.), *The biological bases of personality and individual differences*. New York: Guilford Press.

Kunzmann, U., Kupperbusch, C. S., & Levenson, R. W. (2005). Behavioral inhibition and amplification during emotional arousal: A comparison of two age groups. *Psychology and Aging, 20*, 144–158.

Labouvie-Vief, G. & Medler, M. (2002). Affect optimization and affect complexity: Modes and styles of regulation in adulthood. *Psychology and Aging, 17*, 571–588.

Lang, P. J., Bradley, M. M., & Cuthbert, B. N. (Artist) (1995). *The international affective picture system (IAPS): Photographic slides.*

Lawton, M. P., Kleban, M. H., Rajagopal, D., & Dean, J. (1992). Dimensions of affective experience in three age groups. *Psychology and Aging, 7*, 171–184.

Leigland, L. A., Schulz, L. E., & Janowsky, J. S. (2004). Age related changes in emotional memory. *Neurobiology of Aging, 25*, 1117–1124.

Levenson, R. W., Carstensen, L. L., & Gottman, J. M. (1994). The influence of age and gender on affect, physiology, and their interrelations: A study of long-term marriages. *Journal of Personality and Social Psychology, 67*, 56–68.

Levenson, R. W., Friesen, W. V., Ekman, P., & Carstensen, L. L. (1991). Emotion, physiology, and expression in old age. *Psychology and Aging, 6*, 28–35.

Levine, L. J. & Bluck, S. (1997). Experienced and remembered emotional intensity in older adults. *Psychology and Aging, 12*, 514–523.

Levine, L. J. & Safer, M. A. (2000). Sources of bias in memory for emotions. *Current Directions in Psychological Science, 11*, 169–173.

McGaugh, J. L. (2000). Memory: A century of consolidation. *Science, 287*, 248–251.

MacLeod, C. M., Mathews, A., & Tata, P. (1986). Attentional bias in emotional disorders. *Journal of Abnormal Psychology, 95*, 15–20.

Mast, B. T., Yochim, B., MacNeill, S. E., & Lichtenberg, P. A. (2004). Risk factors for geriatric depression: The importance of executive functioning within the vascular depression hypothesis. *Journals of Gerontology Series A: Biological Sciences and Medical Sciences, 59*, 1290–1294.

Mather, M. (2004). Aging and emotional memory. In D. Reisberg & P. Hertel (Eds.), *Memory and emotion* (pp. 272–307). Oxford: Oxford University Press.

Mather, M., Canli, T., English, T., Whitfield, S. L., Wais, P., Ochsner, K. N., Gabrieli, J. D. E., & Carstensen, L. L. (2004). Amygdala responses to emotionally valenced stimuli in older and younger adults. *Psychological Science, 15*, 259–263.

Mather, M. & Carstensen, L. L. (2003). Aging and attentional biases for emotional faces. *Psychological Science, 14*, 409–415.

Mather, M. & Carstensen, L. L. (2004). *Aging and memory for health care decisions.* Unpublished manuscript.

Mather, M. & Johnson, M. K. (2000). Choice-supportive source monitoring: Do our decisions seem better to us as we age? *Psychology and Aging, 15*, 596–606.

Mather, M. & Knight, M. (2005). Goal-directed memory: The role of cognitive control in older adults' emotional memory. *Psychology and Aging, 20*, 554–570.

Mather, M. & Knight, M. R. (2006). Angry faces get noticed quickly: Threat detection is not impaired among older adults. *Journal of Gerontology: Psychological Sciences, 61*, 54–57.

Mather, M., Knight, M., & McCaffrey, M. (2005). The allure of the alignable: Younger and older adults' false memories of choice features. *Journal of Experimental Psychology: General, 134*, 38–51.

Mather, M., Shafir, E., & Johnson, M. K. (2000). Misremembrance of options past: Source monitoring and choice. *Psychological Science, 11*, 132–138.

Mather, M., Shafir, E., & Johnson, M. K. (2003). Remembering chosen and assigned options. *Memory & Cognition, 31*, 422–434.

Matlin, M. W. & Stang, D. J. (1978). *The Pollyanna principle.* Cambridge, MA: Schenkman.

Muraven, M., Tice, D. M., & Baumeister, R. F. (1998). Self-control as limited resource: Regulatory depletion patterns. *Journal of Personality and Social Psychology, 74*, 774–789.

Ochsner, K. N. & Gross, J. J. (2004). Thinking makes it so: A social cognitive neuroscience approach to emotion regulation. In R. F. Baumeister & K. D. Vohs (Eds.), *Handbook of self-regulation: Research, theory, and applications* (pp. 229–255). New York: Guilford Press.

Ochsner, K. N., Ray, R. D., Cooper, J. C., Robertson, E. R., Chopra, S., Gabrieli, J. D. E., & Gross, J. (2004). For better or for worse: Neural systems supporting the cognitive down- and up-regulation of negative emotion. *Neuroimage, 23*, 483–499.

Öhman, A. (2002). Automaticity and the amygdala: Nonconscious responses to emotional faces. *Current Directions in Psychological Science, 11*, 62–66.

Öhman, A., Flykt, A., & Esteves, F. (2001). Emotion drives attention: Detecting the snake in the grass. *Journal of Experimental Psychology: General, 130*, 466–478.

Park, D. C. & Gutchess, A. H. (2005). Long-term memory and aging: A cognitive neuroscience perspective. In R. Cabeza, L. Nyberg, & D. Park (Eds.), *Cognitive neuroscience of aging: Linking cognitive and cerebral aging* (pp. 218–245). Oxford: Oxford University Press.

Phan, K. L., Wager, T., Taylor, S. F., & Liberzon, I. (2002). Functional neuroanatomy of emotion: A meta-analysis of emotion activation studies in PET and fMRI. *NeuroImage, 16*, 331–348.

Phelps, E. A. (2004). Human emotion and memory: Interactions of the amygdala and hippocampal complex. *Current Opinion in Neurobiology, 14*, 198–202.

Phelps, E. A., LaBar, K. S., Anderson, A. K., O'Connor, K. J., Fulbright, R. K., & Spencer, D. D. (1998). Specifying the contributions of the human amygdala to emotional memory: A case study. *Neurocase, 4*, 527–540.

Rahhal, T., May, C. P., & Hasher, L. (2002). Truth and character: Sources that older adults can remember. *Psychological Science, 13*, 101–105.

Revelle, W. & Loftus, D. A. (1992). The implications of arousal effects for the study of affect and memory. In S.-Å. Christianson (Ed.), *The handbook of emotion and memory: Research and theory* (pp. 113–149). Hillsdale, NJ: Erlbaum.

Ross, M. & Wilson, A. E. (2000). Constructing and appraising past selves. In D. L. Schacter & E. Scarry (Eds.), *Memory, brain, and belief* (pp. 231–258). Cambridge, MA: Harvard University Press.

Ross, M. & Wilson, A. E. (2003). Autobiographical memory and conceptions of self: Getting better all the time. *Current Directions in Psychological Science, 12,* 66–69.

Rozin, P. & Royzman, E. B. (2001). Negativity bias, negativity dominance, and contagion. *Personality and Social Psychology Review, 5,* 296–320.

Sanitioso, R., Kunda, Z., & Fong, G. T. (1990). Motivated recruitment of autobiographical memories. *Journal of Personality and Social Psychology, 59,* 229–241.

Sharot, T. & Phelps, E. A. (2004). How arousal modulates memory: Disentangling the effects of attention and retention. *Cognitive, Affective, & Behavioral Neuroscience, 4,* 294–306.

Stuss, D. T., Alexander, M. P., & Benson, D. F. (1997). Frontal lobe functions. In M. R. Trimble & J. L. Cummings (Eds.), *Contemporary behavioral neurology: Blue books of practical neurology* (Vol. 16, pp. 169–187). Woburn, MA: Butterworth–Heinemann.

Taylor, S. E. (1991). Asymmetrical effects of positive and negative events: The mobilization-minimization hypothesis. *Psychological Bulletin, 110,* 67–85.

Thomas, A. J., Ferrier, I. N., Kalaria, R. N., Davis, S., & O'Brien, J. T. (2002). Cell adhesion molecule expression in the dorsolateral prefrontal cortex and anterior cingulite cortex in major depression in the elderly. *British Journal of Psychiatry, 181,* 129–134.

Tsai, J. L., Levenson, R. W., & Carstensen, L. L. (2000). Autonomic, subjective, and expressive responses to emotional films in older and younger Chinese Americans and European Americans. *Psychology and Aging, 15,* 684–693.

Wagenaar, W. A. & Groeneweg, J. (1990). The memory of concentration camp survivors. *Applied Cognitive Psychology, 4,* 77–87.

Walker, W. R., Skowronski, J. J., Gibbons, J. A., Vogl, R. J., & Thompson, C. P. (2003). On the emotions that accompany autobiographical memories: Dysphoria disrupts the fading affect bias. *Cognition & Emotion, 17,* 703–723.

Walker, W. R., Skowronski, J. J., & Thompson, C. P. (2003). Life is pleasant – and memory helps to keep it that way! *Review of General Psychology, 7,* 203–210.

Wegner, D. M. (1994). Ironic processes of mental control. *Psychological Review, 101,* 34–52.

Wegner, D. M., Erber, R., & Zanakos, S. (1993). Ironic processes in the mental control of mood and mood-related thought. *Journal of Personality and Social Psychology, 65,* 1093–1104.

Yarrow, M. R., Campbell, J. D., & Burton, R. V. (1970). Recollections of childhood: A study of the retrospective method. *Monographs of the Society for Research in Child Development, 35,* 1–83.

Zacks, R. T., Hasher, L., & Li, K. Z. H. (2000). Human memory. In F. I. M. Craik & T. A. Salthouse (Eds.), *The handbook of aging and cognition* (pp. 293–357). Mahwah, NJ: Erlbaum.

8

Age-Related Changes in the Encoding and Retrieval of Emotional and Non-Emotional Information

Bob Uttl and Peter Graf

Abstract

According to theoretical claims, memory for emotional events and experiences seems to show either no decline or even improvements with age. This chapter presents a meta-analysis and critical review of previous research on age-related changes in memory for emotional events and experiences. The review highlights a number of serious methodological problems that limit interpretation of the results from previous investigations. Next, the chapter reports a new study on age-related changes in the encoding and retrieval of emotional versus non-emotional information. The results provide strong evidence that memory for emotional information shows no age declines, at least under some circumstances. Moreover, the findings reveal that the presence or absence of age declines occurs at the time of memory encoding rather than during retrieval.

According to popular belief, declines in memory are an inevitable consequence of aging. This belief is universally accepted, propagated, and buttressed by a large body of scientific research showing that when assessed by means of standardized tests, older adults remember fewer words, pictures, or designs than younger adults. The textbook explanation for this decline is discouraging and blames it on brain changes that are an inevitable consequence of physical aging. However, a comprehensive reading of the relevant literature paints a different and more encouraging picture. It reveals that while some aspects of memory inevitably decline with aging, other aspects show no evidence of decline and some show improvements well into late adulthood.

Research on memory for emotional events and experiences seems to show the latter pattern – either no decline or even improvements with age – and this finding has sparked unique theoretical claims about age-related changes in memory for emotional versus non-emotional information (Carstensen, 1995; Carstensen & Turk-Charles, 1994; Labouvie-Vief, DeVoe, & Bulka, 1989). Our main goal in this chapter is to examine this claim, and to explore the empirical support that has been advanced in its support.

The chapter is divided into three main sections. The first section is a brief review of mainstream memory research for non-emotional, neutral materials, showing age-related declines under some testing conditions, together with no declines or even improvements under other testing conditions. We also briefly review the theoretical accounts that have been offered for this pattern of age effects. The second section critically reviews previous research on age-related changes in memory for emotional events and experiences. Our review highlights a number of serious methodological problems that limit interpretation of the results from previous investigations. More important, we argue that if we discount the results from studies with methodological problems, the remaining evidence gives a less compelling portrait about the uniqueness of memory for emotional events and experiences. In the third and final section of the chapter, we report a new study on age-related changes in the encoding and retrieval of emotional versus non-emotional information. The results provide strong evidence that memory for emotional information shows no age declines, at least under some circumstances. The results also show that the presence/absence of age declines occurs at the time of memory encoding rather than during retrieval, a finding that needs to be accommodated by comprehensive theoretical accounts of age declines in memory.

 AGE-RELATED CHANGES IN MEMORY FOR NON-EMOTIONAL INFORMATION

Basic findings

According to a widespread stereotype, aging is the time of memory decline, but a more careful summary of the evidence reveals that different aspects of memory show different trajectories across the adult lifespan. The stereotype applies to performance on explicit episodic memory tasks, such as free recall and cued recall; on these tests, performance shows substantial age-related declines. By contrast, on implicit memory tests such as word completion, word identification, and picture identification, performance shows no decline or only a minimal decline with age, and on semantic memory tasks, such as word meaning identification and word pronunciation tests, performance even shows some gains (Graf & Ohta, 2002). Another important albeit less researched high-level cognitive function, prospective memory – the ability to bring back to awareness previously formed plans and intentions at the right place and time (Graf

& Uttl, 2001) – also shows substantial declines with age when it is assessed under standard laboratory conditions (Uttl, 2005a).

Figure 8.1 shows the typical adult lifespan trajectories for performance on explicit episodic memory tests, implicit episodic memory tests, semantic memory tests, and episodic prospective memory tests. The results in figure 8.1a come from 351 adults between 18–91 years of age who completed the delayed free recall trial test of a modified version of the Rey Auditory Verbal Learning test (Spreen & Strauss, 1991; see Uttl, 2005b, for modified version). The figure also shows old/new recognition test performance by the same subject group (M-RAVLT; Uttl, 2005b, 2005c), as well as cued recall test performance on a 15-item verbal paired associate test (Uttl, Graf, & Richter, 2002). The figure underscores the substantial age-related declines on all three types of tests, with declines ranging from 1.2 to 1.5 standard deviation units.

Figure 8.1b shows performance by the same 351 adults (Uttl, 2002) on two indexes of semantic memory, the North American Adult Reading Test (Blair & Spreen, 1989; Spreen & Strauss, 1991) and the WAIS-R Vocabulary test (Wechsler, 1987). In contrast to the age declines on measures of explicit episodic memory, both indexes of semantic memory reveal age-related gains ranging from 0.2 to 0.6 standard deviation units.

Figure 8.1c shows performance on two classical indexes of implicit memory: picture naming and word stem completion. The results, obtained from Mitchell and Bruss (2003), show no age-related decline on the picture naming test and only a small age-related decline on the word stem completion test (−0.2 standard deviation units).

Figure 8.1d shows the size of age effects reported in several published studies that compared the performance of younger and older adults on various indexes of event-cued prospective memory in the laboratory. For this figure, age effects were computed with respect to the performance of the older adults. The figure demonstrates that, contrary to the frequent claim of no age declines on prospective memory tasks (e.g., Einstein & McDaniel, 1990; Cherry & LeCompte, 1999; McDaniel et al., 2003), such age declines are large, although they are sometimes missed because of severe performance ceiling effects (Uttl, 2005a, 2005b, in press).

Theoretical views

Global slowing: Age-declines in the speed of executing mental operations

One universal finding in cognitive aging research is that aging lowers performance on a variety of tasks such as finger tapping tests, reaction time tests, simple

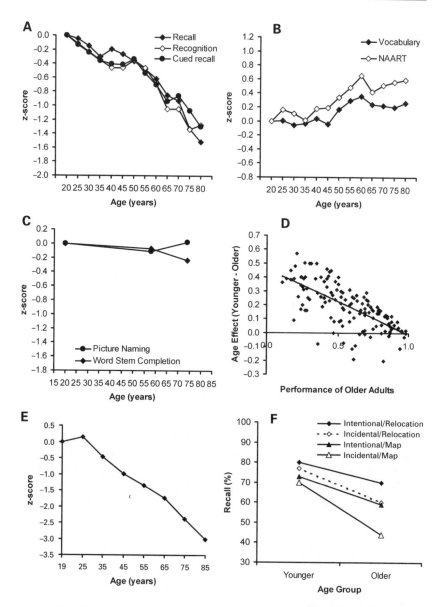

Figure 8.1 Figure 8.1a shows performance of 351 adults from 18–91 years of age on three tests of explicit memory: free recall, old/new recognition, and cued recall (see Uttl, Graf, & Richter, 2002); figure 8.1b shows performance of the same 351 adults on two indexes of word knowledge/semantic memory: North American Adult Reading Test and WAIS-R Vocabulary test (see Uttl, 2002); figure 8.1c shows performance on two classical indexes of implicit memory – picture naming and word stem completion – obtained by Mitchel and Bruss

decision-making tests, and digits symbol copying tests (Uttl, Graf, & Cosentino, 2000; see figure 8.1e). Moreover, an examination of the relationships between age declines on these indexes of processing speed and age declines on indexes of memory and other higher-order cognitive tasks reveals that a substantial portion of age declines in explicit episodic memory performance can be accounted for by age declines in processing speed (Salthouse, Kausler, & Saults, 1988). Collectively, these findings have been used to argue that age declines on explicit episodic memory and other high-level cognitive tasks are due to the age-related slowing of mental operations (i.e., global slowing; Cerella, 1985; Cerella, Poon, & Williams, 1980; Salthouse, 1985, 1988, 1991). In turn, age declines in the speed of executing mental operations have been attributed to age-related declines in the underlying hardware, in the brain, perhaps caused by decreases in neural connectivity, the attrition of neurons, or neural conductivity (Grady & Craik, 2000; Lindenberger & Baltes, 1994; Baltes & Lindenberger, 1997). To capture these various possibilities, Salthouse has proposed that age-related declines in high-level cognition are due to global slowing; he suggested that "the central nervous system is functioning at a slower rate in older adults, [and consequently] mental operation time may be the principle mechanism behind age differences in nearly all aspects of cognitive functioning" (Salthouse, 1980, p. 61).

Age declines in self-initiated processing

To explain differences in the magnitude of age declines across a broad range of memory tasks (see figure 8.1), Craik (1983, 1986) suggested that all memory tests can be arranged on a continuum according to the degree to which they provide environmental support (e.g., cues, encoding instructions) with tasks providing little or no environmental support requiring the greatest amount of subject-initiated processing. Implicit memory tests are located at the end of the continuum where environmental support is at a maximum, whereas free recall tests and laboratory-based prospective memory tests are located at the other end where performance is assumed to make extensive demands on

(2003); figure 8.1d shows the size of age effect plotted against performance of older adults in published studies comparing younger and older adults on various indexes of event-cued prospective memory – the figure shows that age declines on ProM tasks are large, limited only by the severity of ceiling effects (see Uttl, 2005a, 2005b); figure 8.1e shows performance of 351 adults from 18–91 years of age on WAIS-R Digit Symbol test, a frequently used index of processing speed (see Uttl, Graf, & Richter, 2002); and figure 8.1f shows performance of young and older adults on a map vs. relocation spatial memory test under incidental vs. intentional encoding instructions (Uttl & Graf, 1993).

self-initiated processing. By this view, augmented by the assumption that aging results in a reduction of processing resources (e.g., attentional resources, processing speed), memory tasks that offer little or no environmental support are expected to show the largest age-related declines in performance. Craik's environmental support view has received a wealth of empirical support. To illustrate, in one of our studies (Uttl & Graf, 1993) we found that age declines were reduced on a spatial memory test that required participants to place to-be-remembered objects in their study location when they were asked to perform this test in the physical context of a real office rather than in the abstract context of an outline map of the same office.

Age declines in sensory functions

A number of recent investigations have revealed substantial age-related declines in sensory and perceptual processes (e.g., visual acuity, auditory acuity), and they have been used to argue that age-related declines in performance on a variety of high-level cognitive tasks may be the result of age-related declines in sensory functions (Anstey, Stankov, & Lord, 1993; Baltes & Lindenberger, 1997; Lindenberger & Baltes, 1994; Pichora-Fuller, Schneider, & Daneman, 1995; Salthouse et al., 1996; Schneider & Pichora-Fuller, 2000). According to this view, age declines in sensory functions lead to impoverished or inaccurate representations of stimuli. In turn, in order to use these impoverished representations in connection with another task (i.e., a later memory test), more top-down processing is required, thereby further drawing on already limited processing resources, and resulting in the degradation of other resource-demanding cognitive activities. In Craik's (1983) terms, age declines in sensory functions reduce the availability of environmental support, thus increasing the demand for self-initiated processing. However, it is also possible that declines in both cognitive and sensory functions may be caused by a third factor, for example, by widespread neural degeneration, by decrements in the vascular system, or by a loss of temporal synchrony (Lindenberger & Baltes, 1994; Salthouse et al., 1996).

Age declines in encoding

Consistent with the general claim that aging is accompanied by declines in effective sensory/perceptual processing, several lines of evidence suggest that age declines on explicit episodic memory tests arise from older adults' failure to encode to-be-remembered (TBR) information rather than from their failure to remember encoded events. First, a number of studies have revealed that older adults are less likely to engage in deep, elaborative processing of TBR information when left to their own devices (Hultsch, 1969; Bäckman, 1986).

To illustrate, Uttl and Graf (1993) found that age declines on both the relocation and the map test were reduced under intentional versus incidental
encoding conditions. While participants in both conditions were informed that
their memory (in general) would be tested later, only the participants in the
intentional condition were given the specifics and told about the importance
of encoding the *spatial* locations: "as a secretary, you need to remember where
you put things so that you can find them again. When you are finished, I will
ask you about the spatial location of all the objects that you used." In contrast, the participants in the incidental condition performed the scripted
secretarial task without knowing what specifically they would be asked about
on the later test.

Second, additional evidence that favors an encoding-deficit view of age effects
comes from studies showing that, on explicit memory tests, dividing attention
at encoding rather than retrieval results in larger performance decreases; dividing attention at the time of retrieval seems to have minimal or no cost on performance (Baddeley et al., 1984; Craik et al., 1996; Naveh-Benjamin et al., 2005).
This larger cost due to dividing attention at encoding versus retrieval has been
observed with both younger and older adults (e.g., Macht & Buschke, 1983;
Park et al., 1989). The results of some studies show larger divided-attention
costs for older than younger adults, but the specific conditions that produce
this pattern of effects are not yet clear (Park, Puglisi, & Smith, 1986; Naveh-
Benjamin et al., 2005).

Third, Baltes (1987) put forward a meta-theoretical view of lifespan development, highlighting the multidimensionality and multidirectionality of development as well as the co-occurrence of growth (gains) and declines (losses) at
any and all stages of development. Multidimensionality and multidirectionality are illustrated by figures 8.1a and 8.1b. Whereas performance on explicit
episodic memory tests, indexes of fluid intelligence, declines across the adult
lifespan, performance on semantic memory/word knowledge tests or indexes
of crystallized intelligence increases across the adult lifespan. Baltes' view con-
ceptualizes lifespan development as an interplay between losses and gains, even
if losses become increasingly more dominant in old age. Drawing on this meta-
theoretical view, Baltes and Baltes (1990) put forward a theory known as Selective
Optimization with Compensation (SOC). The view highlights that individuals'
resources and goals change over the lifespan and these changes necessitate
changes in the allocation of resources to maintain effective functioning in the
areas selected by each individual. In summary, the lifespan orientation view
contradicts the notion that aging is accompanied by a unidirectional global
decline until death.

Fourth, starting from the lifespan orientation view, a number of researchers
and theorists have suggested that aging brings about increased emotional

maturation and a shift from a focus on information seeking and knowledge acquisition that characterizes younger adults to a focus on emotional satisfaction and on the meaning of life events (Labouvie-Vief, DeVoe, & Bulka, 1989; Carstensen, 1995). It has been suggested that one driving force behind this reprioritization of goals is the perception of a limited future due to one's mortality (e.g., Carstensen, 1995). Concretely, Carstensen (1995) argues that the perception of a limited future causes older adults to focus more on immediate rather than distant goals, and thus, older adults are more concerned with regulating their immediate emotional states, whereas younger adults are more concerned with the acquisition of information and future goals. She posits that older adults may focus on and remember more of the emotional aspects of encountered events rather than on their information value, and that in order to maintain positive affect, older adults focus more on positive rather than negative aspects of emotional events (see also Mather, this volume).

Section summary

Whereas some aspects of memory decline across the lifespan, some show no changes, and some show age-related gains. Moreover, several lines of evidence suggest that age declines observed on explicit memory tests used in typical laboratory investigations arise, at least in part, from older adults' inferior encoding of to-be-remembered materials. A lifespan perspective that emphasizes the multidimensionality and multidirectionality of adult development suggests that age declines on explicit memory tests need not be universal but, due to developmental changes in such factors as personal goals, interests, motivation, and context, may vary across individuals and his or her particular developmental context. Thus, aging may be accompanied by pronounced declines in memory for information that is not of interest to a particular individual within a particular developmental context, while also resulting in memory increases for other information that is more important and interesting. Several authors have suggested that older adults may be more interested in focusing their attention on emotional aspects as well as on the interpretation or meaning of to-be-remembered events, whereas younger adults may be more interested in processing primarily objective information such as the presence of objects, their attributes, numbers, and logical relations. If so, one may see smaller age-related declines or even increases in memory for emotional information. Moreover, according to some suggestions in the literature, older adults focus on maintaining positive affect (e.g., see Mather, this volume), and if so, they may be more likely to focus on positive emotional information and ignore or forget negative emotional information.

AGE-RELATED CHANGES IN MEMORY FOR EMOTIONAL INFORMATION

Does memory for emotional information decline with age or is it somehow special, not changing or even increasing with age? Are older adults more likely to remember emotional aspects of previously encountered events and materials than younger adults? Are younger adults more focused on negative rather than positive information? Are older adults more focused on positive rather than negative information? Figure 8.2 illustrates a hypothetical experiment on age-related differences in memory for non-emotional (neutral) and emotional (negative and positive) information. First, consistent with prior research, the figure shows the expected age declines for neutral, non-emotional information. Second, the figure also illustrates age declines for both negative and positive information. Third, the figure illustrates the possibility that younger adults enjoy an overall advantage for emotional information (i.e., they recall a greater proportion of both negative and positive information) relative to neutral information, and they also show a *negative bias*, that is, they recall a greater proportion of negative than positive information (i.e., negative minus positive recall is +.15). In contrast, older adults show overall no advantage for emotional information, but they demonstrate

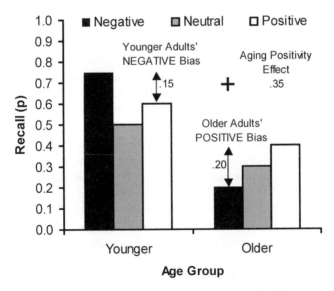

Figure 8.2 Hypothetical experimental results of age-related differences in memory for non-emotional (neutral) and emotional (negative and positive) information.

a *positive bias* (i.e., positive minus negative is +.20). Fourth, corresponding to an ANOVA interaction effect, the data in figure 8.2 reveal an overall +.35 *aging positivity effect* (i.e., younger adults' negative bias plus older adults' positive bias). Using these terms, we will first review prior research and then discuss several methodological issues arising from prior studies.

Review of prior research

In one of the first studies frequently cited as showing that memory for emotional information does not decline with age, Hastroudi, Johnson, and Chrosniak (1990) asked younger and older adults either to perform scripted activities (e.g., packing a picnic basket) or to imagine performing the same activities. One day later and without any prior warning, participants were given the names of each activity and were asked to write everything they could remember about each of them. Participants' descriptions were scored for the occurrence of ideas, colors, objects, non-visual sensory information, spatial references, people, actions, thoughts, and feelings, as well as for making various kinds of evaluative statements. The results showed that compared to younger adults, older adults recalled fewer colors, objects, and references to non-visual sensory information, but they recalled a greater number of thoughts, feelings, and evaluative statements. There was no age difference in the recall of people or of ideas. The authors concluded that "on the recall test, older subjects produced more thoughts and feelings than did younger subjects, whereas younger subjects produced more perceptual and spatial information" (p. 119).

Although this study is often cited as evidence that memory for emotional information does not decline with age (e.g., Carstensen & Turk-Charles, 1994; D'Argembeau & Van der Linden, 2004; Mather, 2004), the results do not justify this conclusion. The main reason for this contrary position is the presence of severe floor effects in performance, which are illustrated in figure 8.3. On most of the items assessed in the Hastroudi, Johnson, and Chrosniak study, the mean scores were within one standard deviation unit of zero, thus unambiguously confounded by performance floor effects (Uttl, 2005b). Most likely, performance on the emotion items did not decline with age because it was already about as low as it could go. This conclusion is not changed by the ANOVA results reported in Hashtroudi et al. (1990); the application of ANOVA with such data is unwarranted and is likely to reveal spuriously significant effects. Moreover, as noted by Hastroudi, Johnson, and Chrosniak (1990), it is also possible that their older participants were not *remembering* thoughts, feelings, and evaluative statements at all, but were merely generating thought and feeling statements at the time of the recall test. Because the study lacked a measure of encoding, it is not possible to conclude that the slightly greater number of thoughts and feelings

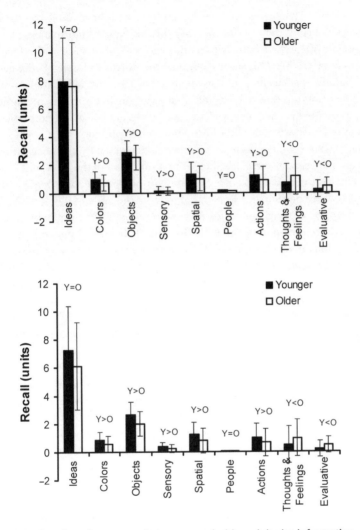

Figure 8.3 Recall performance of younger and older adults by information type and by encoding condition (perceived condition in top panel and imagined condition in bottom panel), in Hastroudi, Johnson, and Chrosniak's (1990) study. The figure highlights the presence of floor effects in most of the recall conditions. Bars represent common standard deviation derived from the published MSe terms and the markers $Y > O$, $Y = O$, and $Y < O$ denote results of statistical inference tests conducted by Hastroudi et al.

and evaluative statements provided by older versus younger adults on the recall test is evidence of their better memory for this type of information.

Another often-cited study with methodological problems was conducted by Adams et al. (1990). This study examined the story recall style of younger and older adults, specifically probing whether younger and older adults differ in the type of information recollected under various test instruction conditions. They presented participants with two narratives, a fable and a non-fable, and then tested memory under four instruction conditions: total recall – where participants were required to write as much as they could remember, summary – where participants were asked to write a summary of the fable, gist – where participants were asked to write only the gist of the fable, and finally gist plus moral – where participants were asked to write the gist and moral of the fable. Recall protocols were scored for text information, for information units that preserved the meaning of the fable, for knowledge-based integrations or the recall of units that were not directly tied to the text but were plausible inferences from it, and for interpretations or the recall of units that were consistent with but went beyond the text. The authors reported their results from the non-fable conditions as showing that older adults provided more integrative or interpretive units than younger adults and that young adults offered primarily text-based details. However, a close inspection of the data undermines this summary and any conclusion based on it. Statistical analysis of the data showed that the difference between the older and younger adults in the number of recalled integration units was only marginally significant. More important, any possible differences between older and younger adults were again obscured by floor effects; in this case, mean scores of zero in four of the eight critical conditions of the experiment. And finally, as was the case with the Hastroudi, Johnson, and Chrosniak (1990) study, the method used by Adams et al. provides no basis for ascertaining whether differences between younger and older adults should be attributed to encoding and/or retrieval phase processes.

Carstensen and Turk-Charles (1994) asked young, middle-aged, and older participants to read two prose passages selected from popular novels, each about 650 words long, and to "try to identify with one of the characters" in the text. Participants were informed that they would be asked questions about the story later. After several intervening tasks, participants were required to recall as much as they could remember about each passage and correctly recalled information was coded either as being emotional or neutral. The authors found no change across age groups in the total amount of information recalled, together with an age-related increase in recollection of emotional information. Specifically, they found that the proportion of the total recall that was emotional was 0.20 for the youngest subject group (20–29 years of age) versus 0.34 for the oldest (70–83 years) group. Unfortunately, the report does not include the actual (non-proportionalized) recall test data for neutral and emotional information, and thus, we cannot determine exactly what aspects of performance gave rise to the age-related increases in the proportion of recalled information that was emotional. In particular, it is not clear whether the proportional increase in the recall of information that was emotional reflects an actual age-related increase in memory for emotional information, or whether it is a consequence of an age-related decrease in the recollection of neutral information.

Our concerns about the interpretation of the proportional scores in Carstensen and Turk-Charles' study are fueled, in part, by the different conclusion that seems justified on the basis of the recall scores and the proportional scores published in Fung and Carstensen (2003). Fung and Carstensen presented younger and older adults with six advertisements: two ads which were accompanied by an emotional slogan (e.g., "Capture those special moments"), two ads that were accompanied by knowledge-related slogans (e.g., "Capture the unexplored world"), and two ads that were not accompanied by any slogan. After viewing the ads, participants were given a list of products, a list of slogans, and a list of brand names, and they were asked to match the slogans and brand names to the products. On this recognition memory test, the score for each condition could range from 0 to 2. The authors reported raw memory scores, but analyzed the data using "proportional scores," which were obtained "by dividing the number of correct recognition scores [i.e., raw memory score] for that version [of the ad] by the total number of correct recognition for all three versions, following the practice in prior studies" (e.g., Carstensen & Turk-Charles, 1994, p. 166). Unfortunately, the two kinds of scores lead to opposite conclusions about age-related changes in memory for emotional versus non-emotional information, as illustrated by Figure 8.4. The top panel of Figure 8.4 shows the proportional scores, the data used by Fung and Carstensen (2003) to claim that "older participants remembered a greater proportion of information from the emotionally meaningful version of advertisements" (p. 168). In contrast, the bottom panel of the figure shows the raw memory scores also reported on page 168 of Fung and Carstensen (2003); that is, it shows the data they used to compute the proportional scores in the top panel. Clearly, the bottom panel data show no age-related change in the recall of advertisements with knowledge-related slogans versus emotional slogans. For a number of different reasons (e.g., incomplete counterbalancing of materials across conditions and within individuals, inability to distinguish between encoding versus recall effects), we are not convinced by the proportional scores in Figure 8.4 and have serious reservations about their interpretation. The most important concern comes from the fact that transforming raw scores into proportion scores should have the same effect on two conditions with identical raw scores (for example, older adults' memory performance on the emotion- and knowledge-biased ads). Deviations from this expectation occur only under conditions where performance is confounded by either floor or ceiling effects or by other factors.

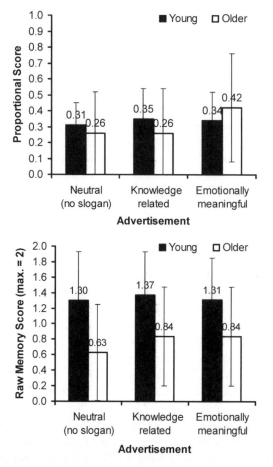

Figure 8.4 Performance of young and older adults in Fung and Carstensen's (2003) study. The top panel shows proportional scores and the bottom panel shows raw memory scores. Suprisingly, for the older adults the mean proportional scores are higher for emotionally meaningful vs. knowledge-related ads even though the mean raw memory scores are identical (see text for discussion of this issue).

Following in the footsteps of Hastroudi, Johnson, and Chrosniak (1990), Adams et al. (1990), and Carstensen and Turk-Charles (1994), a number of investigators examined memory for emotional words, pictures, faces, and prose in younger versus older adults using both negative and positive versions of to-be-remembered materials. The main parameters and the outcomes of these studies are summarized in Table 8.1. For each study, the table shows the nature of the to-be-remembered (TBR) materials that were used (e.g., words, pictures, faces), the number of TBR items in each emotional category, the type of memory test (e.g., free recall, old/new recognition), the size of the age decline for negative materials (i.e., performance of younger minus performance of older adults on negative items), the size of the age decline for positive materials (i.e., performance of younger minus performance of older adults on positive materials), the magnitude of young adults' negative bias (i.e., young adults' performance on negative items minus their performance on positive items), the magnitude of older adults' positive bias (i.e., older adults' performance on positive items minus their performance on negative items), and the size of the effect due to the age by material valence interaction, as well as the statistical significance of this interaction effect. In addition, the table also notes any special circumstances that might limit interpretation of each study's findings, including the presence of ceiling or floor effects (C&F), two study opportunities for older but not for younger adults (O2x), and other possible age-related confounds (e.g., younger adults scoring much higher on depression than older adults (YD)).

An examination of those columns in Table 8.1 that focus on age declines for negative information and age declines for positive information suggests that in contrast to the conclusions offered by Hastroudi, Johnson, and Chrosniak (1990), Adams et al. (1991), and Carstensen and Turk-Charles (1994), older adults' memory for emotional material declines with age. If anything, it appears that when age declines were not observed, the outcome was confounded (by design) with the number of study/learning opportunities provided to young and older adults. On the whole, the results summarized in Table 8.1 do not support the claim that younger adults remember negative information better than positive information (i.e., have a negative bias). Similarly, the data in Table 8.1 fail to support the notion that older adults remember positive information better than negative information (i.e., have a positive bias). The age by material valence interaction effects in the raw data also fail to support the notion of better memory for positive information in older than younger adults; the interaction raw effect came out positive (i.e., in support of older adults' positive bias relative to younger adults) only about half the time in both the recall and old/new recognition test data (i.e., if we disregard all non-interpretable outcomes).

Methodological issues

The preceding review of prior research reveals additional methodological issues that undermine the interpretation of the findings from many of the published studies. First, as already noted above, it is necessary to avoid floor and ceiling effects that automatically diminish any differences between emotional and non-emotional materials in the affected conditions that may lead to spurious

Table 8.1 Research on effects of emotional content in episodic explicit memory.

	Material Type	Number of Negative/Neutral/Positive Items	Memory Test[1]	Age Decline for Negative[2]	Age Decline for Positive[3]	Negative Bias of Young[4]	Positive Bias of Old[5]	Age × Valence Effect (raw)[6]	Found Age × Valence Interaction[7]	Notes[8]
Charles '03, Exp. 1[9]	Pictures	8/16/8	FR	-0.42	-0.15	0.01	0.26	0.27	Yes	
			Recog.	-0.10	-0.01	0.09	0.00	0.09	Yes	
Charles '03, Exp. 2	Pictures	26/26/26	FR	-0.24	-0.15	0.12	-0.03	0.09	Yes	
			Recog.	-0.10	-0.06	0.10	-0.06	0.04	Yes	
D'Argembeau '04	Faces	6/0/6	Recog.	-0.20	-0.24	-0.06	0.03	-0.04	No	
Denburg '03[10]	Pictures	5/5/5	FR/24 hrs	-0.48	-0.24	0.36	-0.12	[0.24]	No	F&C
			MC	-0.15	-0.07	0.04	0.03	0.07	No	
			FC	-0.17	-0.19	-0.13	0.11	-0.02	No	
			FR/LTR	-0.74	-0.56	0.15	0.03	[0.18]	No	F&C
			MC/LTR	-0.04	-0.02	0.01	0.01	[0.01]	No	F&C
			Recog.	-0.15	-0.10	0.00	0.02	[0.05]	No	F&C
Kensinger '02	Pictures	15/15/15	FR	[0.00]	[0.06]	0.06	0.00	0.06	No	O2x
	Words	9/9/9	FR	[0.00]	[-0.08]	-0.06	-0.02	-0.08	No	O2x
Kensinger '04	Story	1/0/1	FR	-0.11				0.00	No	C&F
	Story	1/0/1	FC	[0.00]				[0.00]	No	
	Story	1/0/1	FR	-0.08				0.02	No	
	Story	1/0/1	FC	-0.03				-0.04	No	
Knight '02[11]	Words	12/0/12	FR/Im.	[-0.05]	[0.04]	[0.00]	[0.09]	[0.09]	?	YD,NM
			FR/Del.	[-0.07]	[0.04]	[-0.06]	[0.17]	[0.11]	?	YD,NM
Leighland '04, Exp. 1	Story	21/25/3	FR	-0.06	0.00	N/A	N/A	N/A	No	
	Words	9/9/9	FR/1 min	-0.01	-0.04	-0.06	0.03	-0.03	No	
			FR/30 min	-0.03	0.00	-0.14	0.17	0.03	No	
			Recog.	0.01	0.02	0.00	0.01	0.01	No	

Leighland '04, Exp. 2	Faces	6/6/6	Recog.	−0.05	0.02	−0.08	0.15	0.07	No	
Mather '03, Exp. 1	Faces	10/10/10	Recog.	−0.14	−0.02	−0.01	0.13	0.12	Yes	
			Recog.	−0.12	−0.22	−0.11	0.01	−0.10	Yes	
Mather '03, Exp. 2	Faces	10/10/10	Recog.	−0.12	−0.17	−0.04	−0.01	−0.05	Yes	
			Recog.	−0.19	−0.10	−0.01	0.10	[0.09]	Yes	C&F

Notes

[ ] = Values in squared brackets are impossible to interpret (see Notes).

[1] FR = free recall test, FC = forced choice test, MC = multiple choice test, Recog. = old/new recognition test.

[2] Age decline for negative items = performance of old minus performance of young on negative items.

[3] Age decline for positive items = performance of old minus performance of young on positive items.

[4] Negative bias of young = performance on negative minus positive items for young.

[5] Positive bias of old = performance on positive minus negative items for old.

[6] Age × Valence Effect (raw) = (Young/Negative − Young/Positive) − (Old/Negative − Old/Positive), except for Kensinger '04 where performance on Neutral items was used instead of performance on Positive items.

[7] Reported Age × Valence interaction.

[8] NM = not a memory test because scores included both correct memory, intrusions, and errors; C&FD = ceiling or floor effects, O2x = older adults were given two study exposures whereas younger adults were not, YD = younger adults had substantially higher scores on CES-D than older adults and higher than normal (see Gatz & Hurwicz, 1990).

[9] Charles '03: Instructions in Charles '03 Experiment 1 asked participants "to write down a description of as many of the images as they could recall," but participants were also told that "a short description was sufficient and not to dwell on details." Subsequently, the coders were unable to match the descriptions to the images and the proportion of the descriptions not matched to the images increased with participants' age – it was larger for older (13 percent) than younger adults (2 percent). Moreover, in Experiment 1, half of the participants received the old/new recognition test first and half received the free recall test first. When old/new recognition was first, participants recalled many more items on the subsequent recall test. Although Charles '03 also included a middle-aged group of adults in Experiment 1, only young and old groups' performance is used here.

[10] Denburg '03: Free Recall 24 hour data reported in figure 4, p. 245, show recall scores ranging up to 8.8 items even though only 5 items were presented. For the purposes of this review, we assume that the scores reflect the sum of correctly recalled items across *two* raters although the method is not clear on this point. Although the study included a middle age group of adults, we use only young and old adults in this review.

[11] Knight '02: The review includes data for neutral mood conditions only.

interaction effects, and in general, make the interpretation of the data imposs-ible in all but rare circumstances (see Uttl, 2005b).

Second, the extant research reveals that emotion effects on memory are driven at least in part by arousal (e.g., see Reisberg, this volume). However, the stud-ies reviewed above typically did not collect arousal ratings from older versus younger adults (but see Denburg et al., 2003; Kensinger et al., 2002). Thus, the findings – negative as well as positive – could be due to differences in younger versus older adults' arousal evoked by negative versus positive materials in each particular study.

Third, Talmi and Moscovitch (2004) observed that emotional stimuli used in various investigations of emotional memory tend to be more interrelated than neutral stimuli. Because semantically related stimuli are easier to recall than unrelated stimuli (Mandler, 1967; Tulving & Perlstone, 1966), they argued that the recall advantage for emotional stimuli over neutral stimuli could be due to confounding semantic relatedness with stimulus emotionality. In a series of elegant experiments, Talmi and Moscovitch showed that the recall advant-age for emotional words disappeared when semantic relatedness was equated between emotional and neutral materials. However, none of the reviewed studies discussed or controlled the semantic relatedness of the emotional and non-emotional materials that were employed.

Fourth, a wealth of prior research shows a memory advantage for distinctive items, especially when they occur in the context of mixed lists, that is, lists consisting of many different kinds of items (McDaniel, DeLosh, & Merritt, 2000; Schmidt, 1991). Emotional items may be more distinctive in the context of mixed lists, and thus, the recall advantage for emotional versus neutral items may be due to their distinctiveness rather than their emotion value. Consistent with this reasoning, Dewhurst and Parry (2000) found an advantage of emo-tional words over neutral words in recognition memory test performance when participants studied mixed lists but not when they studied pure lists. Because all the studies listed in Table 8.1 used mixed lists, the previously reported mem-ory advantage of emotional items may be due to their distinctiveness rather than their emotionality.

Fifth, the data in Table 8.1 also show that whereas some studies used a relatively large number of items, other studies used only a few items in each emotional category. The findings from the later kind of study may not gen-eralize to other sets of materials.

Section summary

Memory for emotional information may not decline with aging under some circumstances. However, the weight of the evidence suggests that at least within the laboratory paradigms used for previous investigations, both recall and recognition test performance for emotional materials shows an age-related decline, and this decline seems to persist across the adult lifespan. The evidence summarized in Table 8.1 does not support the claim that younger adults preferentially tend to retain negative information whereas older adults preferentially tend to remember positive information. Any claims about a negativity bias in young adults and a positivity bias in older adults must be tempered by an awareness of the serious methodological flaws that undermine previous investigations.

Our selective review of previous research also suggests that to date, no study has directly examined age-related changes in the encoding of emotional versus non-emotional materials, as opposed to exploring whether such age effects occur during the retrieval phase. Consequently, the existing evidence does not provide a basis for claiming that older adults are more likely to remember positive information as opposed to non-emotional or neutral information, nor does it provide a basis for speculating about the cause of a positivity bias in old age.

We have recently embarked on an effort to furnish the kinds of findings required for claiming that old age is accompanied by a memory positivity bias. In the next section, we briefly describe a study that focused on age-related changes in both the encoding and the retrieval of emotional versus non-emotional materials. This study was conducted under conditions that are familiar to both younger and older adults and that allow participants to focus on the encoding of whatever information they deem to be important.

AGE-RELATED CHANGES IN THE ENCODING AND RETRIEVAL OF COMPLEX SCENES

We conducted a study that asked the following questions: Is the pattern of age declines different for emotional versus non-emotional information? To what extent are age differences in explicit episodic memory due to encoding versus retrieval processes? Does the intentional recollection of information about pictures reflect the same underlying processes as that required for standardized tests of memory such as the Rey Auditory Verbal Learning Test? Do age changes in basic resources, such as processing speed, processing capacity, and verbal intelligence, account for age differences in explicit memory retrieval for both emotional and non-emotional information?

To answer these questions, we recruited 162 healthy community-dwelling adults ranging from 16 to 83 years of age. For the study, we showed pictures of common, everyday scenes to the participants and asked them to describe each picture on two occasions, first while viewing the picture and then from memory. We recorded and later coded participants' descriptions of the pictures for the occurrence of various types of information. Consistent with Rundus (1973), we used participants' descriptions as an index of what they had focused on, and thus presumably processed and encoded into memory, and then later retrieved from memory. By this picture description method, we are able to examine participants' encoding as well as their retrieval of familiar materials under task conditions that are highly familiar and let participants choose on what aspects of materials to focus their attention.

Picture description method

Participants were presented with a series of six different 8.5 by 11 inch color pictures, each showing a common scene such as a picnic at a beach. Participants were required to describe aloud each picture while looking at it and then after a delay of either 15 or 60 minutes, they had to re-describe each picture from memory. All picture descriptions were recorded and later transcribed and scored for the occurrence of different types of information: the frequency of mentioning things (e.g., people, objects, or their attributes, such as color or size), actions (actions and passive states: "The couple are *having a conversation*, the man is *speaking.*"), emotional attributes and reactions (e.g., "The grandmother seems *content* although she isn't *smiling*"), and inferences (e.g., era attributes, analogies: "The lady in the library looks about *fiftyish*"). We computed separate scores for the encoding and retrieval phase of the study. In addition, we also computed match scores, that is, scores for information units that occurred in both the encoding and retrieval phase protocols. In turn, with the aid of the encoding phase, retrieval phase, and encoding-retrieval match scores, we calculated two derived scores, one for gains and one for losses. Losses refer to information units that were included in the encoding transcripts but not in the retrieval transcripts; they reflect the information that participants encoded but failed to recall during the retrieval. Gains refer to information units that were included in the retrieval transcripts but not in the encoding transcripts and they reflect the information that participants correctly remembered about the pictures but did not mention during the encoding phase.

Our target pictures were chosen to represent a broad range of topics, to appeal to participants from all age groups (young, middle, old), and to capture either social or asocial situations: one picture showed a friendly boat race (see Figure 8.5), one showed a couple in a living room, one showed two old women with a skein of wool, one showed a young woman in her bedroom, one show a middle-aged woman in a library, and the last one showed an old tractor driving down a village street.

Figure 8.5 An example of a photo used in our picture description study. Participants were shown this photo printed in color on standard 8.5 × 11 letter-sized paper.

Participants

The participants were 162 community dwelling adults between 16 and 83 years of age (19 16–29 years old, 23 30–39 years old, 29 40–49 years old, 30 50–59 years old, 29 60–69 years old, and 32 70–83 years old) who were recruited for the study through newspaper advertising and by word of mouth. They either volunteered (77 percent) or were paid for attending a single session that lasted about 2.5 hours. The participants were largely women and the majority had at least a few years of college or university education. All age groups rated themselves as being in good to excellent health and as having good to excellent corrected vision and hearing.

Procedure

Each participant was tested individually in a small office of a community center located in an upper-middle class neighborhood in the city of Vancouver,

British Columbia, Canada. At the beginning of each test session the experimenter outlined the main goals of the study and the sequence of tests involved, and participants could ask questions prior to giving their written consent.

Participants completed a long battery of cognitive and neuropsychological tests and experimental tasks, including picture descriptions during the encoding and retrieval phase. Following consent and completion of a demographic questionnaire, the battery included the following tasks in this order: North American Adult Reading Test (NAART; Spreen & Strauss, 1991), Rey Auditory Verbal Learning Test (RAVLT; Spreen & Strauss, 1991), Picture Descriptions/Encoding, 5–10 minute break, RAVLT Delayed Recall and Recognition, Picture Description/Retrieval (10-minute delay for half of the participants), A/B Card Sorting (Uttl, Graf, & Cosentino, 2000), Finger Tapping (Uttl, Graf, & Cosentino, 2000), Color-Word Stroop test (Uttl & Graf, 1997), Color Vision Screening Inventory (Coren & Hakstian, 1988), Hearing Screening Inventory (Coren & Hakstian, 1992), Simple Reaction (Uttl, Graf, & Cosentino, 2000), A/B Decisions (Uttl, Graf, & Cosentino, 2000), Optional break (max. 5 minutes), Picture Descriptions/Retrieval (60-minute delay for half of the participants), and Big Five Inventory (John & Srivastave, 1999), followed by several optional tests. Thus, the retrieval-phase picture descriptions were given either about 10 or 60 minutes after the encoding-phase. The two breaks were unfilled, spent quietly or in conversations, and participants were offered refreshments.

Encoding and retrieval of emotional vs. non-emotional information

The left column of Figure 8.6 shows the encoding, retrieval, and match scores by age groups for things and actions (i.e., non-emotional information, top row), for inferences (middle row), and for emotional reactions (i.e., emotional information, bottom row). The right column shows loss and gain scores by age group for non-emotional information, inferences, and emotional information. For non-emotional information, retrieval, encoding and match scores all show substantial age-related declines. Moreover, age-related declines in memory for non-emotional information are also highlighted by an age-related increase in losses but not in gains. For inferences, encoding, retrieval, and match scores reveal much smaller age declines and no age-related changes in losses or gains. In contrast, for emotional information, encoding, retrieval, and match scores reveal small but statistically insignificant gains over the adult lifespan and no overall age changes in losses or gains (although losses show a statistically significant curvilinear pattern with higher losses for the youngest and oldest adults).

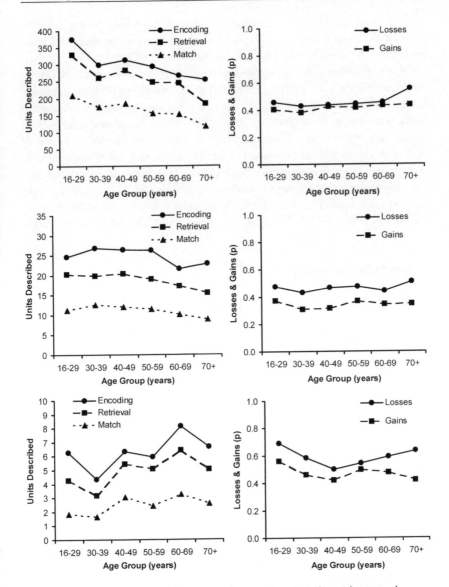

Figure 8.6 The left column shows encoding, retrieval, and match scores by age group for things and actions (i.e., non-emotional information, top row), for inferences (middle row), and for emotional reactions (i.e., emotional information, bottom row). The right column shows loss and gain scores by age group for non-emotional information, inferences, and emotional information.

Correlational analyses revealed that encoding and retrieval were highly correlated for things and actions (r = .82), inferences (r = .86), and emotional information (r = .78), highlighting that for all three kinds of information the best predictor of performance at retrieval was performance at encoding. Correlational analyses also showed that retrieval scores correlated with performance on a psychometric test of explicit episodic memory for non-emotional information, less so for inferences, and minimally for emotional information. Specifically, correlations between retrieval scores and the first three trials of Rey Auditory Verbal Learning test were .50, .35, and .07. Consistent with prior research, correlations between various measures of processing speed and retrieval scores for non-emotional information were also moderately high: .44 for Digit Symbol (Wechsler, 1987), .36 for A/B Card Sorting (Uttl, Graf, & Cosentino, 2000) and .36 for Simple Reactions (Uttl, Graf, & Cosentino, 2000).

Section summary

In combination, the findings from the present study allow several important conclusions. First, age-related declines on explicit episodic memory tests are not universal but depend on the type of to-be-remembered information. They are large for non-emotional information, smaller for inferences, and non-existent for emotional information. Second, age-related declines in retrieval are indirect, mediated by age-related declines in encoding; the age-related pattern of performance on explicit episodic memory tests is almost completely determined by the age-related pattern of performance at encoding. Third, relative to encoding, age-related increases in losses are explained by only a small or no portion of age-related declines in retrieval scores. Fourth, consistent with prior research with psychometric measures of explicit memory, various indexes of processing resources explain a substantial portion of age-related declines in retrieval scores for non-emotional information and inferences (when encoding scores are ignored) but, due to no age declines, they are uninformative in explaining retrieval of scores for emotional information.

■ CONCLUSIONS

This chapter was motivated by the interesting and provocative theoretical claim that aging is accompanied by a shift in memory for emotional or affectively valenced information versus neutral information, and, more concretely, by the possibility that young adults are future-oriented and focused on knowledge acquisition, whereas older adults are present-oriented and relatively more concerned with satisfying their immediate social and emotional needs (Carstensen, 1995;

Carstensen & Turk-Charles, 1994; Labouvie-Vief, DeVoe, & Bulka, 1989). Our goal was to lay out the pattern of data that would be consistent with this theoretical stance. In order to determine whether these theoretically predicted data patterns are unique, thus constituting indisputable evidence in support of an age-related bias toward emotional information, we briefly reviewed research on age-related changes in memory for neutral information. This review showed that the predicted pattern of data is not unique to memory for emotional information, that the same pattern has also been demonstrated in memory for neutral information. Thus, in the absence of corollary evidence or assumptions, we question the need for new theoretical accounts for age-related changes in memory for emotional information. At the very least, in keeping with the principle of parsimony, we recommend that future investigations on age-related changes in memory for emotional information focus on the contrasting predictions derived for general theories about age-related changes in memory versus specific theoretical claims about late life changes in processing emotional events and experiences.

A secondary aim of our chapter was to review critically the existing research on age-related changes in memory for emotional versus neutral information. Our review revealed a number of factors, including methodological and data problems, that undermine the empirical foundation for the general theoretical claim that aging is accompanied by a shift in favor of processing relatively more of the positive emotional aspects of events and experiences. We are impressed by the clever methods researchers have devised to explore this claim, but we are not convinced by the existing evidence.

In the final section of the chapter we report a recent study on age-related changes in the processing of different kinds of information (e.g., neutral, interpretive, emotional), focusing especially on whether such differences, if they exist, occur during the encoding or retrieval phase of a memory experiment. The results from the encoding phase of the study were the more interesting; they showed clear age-related changes for some kinds of information but not for other kinds. Correlation analyses showed that performance in the encoding phase predicted most of the age-related changes that appeared in the recall phase data. This latter finding is important by focusing attention on age-related changes in perception, on the manner in which information is sampled or selected from the environment, rather than on age-related changes in memory retrieval processes. This focus on perception seems broadly consistent with Carstensen's (1995; Carstensen, Isaacowitz, & Charles, 1999) socioemotional selectivity theory. It is also consistent with recent theoretical claims about age-related changes in memory for neutral information (theories that attribute age effects to encoding-related processes). We believe that a marriage of these theoretical efforts may be optimal for advancing understanding of age-related changes in memory for different kinds of materials.

AUTHOR NOTES

We thank Jennifer Shapka, Angie Birt, Monica Mori, Arsalan Ghani, and Daniela Pacheva for assistance with data collection, data coding, transcriptions, and other assistance with the study. We thank Amy L. Siegenthaler for insightful comments on the manuscript. Correspondence concerning this chapter should be addressed to Bob Uttl, Brain Science Research Center, Tamagawa University, Machida, Tokyo, Japan. Email: uttlbob@gmail.com.

REFERENCES

Adams, C., Labouvie-Vief, G., Hobart, C. J., & Dorosz, M. (1990). Adult age group differences in story recall style. *Journals of Gerontology, 45*, P17–P27.

Anstey, K. J., Stankov, L., & Lord, S. R. (1993). Primary aging, secondary aging, and intelligence. *Psychology and Aging, 8*, 562–570.

Backman, L. (1986). Adult age differences in cross-modal recoding and mental tempo, and older adults' utilization of compensatory task conditions. *Experimental Aging Research, 12*, 135–140.

Baddeley, A. D., Lewis, V., Eldridge, M., & Thomson, N. (1984). Attention and retrieval from long-term memory. *Journal of Experimental Psychology: General, 13*, 518–540.

Baltes, P. B. (1987). Theoretical propositions of life-span developmental psychology: On the dynamics between growth and decline. *Developmental Psychology, 23*, 611–626.

Baltes, P. B. & Baltes, M. M. (1990). Plasticity and variability in psychological aging: Methodological and theoretical issues. In G. Gurski (Ed.), *Determining the effects of aging on the central nervous system* (pp. 41–60). Berlin: Schering.

Baltes, P. B. & Lindenberger, U. (1997). Emergence of a powerful connection between sensory and cognitive functions across the adult life span: A new window to the study of cognitive aging? *Psychology and Aging, 12*, 12–21.

Blair, J. R. & Spreen, V. (1989). Predicting premorbid IQ: A revision of the National Adult Reading Test. *Clinical Neuropsychologist, 3*, 129–136.

Carstensen, L. L. (1995). Evidence for a life-span theory of socioemotional selectivity. *Current Directions in Psychological Sciences, 4*, 151–156.

Carstensen, L. L., Isaacowitz, D. M., & Charles, S. T. (1999). Taking time seriously: A theory of socioemotional selectivity. *American Psychologist, 54*, 165–181.

Carstensen, L. L. & Turk-Charles, S. (1994). The salience of emotion across the adult life span. *Psychology and Aging, 9*, 259–264.

Cerella, J. (1985). Information processing rates in the elderly. *Psychological Bulletin, 98*, 67–83.

Cerella, J., Poon, L. W., & Williams, D. M. (1980). A quantitative theory of mental processing time and age. In L. W. Poon (Ed.), *Aging in the 80s: Selected contemporary issues in the psychology aging*. Washington, DC: American Psychological Association.

Charles, S. T., Mather, M., & Carstensen, L. L. (2003). Aging and emotional memory: The forgettable nature of negative images for older adults. *Journal of Experimental Psychology: General, 132*, 310–324.

Cherry, K. E. & LeCompte, D. C. (1999). Age and individual differences' influence on prospective memory. *Psychology and Aging, 14*, 60–76.

Coren, S. & Hakstian, A. R. (1988). Color vision screening without the use of technical equipment: Scale development and cross-validation. *Perception & Psychophysics, 43*, 115–120.

Coren, S. & Hakstian, A. R. (1992). The development and cross-validation of a self-report inventory to assess pure-tone threshold hearing sensitivity. *Journal of Speech & Hearing Research, 35*, 921–928.

Craik, F. I. M. (1983). On the transfer of information from temporary to permananent memory. *Philosophical Transcactions of the Royal Society of London, B302*, 341–359.

Craik, F. I. M. (1986). A functional account of age differences in memory. In F. Klix & H. Hagendorf (Eds.), *Human memory and cognitive capabilities: Mechanisms and performances* (pp. 409–422). New York: Elsevier.

Craik, F. I. M., Govoni, R., Naveh-Benjamin, M., & Anderson, N. D. (1996). The effects of divided attention on encoding and retrieval processes in human memory. *Journal of Experimental Psychology: General, 125*, 159–180.

D'Argembeau, A. & Van der Linden, M. (2004). Identity but not expression memory for unfamiliar faces is affected by aging. *Memory, 12*, 644–654.

Denburg, N. L., Buchanan, T. W., Tranel, D., & Adolphs, R. (2003). Evidence for preserved emotional memory in normal older persons. *Emotion, 3*, 239–253.

Dewhurst, S. A. & Parry, L. A. (2000). Emotionality, distinctiveness, and recollective experience. *European Journal of Cognitive Psychology, 12*, 541–551.

Einstein, G. O. & McDaniel, M. A. (1990). Normal aging and prospective memory. *Journal of Experimental Psychology: Learning, Memory and Cognition, 16*, 717–726.

Fung, H. & Carstensen, L. L. (2003). Sending memorable messages to the old: Age differences in preference and memory for advertisements. *Journal of Personality and Social Psychology, 85*, 163–178.

Gatz, M. & Hurwicz, M. (1990). Are old people more depressed? Cross-sectional data on Center for Epidemiological Studies Scale factors, *Psychology & Aging, 5*, 284–290.

Graf, P. & Uttl, B. (2001). Prospective memory: A new focus for research. *Consciousness & Cognition, 10*, 437–450.

Grady, C. L. & Craik, F. I. M. (2000). Changes in memory processing with age. *Current Opinion in Neurobiology, 10*, 224–231.

Graf, P. & Ohta, N. (Eds.) (2002). *Lifespan memory development*. Cambridge, MA: MIT Press.

Hastroudi, S., Johnson, M. K., & Chrosniak, L. D. (1990). Aging and qualitative characteristics of memories for perceived and imagined complex events. *Psychology and Aging, 5*, 119–126.

Hultsch, D. F. (1969). Adult age differences in the organization of free recall. *Developmental Psychology, 1*, 673–678.

John, O. P. & Srivastave, S. (1999). The Big Five Trait taxonomy: History, measurement, and theoretical perspectives. In L. A. Pervin & O. P. John (Eds.), *Handbook of personality: Theory and research* (2nd ed., pp. 102–138). New York: Guilford Press.

Kensinger, E. A., Anderson, A., Growdon, J. H., & Corkin, S. (2004). Effects of Alzheimer's disease on memory for verbal emotional information. *Neuropsychologia, 42*, 791–800.

Kensinger, E. A., Brierley, B., Medford, N., Growdon, J. H., & Corkin, S. (2002). Effects of normal aging and Alzheimer's disease on emotional memory. *Emotion, 2*, 118–134.

Knight, B. G., Maines, M. L., & Robinson, G. S. (2002). The effects of sad mood on memory in older adults: A test of the mood congruence effect. *Psychology and Aging, 17*, 653–661.

Labouvie-Vief, G., DeVoe, M., & Bulka, D. (1989). Speaking about feelings: Conceptions of emotion across the life span. *Psychology & Aging, 4*, 425–437.

Leigland, L. A., Schulz, L. E., & Janowsky, J. S. (2004). Age related changes in emotional memory. *Neurobiology of Aging, 25*, 1117–1124.

Lindenberger, U. & Baltes, P. (1994). Sensory functioning and intelligence in old age: A strong connection. *Psychology and Aging, 9*, 339–355.

McDaniel, M. A., DeLosch, E. L., & Merritt, P. S. (2000). Order information and retrieval distinctiveness: Recall of common versus bizarre material. *Journal of Experimental Psychology: Learning, Memory, & Cognition, 26*, 1045–1056.

McDaniel, M. A., Einstein, G. O., Stout, A. C., & Morgan, Z. (2003). Aging and maintaining intentions over delays: Do it or lose it. *Psychology and Aging, 18*, 823–835.

Macht, M. L. & Buschke, H. (1983). Age differences in cognitive effort in recall. *Journal of Gerontology, 28*, 695–700.

Mandler, G. (1967). Organization and memory. In K. W. Spence & J. T. Spence (Eds.), *The psychology of learning and motivation* (Vol. 1, pp. 327–372). New York: Academic Press.

Mather, M. (2004). Aging and emotional memory. In D. Reisberg & P. Hertel (Eds.), *Memory and emotion* (pp. 272–307). Oxford: Oxford University Press.

Mather, M. & Carstensen, L. L. (2003). Aging and attentional biases for emotional faces. *Psychological Science, 14*, 409–415.

Mitchell, D. B. & Bruss, P. J. (2003). Age differences in implicit memory: Conceptual, perceptual, or methodological? *Psychology and Aging, 18*, 807–822.

Naveh-Benjamin, M., Craik, F. I. M., Guez, J., & Kreuger, S. (2005). Divided attention in younger and older adults: Effects of strategy and relatedness on memory performance and secondary task costs. *Journal of Experimental Psychology: Learning, Memory, and Cognition, 31*, 520–537.

Park, D. C., Puglisi, J. T., & Smith, A. D. (1986). Memory for pictures: Does an age-related decline exist? *Psychology and Aging, 1*, 11–17.

Park, D. C., Smith, A. D., Dudley, W. N., & Lafronza, V. N. (1989). Effects of age and a divided attention task presented during encoding and retrieval on memory. *Journal of Experimental Psychology: Learning, Memory, and Cognition, 15*, 1185–1191.

Pichora-Fuller, M. K., Schneider, B. A., & Daneman, M. (1995). How young and old adults listen to and remember speech in noise. *Journal of Acoustic Society of America, 97*, 593–608.

Rundus, D. (1973). Negative effects of using list items as recall cues. *Journal of Verbal Learning & Verbal Behavior, 12*, 43–50.

Salthouse, T. A. (1980). Age and memory: Strategies for localizing the loss. In L. W. Poon, J. L. Fozard, L. S. Cermak, D. Arenberg, & L. W. Thompson (Eds.), *New directions in memory and aging: Proceedings of the George A. Talland Memorial Conference* (pp. 47–65). Hillsdale, NJ: Erlbaum.

Salthouse, T. A. (1985). *Theory of cognitive aging*. Amsterdam: North-Holland.

Salthouse, T. A. (1988). Resource-reduction interpretation of cognitive aging. *Developmental Reviews, 8*, 238–272.

Salthouse, T. A. (1991). Mediation of adult age differences in cognition by reduction in working memory and speed of processing. *Psychological Science, 2*, 179–183.

Salthouse, T. A., Hancock, H. E., Meinz, E. J., & Hambrick, D. Z. (1996). Interrelations of age, visual acuity, and cognitive functioning. *Journals of Gerontology, 51B*, P317–P330.

Salthouse, T. A., Kausler, D. H., & Saults, J. S. (1988). Utilization of path-analytic procedures to investigate the role of processing resources in cognitive aging. *Psychology and Aging, 3*, 29–37.

Schmidt, S. R. (1991). Can we have a distinctive theory of memory? *Memory & Cognition, 19*, 523–542.

Schneider, B. A. & Pichora-Fuller, M. K. (2000). Implications of perceptual deterioration for cognitive aging research. In F. I. M. Craik & T. A. Salthouse (Eds.), *The handbook of cognitive aging* (2nd ed., pp. 155–219). Mahwah, NJ: Erlbaum.

Spreen, O. & Strauss, E. (1991). *A compendium of neuropsychological tests* (1st ed.). New York: Oxford University Press.

Talmi, D. & Moscovitch, M. (2004). Can semantic relatedness explain the enhancement of memory for emotional words? *Memory & Cognition, 32*, 742–751.

Tulving, E. & Pearlstone, Z. (1966). Availability versus accessibility of information in memory for words. *Journal of Verbal Learning & Verbal Behavior, 5*, 381–391.

Uttl, B. (2002). North American Adult Reading Test: Age norms, reliability, and validity. *Journal of Clinical and Experimental Neuropsychology, 24*, 1123–1137.

Uttl (2005a). Age-related changes in event cued prospective memory proper. In N. Ohta, C. M. MacLeod, & B. Uttl (Eds.), *Dynamic cognitive processes* (pp. 273–303). Tokyo: Springer.

Uttl (2005b). Measurement of individual differences: Lessons from memory assessment in research and clinical practice. *Psychological Science, 16*, 460–467.

Uttl, B. (2005c, submitted). *A window to explicit episodic memory: A modified Rey Auditory Verbal Learning Test.*

Uttl, B. (in press). Age-related changes in event-cued prospective memory. *Aging, Neuropsychology and Cognition.*

Uttl, B. & Graf, P. (1993). Episodic spatial memory in adulthood. *Psychology and Aging, 8*, 257–273.

Uttl, B. & Graf, P. (1997). Color-word Stroop test performance across the adult lifespan. *Journal of Clinical and Experimental Neuropsychology, 19*, 405–420.

Uttl, B., Graf, P., & Cosentino, S. (2000). Exacting assessments: Do older adults fatigue more quickly? *Journal of Clinical and Experimental Neuropsychology, 22*, 496–507.

Uttl, B., Graf, P., & Richter, L. K. (2002). Verbal Paired Associate tests: Limits on validity and reliability. *Archives of Clinical Neuropsychology, 17*, 567–581.

Wechsler, D. (1987). *Wechsler Memory Scale-Revised*. San Antonio, TX: Psychological Corporation.

PART III

MEMORY, EMOTION, AND PSYCHOPATHOLOGY

Anxiety and the Encoding of Emotional Information

Andrew Mathews

Abstract

The influence of individual differences in emotionality on memory is discussed, and it is proposed that many of these effects can be accounted for in terms of selective attention and encoding. Anxious individuals are more likely to encode events in terms of their threat potential, and focus attention on the central emotional content of threatening pictures. Brain areas involved in defensive behavior are differentially activated by fear-related material, to an extent that is related to variations in anxiety. This activation is modulated by encoding instructions, although less so in highly fearful individuals. Together with recent studies of control over encoding via repeated practice, these results demonstrate that the modification of encoding can have important consequences for subsequent emotional responses and experience.

It is well established that the emotional content of events influences their later recall. However, there is considerable debate about the exact nature and form of that influence. When people are asked to recall their previous experience of seeing mixed sets of emotional and neutral pictures, they typically report more of the emotional pictures than those with neutral content (e.g., Bradley et al., 1992; Mathews, Yiend, & Lawrence, 2004). As well as recalling more of the threatening pictures, participants seem to recall particularly the central aspects of emotional scenes compared to the equivalent aspects of non-emotional or neutral scenes (Burke, Heuer, & Reisberg, 1992; Christianson & Loftus, 1991; Heuer & Reisberg, 1990; Libkuman et al., 1999; Reisberg, this volume). Moreover, there is some evidence that peripheral details present in emotional scenes may be remembered less well (e.g., Burke, Heuer, & Reisberg, 1992; although see Libkuman et al., 1999; and Wessel, van der Kooy, & Merckelbach, 2000, for variable findings).

There are several candidate explanations for this effect (Christianson, 1992; Wessel, van der Kooy, & Merckelbach, 2000). First, selective attention to the central emotional focus of a scene may lead to better encoding of information in that location, at the expense of other less attended locations. Second, people may elaborate on the meaning of emotional scenes, leading to more extensive memorial representations and consequently improved retrieval. Third, emotional arousal at the time of processing the scene may directly enhance the durability of the memory trace (Cahill & McGaugh, 1995; Revelle & Loftus, 1990). For reasons to be discussed later, this chapter is concerned particularly with the first possibility – that emotional memory is enhanced by selective attention.

 ## INDIVIDUAL DIFFERENCES IN EMOTIONAL MEMORY

Surprisingly little is known about the effects of individual differences in emotional reactivity on memory for scenes. An early exception was an experiment by Andrews (1990; cited by Burke, Heuer, & Reisberg, 1992), who found that moviegoers generally recalled more central details of emotional scenes in movies than of matched neutral scenes. Of particular interest is that this advantage was present only for participants with moderate or high scores on a self-report measure of individual differences in ease of emotional arousal. Only participants with high arousal scores showed an advantage for emotional details in memory. As Reisberg and Heuer (1992) note, this "implies that emotionality is indeed the key factor in distinguishing the neutral and emotional scenes" (p. 174). They further comment that without this additional finding one might be concerned that the scenes were not matched in some other important way, such as relevance to the plot. Other sources of variation due to (non-emotional) differences in the content of the scenes should apply equally to all participants, rather than only those with relatively high levels of emotional arousal.

Research using other experimental paradigms has already shown that certain individuals (e.g., those prone to anxiety) are indeed more likely than others to selectively attend to and encode emotionally threatening words or pictures (for reviews, see Mathews & MacLeod, 1994, 2005). From now on, the term "emotional encoding" will be employed to refer to the ways in which emotional events are attended to, perceived and understood, and consequently stored in memory. For example, when two pictures differing in emotional valence are displayed simultaneously, anxiety-prone individuals are more likely to attend to the more threatening picture (Yiend & Mathews, 2001). Also, when a single location is cued by either a threatening or neutral picture, followed by a to-be-responded-to target in the same or a different location, anxiety-prone individuals are slower than non-anxious controls to disengage their attention from threatening pictures in order to find the target when it follows in another location (Yiend & Mathews, 2001). Similarly, Fox et al. (2001) used displays of faces varying in emotional expression followed by a to-be-detected target in the same or different location. Participants with higher anxiety scores were slower to respond following an angry face, but only when face and target were in different locations, requiring disengagement of attention. There is thus good reason to expect anxiety-prone individuals to preferentially attend to and encode emotionally threatening aspects of scenes.

Given these differences in attention, one might expect to find parallel differences in memory. Indeed, as expected, studies of clinically depressed individuals have consistently found evidence of relatively better memory for negative emotional information, particularly when it is self-relevant. Unexpectedly, however, in clinical anxiety states evidence for such an effect remains elusive and unconvincing, with the possible exception of panic disorder (for reviews, see MacLeod & Mathews, 2004; Mathews & MacLeod, 2005). As noted above, this seems curious since there is such strong evidence of selective attention towards threatening information in anxiety states.

A number of reasons have been advanced for the lack of an explicit memory bias in anxiety (note: explicit memory refers to the deliberate conscious use of memory, as opposed to unintended or implicit memory effects). It has been suggested that anxiety motivates avoidance of semantic elaboration and/or promotes perceptual encoding of threat information, so that it is stored in nonverbally accessible forms in memory (cf., Brewin, 2001), and thus does not aid in the retrieval of threat representations. It could be that apparently semantic processing of threatening information in anxiety, implied by symptoms such as excessive worry, does not involve making elaborative connections with other information, but rather consists of repetitive rehearsal of imagined dangers, detectable only in tests sensitive to the ease with which previously exposed stimuli are later perceived or identified (priming). However, the implied prediction that implicit memory tasks, particularly those involving perceptual processes, should be more sensitive to anxiety-related effects has similarly lacked consistent support. Findings have been mixed, with some suggesting better implicit memory for threat in anxious individuals (e.g., MacLeod & McLaughlin, 1995), but others finding no such differences (e.g., Russo, Fox, & Bowles, 1999).

An alternative explanation is suggested by the fact that virtually all studies of individual differences in emotional memory have used fixed forms of semantic encoding. For example, participants are typically presented with a series of words and are asked to judge whether each is self-descriptive or not, or to make some other kind of semantic judgment about them. Judgments related to oneself are particularly well recalled, and these effects are stronger for negative than positive stimuli in those prone to negative affect (see below). To the extent that the words presented are variably represented within knowledge structures in memory, this method may indeed be sensitive to pre-existing differences in the type and extent of semantic knowledge (e.g., differences in self-image or self-schema). Words that are consistent with schematic knowledge may be easier to retrieve later, because they are more readily integrated with existing schemas, and because this knowledge can be used intentionally as a retrieval strategy. Depressed participants, who have a predominantly negative self-view, consequently are better able to recall negative emotional words that are particularly related to their existing depressive beliefs or knowledge structures (Mathews & MacLeod, 1994).

On the other hand, forced semantic encoding may be particularly *insensitive* to differences attributable to people spontaneously using different methods of *encoding* emotional stimuli. Thus, if people prone to anxiety tend to encode stimuli in terms of their potential threat value, while other people select alternative types of encoding, then using a fixed semantic encoding task could completely obscure any differences between high and low anxious groups that might otherwise be apparent. There are in fact good reasons to believe that high and low anxious individuals do indeed differ in their default encoding styles, in addition to the evidence of attention differences discussed previously. Pury and Mineka (2001) required high and low anxious participants to decide as rapidly as possible whether words were (a) related to physical or social domains, or (b) were positive or negative in meaning. The same word set was used for both tasks so that in task (a), the words *disease* and *health* were to be categorized as physical and the words *insult* and *praise* were to be categorized as social. In task (b), however, *disease* and *insult* were to be judged negative and *health* and *praise* as positive. The nature of the decision required was not signaled until the start of each trial, and varied unpredictably from trial to trial. Under these conditions, anxious participants were faster to make emotional (positive/ negative) judgments. This finding is consistent with the notion that highly anxious individuals have a "default preference" for emotional encoding. Because emotional material tends to be better recalled than non-emotional information, a preference for emotional encoding could thus improve memory.

In a previous review (MacLeod & Mathews, 2004), we noted two striking exceptions to the general pattern of failure to find memory differences due to anxiety; one involving patients with generalized anxiety disorder (Friedman, Thayer, & Borkovec, 2000), and the other involving students varying in trait anxiety (Russo et al., 2001). Both used unusual encoding procedures in that participants were required to perform a superficial task with the stimulus words exposed longer than was required to perform this task, leaving participants free to process these words in whatever other way they chose. For example, Friedman, Thayer, and Borkovec (2000) asked their participants simply to read single words that were displayed for eight seconds, far longer than is required to read them. Under these conditions, the anxious groups showed clearly superior recall of threatening words relative to neutral words, an effect not shown by non-anxious controls. The explanation proposed here attributes such findings of memory differences between groups varying in anxiety level to differential encoding, rather than to differences at retrieval. Similarly, the common failure to find memory differences due to anxiety differences can be attributed to experimental procedures that have imposed the same encoding method on all participants.

To summarize conclusions so far, there is evidence consistent with the hypothesis that individual differences in emotionality – such as vulnerability to anxiety – are associated with the tendency for attention to be held more by emotional (threatening) stimuli, to encode ambiguous stimuli in terms of their emotional meaning, and that better memory in such groups for emotional stimuli can depend on the use of different encoding methods.

However, it is also possible that the attention and memory differences discussed above may arise simply because anxious individuals are more aroused than are others by emotional stimuli, leading to a greater narrowing of attention. The hypothesis that emotional arousal is associated with narrowing of attention is an old one (cf., Easterbrook, 1959). Because high negative emotionality is defined as the tendency of an individual to respond more readily with negative emotions, the anxiety effects discussed so far may simply be a special case of a much more general tendency for emotional arousal to narrow attention to the provoking material. If so, some of these effects should be observable with arousing material even in non-anxious groups. Evidence is presented in the next section suggesting that both views receive some support. Emotionally arousing pictures can indeed narrow attention even in non-anxious people, but anxiety is particularly associated with encoding effects that are specific to threat.

 EMOTIONAL INFLUENCES ON THE BOUNDARY EXTENSION EFFECT

To examine the encoding of emotional pictures, we (Mathews & Mackintosh, 2004) used an experimental paradigm sensitive to a phenomenon referred to as the *boundary extension* effect. In this effect, pictures are nearly always remembered as having more extensive boundaries than they had in fact (e.g., Intraub, 2002; Intraub, Bender, & Mangels, 1992; Intraub & Richardson, 1989). Thus, if people view a picture of an object against a background and then draw the scene from memory, they typically include more background than was shown in the original. Similar effects occur when participants have to select the original picture from a recognition set having more or less extended boundaries, even when warned to guard against such errors (Intraub & Bodamer, 1993). Intraub and her colleagues have argued that this ubiquitous boundary extension effect arises because pictures are perceived as being part of the real world, which has space extending beyond the limits of the displayed picture (the *perceptual schema* hypothesis). When reproducing or recognizing a picture, the perceptual schema invoked leads the viewer to remember the original as more extended in space than it was in fact.

Safer et al. (1998) argued that selective processing of central emotional aspects should work against the boundary extension effect. They showed participants one of two sets of slides in sequence that differed only with respect to two critical slides appearing in the middle of the sequence. One group saw a version in which the two slides showed the man holding a bloody knife, followed by a scene with the woman lying with a slashed throat. The other group saw a neutral version in which the man is handing the woman some keys, followed by a scene with the woman picking flowers. Ten minutes later, participants were asked to select the critical slides from among a set of four varying only in whether the boundary was the same, more, or less extensive than in the original.

Errors in the group that saw the neutral slides nearly always involved selecting the distracter with more extensive boundaries (i.e., the standard boundary extension effect). The less common errors in which participants picked distracters with reduced boundaries occurred more frequently in the group that saw emotional slides. This finding is consistent with the hypothesis of a reduction in boundary extension for emotional pictures, although conclusions were limited by the fact that only two critical emotional pictures were used, and only one of these ever revealed the predicted effect. In discussing possible reasons for this finding, Safer et al. (1998) suggest that elaboration on emotional meaning may interfere with the processes underlying the boundary extension effect. However, it seems equally if not more plausible that central emotional aspects are attended to, to the detriment of more peripheral regions, thus reducing boundary extension. To clarify this argument, suppose that only the central portion of a picture is encoded, then boundary extension would presumably have to progress outward from this area, as if the perceived picture had been smaller. Consequently, the boundaries subsequently recalled would be less extended than usual. We suggest that an attenuated form of this restriction could occur if more distal regions were simply not well attended, rather than never encoded at all.

In contrast to the results reported by Safer et al. (1998), Candel, Merckelbach, and Zandbergen (2003) found that neutral and emotional pictures produced equivalent boundary extension effects. Participants were shown either four neutral pictures (previously used by Intraub and colleagues) or four unpleasant pictures (e.g., a wounded hand) from the International Affective Picture

System (IAPS; see Lang, Bradley, & Cuthbert, 1995). In one experiment, later drawings from memory showed boundary extension, with no differences due to emotionality of the pictures. In a second study, participants judged if recognition items appeared closer up, the same, or further away than did the originals (actually, they were all the same as the original). Those participants who made errors were more likely to judge pictures as being closer up than as further away from the original, indicating a degree of boundary extension, but again with no differences between neutral or emotional pictures.

In discussing their findings, neither Safer et al. (1998) nor Candel, Merckelbach, and Zandbergen (2003) consider the possibility that effects might vary with individual differences in emotionality or arousal. In previous work (Mathews, 1996) we found that variations in emotional reactivity can indeed influence the extent of boundary extension. Participants were shown news photographs varying in emotionality (e.g., starving children, cheering crowds) and asked to rate them for pleasantness/unpleasantness. They were then given a choice between two versions of each picture, one that showed a slightly more close-up view, and one that showed a slightly more distant view, so as to include more of the background. Participants were asked to pick which version they thought was more similar to the one they had seen earlier. Consistent with the perceptual schema hypothesis (Intraub, Bender, & Mangels, 1992), participants chose the more extended picture more frequently than the closer version by 72 percent to 28 percent. Furthermore, consistent with Candel and colleagues' finding, once again there were no apparent overall differences due to type of picture.

Despite this, exploratory analyses taking individual differences into account (based on the trait version of the Positive and Negative Affectivity Scales; Watson, Clark, & Tellegen, 1988) revealed some more subtle effects of emotion. For pictures rated as "very unpleasant," negative emotionality scores were correlated with the probability of picking the picture with restricted boundaries ($r = 0.54$, $p < 0.01$). Similarly, difference scores, computed for each participant by subtracting pleasantness ratings for pictures selected in their restricted versus extended boundary versions, were significantly correlated with negative affectivity ($r = 0.58$). That is, pictures judged to be most unpleasant were more likely to lead to the restricted boundary version being selected, but only in subjects with high negative affectivity scores.

In a further study (Mathews & Mackintosh, 2004), we recruited participants with high versus low scores on a measure of trait anxiety. We used a larger set of pictures than before, selected on the basis both of normative ratings for pleasantness/unpleasantness and for evoked feelings of arousal, to explore the respective roles of emotional valence and arousal in reducing boundary extension. For example, pictures of violent assault scenes are typically rated as unpleasant and arousing, whereas an equally unpleasant scene of a body

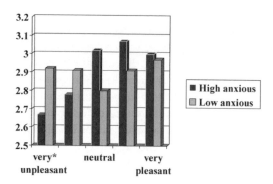

Figure 9.1 Mean boundary extension scores (with 1 = least to 4 = most) for picture sets divided according to pleasantness/unpleasantness ratings given by each participant. (* Less boundary extension for very unpleasant pictures in the high anxious group, $p < 0.05$.)

may receive a lower arousal rating. Pleasant (or neutral) scenes can also vary in their arousing properties. For example, pictures of exciting sporting events such as sky-diving can be rated as being pleasant or neutral in valence, but also as highly arousing, while other neutral scenes of relaxing situations can be rated as low in arousal.

Participants looked at each picture and rated it for pleasantness (using a 5-point scale, 1 = very unpleasant to 5 = very pleasant). In the subsequent recognition test, they were shown four versions and asked to select the one that was most similar to the original. In fact, two of the recognition items had extended boundaries (by 10 percent or 20 percent, scored as 3 or 4) and two had boundaries reduced by the same amount from the original (scored as 2 or 1). If no boundary extension occurred on average, the mean score expected would thus be 2.5. Each participant's pleasantness ratings were used to group the pictures into five sets, according to their score on the 1–5 scale. Pictures rated as "very unpleasant" showed a less marked boundary extension effect in the high than in the low trait anxious group, replicating our earlier results (see figure 9.1).

Further analyses based on the IAPS norms for rated pleasantness (valence) and arousal revealed a more general interaction between valence and arousal across all participants. For pictures classified as negative or neutral, the boundary extension was less marked for highly arousing than for less arousing pictures (see figure 9.2). For positive pictures there was a slight but non-significant effect in the reverse direction.

This finding suggests that the emotional valence of an arousing scene has effects on how it is encoded and remembered. For very unpleasant threatening scenes,

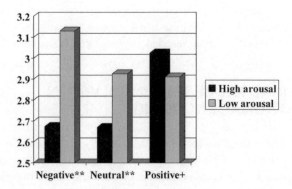

Figure 9.2   Mean boundary extension scores with picture sets divided by normative valence and arousal ratings. (** Less extension for high arousal pictures, $p < 0.01$; + reverse trend for positive pictures, $p < 0.1$.)

boundary extension was reduced more in highly anxious individuals. Furthermore, highly arousing pictures reduced boundary extension across all participants, except for pictures with positively valenced content. It thus seems that arousal interacts with emotional valence in restricting boundary extension.

Turning to possible mechanisms that could account for these data, it is suggested here that a combination of narrowed focus of attention and selective encoding can provide the most parsimonious explanation. Because the threatening or emotionally arousing aspects of pictures were placed centrally within each picture, selective attention and encoding of information in these areas may lead to less attention being accorded to information in more peripheral regions. Regions near the picture boundary may thus be less well encoded as a result, and boundary extension will be limited, because, as was argued earlier, the picture will have been perceived as if it were in fact smaller.

If so, however, then why did positive content not have similar effects in reducing boundary extension? It appears that positive emotional arousal differs in its effect on attention and encoding. In other experiments, in which to-be-responded-to target stimuli were flanked on either side by to-be-ignored distracter stimuli, negative emotional arousal was associated with reduced interference from these distracters, consistent with a more narrow focus of attention on targets. In contrast, positive emotional arousal increased interference due to flanking distracters, consistent with a less narrow focus of attention (Fenske & Eastwood, 2003). It thus seems that positive emotional arousal can actually broaden the focus of attention rather than narrowing it, as does negative arousal.

In summary, the more that emotionally negative arousing aspects of scenes focus attention in the central location, the more attention to more peripheral aspects will be restricted. This focus on only the central aspects of (non-positive) scenes has the effect of reducing our usual sense of surrounding space and thus makes the perceived scene be recalled as closer that it would be otherwise.

 # NEURAL PROCESSES INVOLVED IN EMOTIONAL ENCODING

Until now this discussion has focused on how emotional differences may influence encoding. In fact, the relationship between emotion and encoding could operate in both directions. That is, different types of encoding might influence emotion, as well as emotion influencing the type of encoding. One method of investigating the former direction of influence is to instruct people in how to encode potentially emotional information and then test the psycho-physiological and neural consequences. Another method we have used is to "train" people in how to encode ambiguously emotional information by using extended practice in accessing valenced meanings (Mathews & Mackintosh, 2000).

The extent of control over the neural systems underlying emotional arousal has been the topic of considerable debate. Öhman and Mineka (2001, 2003) have proposed a brain module for fear, centered on the amygdala, that is "cognitively impenetrable" or "relatively encapsulated from more advanced human cognition" (see Fodor, 1983, for a discussion of modules in cognition). In support of this view, angry faces continue to elicit amygdala activation despite attention being directed to other attributes (e.g., gender; see Iidaka et al., 2001) or to other flanking stimuli (Vuilleumier et al., 2001).

More critically, amygdala activation to angry faces occurs even if the faces are presented briefly and then backward masked by superimposition of neutral stimuli to limit awareness (Morris, Öhman, & Dolan, 1999; Öhman, 2002; Whalen et al., 1998). Furthermore, lesions to the visual cortex resulting in functional blindness do not eliminate differential amygdala response to fearful and fear-conditioned faces ("affective blindsight"; see Morris et al., 2001). In summary, the above studies suggest that brain regions involved in processing fear-related stimuli are activated in an obligatory fashion, without the need for directed attention or awareness. Such an obligatory effect is likely to provide an evolutionary advantage, in that defensive behaviours such as escape from potentially lethal dangers would be more certain and rapid as a result.

The finding that amygdala activation can occur in the absence of awareness, however, is not necessarily inconsistent with the idea that fear-related processing can be influenced by higher-level control operations. Several studies have shown that both emotional and non-emotional judgments about fear-related pictures or faces can reduce the enhanced amygdala activation (relative to neutral stimuli) that is seen during passive viewing of the same stimuli

(Lange et al., 2003; Taylor et al., 2003). Pessoa, Kastner, and Ungerleider (2002) made the even stronger claim that attention-demanding judgments can eliminate fear-related activation of the amygdala entirely. They found that the usual differential response to fearful versus neutral faces seen during gender judgments was apparently eliminated when participants had to make difficult perceptual judgments about flanking stimuli.

In discussing selective attention to threatening information, we (Mathews, Mackintosh, & Fulcher, 1997) have proposed that such attention depends on the interaction between two individual difference variables: sensitivity to threat and the ability to control attention. Threat sensitivity depends on the activation threshold within a neural system specialized for the early detection of danger. In addition to the amygdala, regions likely to be involved include the hippocampus (Gray & McNaughton, 2000) and prefrontal cortex (Kalin et al., 2001; Zald, Mattson, & Pardo, 2002). Excessive distraction from very mild threat cues, such as words or pictures, is thought to be modulated by activity of an attentional control system involving the anterior cingulate and dorsolateral prefrontal cortex (Botvinick et al., 2001; Bush, Luu, & Posner, 2000). A degree of control over obligatory responding to very mild and non-urgent threat cues would have the advantage of reducing constant distraction from emotional cues that do not signal any current threat. If so, then optimal functioning involves rapid responding to threats that could signal current danger (e.g., due to the amygdala), balanced by control systems in other areas that can reduce unnecessary false alarms.

To address the question of the extent to which the neural processing involved in encoding fear-related stimuli is obligatory or optional, we (Mathews, Yiend, & Lawrence, 2004) compared emotional ("more frightening than the previous picture?") with non-emotional judgments ("required more planning by the photographer than the previous picture?"), against a baseline uninstructed viewing condition, in which no particular judgment was specified. In planned comparisons across the judgment conditions used, we contrasted fear-related and neutral pictures, while holding the instructed (non-emotional) encoding task constant, with the intention of revealing any obligatory emotional activation to fear-related pictures. We then contrasted emotional versus non-emotional encoding conditions, while holding the (fear-related) picture content constant, with the intention of revealing any optional effects due to top-down cognitive control.

Initial analyses comparing activation during uninstructed viewing of fear-related versus neutral pictures revealed a number of brain regions where activation was significantly greater for fear-related than neutral pictures, including the visual cortex, precentral gyrus, amygdala, hippocampus, and thalamus. There is a striking similarity between these areas and the hierarchically organized system known to mediate defensive behavior in animals, leading to rapid flight or freezing (e.g., Gray & McNaughton, 2000; LeDoux, 1996; Mongeau, Miller,

Chiang, & Anderson, 2003). In addition, areas within the dorsomedial prefrontal cortex and the rostral anterior cingulate were activated by the fear-related pictures.

Those participants with high fearfulness scores (on the Behavioral Inhibition Scale (BIS); Carver & White, 1994) had more pronounced activation due to fear-related versus neutral pictures in several of these locations: specifically, the hippocampus, amygdala, pulvinar of the thalamas, and the periaqueductal gray (PAG). Thus, as expected, those individuals reporting greater anxiety (or sensitivity to threat) did indeed respond with relatively greater activation in areas already found to be associated with fear-related pictures. Significant correlations were also found between self-reported ability to control attention (using the Attention Control Questionnaire; Derryberry & Reed, 2002) and activation in medial prefrontal cortex and anterior cingulate when viewing fear-related versus neutral pictures. As noted earlier, these are areas thought to be part of a system involved in the control of attention under conditions of competition or conflict between responses.

Results of analyses comparing activation due to emotional versus neutral pictures, holding (non-emotional) encoding constant, showed more activation to fear-related than neutral pictures in occipital cortex and amygdala, although the latter was now significant only by one-tailed test and only on the left side. No other brain region revealed significant differences. Thus, when participants were instructed to encode non-emotional aspects of the pictures, most of the greater activation to emotional pictures was no longer significant. Apparently, voluntary effects to direct attention to non-emotional aspects substantially reduced the activation differences due to picture type, but did not eliminate them entirely. Similarly, most of the correlations between individual difference in fearfulness and greater activation due to fear-related versus neutral pictures were no longer significant under non-emotional encoding conditions. Two exceptions were the correlations between BIS scores and activation in the right hippocampus/ parahippocampal cortex area, and between the Attention Control Questionnaire and activation in the anterior cingulate cortex.

Analysis of the activation during emotional versus non-emotional encoding of fear-related pictures only, revealed differential activation in brain regions that overlapped considerably with those distinguishing between pictures with different emotional content during uninstructed viewing. Specifically, emotional encoding was associated with greater activation in dorsomedial prefrontal and anterior cingulate cortex, visual cortex, amygdala, hippocampus, and the pulvinar. Activation differences in right hippocampus and left PAG, due to the type of encoding with picture content held constant (i.e., fear-related), were positively correlated with BIS scores. That is, more fearful participants had greater activation in these brain areas when they were encoding fear-related pictures using emotional rather than non-emotional judgments. Activation in

anterior cingulate cortex, again due to type of encoding, was positively correlated with attentional control, but was *negatively* correlated with BIS scores.
It seems that highly anxious people respond with more hippocampal activation to fear-related pictures, and particularly when attending to their threatening aspects, but are less reactive in areas related to attentional control.

In general, these findings are consistent with expectations from previous studies of the brain regions recruited when viewing pictures of fear-related scenes
versus perceptually similar but more emotionally neutral scenes. Most critically, for our present purposes, we confirmed that fear-related pictures elicited
more activation in the amygdala than did neutral pictures.

The fact that differential activation in areas such as the hippocampus and
amygdala were correlated with BIS scores provides evidence that trait-like individual differences in sensitivity to threat are underpinned by differential responsiveness in the brain system proposed by Gray and McNaughton (2000)
to underlie anxiety. The residual visual cortex and amygdala activation due
to fear-related rather than neutral pictures, even when holding instructions to
make non-emotional judgments constant, suggests that some of the differential
processes involved were obligatory. Nonetheless, loss of most of the differential activations seen previously suggests that the type of optional encoding used
does have important effects.

Turning to the final comparison, the critical finding was that many of
the areas more activated during uninstructed viewing of fear-related versus
neutral pictures remained more active during emotional encoding than non-
emotional encoding, even when holding the picture content constant, consistent with substantial higher-level cognitive control over fear-related neural
activation. Modulation of fear-related activation in many areas often believed
to be part of a largely automatic fear module, suggests they can in fact be
modified by optional cognitive processes, showing that the encoding of emotional events is not immune from top-down attentional control (Pessoa,
Kastner, & Ungerleider, 2002). Furthermore, activation associated with fear-
related encoding was positively related to individual differences in fearfulness,
but (in some areas) negatively correlated with attentional control.

 ## EMOTIONAL CONSEQUENCES OF LEARNED CONTROL OVER ENCODING

The foregoing discussion suggests that optional attention to different aspects
of meaning can have important effects on neural activation in areas thought
to be critical in fear and anxiety. These data imply, but do not conclusively
demonstrate, that control over emotional encoding might have important consequences for the experience of emotion, or for emotional vulnerability. This

expectation has led us (e.g., Mathews & MacLeod, 2002) to conduct a number of studies in which participants engage in tasks designed to promote particular styles of emotional encoding. Some of these studies have utilized attentional tasks in which two stimuli appear, one threatening and one neutral, followed by a to-be-detected target that consistently replaces either the threatening or the neutral stimulus (e.g., MacLeod et al., 2002). Participants who were assigned to the condition in which the to-be-detected target always replaced the threatening word, were expected to learn to attend to threatening words in preference to neutral words. Comparisons of this "attend-threat" condition with the alternative "avoid-threat" condition (in which targets always replaced neutral words) have shown that participants do indeed learn to attend to threatening or neutral words, depending on their assigned experimental condition.

More importantly, although there were no immediately measurable emotional consequences of prolonged practice on such a task, subsequent reactions to stress were markedly different. Specifically, those trained to attend to threatening words reacted with greater increases in negative mood to the subsequent experience of failure in a cognitive test than did those trained to avoid threatening words. Perhaps, therefore, learning to differentially encode threat words leads to greater emotional vulnerability to stress.

Vulnerability to anxiety is also associated with a tendency to encode ambiguous stimuli in terms of their more threatening meaning. In a study by Richards and French (1992), high and low trait anxious individuals completed a lexical decision task in which a homograph prime, having both a threatening and a non-threatening meaning (e.g., growth, which could refer to becoming larger, or to a tumor), was followed by an associated word matching either meaning. With a 750 ms interval between the onset of primes and targets, high trait anxious participants displayed disproportionately greater priming of lexical decision latencies for targets related to the threat rather than the non-threat meanings of these homographs.

It is possible, however, that anxiety vulnerability and encoding bias might not be causally related but might both be independently caused by some third factor. To investigate whether the relationship is causal requires the use of designs in which encoding is manipulated experimentally, so as to test if emotional vulnerability has been modified accordingly.

In a study of whether such an encoding bias could be induced experimentally, Grey and Mathews (2000) modified the semantic priming paradigm employed by Richards and French (1992) by presenting volunteers with a word prime, followed 750 ms later by a word fragment that could be completed to yield a word associated with the meaning of the preceding prime. Participants were assigned at random to conditions in which the target fragment always corresponded to the threatening or to the non-threatening meaning of the prime.

That is, within the non-threat training condition, all word-fragment targets permitted only completions associated with the non-threatening meanings of the preceding homograph primes. Conversely, within the threat training condition, all word-fragment targets permitted only completions associated with the threatening meanings of the preceding homographs.

In subsequent test trials, participants exposed to the threat training condition were faster to complete fragments yielding words associated with the threatening meaning of new homograph primes, whereas the reverse was true for participants exposed to the non-threat training condition. Similarly, threat-trained participants were faster to identify threat-related targets in a lexical decision task, when primed with new homographs. It thus appeared that training caused participants to acquire a differential tendency to encode ambiguous stimuli in terms of either their threatening or non-threatening meanings.

As previously indicated, in order to examine the hypothesis that encoding bias can make a causal contribution to anxiety vulnerability, it is necessary to assess the emotional consequences of experimentally manipulating this bias. In a study designed to test this hypothesis (Mathews & Mackintosh, 2000), we trained participants to encode descriptions of emotionally ambiguous events in a threatening or non-threatening fashion, and rated their anxious mood state at the outset and end of the training session. Anxious mood state increased in those exposed to the threat training condition, but tended to decrease in the group exposed to the non-threat training condition. This finding suggests that the manipulation of encoding bias served to modify anxiety vulnerability, so that participants who acquired a tendency to encode events as threatening consequently became more susceptible to experiencing elevated anxiety.

In a subsequent study, Wilson, MacLeod, and Mathews (2006) followed the training method described by Grey and Mathews (2000) but then tested emotional vulnerability in participants assigned to different training groups by assessing their reaction to a video showing emergency personnel attempting to rescue victims of serious accidents. Importantly, after training with single homographs (rather than with realistic event descriptions as used by Mathews & Mackintosh, 2000) there were no immediate changes in mood as a function of the assigned training conditions. After training, however, when participants were exposed to the video depicting real-life rescue operations, those whose prior training had been designed to induce an encoding bias favoring threatening meanings reported a greater anxiety response than did those in the alternative condition, who had been induced to encode ambiguity in a non-threatening way. Thus it appears that induction of an encoding bias does not necessarily in itself produce any changes in emotional state. Rather, it is only when the induced encoding bias serves to influence how potentially emotional events are processed that differences in emotional vulnerability are revealed.

▉ SUMMARY AND CONCLUSIONS

This chapter has been concerned with variations in how emotional stimuli and events are encoded into memory. Given the fairly consistent evidence that emotionally arousing events are recalled better than non-emotional events, it seems surprising that the evidence of parallel memory effects due to individual differences in emotionality is so inconsistent. Specifically, although depressed individuals often show relatively better recall of negative (self-relevant) information, most studies of those prone to anxiety show either no such effects, or sometimes even poorer recall of emotional stimuli than do non-anxious individuals (see MacLeod & Mathews, 2004). However, we have argued here that these apparently paradoxical findings depend on the imposition of fixed semantic encoding procedures. In some recent studies in which individuals were left free to employ different encoding methods, recall differences were more consistent with expectations. Anxiety seems to be associated with selective encoding of emotional meanings (particularly when associated with threat). Thus, when individuals are free to encode events in any way they select, those who are prone to anxiety do indeed recall more threatening information.

It was also argued that this differential encoding is related to the well established finding that anxiety is associated with selective attention to threat. Such selective attention may be partly responsible for differential encoding and subsequent better memory for threatening content. A specific example occurs when people remember emotionally arousing pictures that they saw previously. As predicted, the normal boundary extension effect, in which pictures are remembered as being more extended in space than they were in fact, was reduced when emotionally arousing content occupies the spatial center of the picture. A similar effect, specific to anxiety-prone individuals, occurred with particularly threatening pictures. Such findings are consistent with the view that selective attention can result in differential encoding of, and better memory for, emotionally arousing and threatening aspects of events.

As well as individual differences influencing how emotional events are encoded, the manner in which events are encoded can lead to emotional consequences. Instructions to judge pictures in different ways were found to have clearly significant effects on the pattern of brain activation seen in response to fear-related versus neutral pictures. Thus, for example, activation in brain areas such as the amygdala was greater when viewing fear-related pictures than when viewing neutral pictures, but this difference was reduced when attending to non-emotional aspects. It seems that such activation is not completely automatic, but can be influenced by top-down control over attention, although both this activation and its control varies according to individual differences.

Other evidence suggests that control over emotional encoding can be learned via training. When encoding is modified by practice in accessing specific valenced meanings, there are important effects on subsequent responses to potentially emotional events. Specifically, practice in the selective encoding of negative meaning leads to greater emotional vulnerability to threatening events. In summary, it appears that there is a causal relation between emotional encoding and emotional arousal that can operate in either direction. On the one hand, we have shown that higher levels of (negative) emotional arousal are associated with better encoding of threatening stimuli, and greater activation in the brain regions involved in such encoding. On the other hand, we have also shown that this brain activation, and the associated preferential encoding of emotional information, can be brought under experimental control. Importantly, this control over encoding has been shown to have causal effects on the later experience of emotion in response to stressful events. Consequently, learned control over emotional encoding has implications both for better theoretical understanding of the link between selective encoding and emotion, and for the prevention or modification of adverse emotional states.

AUTHOR NOTE

Correspondence concerning this chapter should be addressed to Andrew Mathews, Department of Psychology, University of California, Davis, One Shields Avenue, Davis, CA 95616-6868, USA.

REFERENCES

Botvinick, M. M., Braver, T. S., Barch, D. M., Carter, C. S., & Cohen, J. D. (2001). Conflict monitoring and cognitive control. *Psychological Review, 108*, 624–652.

Bradley, M. M., Greenwald, M. K., Petry, M. C., & Lang, P. J. (1992). Remembering pictures: Pleasure and arousal in memory. *Journal of Experimental Psychology: Learning, Memory, and Cognition, 18*, 379–390.

Brewin, C. R. (2001). A cognitive neuroscience account of post-traumatic stress disorder and its treatment. *Behaviour Research and Therapy, 39*, 373–393.

Burke, A., Heuer, F., & Reisberg, D. (1992). Remembering emotional events. *Memory and Cognition, 20*, 277–290.

Bush, G., Luu, P., & Posner, M. I. (2000). Cognitive and emotional influences in anterior cingulate cortex. *Trends in Cognitive Sciences, 4*, 215–222.

Cahill, L. & McGaugh, J. L. (1995). A novel demonstration of enhanced memory associated with emotional arousal. *Consciousness and Cognition, 4*, 410–421.

Candel, I., Merckelbach, H., & Zandbergen, M. (2003). Boundary distortions for neutral and emotional pictures. *Psychonomic Bulletin & Review, 10*, 691–695.

Carver, C. S. & White, T. L. (1994). Behavioral inhibition, behavioral activation, and affective responses to impending reward and punishment – the BIS BAS scales. *Journal of Personality and Social Psychology, 67*, 319–333.

Christianson, S.-Å. (1992). Emotional stress and eyewitness memory: A critical review. *Psychological Bulletin, 112*, 284–309.

Christianson, S.-Å. & Loftus, E. (1991). Remembering emotional events: The fate of detailed information. *Cognition & Emotion, 5*, 81–108.

Derryberry, D. & Reed, M. A. (2002). Anxiety-related attentional biases and their regulation by attentional control. *Journal of Abnormal Psychology, 111*, 225–236.

Easterbrook, J. A. (1959). The effect of emotion on cue utilization and the organization of behavior. *Psychological Review, 66*, 183–201.

Fenske, M. J. & Eastwood, J. D. (2003). Modulation of focused attention by faces expressing emotion: Evidence from flanker tasks. *Emotion, 3*, 327–343.

Fodor, J. A. (1983). *The modularity of mind: An essay on faculty psychology*. Cambridge, MA: MIT Press.

Fox, E., Russo, R., Bowles, R., & Dutton, K. (2001). Do threatening stimuli draw or hold visual attention in subclinical anxiety? *Journal of Experimental Psychology: General, 130*, 681–700.

Friedman, B. H., Thayer, J. F., & Borkovec, T. D. (2000). Explicit memory bias for threat words in generalized anxiety disorder. *Behavior Therapy, 31*, 745–756.

Gray, J. A. & McNaughton, N. (2000). *The neuropsychology of anxiety* (2nd ed.). Oxford: Oxford University Press.

Grey, S. & Mathews, A. (2000). Effects of training on interpretation of emotional ambiguity. *Quarterly Journal of Experimental Psychology, 53A*, 1143–1162.

Heuer, F. & Reisberg, D. (1990). Vivid memories of emotional events: The accuracy of remembered minutiae. *Memory and Cognition, 18*, 496–506.

Iidaka, T., Omori, M., Murata, T., Kosaka, H., Yonekura, Y., Okada, T., & Sadato, N. (2001). Neural interaction of the amygdala with the prefrontal and temporal cortices in the processing of facial expressions as revealed by fMRI. *Journal of Cognitive Neuroscience, 13*, 1035–1047.

Intraub, H. (2002). Anticipatory spatial representation of natural scenes: Momentum without movement? *Visual Cognition, 9*, 93–119.

Intraub, H., Bender, R. S., & Mangels, J. A. (1992). Looking at pictures but remembering scenes. *Journal of Experimental Psychology: Learning, Memory and Cognition, 18*, 180–191.

Intraub, H. & Bodamer, J. L. (1993). Boundary extension: Fundamental aspect of pictorial representation or encoding artifact? *Journal of Experimental Psychology: Learning, Memory and Cognition, 19*, 1387–1397.

Intraub, H. & Richardson, M. (1989). Wide-angle memories of close-up scenes. *Journal of Experimental Psychology: Learning, Memory and Cognition, 15*, 179–187.

Kalin, N. H., Shelton, S. E., Davidson, R. J., & Kelley, A. E. (2001). The primate amygdala mediates acute fear but not the behavioral and physiological components of anxious temperament. *Journal of Neuroscience, 21*, 2067–2074.

Lang, P. J., Bradley, M., & Cuthbert, B. N. (1995). *International affective picture system (IAPS)*. NIMH Centre for the Study of Emotion and Attention, University of Florida.

Lange, K., Williams, L. M., Young, A. W., Bullmore, E. T., Brammer, M. J., Williams, S. C. R., Gray, J. A., & Phillips, M. L. (2003). Task instructions modulate neural responses to fearful facial expressions. *Biological Psychiatry, 53*, 226–232.

LeDoux, J. E. (1996). *The emotional brain*. New York: Simon & Schuster.

Libkuman, T. M., Nichols-Whitehead, P., Griffith, J., & Thomas, R. (1999). Source of arousal and memory for detail. *Memory and Cognition, 27,* 166–190.

MacLeod, C. & Mathews, A. (2004). Selective memory effects in anxiety disorders: An overview of research findings and their implications. In D. Reisberg & P. Hertel (Eds.), *Memory and emotion* (pp. 155–185). New York: Oxford University Press.

MacLeod, C. & McLaughlin, K. (1995). Implicit and explicit memory bias in anxiety: A conceptual replication. *Behaviour Research and Therapy, 33,* 1–14.

MacLeod, C., Rutherford, E., Campbell, L., Ebsworthy, G., & Holker, L. (2002). Selective attention and emotional vulnerability: Assessing the causal basis of their association through the experimental manipulation of attentional bias. *Journal of Abnormal Psychology, 111,* 107–123.

Mathews, A. (1996). Selective encoding of emotional information. In D. Herrman, C. McEvoy, C. Hertzog, P. Hertel, & M. K. Johnson (Eds.), *Basic and applied memory research* (Vol. 2, pp. 287–300). Mahwah, NJ: Erlbaum.

Mathews, A. & Mackintosh, B. (2000). Induced emotional interpretation bias and anxiety. *Journal of Abnormal Psychology, 109,* 602–615.

Mathews, A. & Mackintosh, B. (2004). Take a closer look: Emotion modifies the boundary extension effect. *Emotion, 4,* 36–45.

Mathews, A., Mackintosh, B., & Fulcher, E. (1997). A cognitive model of selective processing in anxiety. *Cognitive Therapy and Research, 22,* 539–560.

Mathews, A. & MacLeod, C. (1994). Cognitive approaches to emotion and emotional disorders. *Annual Review of Psychology, 45,* 25–50.

Mathews, A. & MacLeod, C. (2002). Induced processing biases have causal effects on anxiety. *Cognition and Emotion, 16,* 331–354.

Mathews, A. & MacLeod, C. (2005). Cognitive vulnerability to emotional disorders. *Annual Review of Clinical Psychology, 1,* 167–195.

Mathews, A., Yiend, J., & Lawrence, A. D. (2004). Individual differences in the modulation of fear-related brain activation by attentional control. *Journal of Cognitive Neuroscience, 16,* 1683–1694.

Mongeau, R., Miller, G. A., Chiang, E., & Anderson, D. J. (2003). Neural correlates of competing fear behaviors evoked by an innately aversive stimulus. *Journal of Neuroscience, 23,* 3855–3868.

Morris, J. S., DeGelder, B., Weiskrantz, L., & Dolan, R. J. (2001). Differential extrageniculostriate and amygdala responses to presentation of emotional faces in a cortically blind field. *Brain, 124,* 1241–1252.

Morris, J. S., Öhman, A., & Dolan, R. J. (1999). A subcortical pathway to the right amygdala mediating "unseen" fear. *Proceedings of the National Academy of Science, 96,* 1680–1685.

Öhman, A. (2002). Automaticity and the amygdala: Nonconscious responses to emotional faces. *Current Directions in Psychological Science, 11,* 62–66.

Öhman, A. & Mineka, S. (2001). Fears, phobias, and preparedness: Towards an evolved module of fear and fear learning. *Psychological Review, 108,* 483–522.

Öhman, A. & Mineka, S. (2003). The malicious serpent: Snakes as a prototypical stimulus for an evolved module of fear. *Current Directions in Psychological Science, 12,* 5–9.

Pessoa, L., Kastner, S., & Ungerleider, L. G. (2002). Attentional control of the processing of neutral and emotional stimuli. *Cognitive Brain Research, 15,* 31–45.

Pury, C. L. S. & Mineka, S. (2001). Differential encoding of affective and nonaffective content information in trait anxiety. *Cognition & Emotion, 15,* 659–693.

Reisberg, D. & Heuer, F. (1992). Remembering the details of emotional scenes. In E. Wingrad & U. Neisser (Eds.), *Affect and accuracy in recall: Studies of "flashbulb" memory* (pp. 162–190). New York: Cambridge University Press.

Revelle, W. & Loftus, D. A. (1990). Individual differences and arousal: Implications for the study of mood and memory. *Cognition and Emotion, 3,* 209–237

Richards, A. & French, C. C. (1992). An anxiety-related bias in semantic activation when processing threat/neutral homographs. *Quarterly Journal of Experimental Psychology, 45A,* 503–525.

Russo, R., Fox, E., Bellinger, L., & Nguyen-Van-Tam, D. P. (2001). Mood-congruent free recall bias in anxiety. *Cognition & Emotion, 15,* 419–433.

Russo, R., Fox, E., & Bowles, R. J. (1999). On the status of implicit memory bias in anxiety. *Cognition & Emotion, 13,* 435–456.

Safer, M. A., Christianson, S., Autry, M. W., & Osterland, K. (1998). Tunnel memory for traumatic events. *Applied Cognitive Psychology, 12,* 99–117.

Taylor, S. T., Phan, K. L., Decker, L. R., & Liberzon, I. (2003). Subjective rating of emotionally salient stimuli modulates neural activity. *Neuroimage, 18,* 650–659.

Vuilleumier, P., Armony, J. L., Driver, J., & Dolan, R. J. (2001). Effects of attention and emotion on face processing in the human brain: An event-related fMRI study. *Neuron, 30,* 829–841.

Watson, D., Clark, L. A., & Tellegen, A. (1988). Development and validation of brief measures of positive and negative affect: The PANAS scales. *Journal of Personality and Social Psychology, 54,* 1063–1070.

Wessel, I., van der Kooy, P., & Merckelbach, H. (2000). Differential recall of central and peripheral details of emotional slides is not a stable phenomenon. *Memory, 8,* 95–109.

Whalen, P. J., Rauch, S. L., Etcoff, N. L., McInerey, S. C., Lee, M. B., & Jenicke, M. A. (1998). Masked presentations of emotional facial expressions modulate amygdala activation without explicit knowledge. *Journal of Neuroscience, 18,* 411–418.

Wilson, E., MacLeod, C., & Mathews, A. (2006). The causal role of interpretative bias in vulnerability to anxiety. *Journal of Abnormal Psychology.*

Yiend, J. & Mathews, A. (2001). Anxiety and attention to threatening pictures. *Quarterly Journal of Experimental Psychology, 54A,* 665–681.

Zald, D. H. (2003). The human amygdala and the emotional evaluation of sensory stimuli. *Brain Research Reviews, 41,* 88–123.

Zald, D. H., Mattson, D. L., & Pardo, J. V. (2002). Brain activity in the ventromedial prefrontal cortex correlates with individual differences in negative affect. *Proceedings of the National Academy of Sciences, 99,* 2450–2454.

Memory, Emotion, and Psychotherapy: Maximizing the Positive Functions of Self-Defining Memories

Jefferson A. Singer

Abstract

Emotional memories are likely to emerge across all forms of psychotherapies, whether during the initial history or over ensuing sessions. This chapter presents one such memory from a clinical case study, identifying it as an example of an extensively researched autobiographical memory – the self-defining memory. I review laboratory support for five key features of self-defining memories and then locate self-defining memories in a conceptual model of autobiographical memory and the self. Drawing on this model, the chapter demonstrates how self-defining memories can potentially serve directive, communicative, and self-regulatory functions for individuals. Linking this theory and research back to the clinical arena, I return to the previously discussed case study and illustrate how psychotherapeutic interventions can maximize emotional memories' positive functions.

All psychotherapies, regardless of orientation, require clients to recount the history of the presenting problem along with some general background of their lives. In the course of providing these details from the past, it is likely that clients will recall emotional memories that convey critical concerns or conflicts relevant to their current struggles (Pennebaker, 1995). This chapter focuses on the nature of these potent memory narratives and the role they occupy in the general personality of individuals, as well as the potential role they may play in insight and intervention in psychotherapy. Specifically, I address the functions that these emotional memories serve for clients and then place them in a conceptual framework based in personality and memory research. Having provided this theoretical context, I review research studies from my laboratory that demonstrate the functional role of emotional memories in lesson-learning, interpersonal communication, and mood regulation. Finally, I return to the clinical setting and illustrate how clients may avail themselves of these functions by enlisting their emotional memories as sources of growth and change in psychotherapy.

 AN EMOTIONAL MEMORY DISCLOSED IN PSYCHOTHERAPY

To ground our discussion of emotional memories narrated in psychotherapy, I draw on the following memory from a female client, Tina (name and details changed to protect anonymity), who was undergoing couples therapy with her husband, James. Tina had a history of her own psychological difficulties, including an eating disorder, bouts of depression, and several obsessive-compulsive characteristics. Her tension with James centered on his perceived passivity and failure to "step up to the plate and take care of her and their children effectively." She questioned James's competence and in response he seemed withdrawn, tentative, and defeated. In expanding on her difficulties with James's shortcomings, she described the following memory of her father by way of contrast:

> My dad was in the military and we moved nearly every year when I was growing up; sometimes we even moved two to three times in the same year. When my dad was home, he was our superhero and we all did everything we could to please him. In turn, he seemed to know all the answers and how to fix anything that needed fixing.
>
> I remember one specific time when I sprained my ankle badly at school. That night my dad came home late and found me still in pain on the couch. He carried me to the car, brought me to get an ice cream cone, and had me singing with the radio on the drive home. I felt so safe when he tucked me into bed that night. It was almost like he had healed my ankle with magic powers. This memory reminds me of how much I like to have someone take care of me.

Tina's voice showed strong feeling as she recalled this vivid memory and it marked a powerful contrast to the many times that she felt disappointed by James's lack of assertiveness in their current relationship. Since she returned to this memory more than once over the course of the early sessions of the couples therapy, let us ask what functions the recollection of this kind of emotional memory might serve for Tina.

In recent work on autobiographical memory, David Pillemer (1992, 1998, 2003) and Susan Bluck (Alea & Bluck, 2003; Bluck, 2003; Bluck & Alea, 2002) have highlighted functional analyses of narrative memories (see also earlier articles by Bruce, 1989; Hyman & Faries, 1992). Bluck (2003) has particularly emphasized three important functions of autobiographical memory: (1) *directive* (meaning-making, lesson-learning, problem-solving); (2) *social* (intimacy, teaching, empathy); and (3) *self* (self-continuity, self-esteem maintenance, emotion regulation). Any autobiographical memory might perform one or more of these functions, but clearly Tina's memory holds a particular power for her, given its emotional resonance and her repeated return to it over the course of therapy. Its centrality to significant themes in her relationships to others and in her own self-understanding heighten its power as a source of meaning-making, interpersonal communication, and emotion regulation.

Such touchstone memories can be considered *self-defining memories* and they have been the focus of my research efforts and clinical case studies for the past 15 years (Blagov & Singer, 2004; Moffitt & Singer, 1994; Singer, 1995, 2004; Singer & Moffitt, 1991–2; Singer & Salovey, 1993, 1996). In order to understand the influential functions of direction, communication, and emotion regulation that self-defining memories can perform, I offer a comprehensive description of self-defining memories and their role in the memory and self system of the personality (Conway & Pleydell-Pearce, 2000).

 ## CHARACTERISTICS OF SELF-DEFINING MEMORIES

In previous work, I have defined self-defining memories (SDMs) as consisting of five key characteristics: (1) vividness; (2) emotionality; (3) repetition; (4) linkage to similar memories; and (5) relationship to enduring concerns or unresolved conflicts (Singer & Moffitt, 1991–2; Singer & Salovey, 1993). Before reviewing each of these characteristics and empirical evidence for them, let us locate self-defining memories in the larger framework of autobiographical memory. Self-defining memories are autobiographical memories that are *declarative*, *episodic*, and *autonoetic* (see Nelson & Fivush, 2004, for their account of the critical features of autobiographical memory).

By *declarative* (Squire, 1995), I mean that they are conscious memories – memories that individuals are aware of having and that they can clearly see in their mind's eye. By *episodic* (Schacter, Wagner, & Buckner, 2000), I mean that they are of a specific event that is traceable to a defined moment or set of moments in time. However, although the majority of self-defining memories display this specificity and uniqueness of event status, individuals do vary in their capacity to recall specific events vs. more generalized or summary recollections. Singer and Blagov (2002) have developed a reliable and valid scoring system that differentiates single-event from summary memory narratives. These variations can be meaningfully linked to personality characteristics, including depression and defensiveness (Blagov & Singer, 2004). Finally, by *autonoetic* (Tulving &

Lepage, 2000), I draw on Tulving's distinction between one's knowledge of a past event and one's personal experience of having lived through the event as an active participant. While the first type of knowledge might include information one has read about or absorbed through the media, the second type of knowledge (i.e., autonoetic) requires the individual to retain a personal awareness of having actually experienced the event. When the past event is recalled, it is as if the self is reinserted into the narrative of the event.

Self-defining memories may also be considered a form of what Pillemer (1998) has defined as *personal memories*. Pillemer defines personal memories as memories of specific events that include a detailed personal account that contain sensory images. These accounts are linked to moments of insight or greater personal awareness and they are believed to be accurate renderings of the original events (in other words, the individual sees the memory as a reasonably veridical recreation of the past).

What distinguishes a self-defining memory from other types of personal event memories? Pillemer (1998) makes clear that the term "personal event memory" does not in and of itself imply that the memory is always of strong personal relevance and of an enduring nature. Over time specific personal event memories may diminish in affective intensity, and not all of these memories will remain accessible to conscious memory. Even taking into account those memories that persist over time due to strong imagery and emotion, not all of them are necessarily linked to central goals and thematic concerns of the personality.

For example, we can distinguish self-defining memories from one form of enduring and emotionally charged personal memory. *Flashbulb memories* (Brown & Kulik, 1977; Conway, 1995; Conway et al., 1994; Smith, Bibi, & Sheard, 2003) have been characterized as particularly vivid and accurate personal memories that are usually formed in response to dramatic and emotionally charged news (e.g., news of President Kennedy's assassination, the *Challenger* crash, September 11, 2001). The shock of learning of the event is presumed to set off a "now print" mechanism in the brain that preserves the details of the moment associated with the revelation in an almost iconic fashion (e.g., who you were with, clothes you were wearing, what activity you were doing, etc.).

Self-defining memories share a number of common characteristics with flashbulb memories. Both types of memories are vivid, emotional and are likely to return repeatedly to one's thoughts over time. However, flashbulb memories may also vary from self-defining memories in significant ways. For example, while I have a powerful memory of where I was when I heard the news of September 11, 2001, this memory has not continued to resonate in my thoughts except for when individuals ask me about my whereabouts during that day. In the same way I do not see my September 11 memory as particularly linked to a network of similarly themed memories about threat or danger in my life (in a narrow sense, however, the memory is linked to other flashbulb memories that have captured my attention over my lifetime). Lastly, since I was not directly involved with the victims of the attacks on the World Trade Center or the Pentagon, and terrorism does not figure prominently in my personal life, I cannot say that my memory of September 11 connects to an enduring concern or unresolved conflict in my personality. This comparison of flashbulb memories and self-defining memories highlights the latter's emphasis on the linkage of the memory in question to thematic concerns that relate to one's sense of identity and self-understanding. Without this connection to longstanding themes of the personality, memories may be vivid, emotional, and highly accessible, but they will fall short of the self-defining criteria.

 EMPIRICAL EVIDENCE FOR THE FIVE CHARACTERISTICS OF SELF-DEFINING MEMORIES

Since the introduction of the concept of self-defining memories, my colleagues and I have studied them through both clinical case studies and laboratory research. Clinical case studies have highlighted both the identification of these memory narratives in psychotherapy and their role in transference interpretations and more explicit cognitive-behavioral interventions, including guided imagery, role-playing, and reframing (Singer, 1997, Singer 2001, Singer, 2005a, 2005b; Singer & Blagov, 2004a, 2004b).

In laboratory studies, we have used the self-defining memory request (see table 10.1) to collect written narratives of self-defining memories.[1] In the typical study, we will collect from five to ten self-defining memories from a relatively large sample of undergraduate students (usually 100 or more participants). After recording their memories, each participant fills out rating scales from 0 to 6 for their current emotions about each memory (e.g., happiness, pride, anger, sadness, embarrassment, etc.). They also rate the vividness and importance of the memories on the same rating scales, and then indicate how many years ago the memory took place. Once the memories are collected, they may be scored for both structural features (single event vs. summary) and the degree to which they contain "integrative meaning" (self-reflective statements or life lessons). Scoring for structure and integrative meaning is accomplished through use of the *Classification System and Scoring Manual for Self-Defining Autobiographical Memories* (Singer & Blagov, 2002).

Empirical studies of self-defining memories conducted in my laboratory and by other investigators have provided support for the five characteristics that constitute the operationalized definition of self-defining memories.

Table 10.1 Self-defining memory task.

This part of the experiment concerns the recall of a special kind of personal memory called a self-defining memory. A self-defining memory has the following attributes:

1 It is at least one year old.
2 It is a memory from your life that you remembered very clearly and that still feels important to you even as you think about it.
3 It is a memory about an important enduring theme, issue, or conflict from your life. It is a memory that helps explain who you are as an individual and might be the memory you would tell someone else if you wanted that person to understand you in a profound way.
4 It is a memory linked to other similar memories that share the same theme or concern.
5 It may be a memory that is positive or negative, or both, in how it makes you feel. The only important aspect is that it leads to strong feelings.
6 It is a memory that you have thought about many times. It should be familiar to you like a picture you have studied or a song (happy or sad) you have learned by heart.

To understand best what a self-defining memory is, imagine you have just met someone you like very much and are going for a walk together. Each of you is very committed to helping the other get to know the "Real You." You are not trying to play a role or to strike a pose. While, inevitably, we say things that present a picture of ourselves that might not be completely accurate, imagine that you are making every effort to be honest. In the course of the conversation, you describe a memory that you feel conveys powerfully how you have come to be the person you currently are. It is precisely this memory, which you tell the other person and simultaneously repeat to yourself, that constitutes a self-defining memory.

On the following pages you will be asked to recall and write ten self-defining memories.

Vividness and emotionality

SDMs have a strong sensory quality, usually visual, for the participants who recall them. Over the past dozen years of collecting self-defining memories through written and oral protocols (Blagov & Singer, 2004; Moffitt & Singer, 1994; Singer & Moffitt, 1991–2), participants have provided mean vividness ratings of greater than 4.7 on a 0–6 point scale. In three experiments (432 participants), Singer and Moffitt (1991–2) found mean vividness ratings that ranged from 5.08 to 5.34; Moffittt and Singer (1994) obtained a mean vividness of 4.74 from 117 participants; and Blagov and Singer (2004) calculated a 4.83 mean vividness rating based on 103 participants. Participants have described the memory as having the quality of a "movie inside their head" or a particularly evocative daydream.

Similarly, individuals indicate that these memories have the power to affect them emotionally not just in the past, but also at the very moment of recollection. For example, Singer and Moffitt (1991–2) found across three experiments that participants reported over 75 percent of memories to have a current positive or negative emotion rating of greater than 3 on a 6-point scale. Similarly, Moffitt et al. (1994), in a study of 90 participants, obtained mean positive emotion ratings of 4.07 on a 0–6 scale.

Repetition

The self-defining memory request stipulates that individuals recall memories that the individual has "thought about many times. It should be familiar to you like a picture you have studied or a song (happy or sad) you have learned by heart" (Blagov & Singer, 2004; Singer & Blagov, 2002; see table 10.1). In a recent study of SDMs about moments in which college summer interns experienced themselves as "rising to the occasion" (Singer et al., 2002), we explicitly asked participants how often they had thought about these memories in the six months since the events had occurred. On average, participants replied that they had returned to the memory between once a week and once a month during this time, while a few participants indicated they had thought about the memory on a daily basis.

Linkage to similar memories

SDMs, to the extent that they capture characteristic and significant aspects of individuals' self-understanding, are likely to be connected to a network of related memories that share similar goals, outcomes, and affective responses. In support of this assertion, Thorne, Cutting, and Skaw (1998) examined young adults' important relationship memories collected in two interviews over a six-month period. Participants were given license to recall the same or different memories on the second occasion. Raters coded both sets of memories for the predominant social motives (e.g., independence, affiliation, power) that emerged in the memory narratives. Regardless of whether the memories were repeated or unique over the two collection periods, Thorne and colleagues found a significant degree of thematic consistency in the social motives across the memories. In other words, individuals tended to produce clusters of thematically linked memories that reflected similar interpersonal themes.

In related research, Demorest has been able to show that individuals possess emotional and interpersonal scripts that underline the basic plot structures of many of the narratives they recount (see the work of Tomkins, 1979, on script theory). When asked to generate memories or any other self-generated products of their imagination, individuals are likely to rely on these scripts to guide their imagery and narrative output. In an earlier study, Demorest and Alexander (1992) asked participants to recall important emotional memories from their lives. Raters then extracted the key emotional interpersonal scripts from these memories. A month later, participants returned to the laboratory and generated fictional stories from their imagination. Raters once again extracted scripts from this fictional material. In over 60 percent of the cases, the experimenters were able to match the scripts drawn from the actual autobiographical material to the scripts abstracted from the fictional stories. Demorest concluded that these fundamental scripted templates, which contain key information about cognition, emotion, and behavior, organize and help to shape important interpersonal material stored in memory.

More recently, Demorest and Siegel (1996) demonstrated that the language and imagery that B. F. Skinner used in his autobiography to describe early events from his life matched thematically with the same language and imagery that he used to describe rats' behavior in learning chambers in his first book on operant conditioning. Undergraduate raters were able to match the "thematic maps" extracted from these disparate passages, even when they were disguised and interspersed with a variety of other thematic maps extracted from various individuals' personal writings. The combination of Thorne's and Demorest's findings do indeed support the idea that memories and narrative material in general may be linked by a network of shared thematic and affective features.

Relationship to enduring concerns or unresolved conflicts

As stated earlier in this section, what truly distinguishes SDMs from other emotionally charged personal memories is the relationship of these memories to longstanding and developmentally central concerns and conflicts in individuals' lives. In two earlier studies (Moffitt & Singer, 1994; Singer, 1990), we demonstrated that individuals' current affective responses to memories were a function of the memories' relevance to the success or failure of important goals in their lives. These relationships were moderately strong (correlations in the 0.5–0.7 range) and held for both approach and avoidance goals. Interestingly, individuals who had higher percentages of avoidance goals than the rest of the sample also tended to recall more memories about the non-attainment of their goals. In exploring this relationship, it was apparent that highly avoidant individuals recalled memories about the negative consequences of failing to avoid a dreaded outcome. Such memories seemed to serve as cautionary tales and provided reinforcement for their avoidant stances.

Many other researchers, when studying critically important self-defining memories, such as "turning point memories" or "peak experiences," have found a similar strong relationship between the thematic content of the memory and the dominant goals or social motives in the individual. For example, McAdams (1982; McAdams, Hoffman et al., 1996) has demonstrated repeatedly that power-oriented memories are connected to individuals' agentic motives, while intimacy-oriented memories link to communal motives in individuals. Thorne and Michaelieu (1996) identified a correlation between positive and negative relationship memories and respective levels of high and low self-esteem. Most recently, Sutin and Robins (2005), in a longitudinal study over four years, found consistent correlations between enduring personality characteristics and achievement and power motives as scored from self-defining memories. For example, individuals high in self-esteem (Rosenberg, 1965) and conscientiousness (Costa & McCrae, 1992) showed greater themes of achievement motivation in their memories, while individuals who scored high in narcissism on a Narcissistic Personality Inventory (Raskin & Terry, 1988) showed more evidence of power motivation in their SDMs.

To conclude this section, a range of studies over a 15-year period has demonstrated that SDMs are vivid, affectively intense, and return frequently to individuals' conscious thoughts. SDMs are linked to other memories that share underlying scripts and themes within the individuals' overall organization of mental content. Finally, these memories reflect the enduring goals and developmental concerns of personality.

LOCATING SELF-DEFINING MEMORIES IN A CONCEPTUAL MODEL OF AUTOBIOGRAPHICAL MEMORY RETRIEVAL

In recent efforts to describe the relationship of autobiographical memory to a larger network of self-relevant cognition, affect, and behavioral tendencies, Conway and colleagues (Conway & Pleydell-Pearce, 2000; Conway, Singer, & Tagini, 2004) have proposed an encompassing Self-Memory System (SMS). This system consists of three interlocking cognitive-affective subsystems: the Working Self, Episodic Memory System, and the Long-Term Self (see figure 10.1). These three components work together to allow individuals to pursue ongoing short-term goals, create records of this recent activity, and, when necessary,

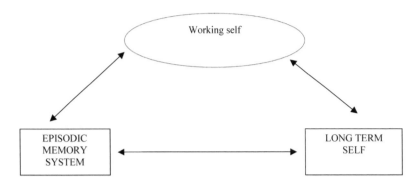

Figure 10.1 The Self-Memory System.

shift into a retrieval mode to draw on an autobiographical knowledge base and semantic information relevant to current task demands.

The working self consists of a complex hierarchy of goals relevant to a current activity. All are active, but vary in their degree of activation depending on the demands of the current task. In addition to the active goals, the working self includes self-images and plans associated with the goals within the particular hierarchy; these images and plans are not necessarily conscious, but may become so, as required by the goal progress. For example, if I am giving a talk at a research meeting, my working self will consist of a goal hierarchy related to the successful presentation of my material. These goals might include a desire to impress the audience, to be organized in the presentation, to be dynamic in the delivery, and to manage time appropriately. As I proceed with the talk, images of previous discussions of my research may be present, as might well-rehearsed strategies that I have learned about how to give emphasis to certain points or to skip others in the interest of time.

As the working self allows me to pursue these immediate goals, my Episodic Memory System is forming short-duration sensory-perceptual affective "summaries" of recent processing. As Conway, Singer, and Tagini (2004) explain, these brief summaries are necessary in order to orient the self as to what actions have been performed and where one stands in the movement toward goal completion. If we were not able to encode brief records of recent activity, we might be doomed to return repetitively to actions that we had already completed, and we would be unlikely to register any completion of a task in process. If I did not form a record of the fact that I displayed a particular figure during my talk, I might repeat the display of this same figure without any knowledge that I had just displayed it. On the other hand, these sensory records would accumulate and flood our cognitive system if we

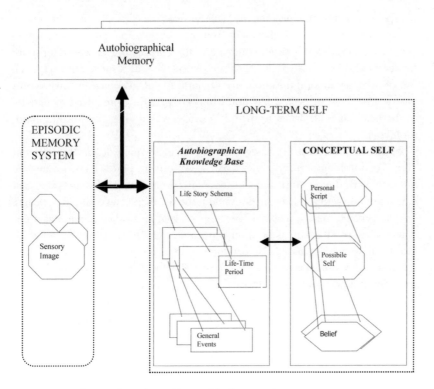

Figure 10.2 Generation of autobiographical memories.

retained every captured summary of ongoing activity. For this reason they are of relatively short duration and fade from permanence unless they are linked to conceptual structures in the Long-Term Self.

The Long-Term Self consists of two primary components: the Auto-biographical Knowledge Base and the Conceptual Self (see figure 10.2). The autobiographical knowledge base contains three temporal units of the self that are aligned in a hierarchy of temporal duration and specificity. At the highest level of this knowledge base is the Life Story Schema (Bluck & Habermas, 2000). The Life Story Schema consists of our sense of the long view of our life and our associated assessments of it as a whole entity. For example, an individual may view her life as a "rags-to-riches" story or a "quest for meaning," or a "story of family devotion." The Life Story Schema takes the chapters and incidents of our life and collects them into a unified whole that provides a sense of purpose or coherence to these smaller units.

At the next level, we find Lifetime Periods, blocks of memory that are defined by distinct epochs or eras of our lives. For example, we might collect a series of experiences under the heading my "college years" or "first job" or "first home." When searching for a specific event from one of these periods, we may often begin by generating this larger context and then proceeding to search for more detailed episodes from within this time period. Still at a more abstract level, but of briefer temporal duration, are General Events. General events encompass weeks, days, or even a few hours and are generally organized by activity or theme, such as "learning to swim," "favorite restaurants," or "turning-point moments."

In order to develop the categories and themes which define the different "bins" of autobiographical knowledge, the Autobiographical Knowledge Base interacts with the semantic units of the Conceptual Self. The Conceptual Self consists of non-temporal abstractions about the self that include attitudes, beliefs, scripts, possible selves, internal working models, and other schematic units. These various self-schemas both influence and are influenced by the autobiographical knowledge base. The products of their reciprocal influence are the relatively stable domains of the Long-Term Self, which highlight the most important temporal periods in an individual's life (e.g., "high school athletics," "work on first book," "early years of marriage," or "time as president of Rotary Club"), along with the dominant themes and concerns (e.g., mastery, intimacy, power).

As figure 10.2 depicts, this Long-Term Self interacts with the records formed by the Episodic Memory System to create the specific and detailed autobiographical memories that come to constitute our memory of our personal past. Episodic memories that share goal themes with the Autobiographical Knowledge Base and the Long-Term Self are likely to be processed more deeply within the overall Self-Memory System and to be retained as enduring memories.

Since we engage in multiple activities and goal pursuits over the course of every day, the usual mode of the Working Self is to inhibit retrieval and processing by the Long-Term Self. The Working Self holds enough motivational and historical information within activated goal hierarchies to function successfully without extensive search through the Autobiographical Knowledge Base or the Conceptual Self. For example, as long as my talk at the research meeting is proceeding smoothly, I have little need to draw on episodes of past talks. In fact, too much attention to complex or emotionally involving memories of previous presentations could distract me or throw me off from the rhythm and pace that I am currently achieving in making my remarks.

On the other hand, when goal activity is frustrated by an obstacle or sudden shift in circumstances (e.g., the LCD projector bulb burns out in the middle of my talk), we are likely to experience an intensified emotional response (see Oatley, 1992, for a theory of emotion based in goal disruption; also Levine & Pizarro, this volume). This emotional response dissolves the inhibitory relationship between the Working Self and the Long-Term Self, and the Self-Memory System shifts into a retrieval mode. If the goal in question is relevant to a developmentally significant theme within the self-concept (e.g., with regard to my talk – mastery and achievement), then the memory search process will prime activation of conceptual structures and autobiographical memories relevant to this emotionally charged developmental goal. At such moments, self-defining memories with their compact linkage of emotion, thematic concerns, and concrete specific past experience are likely to be activated and dominate processing (e.g., suddenly, my memory of when I gave a talk in front of a hostile former professor surfaces and reminds me of how I must keep my cool under pressure). With the emergence of the self-defining memory in the processing sequence of the self-memory system, we are now ready to complete our exploration of the place of self-defining memories in a conceptual model of autobiographical memory.

Self-defining memories are integrative units of the personality that contain vivid images and thematic information about goals and conflicts in our lives. In the course of current goal pursuits, obstacles or challenges can activate recall of these memories as a means of providing a swift and schematic response to situational demands. Due to repetitive recall of these memories and their entrenched relationship to memories that share similar thematic content, the scripted sequences of cognition, emotion, and behavior underlying these memories tend to be rather simplistic and inflexible (for more elaboration on the nature of scripts underlying memories, see Tomkins, 1979).

Their reductive simplicity is clearly both a virtue and a vice. On the positive side, they provide an immediate tangible template for decision and action, based in a past concrete experience. When individuals are in a state of struggle and emotional arousal, this emphatic message diminishes ambiguity and allows for a quick and defined response. On the negative side, their schematic organization tends to disregard nuance and to press new situations into the narrow confines of older circumstances. For instance, in my research talk example, when the projector bulb burns out and I suddenly conjure up the memory of my hostile former professor in the audience, I may be misreading the potential responses of my highly sympathetic audience. Although the previous experience reminds me of my ability to triumph in adverse circumstances, it may also amplify my anxiety unnecessarily. In sum, self-defining memories take charge of processing during challenging situations for better or worse.

 ## RETURNING TO TINA'S SELF-DEFINING MEMORY AND ITS FUNCTIONS IN HER LIFE

We can now return to Tina's memory and consider it in light of what we have established about the role of SDMs in the self-memory system of personality. When her husband James disappoints Tina, frustrating her central goal of feeling in control and leaving her in doubt that the male in her life can take care of her, she is likely to become emotional and summon up relevant SDMs. Her memory of her ankle injury and her father's "heroic" arrival and transformation of her pain and unhappiness looms large in her consciousness. With imagery and emotion associated with this memory now guiding her thoughts, she is likely to find herself dismissive of James and angry about her marriage. This anger fuels her tendency to seek control unilaterally, aggravating her perfectionism and disordered eating, as well as her depressive mood.

Given this prominent role for her SDM, we can legitimately ask about the Directive, Communicative, and Self functions this memory is serving for Tina. From the Directive standpoint, Tina's memory provides her with a powerful "lesson" – that she requires control in her life and James is not the man her father was. From the Communicative standpoint, the memory is an opportunity to "teach" James about what a "real provider" might have to offer and how he lets her down in his inadequate efforts. With regard to the Self function of emotion regulation, the memory serves a brief function of reminding her of the pleasant past, but ultimately leads to negative rumination (Nolen-Hoeksema, 2000) and increased depressive mood.

My goal as a therapist is to help Tina derive more adaptive functions for this SDM, as well as for other memories that she might enlist during emotionally challenging moments. Is this a realistic goal or must SDMs inevitably perform regressive and destructive roles in individuals' lives? My answer is that such positive applications of SDMs are indeed possible and constitute a major outcome of many successful therapies. In order to support this assertion, I return briefly to the laboratory and provide empirical demonstrations of the role of SDMs in more adaptive directive, communicative, and self memory functions.

LABORATORY EVIDENCE FOR POSITIVE DIRECTIVE FUNCTIONS OF SDMS

Blagov and Singer (2004) recently examined the connection of lesson-learning in SDMs to healthy adjustment. We collected 10 memories apiece from over 100 participants and used the Singer and Blagov (2002) coding manual to identify memories that contained statements of insight, lesson-learning, and meaning-making. We called these memories "integrative memories." In addition to collecting the memories, we asked participants to fill out the Weinberger Adjustment Inventory Short Form (WAI-SF; Weinberger, 1997, 1998). This inventory measures two primary dimensions of subjective distress and self-restraint. Weinberger (1998) has demonstrated that individuals who show moderate levels of self-restraint display more successful adjustment in terms of both psychological and physical health. Individuals who are low in self-restraint lean toward impulsive and anti-social tendencies, while individuals who score high in self-restraint are prone to emotional rigidity and repressive tendencies. As predicted, we found that individuals who were able to step back from their SDMs and extract meaningful lessons or insights showed optimal levels of adjustment (moderate self-restraint) on the WAIS-SF. In contrast, both low and high self-restraint individuals recalled fewer integrative SDMS. The ability to find some distance from the SDM and extract a useful lesson from its powerful imagery was clearly associated with healthier adjustment. In therapeutic terms, practitioners need to engage the emotional immediacy of SDMs, but balance their intensity by teaching clients to draw insights and lessons from their potent imagery.

 ## LABORATORY EVIDENCE FOR POSITIVE COMMUNICATIVE FUNCTIONS OF SDMS

In Tina's case, she persisted in using her memory of her father to communicate her disappointment and anger to her spouse. Yet SDMs can be sources of supportive and affirming communication within relationships. Hayden, Singer, and Chrisler (2004) demonstrated this point by studying female college students' narratives of their birth, as recounted to them by their mothers. We collected over 70 of these birth stories and then had raters code them for descriptiveness and emotional quality. We also asked the college student participants to estimate how many times their mothers had shared the story with them. In addition to collecting the narratives, we asked the students to fill out a self-esteem inventory and measure of mother–daughter bonding. Our results indicated that daughters with more positive birth narratives showed higher self-esteem, while at the same time daughters with more frequently told and descriptive stories showed closer relationships with their mothers on several dimensions of the mother–daughter bonding inventory.

We also asked a subset of mothers to provide us with their first-person accounts of their daughters' births. Once again, raters coded these narratives for emotional quality and descriptiveness. The results paralleled our findings for the daughters – more positive and descriptive stories, as told by the mothers, were linked to higher self-esteem and more secure maternal bonding in the daughters. Finally, we asked raters, blind to the identity of the narrators, to match pairs of birth narratives. As predicted, daughters with high self-esteem and stronger maternal bonding were more likely to have their birth stories matched with their mothers' stories.

These various results argue strongly that significant memory narratives can serve a communicative function of conveying intimacy and bonding within a relationship. The therapist's goal in this regard is to locate positive memories within a client's relationships that can be used as healthy touchstones and vehicles for conveying connection rather than discord.

LABORATORY EVIDENCE FOR POSITIVE SELF FUNCTIONS OF SDMS

One of the most important self functions that autobiographical memories can serve is emotion regulation. Tina was unfortunately taking a positive memory from her life and using it to highlight her current frustration. In this sense, rather than using personal memories to regulate or repair dysphoric states, Tina was engaging in a ruminative process of perpetuating her negative mood.

Josephson, Singer, and Salovey (1996) studied the process of mood repair by inducing negative moods in participants (using a montage of painful scenes from *Terms of Endearment*, a film in which a young woman, played by Debra Winger, dies of cancer) and then asking them to recall two consecutive autobiographical memories. All participants had previously filled out the Beck Depression Inventory. As hypothesized, participants who recalled a negative memory, followed by a positive memory, reported a more positive subsequent mood than individuals who recalled two consecutive negative memories. Even more importantly, individuals who recalled two negative memories in a row had depression scores that were almost twice as high as the individuals who recalled a negative–positive memory sequence. (Joormann and Siemer, 2004, recently found a similar difficulty in depressed individuals with regard to their ability to recruit positive memories to repair negative moods.) When we asked participants who followed a negative memory with a positive one why they had recalled their memories in that order, over 60 percent were able to articulate a conscious mood-repair strategy.

We concluded from these results that non-depressed individuals know how to use their personal memories to regulate their emotions and raise their spirits when they experience a temporary negative mood. Translating this finding into the therapeutic arena, therapists can play a clear role in helping their clients to identify SDMs that genuinely improve their moods. Once these memories are selected, clients can learn how to use imagery to enhance the positive emotions and thoughts associated with these mood-repairing memories.

PUTTING THIS ALL TOGETHER: TEACHING TINA THE POSITIVE FUNCTIONS OF SDMS

In my work with Tina's SDM, in the context of her couples therapy, we addressed the negative directive function that she assigned to this memory.

After identifying the ways in which her memory of her father led her to critical judgments of James, we looked at ways to slow down the memory retrieval process and insert questions (in individual therapy, transference interpretations can often be linked to the same thematic pattern that guides the memory; see Singer & Singer, 1992). For example, Tina trained herself to ask, "Is it always fair to compare James to my father?" or "What does James bring to our marriage that my father failed to bring to his?" Most importantly, Tina confronted the fundamental question of whether one could ever hope to be in control of every situation and circumstance in life. In acknowledging her own limits, as well as the limits of those whom she loved, she attached a new integrative message to her memory: "Although it would be wonderful to have a hero solve every problem, adult life is a lot more complicated than that." This new message, which she rehearsed in conjunction with her retrieval of the SDM, enabled her to show a great deal more patience with James. He rewarded this patience by withdrawing less and showing more confidence in asserting himself in the relationship.

One act of assertion that had strong positive effects for the couple was his suggestion that the family try some weekend camping trips in order to build some positive memories together. Tina was reluctant to try this new endeavor at first and showed a great deal of anxiety about James' planning and preparations for these excursions. However, much to her surprise, these trips were highly successful and revealed a major new area of common interest that they could share. As a result of this positive development, the couple now had a new set of highly supportive and affirming memories about positive time spent together. As a powerful example of the communicative function of SDMs, I urged them to recount the stories of their trips to friends and family members. In telling these memories to others and retelling them to each other, they were using their SDMs to build intimacy and expand a sense of empathic connection with each other.

Finally, Tina and I looked carefully at the ruminative and dysphoric effects secondarily evoked by her persistent return to the SDM of her ankle injury and her father's rescue. Despite its apparent positive ending, it failed to promote positive feelings inside her. Additionally, as she talked more about this memory, she also revealed how painful her father's frequent absences due to his military duty were to the family. In fact, in more traditional psychoanalytic terms, there may have been ways in which this memory served as a "screen" for more conflicted and negative feelings that Tina held inside her about her father and the family life he created. Far from reminding her of the joy of security, the memory may also have contained a wish that disguised a deeper frustration with being unable to control the comings and goings of her often-elusive father.

With the troubling aspects of this memory in mind, we agreed to embark on a two-part strategy (for other examples of this approach, see Singer, 2005b).

First, I taught Tina how to employ a traditional behavior therapy tactic of thought-stopping. Using a rubber band around her wrist (actually one of the "Live Strong" wristbands sponsored by Lance Armstrong to raise money for cancer), she gave herself a gentle snap whenever she began to dwell on this particular SDM (her "Don't Go There" memory). She then selected a highly positive and unambivalent SDM that she could consider her "Go-To" memory (she selected one of sitting around the campfire from one of the family's recent camping trips). Whenever she snapped her wrist to break the spell of the negative memory, she was supposed to summon up her "Go-To" memory of the camping trip and allow its imagery to fill her thoughts. With practice, Tina identified other SDMs that detracted from positive moods. She employed her thought-stopping procedure and then drew on an expanding repertory of "Go-To" memories to stabilize and lift her mood.

From all these exercises, we can see that the goal of therapy is not to banish or remove the influence of SDMs. As I have suggested in this chapter, they are an integral part of autobiographical memory and the larger self system. Indeed, they contribute substantially to our overall life story and sense of identity (McAdams, 2001; Singer & Blagov, 2004a, 2004b). However, as with any dynamic component of the personality, their presence can be beneficent or malevolent, depending on the use the individual makes of their influence.

■ CONCLUSION

Self-defining memories are integrative units of personality that link cognitive, affective, and motivational information together in highly imagistic and thematic "packages." They are particularly vivid, emotional, familiar, and well-networked memories that connect to the most enduring goals or unresolved conflicts from individuals' lives. Similar to other autobiographical memories, they can serve directive (e.g., lesson-learning), communicative (e.g., teaching and intimacy-building), and self (e.g., maintenance of self-coherence and emotion regulation) functions. Self-defining memories are likely to be recruited during periods of goal disruption or conflict. When emotional arousal is high and the demand for efficient processing is at a premium, self-defining memories are an immediate source of information and direction for the individual. A key goal for therapy with regard to these emotional memories is to ensure that they function in constructive rather than destructive ways. To achieve this end, therapists may work with clients to enhance the lesson-learning and meaning-making aspects of their memories. They may also help clients to work on the sharing of positive and relationship-affirming memories with intimate others. Finally, therapists can teach clients concrete strategies for distracting themselves from negative rumination about troubling memories, while helping them to focus on positive self-defining memories from their lives. This chapter has drawn on theory, research, and practice to demonstrate the conceptual, empirical, and practical advances that the fields of cognitive psychology, personality psychology, and clinical psychology are making in understanding and harnessing the power of emotional memories. As neuroscience also makes significant inroads into the mapping of the biological correlates of memory retrieval, we can truthfully say that we are in the midst of a revolutionary era in the study of memory and emotion. By continuing to build bridges across the subdisciplines of psychology, including clinical psychology, we will be able to translate these advances into tangible benefits for scientific understanding and clinical application.

AUTHOR NOTES

Correspondence concerning this chapter should be addressed to Jefferson A. Singer, Department of Psychology, Connecticut College, New London, CT 06320, USA. Email: jasin@conncoll.edu.

Figure 10.1 and Figure 10.2 were reprinted with permission from Conway, M. A., Singer, J. A., & Tagini, A. (2004). The self and autobiographical memory: correspondence and coherence. *Social Cognition, 22,* 491–529.

NOTE

1   Other recent investigators who have employed the self-defining memory request include Avril Thorne at the University of California-Santa Cruz, Richard Robins and Gina Sutin at the University of California-Davis, Brent Roberts at the University of Illinois-Urbana-Champaign, Lynn Angus at the University of Toronto, and Michael Conway and Wendy Wood at Concordia University.

REFERENCES

Alea, N. & Bluck, S. (2003). Why are you telling me that? A conceptual model of the social function of autobiographical memory. *Memory, 11,* 165–178.

Blagov, P. S. & Singer, J. A. (2004). Four dimensions of self-defining memories (specificity, meaning, content, and affect) and their relationships to self-restraint, distress, and repressive defensiveness. *Journal of Personality, 72,* 481–511.

Bluck, S. (2003). Autobiographical memory: Exploring its functions in everyday life. *Memory, 11,* 113–123.

Bluck, S. & Alea, N. (2002). Exploring the functions of autobiographical memory: Why do I remember the autumn? In J. D. Webster & B. K. Haight (Eds.), *Critical advances in reminiscence: From theory to application.* New York: Springer.

Bluck, S. & Habermas, T. (2000). The life story schema. *Motivation and Emotion, 24,* 121–147.

Brown, R. & Kulik, J. (1977). Flashbulb memories. *Cognition, 5,* 73–99.

Bruce, D. (1989). Functional explanations of memory. In L. W. Poon, D. C. Rubin, & B. A. Wilson (Eds.), *Everyday cognition in adulthood and late life* (pp. 44–58). Cambridge: Cambridge University Press.

Conway, M. A. (1995). *Flashbulb memories.* Hillsdale, NJ: Erlbaum.

Conway, M. A., Anderson, S. J., Larsen, S. F., Donnelly, C. M., McDaniel, M. A., McClelland, A. G. R., Rawles, R. E., & Logie, R. H. (1994). The formation of flash-bulb memories. *Memory & Cognition, 22,* 326–343.

Conway, M. A. & Pleydell-Pearce, C. W. (2000). The construction of autobiographical memories in the self-memory system. *Psychological Review, 107,* 261–288.

Conway, M. A., Singer, J. A., & Tagini, A. (2004). The self and autobiographical memory: Correspondence and coherence. *Social Cognition, 22,* 491–529.

Costa, P. T. & McCrae, R. R. (1992). *Revised NEO Personality Inventory (NEO–PI–R) and NEO Five Factor Inventory (NEO–FFI) professional manual.* Odessa, FL: Psychological Assessment Resources.

Demorest, A. P. & Alexander, I. E. (1992). Affective scripts as organizers of personal experience. *Journal of Personality, 60,* 645–663.

Demorest, A. P. & Siegel, P. F. (1996). Personal influences on professional work: An empirical study of B. F. Skinner. *Journal of Personality, 64,* 243–261.

Hayden, J., Singer, J. A., & Chrisler, J. (2004). *The transmission of birth stories from mother to daughter: Mother–daughter attachment, self-esteem and attitudes toward childbirth.* Paper presented at the annual meeting of the New England Psychological Association, Providence, RI.

Hyman, I. E., Jr. & Faries, J. M. (1992). The functions of autobiographical memory. In M. A. Conway, D. C. Rubin, H. Spinnler, & W. A. Wagenaar (Eds.), *Theoretical perspectives on autobiographical memory* (pp. 207–221). Amsterdam: Kluwer Academic Publishers.

Joormann, J. & Siemer, M. (2004). Memory accessibility, mood regulation, and dys-phoria: Difficulties in repairing sad mood with happy memories? *Journal of Abnormal Psychology, 113,* 179–188.

Josephson, B., Singer, J. A., & Salovey, P. (1996). Mood regulation and memory: Repairing sad moods with happy memories. *Cognition and Emotion, 10,* 437–444.

McAdams, D. P. (1982). Experiences of intimacy and power: Relationships between social motives and autobiographical memory. *Journal of Personality and Social Psychology, 42,* 292–302.

McAdams, D. P. (2001). The psychology of life stories. *Review of General Psychology, 5,* 100–122.

McAdams, D. P., Hoffman, B. J., Mansfield, E. D., & Day, R. (1996). Themes of agency and communion in significant autobiographical scenes. *Journal of Personality, 64,* 339–377.

Moffitt, K. H. & Singer, J. A. (1994). Continuity in the life story: Self-defining mem-ories, affect, and approach/avoidance personal strivings. *Journal of Personality, 62,* 21–43.

Moffitt, K. H., Singer, J. A., Nelligan, D. W., Carlson, M. A., & Vyse, S. A. (1994). Depression and memory narrative type. *Journal of Abnormal Psychology, 103,* 581–583.

Nelson, K. & Fivush, R. (2004). The emergence of autobiographical memory: A social cultural developmental theory. *Psychological Review, 111,* 486–511.

Nolen-Hoeksema, S. (2000). The role of rumination in depressive disorders and mixed anxiety/depressive symptoms. *Journal of Abnormal Psychology, 109,* 504–511.

Oatley, K. (1992). *The best laid schemes: The psychology of emotions.* Cambridge: Cambridge University Press.

Pennebaker, J. W. (Ed.) (1995). *Emotion, disclosure, and health.* Washington, DC: American Psychological Association.

Pillemer, D. B. (1992). Remembering personal circumstances: A functional analysis. In E. Winograd & U. Neisser (Eds.), *Affect and accuracy in recall: Studies of "flashbulb" memories (Emory symposia in cognition,* 4th ed., pp. 236–264). New York: Cambridge University Press.

Pillemer, D. B. (1998). *Momentous events, vivid memories.* Cambridge, MA: Harvard University Press.

Pillemer, D. B. (2003). Directive functions of autobiographical memory: The guiding power of the specific episode. *Memory, 11,* 193–202.

Raskin, R. & Terry, H. (1988). A principal-component analysis of the Narcissistic Personality Inventory and further evidence of its construct validity. *Journal of Personality and Social Psychology, 54,* 890–902.

Rosenberg, M. (1965). *Society and the adolescent self-image.* Princeton, NJ: Princeton University Press.

Schacter, D. L., Wagner, A. D., & Buckner, R. L. (2000). Memory systems of 1999. In E. Tulving & F. I. M. Craik (Eds.), *The Oxford handbook of memory* (pp. 627–643). New York: Oxford University Press.

Singer, J. A. (1990). Affective responses to autobiographical memories and their relationship to long-term goals. *Journal of Personality, 58,* 535–563.

Singer, J. A. (1995). Seeing one's self: Locating narrative memory in a framework of personality. *Journal of Personality, 51,* 206–231.

Singer, J. A. (1997). *Message in a bottle: Stories of men and addiction.* New York: Free Press.

Singer, J. A. (2001). Living in the amber cloud: A life story analysis of a heroin addict. In D. P. McAdams, R. Josselson, & A. Lieblich (Eds.), *Turns in the road: Narrative studies of lives in transition* (pp. 253–277). Washington, DC: American Psychological Association.

Singer, J. A. (2004). A love story: Using self-defining memories in couples therapy. In D. P. McAdams, R. Josselson, & A. Lieblich (Eds.), *Healing plots: Narrative and psychotherapy.* Washington, DC: American Psychological Association.

Singer, J. A. (2005a). *Memories that matter: How to use self-defining memories to understand and change your life.* Oakland, CA: New Harbinger.

Singer, J. A. (2005b). *Personality and psychotherapy: Treating the whole person.* New York: Guilford Press.

Singer, J. A. & Blagov, P. S. (2002). *Classification system and scoring manual for self-defining autobiographical memories.* Available from the Department of Psychology, Connecticut College, New London, CT, 06320.

Singer, J. A. & Blagov, P. (2004a). The integrative function of narrative processing: Autobiographical memory, self-defining memories and the life story of identity. In D. Beike, J. Lampinen, & D. Behrend (Eds.), *Self and memory: Evolving concepts* (pp. 117–138). New York: Psychology Press.

Singer, J. A. & Blagov, P. (2004b). Self-defining memories, narrative identity, and psychotherapy: A conceptual model, empirical investigation, and case report. In L. E. Angus & J. McLeod (Eds.), *Handbook of narrative and psychotherapy: Practice, theory and research* (pp. 229–246). Thousand Oaks, CA: Sage.

Singer, J. A., King, L. A., Green, M. C., & Barr, S. C. (2002). Personal identity and civic responsibility: "Rising to the occasion" narratives and generativity in community action interns. *Journal of Social Issues, 58,* 535–556.

Singer, J. A. & Moffitt, K. H. (1991–2). An experimental investigation of specificity and generality in memory narratives. *Imagination, Cognition & Personality, 11,* 233–257.

Singer, J. A. & Salovey, P. (1993). *The remembered self: Emotion and memory in personality.* New York: Free Press.

Singer, J. A. & Salovey, P. (1996). Motivated memory: Self-defining memories, goals, and affect regulation. In L. L. Martin & A. Tesser (Eds.), *Striving and feeling: Inter-actions among goals, affect, and self-regulation* (pp. 229–250). Hillsdale, NJ, Erlbaum.

Singer, J. A. & Singer, J. L. (1992). Transference in psychotherapy and daily life: Implications of current memory and social cognition research. In J. W. Barron & M. N. Eagle (Eds.), *Interface of psychoanalysis and psychology* (pp. 516–538). Washington, DC: American Psychological Association.

Smith, M. C., Bibi, U., & Sheard, D. (2003). Evidence for the differential impact of time and emotion on personal and event memories for September 11, 2001. *Applied Cognitive Psychology, 17,* 1047–1055.

Squire, L. R. (1995). Biological foundations of accuracy and inaccuracy in memory. In D. L. Schacter (Ed.), *Memory distortions: How minds, brains, and societies reconstruct the past* (pp. 197–225). Cambridge, MA: Harvard University Press.

Sutin, A. R. & Robins, R. W. (2005). Continuity and correlates of emotions and motives in self-defining memories. *Journal of Personality, 73,* 793–824.

Thorne, A., Cutting, L., & Skaw, D. (1998). Young adults' relationship memories and the life story: Examples or essential landmarks. *Narrative Inquiry, 8,* 237–268.

Thorne, A. & Michaelieu, Q. (1996). Situating adolescent gender and self-esteem with personal memories. *Child Development, 67,* 1374–1390.

Tomkins, S. S. (1979). Script theory: Differential magnification of affects. In H. E. Howe, Jr. & R. A. Dienstbier (Eds.), *Nebraska Symposium on Motivation 1978* (Vol. 26, pp. 201–236). Lincoln: University of Nebraska Press.

Tulving, E. & Lepage, M. (2000). Where in the brain is the awareness of one's past? In D. L. Schacter & E. Scarry (Eds.), *Memory, brain, and belief* (pp. 208–228). Cambridge, MA: Harvard University Press.

Weinberger, D. A. (1997). Distress and self-restraint as measures of adjustment across the lifespan: Confirmatory factor analyses in clinical and nonclinical samples. *Psychological Assessment, 9,* 132–135.

Weinberger, D. A. (1998). Defenses, personality structure, and development: Integrating psychodynamic theory into a typological approach to personality. *Journal of Personality, 66,* 1061–1080.

Trauma and Memory: Normal versus Special Memory Mechanisms

11

Gail S. Goodman and Pedro M. Paz-Alonso

Abstract

The influence of stress and trauma on memory has attracted considerable research attention in recent years. In this chapter, we first review some of the factors that affect memory generally and that have also been shown to play a critical role in the recollection of stressful and traumatic experiences. Also, memory for central versus peripheral information is discussed, as well as the main theoretical approaches used to enlighten the relations between negative emotional arousal and memory. Second, we review studies from our laboratory on memory for child sexual abuse, particularly as relevant to "lost memory," recovered lost memory, and accuracy of memory for childhood sexual trauma. Finally, the implications of normal versus special memory mechanisms on trauma and memory phenomena are discussed.

I don't wanna remember, and I don't wanna have to deal with it.
A victim of child sexual abuse (Goodman et al., 2003)

Even in the midst of a moment of panic, this scene struck me as particularly and memorably bizarre.
Matt Morrison, eyewitness ("Remembering Bloody Sunday," *The Irish People*, January 25, 1997)

These quotations capture some of the many issues that have attracted research interest in trauma and memory. Questions about the effects of trauma on memory abound because of their profound theoretical and applied importance. Such questions include: What factors and characteristics of a traumatic event contribute to making it highly memorable after, for example, 20 years? Does the emotion associated with an event lead to more durable memories? How accurate and malleable is human memory for trauma? Are there important individual differences, such as in psychopathology, that affect memory accuracy for distressing information? Is it possible to lose consciously accessible memory of childhood trauma? If so, do we need to invoke special memory mechanisms, such as repression and dissociation, to explain such memory loss?

The aim of this chapter is to review some of the empirical evidence that addresses questions such as these. First, we review factors that influence memory generally, such as delay, event distinctiveness, personal involvement, and rehearsal, with a focus on how these factors affect memory for stressful events. Also, we discuss memory for central versus peripheral information, and the basic theoretical accounts used to elucidate the complex relations between negative emotional arousal and memory (see also Mathews, this volume; Reisberg, this volume). Second, we review studies from our laboratory on memory for child sexual abuse (CSA), particularly as relevant to "lost memory," recovered lost memory, and accuracy of memory for childhood sexual trauma. Finally, we conclude with a discussion of whether normal memory mechanisms can explain trauma and memory phenomena or whether special memory mechanisms are involved.

Thus, in this chapter, we first consider what is known from research about normal memory processes that can affect recollection of stressful experiences. If normal memory processes can explain trauma memory, then special memory mechanisms are not needed. However, when we next consider memory for traumatic childhood experiences, we will see that, although normal cognitive processes go a long way toward explaining such memory, there are also hints that certain symptoms of psychopathology (e.g., dissociation) play a role and could arguably be associated with what have come to be known as special memory mechanisms.

 MEMORY FOR STRESSFUL AND TRAUMATIC EVENTS

In general, memory for traumatic and highly emotional negative events tends to be reasonably accurate and better retained over time than is memory for more routine experiences. Empirical evidence from eyewitness memory studies, flashbulb memory research, and memory experiments that have used emotional stimuli (i.e., pictures, words) confirms this statement (e.g., Christianson & Hübinette, 1993; Neisser et al., 1996; Oschner, 2000; but see also Talarico & Rubin, 2003). Nevertheless, memories for traumatic and emotional events are often far from error free (e.g., Levine & Pizarro, 2004; Wagenaar & Groeneweg, 1990). Like other experiences, these memories undergo forgetting and are subject to interference (e.g., Barnier, Hung, & Conway, 2004; Neisser & Harsch, 1992; Shane & Peterson, 2004). However, as discussed next, several factors and event characteristics may influence research findings about memory and suggestibility for these sorts of experiences.

Effects of cognitive factors

Time *delay* may influence the accuracy and consistency of traumatic recollections. For example, overall, studies investigating children's memory for traumatic medical procedures and personally salient events have shown impressive recall even after delays of more than one year (e.g., Burgwyn-Bailes et al., 2001; Peterson, 1999; Peterson & Whalen, 2001). However, forgetting and infantile amnesia effects clearly occur even for stressful and traumatic experiences (e.g., Goodman et al., 1991; Quas et al., 1999).

Nevertheless, research on flashbulb memories indicates a slow memory decline over time (e.g., Bernsten & Thomsen, 2005). Unfortunately, in flashbulb memory studies, as in studies of many other real-life events, it is often not possible to evaluate memory reports in relation to an objective record of the startling experience. Thus, these studies have tended to examine the consistency of flashbulb recollections on at least two separate occasions. Although some empirical evidence with children and adults indicates flashbulb memory reporting to be remarkably accurate and stable over periods of time between one and two years (e.g., Er, 2003; Hornstein, Brown, & Mulligan, 2003; Warren & Swartwood, 1992), other studies with similar or longer delays have found flashbulb recollections to be prone to decay and inaccuracies (Bohannon & Symons, 1992; Curci et al., 2001; Neisser & Harsch, 1992; but see Fivush et al., 2004; Kvavilasvili et al., 2003). Terr et al. (1996) reported that children's memories of the *Challenger* explosion were vivid, detailed, and consistent up to 14 months later, but one third of the sample also incorporated misinformation into their memories. Similarly, in their comparison of adults' recollections about a famous, public-trial verdict after 15 and 32 months, Schmolck, Buffalo, and Squire (2000) reported a significant decrease in accuracy and an increase in memory distortions at the longer retention interval. However, using a documentary method, Bernsten and Thomsen (2005) recently found that people who lived through the Danish occupation by German troops during World War II were far more accurate after 60 years than what could be predicted on the basis of cited results from test-retest flashbulb memory studies with shorter delays (for a discussion of flashbulb memories, see Christianson & Engelberg, this volume).

The *distinctiveness* of events is another factor that may facilitate event retention and retrieval over time (for reviews, see Hunt & McDaniel, 1993; Wallace, 1965). Catal and Fitzgerald (2004), for instance, examined autobiographical memories in older adults over a retention interval of 20 years as a function of a continuum from memorable (i.e., unique) to mundane (i.e., routine) event distinctiveness. Results showed that event distinctiveness was associated with better recall. Studies manipulating the conceptual and perceptual distinctive nature of stimuli have also reported similar findings (e.g., Dewhurst & Parry, 2000; Rajaram, 1996; von Restorff, 1933; see also Geraci & Rajaram, 2002).

In the same fashion, the distinctive nature of many traumatic and emotional events may contribute to these experiences being retained and retrieved accurately over time, and to their memory being resistant to false information (e.g., Dodson & Schacter, 2002; Edery-Halpern & Nachson, 2004). However, vividness of the memorable experiences may decline as the trauma and associated emotion lose their distinctiveness. As Howe (1998) pointed out, when emotional experiences are repeated often enough, they can become represented generically (see also Howe, 1997; Lindsay & Read, 1994; and Levine et al., 2002). For example, adolescents may remember their first romantic kiss because it is distinctive, but as romantic kissing becomes more common, they may find each kiss less memorable (Rubin, Rahhal, & Poon, 1998). On the other hand, memory for highly traumatic experiences could remain more distinct, at least relatively, even with repetition. In a study by Goodman et al. (1996) on children's memory for a highly stressful medical procedure known as Voiding Cystourethrogram Fluoroscopy (VCUG), which involves genital catheterization, the number of previous VCUG procedures experienced did not adversely affect the accuracy of children's memory for their last VCUG.

Personal involvement in events at the time of their occurrence has also been highlighted as a predictor of subsequent detailed memory, including of flash-bulb memories at relatively long retention intervals (Conway et al., 1994; Curci et al., 2001; Neisser et al., 1996; Terr et al., 1996; see also Christianson & Engelberg, this volume). Moreover, the positive effect of involvement has been observed in both field and laboratory-based eyewitness studies addressing memory accuracy and suggestibility (e.g., Bates, Ricciardelli, & Clarke, 1999; Christianson & Hübinette, 1993; Tobey & Goodman, 1992). Although the influence of event distinctiveness and personal involvement on memory performance is well documented, the possible mechanisms by which these factors contribute to memory enhancement are still under discussion. Some authors have pointed out the possible role of rehearsal on both event distinctiveness and personal involvement, noting also the difficulty of pulling these factors apart in naturalistic studies (Brewer, 1992; Finkenahuer et al., 1998; Neisser et al., 1996).

Overall, repeated *rehearsal* contributes to "freezing," or at least slowing down, of the normal progress of forgetting (e.g., Bjork, 1988; Dunning & Stern, 1992; Turtle & Yuille, 1994). But, at the same time, repetition of false information can also lead to increased inaccuracies (e.g., Cassel, Roebers, & Bjorklund, 1996; Warren & Lane, 1995). Moreover, the intensity of emotional feeling elicited during traumatic and highly emotional experiences may determine their overt (i.e., social sharing) and covert (i.e., mental rumination) rehearsal, and subsequently the long-term memory of the original events (e.g., Finkenahuer et al. 1998; Philippot & Rime, 1998; Rime et al., 1992). Neisser et al. (1996) proposed that stressful events are likely to be transferred into narrative constructions and frequently rehearsed as such. In the case of flashbulb memories, due to their public nature, media exposure can also contribute to their rehearsal and the maintenance of accurate details, but also of inaccuracies (e.g., Bohannon, 1988; Nachson & Zelig, 2003; Rubin & Kozin, 1984; see also Lewandowsky et al., 2005). Pezdek (2003) found that the participants most involved and distressed by the 9/11 attacks (i.e., New Yorkers) produced more accurate recollections of the event than the least involved and distressed ones (i.e., Californians and Hawaiians). The author concluded that it is the synergy between arousal and rehearsal that affects memory for stressful events, a conclusion that is consistent with studies that have highlighted the role of emotion and rehearsal on flashbulb memories (e.g., Bernsten & Thomsen, 2005; Bohannon & Symons, 1992; Hornstein, Brown, & Mulligan, 2003; Mahmood, Manier, & Hirst, 2004; Otani et al., 2005). But, again, even with high personal involvement and report of strong emotion during the incident, traumatic memories are not immune from forgetting or suggestive influences (Nourkova, Bernstein, & Loftus, 2004; Ost et al., 2002; Pezdek, 2003; see also McNally et al., 2004). Thus, rehearsal may reinforce long-term memory of original events, but it can also modify memory content and contribute to distortions (e.g., Finkenauer et al., 1998; Neisser & Harsch, 1992). It is also important to consider that certain individuals may be more subject to such distortion (e.g., Hyman & Billings, 1998; Shane & Peterson, 2004).

Effects of stress and arousal

In addition to cognitive factors, factors such as arousal and stress are also known to play a role in increasing the salience of emotional memories. Emotional arousal and stress (two terms often used interchangeably in the literature) may also affect memory, perhaps particularly for the type of information inherent in a specific event (for reviews, see Christianson, 1992; Reisberg & Heuer, 2004; Reisberg, this volume). As confirmed by field and laboratory-based research conducted with children and adults, central or salient information that elicits an emotional reaction tends to be especially accurate and persistent in memory (e.g., Christianson & Loftus, 1987; Goodman et al., 1991; Heuer & Reisberg, 1990; Kebeck & Lohaus, 1986; Terr, 1990). Moreover, there is evidence to suggest that, compared to central features, peripheral or more irrelevant details within an emotional scenario, or information preceding and following traumatic events, are often less accurately recalled (e.g., Brown, 2003; Burke, Heuer, & Reisberg, 1992; Loftus & Burns, 1982; Loftus, Loftus, & Messo, 1987; Mathews, this volume; but see Tollestrup, Turtle, & Yuille, 1994). In other words, traumatic and emotional events can be remembered accurately but relatively incompletely, at least in regard to peripheral details (Reisberg

& Heuer, 2004). Other studies on autobiographical memory and on memory in depressed and obsessive-compulsive patients have also suggested that emotional activation, momentary or chronic, is associated with poorer recall of certain specific memory details (e.g., Philippot, Schaefer, & Herbette, 2003; Schaefer & Philippot, 2005; Williams, 1996).

These and previously cited findings indicate that the relation between stress or arousal and memory is complex. Several theoretical accounts have been offered to enlighten our understanding of this relation. Initially, an inverted-U function, as described by Yerkes and Dodson (1908) to explain the association between stimulus strength and the rapidity of habit formation for tasks varying in discrimination difficulty, was applied to human memory for stressful experiences. According to the Yerkes-Dodson Law (see Hanoch & Vitouch, 2004), performance on complex tasks improves with increases in arousal up to some optimal point, and then declines with further increases in arousal (e.g., Deffenbacher, 1983). This theoretical account was later refuted due to empirical evidence that suggested better memory for central details of negative emotional events compared to neutral events (e.g., Christianson, 1992; Deffenbacher, 1994). Researchers also criticized its main focus on physiological activation and the problem of defining what constitutes an "optimal" level of stress (Loftus, 1979; Mandler, 1992; Metcalfe & Jacobs, 2000; Neiss, 1988).

Another classic approach to explaining the effects of emotional arousal on memory is the cue-utilization hypothesis (Easterbrook, 1959), which reinterprets the Yerkes-Dodson law in attentional terms. As arousal increases in intensity, the individual's attention is progressively restricted to the more central or salient aspects of an event, at the expense of decreased memory for information that is out of the focus of attention. In the Wessel and Merckelbach (1998) study, for example, spider phobics showed enhanced memory for central information and impaired memory for peripheral details (see also Brown, 2003; Yuille et al., 1994). Thus, according to the cue-utilization hypothesis and empirical evidence, the relation between stress and memory depends on information centrality. Although this theoretical account is disputed, it has had an influence on the development of criteria for classifying information as central or peripheral in an emotional event (e.g., Christianson & Loftus, 1991; Heuer & Reisberg, 1990; Christianson & Engelberg, this volume). This classification, in turn, can potentially affect research findings and conclusions.

Of importance, based on extensive empirical evidence contradicting the view that high levels of emotional arousal impair memory, Christianson (1992) proposed a modification of Easterbrook's hypothesis. Christianson underlined the importance of differentiating whether the to-be-remembered items of emotional events are dissociated or not from the arousal state. According to the results of a considerable number of laboratory and field-based studies, Christianson concluded that the most negative emotionally arousing conditions improve memory, rather than lead to deterioration, especially in relation to central details and delayed test intervals (e.g., Burke, Heuer, & Reisberg, 1992; Christianson & Loftus, 1991; Goodman, Hepps, & Reed, 1986; Terr, 1979, 1983; Wagenaar & Groeneweg, 1990). In addition, the finding of enhanced memory for central features of emotional events has also received support from studies examining the release and regulation of ß-adrenergic hormones and amygdala activation (e.g., Adolphs, Denburg, & Tranel, 2001; LeDoux, 2000; McGaugh, 2000; McGaugh & Cahill, 2003; Ochsner & Schacter, 2003).

According to Yuille and Tollestrup (1992), there are also factors that may substantially influence this pattern. For instance, memory for details may be, to some extent, a function of whether a witness has focused externally or internally during the occurrence of the emotional event. Whereas an external focus on event information may have a facilitative effect on memory for details, an internal focus on thoughts and emotions could restrict perception and elaboration of event information. Moreover, when Goodman et al. (1996) investigated children's memories of the personally experienced, stressful medical event mentioned earlier (VCUG), parental influence on the children's memory was implicated. Fewer memory errors were associated with the children having parents who comforted the children after the medical procedure and who talked to the children about the event before and after it occurred. Thus, socio-emotional influences, such as coping and discussion factors, may play a role in memory for stressful events. Such factors could differentially affect memory for central versus peripheral information. In their study of tunnel memory for traumatic events, Safer et al. (1998) reported that elaboration of one's emotional reaction enhanced memory for central, emotion-arousing information in an event, and inhibited the processing for peripheral information.

However, Deffenbacher et al. (2004), in a recent review article, reported that high levels of stress negatively impact memory accuracy both for face identification and recall of crime-related information. More specifically, high levels of stress were found to negatively influence interrogative recall more than free recall, and also impair eyewitness recall in adults but not in children. Based on a revision of the Yerkes-Dodson unidimensional continuum of arousal, they noted that cognitive anxiety and physiological activation produce non-linear effects on performance (Fazey & Hardy, 1988; Tucker & Williamson, 1984; see also Deffenbacher, 1994). Also, they proposed that findings of former studies showing facilitated memory for central features of emotional events were due to the experimental manipulations generating an orientating response to stimulus conditions, rather than a defensive response typically produced by a successful manipulation of stress or anxiety. For example, studies with combat veterans have found that memories related to life-threatening experiences may be inconsistent and subject to inaccuracies (Roemer et al., 1998; Southwick et al., 1997; see also Morgan et al., 2004). The presumption is that laboratory studies are likely to elicit an orienting response, whereas life-threatening experiences are likely to elicit a defensive response.

Finally, some researchers have pointed out that in the vast majority of research on traumatic and highly emotional events, emotion is equated with arousal, noting that whereas arousal is an essential component of emotion, certainly affecting memory, emotion is more than arousal (e.g., Levine & Pizarro, 2004, this volume). According to discrete emotion theories, which emphasize that specific emotions are evoked by different interpretations of events and are associated with different motivations and goals (e.g., Ellsworth & Scherer, 2003; Goodman et al., 1991; Oatley & Johnson-Laird, 1987; Smith & Lazarus, 1993; Stein, Trabasso, & Liwag, 2000), information-processing strategies may differ substantially when a person is in a positive emotional state as opposed to a negative one (e.g., Bless et al., 1990; Forgas, 2002; Levine & Bluck, 2004; Park & Banaji, 2000; for a review, see Bless & Schwarz, 1999). For instance, recent studies on emotional autobiographical memories confirm that adults' recollections, and also parent–child conversations, about positive and negative experiences differ substantially in their qualities and contents depending in part on the specific goals and emotions of concern (Bohanek, Fivush, & Walker, 2005; Butler & Wolfner, 2000; D'Argembeau, Comblain, & van der Linden, 2003; Lagattuta & Wellman, 2002; Sales & Fivush, 2003). Also, Bernsten (2002) found that adults report a wide variety of details about their happiest memories, but they focus on central features in their recollections about their most shocking or negative memories. Both types of events may be arousing, and yet different cognitive and memory processes may be involved, perhaps in part due to different motivations and goals being activated. Studies examining adults' and children's memory accuracy and misleading-information acceptance have tended to show better performance for negative than positive emotional events (e.g., Banaji & Hardin, 1994; Bluck & Li, 2001; Ceci et al., 1994; Paz-Alonso et al., 2003), although such studies have often failed to consider the discrete emotions elicited by the events.

Thus, emotional valence may influence people's information-processing strategies, and information that is considered as central in one emotional state may not be necessarily judged as central in another. In fact, differential recall of central versus peripheral information of emotional events is not always a stable phenomenon (e.g., Wessel, van der Koov, & Merckelbach, 2000). However, there are no published studies that have examined whether the results of memory studies vary as a function of comparing *a priori* criteria to classify centrality of information with a more ecological one (i.e., people's ratings of the centrality of information contained in a specific emotional event).

In two recent experiments (Paz-Alonso & Goodman, in preparation), we investigated adults' memory accuracy and suggestibility for central versus peripheral details of a highly negative emotional film as a function of retention interval (immediate versus two weeks). Also, centrality of information was examined on the basis of two different criteria: (1) a recently developed set of criteria that tries to embrace formerly used conceptual (Heuer & Reisberg, 1990) and spatial (Christianson & Loftus, 1991) *a priori* concepts, to distinguish central from peripheral details for information that occurs during the critical incident of the events and/or that is related to the event's main characters (Ibabe & Sporer, 2004); and (2) adults' ratings about centrality of event information obtained via pre-testing (see Heath & Erickson, 1998).

Results were highly consistent across the two experiments. Consistent with previous laboratory-based studies, eyewitness recognition accuracy and compliance were negatively affected by a retention interval of two weeks (e.g., Lipton, 1977; Roebers & Schneider, 2000). However, our data also indicate substantial differences depending on the criteria used to classify centrality of event information. The Critical incident/Main characters criteria were associated with generally higher recognition accuracy for central than peripheral information, at both immediate and two-week retention intervals. Analyses of false information acceptance also showed that at the two-week condition, eyewitness compliance increased in relation to peripheral suggestions contained in misleading questions, but not to central ones. These results fit relatively well with those obtained in former studies, using similar *a priori* concepts to classify information centrality (e.g., Burke, Heuer, & Reisberg, 1992; Cassel, Roebers, & Bjorklund, 1996; Kebeck & Lohaus, 1986). In contrast, when the Adults' Ratings criteria were used, the interactions between delay interval and centrality for recognition accuracy and compliance measures showed a decline of eyewitness performance with delay to central information, but not to peripheral information.

These results highlight that inconsistencies in research findings can be explained, at least in part, by differences in the criteria used to define central and peripheral information (Christianson & Lindholm, 1998). Also, it could be crucial to examine the potential individual and developmental differences in what is judged as central or peripheral in a specific emotional event. For example, as several studies have indicated, female and male witnesses may attend to different details, and the classification schemes of adults and children may not be equivalent (e.g., Ihlebaek et al., 2003; Peterson & Bell, 1996; Shaw & Skolnick, 1994).

In summary, there is evidence to indicate that memories of traumatic and emotional events tend to be well retained over time, especially compared to memory for more mundane events, but the former memories, like the latter ones, are also subject to inaccuracies and forgetting. Distinctiveness and personal involvement are associated with subsequent detailed and accurate recollections, as well as with higher resistance to false information. Rehearsal plays a crucial role in long-term memory of traumatic and emotional experiences, but it can also contribute to the incorporation and maintenance of false information. Finally, central information of emotional events tends to be more accurately remembered than peripheral information. However, there is still debate about how emotional arousal affects event information processing, and what is considered as central or peripheral in relation to a specific emotional event. Overall, we agree with Pezdek and Taylor (2002) that memory for traumatic events in many ways appears to follow the same cognitive principles as memory for distinctive non-traumatic events. However, in some cases, more may be involved. We next turn to research that emphasizes the effects of traumatization on memory and that has explored situations in which special memory mechanisms might be more likely to come into play.

■ TRAUMATIZATION AND MEMORY

Although debate remains, as noted above, Christianson has proposed that during traumatic events, attention becomes focused on the main stressor, which is then remembered particularly well. Studies leading to that conclusion have largely involved one-time exposure to distressing stimuli, such as a photograph of a disfigured face, viewed by college students in a laboratory experiment (e.g., Christianson & Nilsson, 1984). However, what if a person is chronically exposed to traumatic events? And, moreover, what if such exposure starts in childhood? In discussing this issue, we restrict our attention to the trauma of CSA because much of the current debate around trauma and memory focuses on this controversial, difficult-to-prove crime.

One possible result of chronic exposure to stressful events, perhaps especially when such exposure occurs in childhood, is that the person will come to focus on stressors, and their associated cues (i.e., threat or trauma cues), as a general personality or processing strategy. In a meaningful sense, the phenomenon identified by Christianson may become more or less habitual, especially in the face of trauma-related information. In this case, the individual may be hypervigilant to trauma-related information, perhaps as a protective mechanism. The person is, in effect, in a chronic fear state, or at least is more easily transformed into a state of fear than is a nontraumatized person.

This fear state should result in what Foa and her colleagues have termed "fear networks" (Foa et al., 1991; Foa & Rothbaum, 1992). According to Foa, individuals who become traumatized (e.g., develop post-traumatic stress disorder: PTSD) develop fear networks, which are semantic/episodic mental structures for storing trauma-related information. These structures help guide both attention and memory. If a person has PTSD, these fear structures may be all too readily activated, resulting in intrusive memories, such as flashbacks. Consistent with the idea of fear networks, considerable research indicates that traumatized individuals over-focus on trauma cues and have difficulty ignoring trauma stimuli (e.g., McNally et al., 1998).

The traumatized person's knowledge base for trauma-related information might well be more elaborated than that of someone who has never experienced trauma. However, in comparing people who have experienced the same types of traumatic events, it is only the more traumatized ones who show the over-focus-on-trauma effects. Moreover, with successful therapy, the over-focus effects disappear (e.g., Mattia, Heimberg, & Hope, 1993; McNally, Riemann, & Kim, 1990). Thus, normal memory mechanisms associated with knowledge base do not seem to account for these results.

This line of research seems to imply that more traumatized individuals would be most likely to remember their abuse experiences and remember them particularly accurately. They should be least likely to have forgotten the abuse, and thus not likely to experience such memory problems as "repressed memory" or "lost and then recovered memory" of traumas, such as CSA.

Alternatively, it is possible that "special memory mechanisms" like repression and/or dissociation come into play, as has been suggested by several clinical psychologists and psychiatrists (e.g., Terr, 1990; van der Kolk, 1997). These mechanisms are believed to result in lost memory of trauma experiences, especially when such experiences are associated with self-blame, helplessness, and/or repeated trauma. CSA is often characterized by feelings of self-blame and helplessness among victims, and by repeated assaults. Thus, CSA is a prime candidate for repression and/or dissociation.

 PAST PROSPECTIVE STUDIES OF MEMORY FOR CSA

One problem with most studies relevant to testing these ideas is that the reports of CSA are retrospective. Thus, one has to rely on the individual's memory to determine if the abuse ever occurred and then also to gauge the extent of the abuse. Because memory (or lack thereof) is the core issue at stake, it is problematic to have to rely on self-reports of CSA experiences themselves. Instead, it is essential to conduct prospective research in which documented cases of CSA are later studied.

Fortunately, a few prospective studies exist. These studies of memory in CSA victims have concentrated on the issue of lost or repressed memory of CSA. In landmark research, Linda Williams (1994) re-interviewed adults who had participated in one of her earlier research projects concerning CSA. Because Williams had studied the individuals as children at the time their CSA cases were investigated by authorities, Williams had documentation of the alleged acts and the alleged perpetrators. The sample was largely African American and all female. Williams re-interviewed the CSA victims after a 17-year delay, on average. Of note, she found that 39 percent of the women failed to disclose the CSA that had been previously documented. Because many of the women disclosed other embarrassing, traumatic, and/or sexual events, the lack of disclosure was interpreted as not due to unwillingness to report the earlier incidents. Instead, repressed memory was considered a likely reason for the lack of disclosure (see also Widom & Morris, 1997).

The Williams findings were of such importance both from a theoretical and social-policy perspective that further research on the topic was essential. Goodman and her colleagues were fortunate to be able to conduct a similar study and to expand on the ideas further. We turn now to this research on memory in CSA victims. Several core questions were asked: (1) Would Williams' results replicate with a new sample of CSA victims? A possible lost-memory rate of 39 percent is quite striking, potentially indicating that many victims of CSA have no memory of their earlier traumatic experiences. Is it likely that the rate is really that high? (2) For individuals who reported the documented case, how likely is it that they would report a period of prior "lost memory"? This issue is important because it relates to whether or not CSA victims could have periods of time during which they lacked memory of the childhood experience but then recovered it later. (3) For victims who remember the documented CSA, how accurate is their memory, after many years have passed?

 CURRENT PROSPECTIVE RESEARCH ON CHILD SEXUAL ABUSE AND MEMORY IN ADULTS

The memory research we describe next is based on an earlier study conducted in the mid-1980s. At that time, Goodman et al. (1992) examined CSA victims' reactions to criminal court testimony. The main goal of that study was to determine the short-term sequeale for CSA victims of testifying in criminal court. Included in the research were 218 four- to seventeen-year-old alleged CSA victims, whose cases were referred for prosecution in Denver, Colorado. Information was collected on the children's behavioral adjustment at the start of the prosecution. With the nonoffending parents' and prosecutors' consent, the researchers collected data from the prosecutors' files, which included such information as police reports, forensic medical examination results, reports of defendant admissions and confessions, and the like. Although interviews with the children directly about the abuse were not possible, researchers were able

to talk to the nonoffending parent about the allegations, as well as to interview the children about their fears about the legal process. For the subset of
children called to take the stand, the researchers observed the child victim/
witness testify. Thus, substantial documentation existed of the children's CSA
case and legal experiences from the 1980s.

Approximately 14 years later, Goodman and colleagues relocated and re-
interviewed as many of these victims as possible (for details of the study, see
Goodman et al., 2003; Quas et al., in press). In soliciting them for the follow-
up study, it was explained that the researchers were conducting a scientific
investigation of legal attitudes and experiences. For ethical and scientific reasons, participants were not told that the researchers knew about their CSA
histories or legal involvement. A total of 174 of the 218 CSA victims were
located and interviewed.

Following Linda Williams' research on "lost memory" of CSA, the first goal
was to determine how many CSA victims would disclose the target case
(Goodman et al., 2003). In the first interview, which was conducted by phone,
the respondents were asked several times about their victimization experiences,
including of CSA. Despite the "surprise" phone call, 81 percent of the CSA
victims disclosed the target case. Only 15.5 percent clearly failed to disclose
the incident(s). This rate of nondisclosure is substantially lower than that reported
by Williams, who found a 39 percent nondisclosure rate.

There are numerous differences between the two studies that may account
for the discrepancy. For instance, the CSA incidents in Williams' study took
place during a societal time when CSA was still largely shrouded in secrecy
and shame (secrecy and shame may promote "repression"), and the cases she
studied, although reported to authorities, were not from a purely prosecution
sample, as were ours (referral for prosecution and subsequent legal involvement might reinforce memory of CSA). Although these are viable explanations of the difference in our findings, there are two additional factors that
may be of particular importance. One is that Williams' sample was largely
African American, whereas ours was largely European American. When
Goodman et al. examined the disclosure rate of the African Americans in the
sample, a full 30 percent failed to disclose the target CSA case. Thus, the rate
of nondisclosure for this subset of participants was quite similar to that reported
by Williams. Perhaps these individuals did not feel comfortable disclosing the
maltreatment to researchers or perhaps lost memory is especially common in
this subsample of individuals. Another consideration, however, is that Williams
found that 26 percent of her sample reported another case of CSA, but not
the target case, whereas 12 percent indicated that they had never been CSA
victims. In the Goodman et al. study, the latter rate was about the same as
that found by Williams (Goodman et al.'s rate of CSA denial was 10 percent),
but the former rate in the Goodman et al. study was much smaller (4 percent)

than the 26 percent reported by Williams. That is, Goodman and colleagues had a much smaller percentage of people who reported another CSA case but not the target case. The most parsimonious explanation for this discrepancy is that it was easier for Goodman et al. to identify that the case reported was the target case, given the extensive amount of information available on each participant. Thus, it is possible that in the Williams study, more people disclosed the target case than Williams could determine, despite her valiant efforts (for a similar discussion, see Kihlstrom, this volume).

Predictors of lost memory/lack of disclosure were also examined by Goodman and her colleagues. Individuals who were younger when the abuse occurred and who had less maternal support were less likely to disclose. Also, individuals who experienced more severe CSA were more likely to disclose than were individuals who experienced less severe CSA. Findings such as these can be largely explained by normal memory mechanisms (e.g., "infantile amnesia" is common for memory generally; maternal support is associated with discussing the event, which is a form of rehearsal; as we described earlier in this chapter, greater stress is often associated with better memory for main stressors). However, one finding was consistent with the special memory mechanism point of view. Individuals who scored higher on a measure of dissociation (the Dissociative Experiences Scale) were less likely to disclose than were their less dissociative counterparts. Dissociation has been mentioned by clinicians as a "special memory mechanism," and specifically, as a response to the trauma of CSA that could create holes in memory for the traumatic experience. Results of the Goodman et al. research indicate that lost memory of abuse is not as common as that indicated in Williams' study. However, it is impossible to differentiate lack of disclosure from lack of memory. If one assumes that lost memory of CSA is involved, normal memory mechanisms can explain most of the study's findings, but, of importance, such mechanisms do not appear to explain all of the results.

If one believes that memory for childhood trauma can be lost from consciousness, there is still the question of whether such memories can be recovered back into awareness. This issue is important in terms of a theoretical understanding of trauma and memory, but the issue is also important from an applied perspective, because it is typically recovered memories that make their way into the courtroom in repressed memory cases. Therefore, in the Goodman et al. study, individuals who disclosed the target case were asked if there was ever a time during which they had forgotten the CSA incidents (see Ghetti et al., in press). Williams (1995) had asked a similar question in her study. Clearly, the findings are important in relation to the "repressed/recovered memory" controversy.

Ghetti et al.'s results were quite comparable to those of Williams. In their study, 14 percent reported periods of having forgotten the CSA; Williams reported that about 10 percent of her sample had done so. However, it was unclear how the respondents interpreted the question about forgetting. For instance, did they think the interviewer was just trying to ask if there had ever been a time when they were not thinking about the abuse, even though they could have easily retrieved the memory, if only they had tried? Fortunately, Ghetti et al. posed a second question: "During the time when you had no memory for the CSA, if someone had directly asked you about the CSA, would you have remembered it?" To this question, virtually everyone said "yes."

Thus, most of the individuals who were candidates for repressed and then recovered memory indicated that the lost memory really had not been lost at all, at least not in the Freudian sense of a repressed and therefore consciously inaccessible memory. Instead, it appeared that the respondents did not interpret the initial question as implying total amnesia for the CSA. Nevertheless, five of the victims did indicate that there had been a time when, even if asked, they would not have been able to retrieve the CSA memory. These individuals could perhaps have "repressed" the memory. Even so, for most of these cases, the memory recovery occurred in childhood, not in adulthood in a therapist's office, as was often the case in the more controversial "repressed memory cases" that reached the courtroom.

Finally, in the same study by Goodman and her colleagues, the accuracy of the victims' long-term memories of the CSA was examined (Alexander et al., 2005). It had been 12 to 21 years since the CSA had occurred. How accurate were the victims' memories about this childhood experience now that they were older adolescents or adults? What predicted more versus less accurate long-term memory for this childhood trauma?

On average, the victims' memories were fairly accurate (e.g., 72 percent correct, with 14 percent commission errors and another 14 percent omission errors). Moreover, the more traumatic the CSA was, the better was the victims' memory. For instance, CSA victims who said that CSA was the worst thing that had ever happened to them or who had more PTSD symptoms had particularly accurate memories. Why? We believe that the more traumatized individuals had developed "fear networks" (e.g., Foa & Kozak, 1991) that maintained accurate memory. These fear networks arguably reflect the workings of normal and special memory mechanisms. They are normal in the sense of being semantic/episodic memory stores. But they are also special in the sense that they reflect psychopathology and traumatization.

■ CONCLUSION

Debates about the effects of trauma on memory have waged for years, but without sufficient empirical evidence to constrain theory and speculation. We hope our studies enlighten debates about the fate of memory for the trauma of CSA. Although normal memory mechanisms can explain much of the memory and forgetting results obtained with adults who were sexually abused as children, some of whom were traumatized to the point of having PTSD symptoms even many years later, a few "special memory mechanisms" (e.g., dissociative processes) might be involved. However, even these "special memory mechanisms" may have normal memory mechanisms at their base, such as activation of semantic networks (albeit ones that revolve around fear) and avoidance of trauma memories.

AUTHOR NOTES

This chapter is based in part on work supported by the National Science Foundation under Grant No. 0004369 to Dr. Gail S. Goodman, and by a grant from the Program for Research Training (Department of Education, Universities, and Research) of the Basque Government to Dr. Pedro M. Paz-Alonso. Any opinions, findings, conclusions, or recommendations expressed in this chapter are those of the authors and do not necessarily reflect the views of the National Science Foundation. We thank Jodi Quas, Simona Ghetti, Robin Edelstein, Kristen Alexander, Alison Redlich, Ingrid Cordon, and David P. H. Jones for their contributions to research reported in this chapter.

Correspondence concerning this chapter should be addressed to Dr. Gail S. Goodman, Department of Psychology, University of California, 1 Shields Avenue, Davis, CA 95616, USA. Email: ggoodman@ucdavis.edu.

REFERENCES

Adolphs, R., Denburg, N. L., & Tranel, D. (2001). The amygdala's role in long-term declarative memory for gist and detail. *Behavioral Neuroscience, 115*, 983–992.

Alexander, K., Quas, J., Goodman, G. S., Ghetti, S., Edelstein, R., Redlich, A., Cordon, I., & Jones, D. P. H. (2005). Traumatic impact predicts long-term memory of documented child sexual abuse. *Psychological Science, 16*, 33–40.

Banaji, M. R. & Hardin, C. (1994). Affect and memory in retrospective reports. In N. Schwarz & S. Sudman (Eds.), *Autobiographical memory and the validity of the retrospective reports* (pp. 71–86). New York: Springer-Verlag.

Barnier, A., Hung, L., & Conway, M. A. (2004). Retrieval-induced forgetting of emotional and unemotional autobiographical memories. *Cognition & Emotion, 18*, 457–477.

Bates, J. L., Ricciardelli, L. A., & Clarke, V. A. (1999). The effects of participation and presentation media on the eyewitness memory of children. *Australian Journal of Psychology, 51*, 71–76.

Berntsen, D. (2002). Tunnel memories for autobiographical events: Central details are remembered more frequently from shocking than from happy experiences. *Memory & Cognition, 30*, 1010–1020.

Berntsen, D. & Thomsen, D. K. (2005). Personal memories for remote historical events: Accuracy and clarity of flashbulb memories related to World War II. *Journal of Experimental Psychology: General, 134*, 242–257.

Bjork, R. A. (1988). Retrieval practice and the maintenance of knowledge. In M. M. Grueneberg & P. E. Morris (Eds.), *Practical aspects of memory: Current research and issues: Memory in everyday life* (pp. 396–401). Oxford: Wiley.

Bless, H., Bohner, G., Schwarz, N., & Strack, F. (1990). Mood and persuasion: A cognitive response analysis. *Personality and Social Psychology Bulletin, 16*, 331–345.

Bless, H. & Schwarz, N. (1999). Sufficient and necessary conditions in dual process model: The case of mood and information processing. In S. Chaiken & Y. Trope (Eds.), *Dual process theories in social psychology* (pp. 423–440). New York: Guilford Press.

Bluck, S. & Li, K. Z. H. (2001). Predicting memory completeness and accuracy: Emotion and exposure in repeated autobiographical recall. *Applied Cognitive Psychology, 15*, 145–158.

Bohanek, J. G., Fivush, R., & Walker, E. (2005). Memories of positive and negative emotional events. *Applied Cognitive Psychology, 19*, 51–66.

Bohannon, J. N. (1988). Flashbulb memories for the space shuttle disaster: A tale of two theories. *Cognition, 29*, 179–196.

Bohannon, J. N. & Symons, V. L. (1992). Flashbulb memories: Confidence, consistency, and quantity. In E. Winograd & U. Neisser (Eds.), *Affect and accuracy in recall: Studies of "flashbulb" memories, Vol. 4: Emory Symposia in Cognition* (pp. 65–95). New York: Cambridge University Press.

Brewer, W. F. (1992). The theoretical and empirical status of the flashbulb memory hypothesis. In E. Winograd & U. Neisser (Eds.), *Affect and accuracy in recall: Studies of "flashbulb" memories, Vol. 4: Emory Symposia in Cognition* (pp. 247–305). New York: Cambridge University Press.

Brown, J. M. (2003). Eyewitness memory for arousing events: Putting things into context. *Applied Cognitive Psychology, 17*, 93–106.

Burgwyn-Bailes, E., Baker-Ward, L., Gordon, B. N., & Ornstein, P. A. (2001). Children's memory for emergency medical treatment after one year: The impact of individual difference variables on recall and suggestibility. *Applied Cognitive Psychology, 15*, S25–S48.

Burke, A., Heuer, F., & Reisberg, D. (1992). Remembering emotional events. *Memory & Cognition, 20*, 277–290.

Butler, L. D. & Wolfner, A. L. (2000). Some characteristics of positive and negative ("most traumatic") event memories in a college sample. *Journal of Trauma and Dissociation, 1*, 45–68.

Cassel, W. S., Roebers, C. M., & Bjorklund, D. F. (1996). Developmental patterns of eyewitness responses to repeated and increasingly suggestive questions. *Journal of Experimental Child Psychology, 61*, 116–133.

Catal, L. L. & Fitzgerald, J. M. (2004). Autobiographical memory in two older adults over a twenty-year retention interval. *Memory & Cognition, 32*, 311–323

Ceci, S. J., Loftus, E. F., Leichtman, M. D., & Bruck, M. (1994). The possible role of source misattributions in the creation of false beliefs among preschoolers. *International Journal of Clinical and Experimental Hypnosis, 42*, 304–320.

Christianson, S.-Å. (1992). Emotional stress and eyewitness memory: A critical review. *Psychological Bulletin, 112*, 284–309.

Christianson, S.-Å. & Hübinette, B. (1993). Hands up: A study of witnesses' emotional reactions and memories associated with bank robberies. *Applied Cognitive Psychology, 7*, 365–379.

Christianson, S.-Å. & Lindholm, T. (1998). The fate of traumatic memories in childhood and adulthood. *Development and Psychopathology, 10*, 761–780.

Christianson, S.-Å. & Loftus, E. F. (1987). Memory for traumatic events. *Applied Cognitive Psychology, 1*, 225–239.

Christianson, S.-Å. & Loftus, E. F. (1991). Remembering emotional events: The fate of detailed information. *Cognition & Emotion, 5*, 81–108.

Christianson, S.-Å. & Nilsson, L. G. (1984). Functional amnesia as induced by a psychological trauma. *Memory & Cognition, 12*, 142–155.

Conway, M. A., Anderson, S. J., Larsen, S. F., Donnelly, C. M., McDaniel, M. A., McCleland, A., & Rawles, R. E. (1994). The formation of flashbulb memories. *Memory & Cognition, 22*, 326–343.

Curci, A., Luminet, O., Finkenauer, C., & Gisle, L. (2001). Flashbulb memories in social groups: A comparative test–retest study of memory of French President Mitterrand's death in a French and a Belgian group. *Memory, 9*, 81–101.

D'Argembeau, A., Comblain, C., & van der Linden, M. (2003). Phenomenal characteristics of autobiographical memories for positive, negative, and neutral events. *Applied Cognitive Psychology, 17*, 281–294.

Deffenbacher, K. A. (1983). The influence of arousal on reliability of testimony. In S. Lloyd-Bostock & B. R. Clifford (Eds.), *Evaluating witness evidence* (pp. 235–254). Chichester: Wiley.

Deffenbacher, K. A. (1994). Effects of arousal on everyday memory. *Human Performance, 7*, 141–161.

Deffenbacher, K. A., Bornstein, B. H., Penrod, S. D., & McGorty, E. K. (2004). A meta-analytic review of the effects of high stress on eyewitness memory. *Law and Human Behavior, 28*, 687–706.

Dewhurst, S. A. & Parry, L. A. (2000). Emotionality, distinctiveness and recollective experience. *European Journal of Cognitive Psychology, 12*, 541–551.

Dodson, C. S. & Schacter, D. L. (2002). When false recognition meets metacognition: The distinctiveness heuristic. *Journal of Memory and Language, 46*, 782–803.

Dunning, D. & Stern, L. B. (1992). Examining the generality of eyewitness hypermnesia: A close look at time delay and questions type. *Applied Cognitive Psychology, 6*, 643–657.

Easterbrook, J. A. (1959). The effect of emotion on the utilization and organization of behavior. *Psychology Review, 66*, 183–201.

Edery-Halpern, G. & Nachson, I. (2004). Distinctiveness in flashbulb memory: Comparative analysis of five terrorist attacks. *Memory, 12*, 147–157.

Ellsworth, P. C. & Scherer, K. R. (2003). Appraisal processes in emotion. In R. J. Davidson, K. R. Scherer, & H. H. Goldsmith (Eds.), *Handbook of affective sciences* (pp. 93–116). New York: Oxford University Press.

Er, N. (2003). A new flashbulb memory model applied to the Marmara earthquake. *Applied Cognitive Psychology, 17*, 503–517.

Fazey, J. A. & Hardy, L. (1988). *The inverted U-hypothesis: A catastrophe for sport psychology* (British Association for Sports Sciences Monograph No. 1). Leeds: National Coaching Foundation.

Finkenahuer, C., Luminet, O., Gisle, L., El-Ahmadi, A., van der Linden, M., & Philippot, P. (1998). Flashbulb memories and the underlying mechanisms of their formation: Toward an emotional–integrative model. *Memory & Cognition, 26*, 516–531.

Fivush, R., Sales, J. M., Goldberg, A., Bahrick, L., & Parker, J. (2004). Weathering the storm: Children's long-term recall of hurricane Andrew. *Memory, 12*, 104–118.

Foa, E. B., Feske, U., Murdock, T., Kozak, M. J., & McCarthy (1991). Processing of threat-related information in rape victims. *Journal of Abnormal Psychology, 100*, 156–162.

Foa, E. B. & Kozak, M. J. (1991). Emotional processing: Theory, research, and clinical implications for anxiety disorders. In J. D. Safran & L. S. Greenberg (Eds.), *Emotion, psychotherapy, and change* (pp. 21–49). New York: Guilford Press.

Foa, E. B. & Rothbaum, B. O. (1992). Post-traumatic stress disorder: Clinical features and treatment. In R. D. Peters & R. J. McMahon (Eds.), *Aggression and violence throughout the life span* (pp. 155–170). Thousand Oaks, CA: Sage.

Forgas, J. P. (2002). Feeling and doing: Affective influences on interpersonal behaviour. *Psychological Inquiry, 13*, 1–28.

Geraci, L. & Rajaram, S. (2002). The orthographic distinctiveness effect on direct and indirect tests of memory: Delineating the awareness and processing requirements. *Journal of Memory and Language, 47*, 273–291.

Ghetti, S., Edelstein, R., Goodman, G. S., Cordon, I., Quas, J. A., Alexander, K., Redlich, A., Cordon, I., & Jones, D. H. P. (in press). Subjective and objective memory for child sexual abuse. *Memory and Cognition.*

Goodman, G. S., Ghetti, S., Quas, J. A., Edelstein, R., Alexander, K., Cordon, I., & Jones, D. P. H. (2003). A prospective study of memory for child sexual abuse: New findings relevant to the repressed memory controversy. *Psychological Science, 14*, 113–118.

Goodman, G. S., Hepps, D. H., & Reed, R. S. (1986). The child victim's testimony. In A. Haralamic (Ed.), *New issues for child advocates.* Phoenix: Arizona Council of Attorneys for Children.

Goodman, G. S., Hirschman, J. E., Hepps, D., & Rudy, L. (1991). Children's memory for stressful events. *Merrill-Palmer Quarterly, 37*, 109–158.

Goodman, G. S., Quas, J. A., Batterman-Faunce, J. M., Riddlesberger, M. M., & Kuhn, J. (1996). Predictors of accurate and inaccurate memories of traumatic events experienced in childhood. In K. Pezdek & W. P. Banks (Eds.), *The recovered memory/false memory debate* (pp. 3–28). San Diego: Academic.

Goodman, G. S., Taub, E. P., Jones, D. P. H., England, P., Port, L. K., Rudy, L., & Prado. L. (1992). Testifying in criminal court. *Monographs of the Society for Research in Child Development, 57* (5, Serial No. 229), v–142.

Hanoch, Y. & Vitouch, O. (2004). When less is more: Information, emotional arousal and the ecological reframing of the Yerkes-Dodson law. *Theory and Psychology, 14*, 427–452.

Heath, W. P. & Erickson, J. R. (1998). Memory for central and peripheral actions and props after varied post-event presentation. *Legal and Criminological Psychology, 3*, 321–346.

Heuer, F. & Reisberg, D. (1990). Vivid memories of emotional events: The accuracy of remembered minutiae. *Memory & Cognition, 18,* 496–506.

Hornstein, S. L., Brown, A. S., & Mulligan, N. W. (2003). Long-term flashbulb memory for learning of Princess Diana's death. *Memory, 11,* 293–306.

Howe, M. L. (1997). Children's memory for traumatic experiences. *Learning and Individual Differences, 9,* 153–174.

Howe, M. L. (1998). Individual differences in factors that modulate storage and retrieval of traumatic memories. *Development and Psychopathology, 10,* 681–698.

Hunt, R. R. & McDaniel, M. A. (1993). The enigma of organization and distinctiveness. *Journal of Memory and Language, 32,* 421–445.

Hyman, I. & Billings, F. J. (1998). Individual differences and the creation of false childhood memories. *Memory, 6,* 1–20.

Ibabe, I. & Sporer, S. L. (2004). How you ask is what you get: On the influence of question form on accuracy and confidence. *Applied Cognitive Psychology, 18,* 1–16.

Ihlebaek, C., Love, T., Eilertsen, D. E., & Magnussen, S. (2003). Memory for a staged criminal event witnessed live and on video. *Memory, 11,* 319–327.

Kebeck, G. & Lohaus, A. (1986). Effect of emotional arousal on free recall of complex material. *Perceptual and Motor Skills, 63,* 461–462.

Kvavilasvili, L., Mirani, J., Schlagman, S., & Kornbrot, D. E. (2003). Comparing flashbulb memories of September 11 and the death of the Princess Diana: Effects of time delays and nationality. *Applied Cognitive Psychology, 17,* 1017–1031.

Lagattuta, K. H. & Wellman, H. M. (2002). Differences in early parent–child conversations about negative versus positive emotions: Implications for the development of psychological understanding. *Developmental Psychology, 38,* 564–580.

LeDoux, J. (2000). Emotion circuits in the brain. *Annual Review of Neuroscience, 23,* 155–184.

Levine, B., Svoboda, E., Hay, J. F., Winocur, G., & Moscovitch, M. (2002). Aging and autobiographical memory: Dissociating episodic from semantic retrieval. *Psychology & Aging, 17,* 677–689.

Levine, L. J. & Bluck, S. (2004). Painting with broad strokes: Happiness and the malleability of event memory. *Cognition & Emotion, 14,* 559–574.

Levine, L. J. & Pizarro, D. A. (2004). Emotion and memory research: A grumpy overview. *Social Cognition, 22,* 530–544.

Lewandowsky, S., Stritzke, W. G., Oberauer, K., & Morales, M. (2005). Memory for fact, fiction, and misinformation: The Iraq war 2003. *Psychological Science, 16,* 190–195.

Lindsay, D. S. & Read, J. D. (1994). Psychotherapy and memories of childhood sexual abuse: A cognitive perspective. *Applied Cognitive Psychology, 8,* 281–338.

Lipton, J. P. (1977). On the psychology of eyewitness testimony. *Journal of Applied Psychology, 62,* 90–95.

Loftus, E. F. (1979). *Eyewitness testimony.* Cambridge, MA: Harvard University Press.

Loftus, E. F. & Burns, T. E. (1982). Mental shock can produce retrograde amnesia. *Memory & Cognition, 10,* 318–323.

Loftus, E. F., Loftus, G. R., & Messo, J. (1987). Some facts about "weapon focus." *Law and Human Behavior, 11,* 55–62.

McGaugh, J. L. (2000). Memory: A century of consolidation. *Science, 287,* 248–251.

McGaugh, J. L. & Cahill, L. (2003). Emotion and memory: Central and peripheral contributions. In R. J. Davidson, K. R. Scherer, & H. H. Goldsmith (Eds.), *Handbook of affective sciences* (pp. 93–116). New York: Oxford University Press.

McNally, R. J., Lasko, N. B., Clancy, S. A., Mackin, M. L., Pitman, R. K., & Orr, S. P. (2004). Psychophysiological responding during script-driven imagery in people reporting abduction by space aliens. *Psychological Science, 15,* 493–497.

McNally, R. J., Metzger, L. J., Lasko, N. B., Clancy, S. A., & Pitman, R. K. (1998). Directed forgetting of trauma cues in adult survivors of childhood sexual abuse with and without posttraumatic stress disorder. *Journal of Abnormal Psychology, 107,* 596–601.

McNally, R. J., Riemann, B. C., & Kim, E. (1990). Selective processing of threat cues in panic disorder. *Behaviour Research & Therapy, 28,* 407–412.

Mahmood, D., Manier, D., & Hirst, W. (2004). Memory for how one learned of multiple deaths from AIDS: Repeated exposure and distinctiveness. *Memory & Cognition, 32,* 125–134.

Mandler, G. (1992). Memory, arousal and mood: A theoretical integration. In S.-Å. Christianson (Ed.), *The handbook of emotion and memory: Research and theory* (pp. 93–110). Hillsdale, NJ: Erlbaum.

Mattia, J. I., Heimberg, R. G., & Hope, D. A. (1993). The revised Stroop color-naming task in social phobics. *Behaviour Research & Therapy, 31,* 305–313.

Metcalfe, J. & Jacobs, W. J. (2000). "Hot" emotions in human recollection: Toward a model of traumatic memory. In E. Tulving (Ed.), *Memory, consciousness, and the brain: The Tallinn Conference* (pp. 228–242). New York: Psychology Press.

Morgan, III, C. A., Hazlett, G., Doran, A., Garret, S., Hoyt, G., Thomas, P., Baranoski, M., & Southwick, S. M. (2004). Accuracy of eyewitness memory for persons encountered during exposure to highly intense stress. *International Journal of Law and Psychiatry, 27,* 265–279.

Nachson, I. & Zelig, A. (2003). Flashbulb and factual memories: The case of Rabin's assassination. *Applied Cognitive Psychology, 17,* 519–531.

Neiss, R. (1988). Reconceptualizing arousal: Psychological states in motor performance. *Psychological Bulletin, 107,* 101–105.

Neisser, U. & Harsch, N. (1992). Phantom flashbulbs: False recollections of hearing the news about *Challenger.* In E. Winograd & U. Neisser (Eds.), *Affect and accuracy in recall: Studies of "flashbulb" memories, Vol. 4: Emory Symposia in Cognition* (pp. 9–31). New York: Cambridge University Press.

Neisser, U., Winograd, E., Bergman, E. T., Schreiber, C. A., Palmer, S. E., & Weldon, M. S. (1996). Remembering the earthquake: Direct experience vs. hearing the news. *Memory, 4,* 337–357.

Nourkova, V., Bernstein, D. M., & Loftus, E. F. (2004). Altering traumatic memory. *Cognition & Emotion, 18,* 575–585.

Oatley, K. & Johnson-Laird, P. N. (1987). Toward a cognitive theory of emotions. *Cognition and Emotion, 1,* 29–50.

Ochsner, K. N. (2000). Are affective events richly recollected or simply familiar? The experience and process of recognizing feelings past. *Journal of Experimental Psychology: General, 129,* 242–261.

Ochsner, K. N. & Schacter, D. L. (2003). Remembering emotional events: A social cognitive neuroscience approach. In R. J. Davidson, K. R. Scherer, & H. H. Goldsmith (Eds.), *Handbook of affective sciences* (pp. 643–660). New York: Oxford University Press.

Ost, J., Vrij, A., Costall, A., & Bull, R. (2002). Crashing memories and reality monitoring: Distinguishing between perceptions, imaginations and "false memories." *Applied Cognitive Psychology, 16,* 125–134.

Otani, H., Kusumi, T., Kato, K., Matsuda, K., Kern, R. P., Widner Jr., R., & Ohta, N. (2005). Remembering a nuclear accident in Japan: Did it trigger flashbulb memories? *Memory, 13,* 6–20.

Park, J. & Banaji, N. R. (2000). Mood and heuristics: The influence of happy and sad states on sensivity and bias in stereotyping. *Journal of Personality and Social Psychology, 78,* 1005–1023.

Paz-Alonso, P. M. & Goodman, G. S. (in preparation). *Effects of centrality criteria on adult eyewitness memory and suggestibility performance.*

Paz-Alonso, P. M., Goodman, G. S., Ibabe, I., & DePaul, J. (2003). *The influence of emotion on children eyewitness suggestibility.* Poster presented at the 2nd International Psychology and Law Interdisciplinary Conference, Edinburgh, UK.

Peterson, C. (1999). Children's memory for medical emergencies: 2 years later. *Developmental Psychology, 35,* 1493–1506.

Peterson, C. & Bell, M. (1996). Children's memory for traumatic injury. *Child Development, 67,* 3045–3070.

Peterson, C. & Whalen, N. (2001). Five years later: Children's memory for medical emergencies. *Applied Cognitive Psychology, 15,* S7–S24.

Pezdek, K. (2003). Event memory and autobiographical memory for the events of September 11, 2001. *Applied Cognitive Psychology, 17,* 1033–1045.

Pezdek, K. & Taylor, J. (2002). Memory for traumatic events in children and adults. In M. L. Eisen, J. A. Quas, & G. S. Goodman (Eds.), *Memory and suggestibility in the forensic interview. Personality and clinical psychology series* (pp. 165–183). Mahwah, NJ: Erlbaum.

Philippot, P. & Rime, B. (1998). Social and cognitive processing in emotion: A heuristic for psychopathology. In W. F. Flack & J. Laird (Eds.), *Emotions in psychopathology: Theory and research. Series in affective science* (pp. 114–129). Oxford: Oxford University Press.

Philippot, P., Schaefer, A., & Herbette, G. (2003). Consequences of specific processing of emotional information: Impact of general versus specific autobiographical memory priming on emotion elicitation. *Emotion, 3,* 270–283.

Quas, J., Goodman, G. S., Bidrose, S., Pipe, M.-E., Craw, S., & Ablin, D. (1999). Emotion and memory: Children's remembering, forgetting, and suggestibility. *Journal of Experimental Child Psychology, 72,* 235–270.

Quas, J. A., Goodman, G. S., Ghetti, S., Redlich, A., Edelstein, R., Alexander, K., Cordon, I., & Jones, D. P. H. (in press). Child sexual abuse victims: Long-term outcomes after testifying in criminal court. *Monographs of the Society for Research in Child Development.*

Rajaram, S. (1996). Perceptual effects on remembering: Recollective processes in picture recognition memory. *Journal of Experimental Psychology: Learning, Memory, and Cognition, 22,* 365–377.

Reisberg, D. & Heuer, F. (2004). Memory for emotional events. In D. Reisberg & P. Hertel (Eds.), *Memory and emotion* (pp. 3–42). New York: Oxford University Press.

Rime, B., Philippot, P., Boca, S., & Mesquita, B. (1992). Long-lasting cognitive and social consequences of emotion: Social sharing and rumination. In W. Stroebe & M. Hewstone (Eds.), *European review of social psychology* (Vol. 3, pp. 225–258). Oxford: Wiley.

Roebers, C. M. & Schneider, W. (2000). The impact of misleading questions on eyewitness memory in children and adults. *Applied Cognitive Psychology, 14,* 509–526.

Roemer, L., Litz, B., Orsillo, S. M., Ehlich, P. J., & Friedman, M. J. (1998). Increases in retrospective accounts of war-zone exposure over time: The role of PTSD symptom severity. *Journal of Traumatic Stress, 11,* 597–605.

Rubin, D. C. & Kozin, M. (1984). Vivid memories. *Cognition, 16,* 81–95.

Rubin, D. C., Rahhal, T. A., & Poon, L. W. (1998). Things learned in early adulthood are remembered best. *Memory & Cognition, 26,* 3–19.

Safer, M. A., Christianson, S.-Å., Autry, M. W., & Osterlund, K. (1998). Tunnel memory for traumatic events. *Applied Cognitive Psychology, 12,* 99–117.

Sales, J. M. & Fivush, R. (2003). Parental reminiscing about positive and negative events. *Journal of Cognition and Development, 4,* 185–209.

Schaefer, A. & Philippot, P. (2005). Selective effects of emotion on the phenomenal characteristics of autobiographical memories. *Memory, 13,* 148–160.

Schmolck, H., Buffalo, E. A., & Squire, L. R. (2000). Memory distortions develop over time: Recollections of the O. J. Simpson trial verdict after 15 and 32 months. *Psychological Science, 11,* 39–45.

Shane, M. S. & Peterson, J. B. (2004). Self-induced memory distortions and the allocation of processing resources at encoding and retrieval. *Cognition & Emotion, 18,* 533–558.

Shaw, J. J. & Skolnick, P. (1994). Sex differences, weapon focus, and eyewitness reliability. *Journal of Social Psychology, 134,* 413–420.

Smith, C. A. & Lazarus, R. S. (1993). Appraisal components, core relation themes, and the emotion. *Cognition & Emotion, 7,* 233–269.

Southwick, S. M., Morgan, III, C. A., Nicolau, A. L., & Charney, D. S. (1997). Consistency of memory for combat-related traumatic events in veterans of Operation Desert Storm. *American Journal of Psychiatry, 154,* 173–177.

Stein, N. L., Trabasso, T., & Liwag, M. D. (2000). A goal appraisal theory of emotional understanding: Implications for development and learning. In M. Lewis & J. M. Haviland-Jones (Eds.), *Handbook of emotions* (2nd ed., pp. 436–457). New York: Guilford Press.

Talarico, J. M. & Rubin, D. C. (2003). Confidence, not consistency, characterizes flashbulb memories. *Psychological Science, 14,* 455–461.

Terr, L. C. (1979). Children of Chowchilla: A study of psychic trauma. *Psychoanalytic Study of the Child, 34,* 547–623.

Terr, L. C. (1983). Chowchilla revisited: The effects of psychic trauma four years after a schoolbus kidnapping. *American Journal of Psychiatry, 140,* 1543–1550.

Terr, L. C. (1990). *Too scared to cry: Psychic trauma in childhood.* New York: Harper & Row.

Terr, L. C., Bloch, D. A., Michel, B. A., Shi, H., Reinhart, J. A., & Metayer, S. A. (1996). Children's memories in the wake of *Challenger. American Journal of Psychiatry, 153,* 618–625.

Tobey, A. E. & Goodman, G. S. (1992). Children's eyewitness memory: Effects of participation and forensic context. *Child Abuse & Neglect, 16*, 779–796.

Tollestrup, P. A., Turtle, J. W., & Yuille, J. C. (1994). Actual victims and witnesses to robbery and fraud: An archival analysis. In D. F. Ross, J. D. Read, & M. P. Toglia (Eds.), *Adult eyewitness testimony: Current trends and developments* (pp. 144–160). Cambridge: Cambridge University Press.

Tucker, D. M. & Williamson, P. A. (1984). Asymmetric neural control systems in human self-regulation. *Psychological Review, 91*, 185–215.

Turtle, J. W. & Yuille, J. C. (1994). Lost but not forgotten details: Repeated eyewitness recall leads to reminiscence but not hypermnesia. *Journal of Applied Psychology, 79*, 260–271.

van der Kolk, B. A. (1997). Traumatic memories. In P. S. Applebaum & L. A. Uyehara (Eds.), *Trauma and memory: Clinical and legal controversies* (pp. 243–260). New York: Oxford University Press.

von Restorff, H. (1933). Uber die wirkung von bereichsbildungen im spurenfeld. *Psychologische Forschung, 18*, 299–342.

Wagenaar, W. A. & Groeneweg, J. (1990). The memory of concentration camp survivors. *Applied Cognitive Psychology, 4*, 77–88.

Wallace, W. P. (1965). Review of the historical, empirical and theoretical status of the von Restorff phenomenon. *Psychological Bulletin, 63*, 410–424.

Warren, A. R. & Lane, P. (1995). Effects of timing and type of questioning on eyewitness accuracy and suggestibility. In M. S. Zaragoza, J. R. Graham, G. N. C. Hall, R. Hirschman, & Y. S. Ben-Porath (Eds.), *Memory and testimony in the child witness* (pp. 44–60). Thousand Oaks, CA: Sage.

Warren, A. R. & Swartwood, J. N. (1992). Developmental issues in flashbulb memory research: Children recall the *Challenger* event. In E. Winograd & U. Neisser (Eds.), *Affect and accuracy in recall: Studies of "flashbulb" memories, Vol. 4: Emory Symposia in Cognition* (pp. 95–120). New York: Cambridge University Press.

Wessel, I. & Merckelbach, H. (1998). Memory for threat-relevant and threat-irrelevant cues in spider phobics. *Cognition & Emotion, 12*, 93–104.

Wessel, I., van der Koov, P., & Merckelbach, H. (2000). Differential recall of central and peripheral details of emotional slides is not a stable phenomenon. *Memory, 8*, 95–100.

Widom, C. S. & Morris, S. (1997). Accuracy of adult recollections of childhood victimization: Part 2. Childhood sexual abuse. *Psychological Assessment, 9*, 34–46.

Williams, J. M. G. (1996). Depression and the specificity of autobiographical memory. In D. C. Rubin (Ed.), *Remembering our past: Studies in autobiographical memories* (pp. 244–270). New York: Cambridge University Press.

Williams, L. M. (1994). Recall of childhood trauma: A prospective study of women's memories of child sexual abuse. *Journal of Consulting and Clinical Psychology, 62*, 1167–1176.

Williams, L. M. (1995). Recovered memories of abuse in women with documented child sexual victimization histories. *Journal of Traumatic Stress, 8*, 649–673.

Yerkes, R. M. & Dodson, J. D. (1908). The relation of strength of stimulus to rapidity of habit-information. *Journal of Comparative Neurology of Psychology, 18*, 459–482.

Yuille, J. C., Davies, G., Gibling, F., Marxen, D., & Porter, S. (1994). Eyewitness memory of police trainees for realistic role plays. *Journal of Applied Psychology, 79,* 931–936.

Yuille, J. C. & Tollestrup, P. A. (1992). A model of the diverse effects of emotion on eyewitness memory. In S.-Å. Christianson (Ed.), *The handbook of emotion and memory: Research and theory* (pp. 201–215). Hillsdale, NJ: Erlbaum.

<table>
<tr><td>12</td><td># Trauma and Memory Revisited</td></tr>
</table>

12 | Trauma and Memory Revisited

John F. Kihlstrom

Abstract

The idea that trauma causes amnesia by virtue of psychopathological processes such as repression and dissociation has been a fixture of clinical folklore (and popular culture) for more than a century. Repression, suppression, and dissociation are distinguished in conceptual terms, as are "functional" and "psychogenic" amnesia. Modern versions of the trauma-memory argument, involving such concepts as "memory suppression" and the distinction between "hot" and "cool" memory systems, are critically examined. In view of the paucity of evidence that trauma causes amnesia in the first place, laboratory analogs of traumatic amnesia appear to be models in search of a phenomenon in the real world, and theories of traumatic amnesia to be explanations in search of facts.

The idea that psychological trauma can render its victims amnesic for the traumatic event has been a fixture of psychotherapy from its beginnings in the late nineteenth century. It was firmly enshrined in popular culture in the mid-twentieth century in films like *Random Harvest* (1942), *Spellbound* (1945), and *The Snakepit* (1948). Despite the rise of biological psychiatry, and a progressive shift from psychogenic to somatogenic theories of mental illness, the trauma-memory argument – and its companion, recovered-memory therapy – were revived as post-traumatic stress disorder was established as the "new hysteria" of our time – often with a neuroscientific cover story designed to make it more appealing to both professional and nonprofessional consumers of the contemporary psychotherapeutic literature.

The trauma-memory argument proceeds as follows (Kihlstrom, 1996, 1997, 1998; Shobe & Kihlstrom, 1997):

- Traumatic levels of stress sometimes lead victims to invoke mental defenses, such as repression and dissociation, which result in a "psychogenic" or "functional" amnesia for the stressful event itself.
- This amnesia affects explicit memory for the trauma, but spares implicit memory, so that representations of the event persist in symptoms such as "body memories."

- The presence of such symptoms as "body memories" is a sign that a traumatic event occurred, and that a representation of the traumatic event has been encoded, and is available in memory.
- This traumatic memory, ordinarily denied to consciousness, may be recovered, either spontaneously or by means of such techniques as guided imagery, hypnosis, and barbiturate sedation.
- In the absence of independent corroboration, the accuracy of the recovered memory may be inferred from its explanatory value in the context of the person's symptoms – or, simply, from the fact that the person gets better after the memory has been recovered.
- Exhumation of the traumatic memory is essential for coping with the trauma itself.

 A SHORT HISTORY OF REPRESSION AND DISSOCIATION

In one form or another, the trauma-memory argument and recovered-memory therapy have been features of clinical lore since the late nineteenth century, when Pierre Janet and Sigmund Freud announced their respective doctrines of dissociation and repression. In contemporary discourse about trauma, the terms *repression* and *dissociation* are sometimes used interchangeably; or, in other cases, the term *dissociation* seems to be invoked in order to escape the taint of Freudian psychoanalysis.

Historically, of course, the doctrine of dissociation came first (Ellenberger, 1970; Kihlstrom, Tataryn, & Hoyt, 1993). Pierre Janet, trained as both a neurologist and a psychologist, described the elementary structures of the mind as *psychological automatisms*, each representing a complex act, finely tuned to the situation (both external and intrapsychic), preceded by an idea, and accompanied by an emotion (Janet, 1889). Under normal circumstances, a person's entire repertoire of psychological automatisms is bound together into a single unified stream of consciousness. However, under certain circumstances, one or more of these automatisms can be split off from the rest, and function outside phenomenal awareness, voluntary control, or both. In Janet's case of Irene, for example, ideas related to the death of her mother – the sight of her face, the sound of her voice, and the movements of carrying her body – were broken off from the rest of the stream of consciousness. Janet's term for this situation was *désagrégation*, translated into English as *dissociation*. One circumstance promoting dissociation was psychological stress, and the dissociations associated with stress were held to be responsible for the major symptoms of hysteria, one of two major categories of neurosis in Janet's system (Janet, 1907). Another circumstance was hypnosis, leading to the historical association of hypnosis with hysteria (Kihlstrom, 1979; Kihlstrom & McGlynn, 1991).

Enter Sigmund Freud. As is well known, Freud, who also trained as a neurologist, spent a kind of postdoctoral year (1885–6) with Charcot at the Salpetriere clinic in Paris, where he was introduced to the wonders of hysteria and hypnosis, and also began a kind of professional rivalry with Janet. Freud actually made his early reputation with the study of aphasia (Freud, 1891/1953) – and he coined the term *agnosia*. But he took his newly acquired interest in hysteria back to Vienna, and within a couple of years began to develop an alternative account of the syndrome in terms of repression (*Verdrängt*; Breuer & Freud, 1893–5/1953; Freud, 1915/1957) – a concept which Freud had borrowed from Herbart's analysis of unconscious percepts (Herbart, 1816/1881). For Freud, early sexual experiences, which were repressed, combined later with events at the time of puberty to generate symptoms that appear in adulthood. Although Freud's theory of hysteria shifted from a focus on actual sexual trauma to sexual fantasies, repression remained at the heart of the story (Macmillan, 1991/1997). By 1914, Freud had identified repression as "the foundation-stone on which the whole structure of psychoanalysis rests" (Freud, 1914/1957, p. 16). By means of repression, and its supplementary defenses, people deny themselves conscious awareness of primitive sexual and aggressive impulses that conflict with the demands of reality and the strictures of society – "Monsters from the Id," in the lovely phrase of *Forbidden Planet* (1956), my favorite science-fiction movie of all time.

Within just a few years, the psychoanalytic juggernaut had swept Janet and dissociation into the dustbin of history. Janet's views were more recently revived by the late Ernest R. Hilgard, who proposed a "neo-dissociation" theory of multiple controls in human thought and action, to describe hypnosis and related phenomena (Hilgard, 1977; see also Kihlstrom, 1992a). Publication of *Sybil* (Schreiber, 1973) had already renewed popular interest in multiple personality disorder, which had been rather dormant since *The Three Faces of Eve* (Thigpen & Cleckley, 1957; film, 1957) won an Academy Award for Joanne Woodward (in a classic case of "What goes around, comes around" Woodward later played a psychiatrist to Sally Field in the film version of *Sybil*, 1976). There followed a virtual epidemic of multiple personality disorder in the 1980s and 1990s (Boor, 1982) – including an amusing contest, of sorts, between Eve and Sybil to determine who had the most personalities. In 1980, the third edition of the *Diagnostic and Statistical Manual of Mental Disorders* (*DSM-III*) reclassified psychogenic amnesia, psychogenic fugue, and multiple personality disorder (MPD) as "dissociative" disorders (for reviews, see Kihlstrom, 1994; Kihlstrom, 2001, 2005; Kihlstrom, Tataryn, & Hoyt, 1993). In 1984 the International Society for the Study of Multiple Personality and Dissociation held its first annual conference, and the first scholarly monographs on MPD appeared in 1986 (Bliss, 1986; Ross, 1986).

With a growing awareness of the problems of returning Vietnam War veterans, as well as the victims of sexual assault, the *DSM-III* also saw the emergence of a new diagnostic category of *post-traumatic stress disorder* (PTSD). PTSD quickly became a popular diagnosis, as clinicians began noticing its characteristic symptoms – especially anxiety and depression – even in patients who did not appear to have been exposed to the usual sorts of traumas. Increasing societal interest in very real problems of incest and childhood sexual abuse, including the beginnings of the sexual-abuse scandal in the Roman Catholic Church, ignited a revival of Freud's early theory that hysteria was caused by repressed memories of infantile seduction (Masson, 1984). In 1981, a clinical study of father–daughter incest had made no mention of repression, dissociation, or amnesia (Herman, 1981); in 1987, the same author published a study in which more than 25 percent of patients in a therapy group for incest survivors were amnesic for their incest (see also Harvey & Herman, 1994; Herman & Schatzow, 1987).

The idea that trauma could be repressed, and that lifting the repression was critical to full recovery, spread like wildfire through American culture. Popular books like *The Courage to Heal* (Bass & Davis, 1988), probably the best-selling self-help book of all time, fanned the flames:

> If you are unable to remember any specific instances . . . but still have a feeling that something abusive happened to you, it probably did. (p. 21)

> Many survivors suppress all memories of what happened to them as children . . . Coming to believe that the abuse really happened, and that it really hurt you, is a vital part of the healing process. (p. 58)

> If you don't remember your abuse, you are not alone. Many women don't have memories, and some never get any memories. This doesn't mean they weren't abused. (p. 81)

Bass and Davis also published a list of 74 different symptoms ostensibly associated with sexual abuse, so that readers could determine for themselves whether, in fact, they might ever have been abused. A similar list even appeared in a professional book published by the American Psychological Association (Walker, 1994).

And so, after 100 years, we come full circle: Janet and Freud were vindicated, PTSD was the new neurosis, or at least the new hysteria, and dissociation was the new repression. While the traditional diagnosis of PTSD referred to intrusive memories, the boundaries of the disorder were expanded to include amnesia as well. And because trauma caused dissociation, the dissociative disorders could be reconstrued as forms of PTSD. In 2000, the journal *Dissociation* was renamed the *Journal of Trauma and Dissociation*, as if the two were closely related. And in the run up to the publication of *DSM-V*, there is a serious move afoot to reclassify the dissociative disorders as forms of PTSD.

■ THE CURRENT SCENE

The trauma-memory argument is still with us. As recently as 2004, a highly regarded science writer published a book detailing how unconscious traumatic memories exert toxic effects on mind and body, and how secret traumas can be unlocked and overcome by "power therapies" such as Eye Movement Desensitization and Reprocessing, Thought Field Therapy, and the like (Scarf, 2004). As this paper was being written, the *New York Times* (02/08/05) reported that Paul Shanley, a former Catholic priest, had been convicted in Boston of a single count of child sexual abuse based on uncorroborated recovered memories from 20 years before. Shortly thereafter, the *Times* (02/24/05) carried a story about Martha Beck, a sociologist and psychotherapist who writes a self-help column for Oprah Winfrey's *O* magazine, who has written a memoir detailing recovered memories of sexual abuse allegedly perpetrated by her father, Hugh Nibley, a prominent Mormon scholar – claims strongly disputed by Beck's seven siblings (he died at age 94 the day the article was published).

Repression and dissociation compared and contrasted

In the contemporary literature, the terms *repression* and *dissociation* tend to be used interchangeably to refer to a lack of conscious awareness of trauma, conflict, and anxiety (Singer, 1990). In fact, Janet believed that repression was merely a special form of dissociation. But Freud held that dissociation was utterly trivial, and repression was a separate process with its own ontological status. In fact, the two concepts do seem to be different. As Hilgard (1977) noted, dissociation entails a vertical division of consciousness, while in repression the division is horizontal. For Freud (at least the early Freud), available memories are located in the System *Cs* (Conscious) and the System *Pcs* (Preconscious), while repressed memories are buried in the System *Ucs* (Unconscious) underneath a barrier of repression. For Janet, dissociations occur among memories that are normally available to consciousness. For Freud, repressed memories have special emotional and motivational properties, closely bound either to trauma (in his early theorizing) or with primitive sexual and aggressive impulses (in his later work). For Janet, any kind of memory at all can be subject to dissociation.

For Freud, repression is motivated by considerations of defense – the whole point of repression is to prevent us from becoming aware of threats and impulses that would cause us great anxiety. But in Janet's theory, dissociation *just happens* as a result of some weakness, or excessive strain, in the stream of consciousness – much the way a chain, when stretched too tightly, will break at its weakest link. Further, Janet appears to believe that one could gain access to dissociated ideas directly, by techniques such as hypnosis that bridge the dissociative gap. By contrast, Freud seems to argue that repressed mental contents can be known only indirectly, by inference: hence Freud's abandonment of hypnosis and subsequent emphasis on the interpretation of dreams, and of symptoms as symbolic expressions of underlying conflict. In this respect, at least, modern recovered-memory therapy – while certainly inspired by Freud's ideas about repression – is closer to Janet's ideas about dissociation.

Implicit memory of trauma

One point on which both theories agree is that unconscious memories of trauma manifest themselves, unconsciously, in the form of symptoms, dreams, and the like. For Janet, these are the *stigmata* of hysteria (Janet, 1907). For Freud, "Hysterics suffer mainly from reminiscences" (Breuer & Freud, 1893–5/1953, p. 7), and their symptoms are evidence of "the return of the repressed" (Freud, 1896/1962, p. 169). Blume (1990) echoed Freud directly when she wrote:

> Hysterical symptoms . . . represent unremembered trauma or unacknowledged feelings. Because there is a physical distraction, the survivor is at once protected and blocked . . . Her body remembers, but her mind does not. (p. 93)

Similarly, van der Kolk (1994) asserted that unconscious memories of trauma are expressed as somatic symptoms. In his phrase, "the body keeps the score" (p. 253).

Fredrickson (1992) offered a catalog of the various ways in which repressed memories can return to haunt us:

Imagistic memory: incomplete or exaggerated pictures of the abuse scene.
Feeling memory: inexplicable emotions pertaining to the event.
Acting-out memory: including both verbal and bodily acts, as well as actions that occur in dreams.

In modern memory research, we would discuss repression and dissociation in terms of memories of traumatic events that have been encoded, and remain available in storage, but are inaccessible to retrieval. Evidently, the failure of access covers only explicit expressions of traumatic memory; implicit memories of trauma continue to influence the victim's ongoing experience, thought, and action – in the absence of conscious awareness, and independent of conscious control. Van der Kolk (1994) specifically invoked the concept of implicit memory when discussing the aftermath of trauma and abuse:

Research into the nature of traumatic memories indicates that trauma interferes with declarative memory (i.e., conscious recall of experience) but does not inhibit implicit, or nondeclarative, memory, the memory system that controls conditioned emotional responses, skills and habits, and sensorimotor sensations related to experience. (p. 258)

Although the concept of unconscious memory is very old, predating Freud (Butler, 1880/1910), the formal distinction between explicit and implicit memory began to emerge only a century later, in the mid-1980s (Schacter, 1987). Like Hilgard's neo-dissociation theory of divided consciousness (Hilgard, 1977), this new work inadvertently gave intellectual aid and comfort to the recovered memory movement – at last, science had proven that unconscious memories can exist! But there is a big difference between inferring the existence of unconscious memories in the laboratory and doing so in the clinic.

In the laboratory, implicit memories are commonly expressed as priming effects – in which, for example, prior study of the word *ashcan* leads subjects, and even amnesic patients, to complete the word-stem *ash-* with the word *ashcan* rather than the far more common *ashtray*. When subjects who have studied *ashcan* respond with *ashcan* more often then subjects who have not, we can plausibly say that the stem-completion is an implicit expression of memory for the prior study episode. This is because we can tie the subject's task performance to some event in his or her past. A similar logic underlies the inference of unconscious memories from savings or interference effects. But clinicians typically lack the means to independently corroborate what happened to their patients – to confirm the inference that their patients' behaviors are, in fact, implicit memories of past experiences. Without this independent corroboration, the inference that some symptom actually reflects an unconscious traumatic memory is just an opinion. To insist on the correctness of the inference, in the absence of any positive evidence, verges on solipsism.

Consider, for example, a patient, known as Jane Doe, who could not identify herself or give any helpful information about her identity (Lyon, 1985). During an informal test of her ability to recognize and use common objects, the psychologist Lionel Lyon noticed that she dialed the same telephone number repeatedly. When he called the number himself, the person who answered proved to be the patient's mother. Now Lyon's clinical insight was brilliant, but it might have been wrong. Lyon tested his hypothesis, and found that he was right. But suppose that the person on the other end of the line had said that she did not know the patient: Lyon would have had no justification for saying "Yes, you do so too!" But that is the risk trauma therapists take when they persuade their patients, on the basis of symptoms that *might* be implicit memories, that they were in fact traumatized. The general lack of independent corroboration is the Achilles' heel in the trauma-memory argument.

Repression and suppression

In experimental psychology, of course, repression has had a vexed existence almost from the beginning. In contrast to psychodynamically oriented clinicians, researchers who have looked for repression in the laboratory have rarely found it, and even the few ostensibly positive findings are beset by a host of methodological problems (Holmes, 1974, 1990; Mackinnon & Dukes, 1964; Zeller, 1950). In the aftermath of seven decades of negative reviews, it was perhaps no oversight that the *Handbook of Emotion and Memory* did not even include a chapter on repression, and only six entries in the index (Christianson, 1992).

There is a further question about the relationship between repression (or dissociation, for that matter) and suppression or denial. It is one thing to deny that something happened, or to deliberately avoid thinking about something that did happen, and another thing entirely to be unaware of something that happened – or, for that matter, to be unaware that one is avoiding thinking about something that happened. Erdelyi has vigorously argued that Freud used the terms *repression* and *suppression* interchangeably throughout his career, and referred to conscious and unconscious forms of repression. In Erdelyi's view, the restriction of repression to unconscious defense was a later revisionist ploy by his daughter Anna (Erdelyi, 1990; Erdelyi & Goldberg, 1979). Erdelyi's philological legwork is on point, to be sure, but – as both Sigmund and Anna Freud surely understood – the concept of repression, and the technique of psychoanalysis, only make sense if repression is deployed *un*consciously. Rapaport (1942), who should know, seems to identify repression with unconscious defense; and if Wegner (1989; Wegner et al., 1987) is to be believed, unconscious thought suppression is the only kind of thought suppression that can work anyway.

The distinction between unconscious repression and conscious suppression is important because directed forgetting, a variant on conscious thought suppression, has recently been proposed as a model of Freudian repression. In such experiments, subjects study a list of items, and then receive instructions to forget some of them, followed by memory tests. The general finding of such experiments is that instructions to forget do seem to work under some circumstances (Anderson & Green, 2001). This much has long been known (Bjork, 1972, 1978; Kihlstrom, 1983), but Anderson and his colleagues, as well as some other researchers, have repeatedly referred to their experimental results as relevant to Freud's views about the repression of trauma (Anderson & Levy, 2002; Conway, 2001; Freyd et al., 2005; Levy & Anderson, 2002). However, there are a large number of differences between Freudian repression and directed forgetting (Kihlstrom, 2002; see also Schacter, 2001). In the first place, the effect produced on explicit memory was nothing like a full-fledged amnesia: even after 16 suppression trials, the subjects still recalled more than 70 percent of the critical material. Presumably, none of them forgot that they had studied a list of words, much less that they had just been in an experiment. Moreover, the experiment provided no evidence of a persisting influence of unconscious (implicit) memory, or of the reversal of the "amnesia" and recovery of the lost memories – points that are critical to the classical concept of repression. Most important, however, even the small effects observed were the product of *conscious* thought suppression – and conscious thought suppression cannot be a model of repression if repression must be unconscious. Nevertheless, this work has been endorsed as a model of repression by some of the same professionals who criticized the associative memory illusion as a model of false memory (Freyd & Gleaves, 1996; Freyd et al., 2005).

Sincere attempts to study repression in the laboratory have often been rejected as irrelevant by psychoanalysts themselves. Partly, this is due to a methodological problem identified early on by Sears (1936) and Rapaport (1942): repression is not about forgetting the merely unpleasant; it is about the forgetting of vital threat – threat whose intensity simply cannot be reproduced in the laboratory. Even so, to psychoanalysts, repression is obvious in their consulting rooms, and experimental evidence is not necessary. As Freud himself put it in his 1934 note to Saul Rosenzweig, an experimental psychologist quite sympathetic to psychoanalytic thinking (Mackinnon & Dukes, 1964):

> I have examined your experimental studies for the verification of the psychoanalytic assertions with interest. I cannot put much value on these confirmations because the wealth of reliable observations on which these assertions rest make them independent of experimental verification. Still, it can do no harm. (p. 703)

The new dissociation(s)

By contrast with repression, the concept of dissociation has fared somewhat better in its later history. As noted earlier, Hilgard's (1977) neo-dissociation theory of divided consciousness was instrumental in reviving interest in the phenomenon. One important aspect of Hilgard's argument was that divisions of consciousness could occur in normal mental life, without being instigated by trauma. We see dissociative divisions of consciousness all the time in hypnosis, for example (Kihlstrom, 2005). In posthypnotic amnesia, highly hypnotizable subjects cannot remember what they did or experienced while they were hypnotized – yet they show both repetition and semantic priming effects related to those experiences, revealing a dissociation between explicit and implicit memory. Furthermore, they recover the critical memories when the amnesia suggestion is canceled by a prearranged reversibility cue. Spared priming is also observed in hypnotically suggested blindness, revealing a dissociation between explicit and implicit perception. Posthypnotic suggestion also has some of the character of implicit learning: by virtue of posthypnotic amnesia, subjects typically forget that they received the suggestion; yet they respond appropriately to the posthypnotic cue.

Of course, the very existence of the category of *dissociative disorder* in the *DSM* also indicates that the concept of dissociation has attained general acceptance (Kihlstrom, 1992b, 1994). And again, we can see dissociations in the dissociative disorders. The interpersonality amnesia observed in multiple personality disorder, for example, impairs explicit memory but spares at least some forms of implicit memory (Eich et al., 1996). Still, we have to be careful here, because the term "dissociation" can be used in two quite different senses – one descriptive, the other explanatory.

Neuropsychologists use the word in a purely descriptive manner, to refer to a situation where a single independent variable has different effects on two dependent variables. When we say that the amnesic syndrome or posthypnotic amnesia dissociate explicit and implicit memory, we are using the term "dissociation" as a kind of synonym for statistical interaction. This usage goes back at least to William James (Taylor, 1999), who coined the term to refer to a disruption in the normal association between two processes (James, 1890/1980). This is what Janet had in mind when he referred to *désagrégation*, translated as *dissociation* – a usage which entered English in the last years of the nineteenth century. And it's also what *DSM* means, at least on the surface, when it defines the dissociative disorders as entailing disruptions in the normally integrated functions of consciousness.

In either case, dissociation simply describes a situation where some percept, memory, or thought is not accessible to conscious awareness. But *dissociation* can also refer to a psychopathological process. This use of the term as an explanation, rather than a description, began appearing in the 1990s, as the dissociative disorders began to be viewed as syndromes of trauma. Thus, van der Kolk and others have argued that stress-induced increases in corticosteroids interfere with hippocampal function, and thus the storage of an explicit memory of the stressful event, but have no effect on the storage of implicit emotional associations, which is mediated by the amygdala (van der Kolk, 1994; van der Kolk & Fisler, 1993). As a result, trauma victims will respond emotionally to objects and events that somehow resemble the original trauma, without consciously remembering the trauma itself. In this usage, dissociation is an explanatory construct, not a descriptive label. Trauma causes dissociation, which renders the victim amnesic – an amnesia that in turn is characterized by dissociations between explicit and implicit memory.

TRAUMATIC MEMORY: NOT SO SPECIAL AFTER ALL?

The only problem with this assertion, which after all goes back at least as far as Janet, is that everything we know about emotion and memory tells us that emotional involvement makes events *more* memorable, not less (e.g., see Reisberg, this volume). At least, this is true in the mundane circumstances of the *affective intensity effect* familiar in laboratory studies of verbal learning (Kihlstrom et al., 2000). Of course, higher levels of stress, or different kinds of stress, might have different effects. In this way, proponents of the trauma-memory argument and recovered-memory therapy often argue that traumatic memories have special properties that render the usual rules of memory processing inapplicable. For example, it has been proposed that traumas of terror are well remembered, but traumas of betrayal are subject to dissociative amnesia because detecting such betrayals threatens the attachment-based dependency of the victim on his or her primary caregivers (Freyd, 1996). Reviewing this literature in 1997, Shobe and I questioned whether traumatic memories were special, and concluded that the major theories of traumatic memory were either incoherent or inadequately supported by empirical evidence (Shobe & Kihlstrom, 1997).

An anatomy of traumatic memory?

In apparent response to our critique, Nadel and Jacobs (1998) took another tack to support the idea that traumatic memories are special. According to them, different aspects of memories are processed by different memory modules. Furthermore, they argued that emotion, and particularly traumatic stress, affects the function of these memory modules differently. The differential effects of emotion on different memory modules provide the mechanism by which traumatized individuals can forget some aspects of their experiences but not others, resulting in the kinds of fragmentary memories described by van der Kolk and Fisler (1995) in a widely cited paper. Specifically, Nadel and Jacobs propose that traumatic stress enhances the emotional component of the traumatic memory, but impairs the contextual component – resulting in the free-floating "feeling memory" described by Fredrickson (1992): "What distinguishes these intrusive memory states is the absence of the time-and-place contextual information that typically characterizes autobiographical episode memory" (p. 156).[1]

In support of their first proposition, Nadel and Jacobs cited a number of animal studies showing that "various aspects of an episode memory are represented and stored in dispersed neocortical modules," collected by a "hippocampal ensemble" (p. 155). As far as it goes, this view of the neural substrates of memory is unobjectionable. The distributed nature of memory processing – in which, for example, emotional valence is contributed by the amygdala, recognition mediated by the rhinal cortex, spatial context by the parahippocampal gyrus, and the whole trace bound together by the hippocampal formation – is widely accepted within cognitive neuropsychology and cognitive neuroscience.

In principle, the fact that different aspects of a memory are processed by different brain structures could provide the foundation for the fragmentary nature of emotional memory noted by van der Kolk and Fisler, among other proponents of the trauma-memory argument and recovered-memory therapy. If one module were impaired (for example, by the biological consequences of traumatic stress), the information processed by that module might well be missing from the resulting memory. However, this proposition must be considered purely speculative, because Nadel and Jacobs offer no evidence in support of the second proposition, that the functioning of these cortical subsystems, or the representational components generated by them, are differentially impaired by traumatic stress. On the contrary, there are good reasons to think that the amygdala is activated by stress, resulting in robust, lasting memory for emotional events, as demonstrated convincingly by Cahill and his colleagues, in widely known research that Nadel and Jacobs failed to cite (e.g., Cahill & McGaugh, 1996, 1998; Cahill et al., 2004). The trauma-memory argument seeks to explain why people forget trauma; it cannot be supported by evidence that the involvement of the amygdala makes events *more* memorable.

Nadel and Jacobs do cite a number of animal studies showing that increased stress impairs hippocampal functioning, and thus memory. But the stress in question is chronic stress (e.g., 21 days of restraint) and the memory task in question is unrelated to the stressful event (e.g., maze learning). It is highly plausible, as Sapolsky (1996) and others (e.g., Bremner, 2002) have suggested, that exposure to chronic stress releases neurotoxins which damage the hippocampus and consequently impair memory. But this memory impairment would be general in nature, not specific to the trauma, and would include memories unrelated to the trauma. The amnesia would be anterograde in nature, not including the initial trauma itself (the retrograde effects of hippocampal damage remain highly controversial), and it would be progressive, producing denser amnesic lacunae as the stress continued. There is no evidence from controlled research on either humans or animals that stress specifically impairs memory for the central details of the stressful event itself – which is what the claim of "repressed" or "dissociated" traumatic memories is all about.

Fragmentary memories?

Nadel and Jacobs' third proposition, that traumatic memory is fragmentary, is the outcome to be explained by the first two propositions. But if the second of these propositions is invalid, what is there to be said about the third? In fact, Nadel and Jacobs seem to base their third proposition entirely on the work of van der Kolk and Fisler:

> Within a certain range, stress could enhance all forms of explicit memory, but high levels of stress could enhance some aspects of explicit memory while impairing others. And here is the critical point: When stress is high enough to impair the function of the hippocampus, resulting memories will be different from those formed under more ordinary circumstances. These empirical data may be available as isolated fragments rather than as coherently bound episodes (e.g., van der Kolk & Fisler, 1995). This hypothesis contrasts with the position espoused by Shobe and Kihlstrom (1997), who did not take into account the differential effects of stress on the various memory modules. (p. 156)

Note, first, that the material quoted is presented only as a "hypothesis" and it is qualified with hedge words such as "could" and "may." In fact, nowhere in their paper do Nadel and Jacobs offer any evidence that stress has the predicted effect on memory; it is not clear why they should criticize us for failing to take into account evidence that did not exist at the time, and apparently still does not exist.

It is ironic that, in bolstering their "hypothesis" concerning the fragmentary nature of traumatic memories, Nadel and Jacobs rely heavily on van der Kolk and Fisler (1995), because – as Shobe and I discussed in some detail – this study is badly confounded, and no conclusions about the qualities of traumatic memory should be drawn from it. These investigators recruited subjects for their study by advertising in a local newspaper for individuals who were "haunted by memories of terrible life experiences" (p. 514), which they then compared to self-selected memories for events such as weddings and graduations. To make things worse, most of the traumatic events were reported to have occurred in childhood, while most of the nontraumatic events occurred in adulthood. As Shobe and I wrote: "the poor narrative quality of the traumatic memories, and even the periods of amnesia, may have been due to normal processes associated with infantile and childhood amnesia, rather than any special qualities of traumatic memory" (Shobe & Kihlstrom, 1997, p. 72). In fact, subsequent, more carefully constructed comparisons of traumatic and nontraumatic memories have largely failed to confirm the assertions of van der Kolk and Fisler (e.g., Berntsen, 2001; Berntsen, Willert, & Rubin, 2003;

Bohanek, Fivush, & Walker, 2005; Byrne, Hyman, & Scott, 2001; Peace & Porter, 2004; Porter & Birt, 2001). Traumatic memories differ from positive memories in some respects, but they are far from fragmentary.[2]

"Hot" and "cool" memory systems?

Nadel and Jacobs also cited a paper by Metcalfe and Jacobs (1996; see also Metcalfe & Jacobs, 1998, 2000) which proposes that there are separate "cool" and "hot" memory systems that are affected differently by stress. Metcalfe and Jacobs propose:

> As stress increases, the cool-memory system at first becomes increasingly responsive but then, as the level continues to grow, becomes less responsive until, at traumatic levels of stress, it becomes dysfunctional . . . In contrast, the hot system becomes increasingly responsive to increasing levels of stress in a mono-tonic manner up to and including very extreme levels, breaking down only at extremely high levels. (pp. 205–6)

Presumably, the cool memory system processes information about the context in which the trauma occurred, while the hot memory system processes information about its emotional content.

Like Nadel and Jacobs, Metcalfe and Jacobs seem to be invoking something like the Yerkes-Dodson Law, the famous inverted U-shaped function that relates arousal to performance (Yerkes & Dodson, 1908). According to the law, there is some moderate level of arousal that leads to optimum performance on any task. Extremely high levels of arousal impair performance, perhaps by activating competing responses that are ordinarily inhibited (their original idea), or perhaps by reducing the number of cues that the organism can process (Easterbrook, 1959). Either way, high levels of arousal might produce just the kinds of fragmentary memories described by van der Kolk and Fisler. But fragmentary memory is not the absence of memory. High levels of arousal might impair the victim's memory for peripheral details, but there is no reason to think they might impair memory for central details, like the event itself.

Still, even the assertion of a new Yerkes-Dodson Law takes the form of a hypothesis. Metcalfe and Jacobs (1998) review available evidence that low levels of stress can enhance processing of both the "cool" (hippocampus-based) and "hot" (amygdala-based) memory systems, as well as available evidence that moderate levels of stress can enhance "hot" memory while impairing "cool" memory to some degree. However, they offer no evidence for the critical prediction that traumatic stress can produce profound amnesia for the spatiotemporal components of memory processed by the "cool" system. Aside from two anecdotal case reports of unknown representativeness, Metcalfe and Jacobs, like Nadel and Jacobs, rely entirely on the study by van der Kolk and Fisler (1995) – the same study that Shobe and I had already criticized in considerable detail, and that subsequent research has undermined.

It is important to understand precisely what is going on here. Nadel and Jacobs offer no empirical support for their prediction that individuals subjected to traumatic levels of stress can retain strong memories for their emotional state while forgetting the spatiotemporal context in which this emotion was aroused. Although they refer to papers by Jacobs et al. (1996) and Metcalfe and Jacobs (1998) as if they presented such evidence, these papers both rely solely on the highly questionable study by van der Kolk and Fisler (1995). As such, their hypothesis remains just that – a hypothesis that has no grounding in actual empirical data. A hypothesis (Nadel & Jacobs, 1998) cannot be supported merely by repetitions of the same hypothesis in other publications (Jacobs et al., 1996; Metcalfe & Jacobs, 1998).

Nevertheless, six years later Jacobs, Nadel, and their colleagues repeated essentially the same argument (Payne et al., 2004). Once again, they conflated memory and cognitive difficulties that might be caused by the neurotoxic effects of chronic stress with traumatic amnesia mediated by repression or dissociation. Once again, they relied on the van der Kolk and Fisler (1995) study for evidence that "traumatic events are remembered initially as disconnected images and waves of disjointed sensations" (p. 97) – plus a description of a "hypothetical traumatic war experience" (p. 95). Once again, they proposed that "If high levels of cortisol disrupt normal neuronal function [of the hippocampus] . . . then coherent memories of trauma will be rendered inaccessible" (p. 97). This time, at least, the proposal by Metcalfe and Jacobs of two memory systems, one hot and one cool, is clearly labeled "speculative" (p. 98), and the notion of traumatic amnesia is acknowledged to be "controversial" (p. 113). Nevertheless, these authors conclude that "Intense stress is associated with memory disruption, either partial or complete, relating to the trauma itself or to episodic memory in general" (p. 102), and that "Trauma appears to disrupt memory for the context and the details of experienced events" (p. 111).

Recovery and reconstruction

Despite the lack of pertinent evidence, Nadel and Jacobs (1998) concluded that "Traumatic stress can cause amnesia for the autobiographical context of stressful events, but stronger than normal recall for the emotional memories produced by them" (p. 156). But they went even further, concluding that despite the allegedly fragmentary nature of traumatic memories, "an autobiographical memory eventually emerges" by a process of "inferential narrative smoothing whereby disembodied fragments are knit together into a plausible auto-biographical episode . . . The present analysis suggests that at least some memories 'recovered' during therapy should be taken seriously" (p. 156). The evidence provided that memory fragments can be knitted into autobiograph-ical narratives was, once again, the study by van der Kolk and Fisler (1995). Unfortunately, as noted by Shobe and myself, van der Kolk and Fisler did not attempt to corroborate their subjects' narratives against independent records of the traumatic events in question. Accordingly, we have no idea how much of their subjects' narratives were accurate accounts of the traumatic events in question – or, frankly, even that the events occurred at all.

Nadel and Jacobs (1998) concede as much: "The narratives associated with [recovered traumatic] memories are less likely to be veridical in their entirety" (p. 156). Given that, according to their own hypothesis, the contextual informa-tion underlying these narratives was not properly encoded at the time that the events ostensibly occurred, this would seem to be an understatement. If, as they propose, extremely high levels of arousal impaired the processing of central as well as peripheral details, and included the emotional response to the event as well as the contextual features of the event, such a massive encod-ing failure would render attempts to recover traumatic memories pointless: there would be no traumatic memory available to recover.

It is a cardinal principle of memory that encoding constrains retrieval (Morris, Bransford, & Franks, 1977; Tulving & Thomson, 1973). To put it bluntly, if something is not encoded in memory at the outset, it cannot be retrieved later (see also Uttl & Graf, this volume). If the Yerkes-Dodson law impairs encod-ing to such a degree as to render someone amnesic for even the central details of a traumatic event, then these details are simply not available in memory for later retrieval. To speak of such memories as "recovered" is, therefore, to make a category mistake – which Ryle (1949, p. 17) referred to as "one big mistake and a mistake of a special kind." If some sort of Yerkes-Dodson pro-cess impairs the encoding of the various features of a traumatic event, then the prospects of recovering such an event are nil. Any such "recovery" would be a reconstruction, based more on imagination than on the retrieval of trace information. No matter how "plausible" such memories may be, they should not be "taken seriously" (Nadel & Jacobs, 1998, p. 156) unless and until they have been subjected to independent corroboration.

 ## DOES TRAUMA CAUSE AMNESIA AFTER ALL?

Much of the literature on the effects of very high levels of stress cited by Nadel and Jacobs (1998) and other theorists sympathetic to the trauma-memory argument is animal research, and studies of animal memory are often open to interpretation as pertaining to *implicit*, or at least nonverbal, memories. Under this gambit the very literature that McGaugh (2004) cites as evidence that stress improves memory can be cited in favor of the trauma-memory argument, on the assumption that high levels of stress impair the encoding of explicit, consciously accessible memories of the sort that might be expressed in free recall, but enhance the encoding of implicit, unconscious ones that might be expressed in priming and other aspects of behavior. Of course, such a reconstrual risks confusing unconscious implicit memories with conscious explicit memories that are simply nonverbal in nature. Setting this nontrivial problem aside, in the final analysis, it all comes down to a simple question: Is there any evidence that psychological trauma actually causes functional or psychogenic amnesia – that is, a profound loss of explicit memory for traumatic and peritraumatic events?

Although traumatic amnesia has been part of the folklore of psychiatry and clinical psychology since the nineteenth century (Janet and Freud both made it a central part of their theories of neurosis and psychotherapy), the best that can be said is that after more than 100 years even the best evidence favoring the existence of traumatic amnesia is highly debatable (Crews, 1995, 2004). Even amnesia in war neurosis – perhaps the prototype of stress-induced functional or psychogenic amnesia (Arrigo & Pezdek, 1997; Brown, Scheflin, & Hammond, 1998) – rests on an unsecured empirical base. As Pendergrast (1998) has pointed out, the classic monographs of Kardiner and Spiegel (1941/1947) and Grinker and Spiegel (1943/1945) each include only a single detailed case report of traumatic amnesia (for detailed critiques of the war neurosis literature, see also Giglio, 1998; Lilienfeld, 1998; Piper, 1998). Amnesia may occasionally occur in the context of war neurosis, but apparently it does not happen often enough to permit clinicians who were actively looking for it to report a series of cases. Moreover, as Pendergrast also pointed out, the general failure of clinicians to independently corroborate memories of war-related trauma recovered through such means as hypnosis and the amytal interview (e.g., Fisher, 1945) raises the possibility that many, if not most, of these memories are confabulations.

Disaster and terror

In view of the problem of obtaining independent corroboration of retrospective reports of trauma, it would seem that the best evidence for trauma-induced amnesia would be provided by prospective studies of actual trauma survivors. In a comprehensive review of the available literature, Pope and his colleagues surveyed 63 studies of more than 10,000 trauma survivors, everything from the Holocaust and war to accidents and natural disasters, and concluded that they recorded "not a single instance" of a psychogenic amnesia caused by processes such as repression or dissociation (Pope et al., 1998, p. 213). Most victims apparently remembered their experiences all too well. Those who did not could be accounted for by organic amnesia, or by normal memory processes such as infantile and childhood amnesia or time-dependent forgetting (Pope, Oliva, & Hudson, 2000).

By contrast, Brown and his colleagues reviewed much of the same literature in a massive tome of almost 800 pages, leading toward quite the opposite conclusion (Brown, Scheflin, & Hammond, 1998). For example, they concluded that "A significant subpopulation of traumatized individuals retain no or little narrative memory for the trauma" (p. 200). Although the exigencies of publication prevented Brown and his colleagues from confronting Pope's analysis directly, they did so in a further paper, more than 150 pages long, just the next year (Brown, Scheflin, & Whitfield, 1999). After rejecting 42 of the 63 studies as "irrelevant" to the question of amnesia, Brown et al. concluded that "all 21 [of the remaining studies] show that trauma significantly affected memory – and 18 demonstrate amnesia either for the traumatic event or for injuries related to the trauma" (p. 29). As it happens, the 21 allegedly positive studies were a mixed bag, including evidence for general memory disturbance of the sort often seen in PTSD, or for "cognitive avoidance" of the trauma, rather than amnesia per se. But Brown et al. did assert that "Nine studies actually present *data in favor of the existence of traumatic amnesia* [emphasis added]" (p. 28).

In response, Piper and his colleagues re-analyzed those nine studies and reaffirmed the conclusions of Pope et al. (see also McNally, 2003; Piper, Pope, & Borowiecki, 2000). For example, two individuals who were amnesic for a lightning strike were "side-flash" victims who probably received the equivalent of electroconvulsive shock. Some of the children who forgot a flood disaster were as young as two years old at the time of the incident. And while approximately one-third of older children who were earthquake survivors were reported as showing psychogenic amnesia for the event, more than two-thirds of a control group of children who were not directly exposed to the trauma met the same criterion. One study did report a high rate of dissociative symptoms, as measured by the DES, among those who experienced the Loma Prieta earthquake of 1989, but these were most likely common experiences of depersonalization and derealization; there was no evidence that any subject forgot the earthquake.

Incest and child sexual abuse

In the face of such evidence, the trauma-memory argument is sometime revised to take special note of trauma associated with incest and other childhood sexual abuse (Brown, Scheflin, & Hammond, 1998; Scheflin & Brown, 1996). For example, Freyd (1996) has proposed that traumas of terror, such as natural disasters, are remembered well, while traumas of betrayal, such as incestuous sexual abuse, are dissociated from conscious recollection. Brown and his colleagues reviewed the literature on "naturally occurring dissociative or traumatic amnesia for childhood sexual abuse," and concluded that "Not a single one of the 68 data-based studies failed to find it" (Brown, Scheflin, & Whitfield, 1999, p. 127; see also p. 67).

Unfortunately, these studies suffer from a host of methodological problems, including, in many cases, an unhealthy reliance on self-reports – both that the trauma in question actually occurred, and that it was actually forgotten (Kihlstrom, 1996, 1998; Loftus, Garry, & Feldman, 1994; Pendergrast, 1996; Pope & Hudson, 1995a). Even where there is independent verification of the abuse, there is often a failure to distinguish between amnesia and the normal forgetting that occurs with the passage of time – not to mention infantile and childhood amnesia. Typically, there is also a failure to distinguish between actual forgetting and failures of self-disclosure. For example, Brown, Scheflin, and Hammond (1998) cited a massive study by Widom and Morris (1997) of "full amnesia" in 37 percent of 1,114 adult survivors of "court-substantiated" childhood sexual abuse (p. 196) – despite the fact that Widom and Morris themselves specifically disavowed such an interpretation, and attributed their reporting failures as lack of disclosure rather than amnesia. In view of these problems, perhaps a more accurate statement would be that *not a single one of the studies in question convincingly showed it.*

When researchers take account of these sorts of factors, the incidence of "amnesia" for child abuse goes way down. In a study of victims of docu-mented child sexual abuse (CSA), Goodman and her colleagues reported that only 15.5 percent of abuse victims failed to report the target incident during a telephone interview conducted an average of 13 years after the events in question (Goodman et al., 2003). Nondisclosure dropped to 8.3 percent after follow-up by a mailed questionnaire and a telephone interview. Both rates of reporting failure are markedly lower than that yielded by earlier, less rigor-ous studies (e.g., Williams, 1994).

Although an 8 percent disclosure failure might be interpreted in terms of traumatic amnesia, it should be understood that this figure represents an upper limit, because the failure to report may be for reasons other than repression or dissociation. Goodman's detailed analysis supports more prosaic inter-pretations in terms of infantile and childhood amnesia, depth of processing, time-dependent forgetting, and a simple unwillingness to disclose personal tragedy to a stranger. Accordingly, Goodman et al. concluded:

> These findings do not support the existence of special memory mechanisms unique to traumatic events, but instead imply that normal cognitive operations under-lie long-term memory for CSA. (p. 117)

Goodman (this volume) has provided a further analysis of these data that provides more evidence against the trauma-memory argument. When directly questioned, 21 of the 142 respondents who completed the telephone interview reported that there had been some period of time when they had forgotten about the abuse. Of these, most engaged in conscious suppression: only 5 of 138 subjects who answered the question indicated that they would not have remembered the target incident if they had been asked directly about it, and a sixth was not sure – yielding a reduced estimate of 3.6 percent for the incidence of traumatic amnesia.

Although this estimate is an order of magnitude below Williams' figure of 38 percent, it should be underscored that even this vastly reduced estimate is an upper bound. Goodman and her colleagues have reported that at least two of these subjects were very young at the time the target incident occurred – again raising the likelihood of infantile and childhood amnesia. Another victim was asleep at the time of the incident, and thus was not even aware of it at the time it occurred. That leaves only two individuals, at most 1.5 percent of the sample, who might conceivably have suffered from traumatic amnesia. Similarly, Porter and Birt (2001) reported that 14 of 306 subjects (4.6 percent) reported an extended time period during which they did not recall their traumatic experience. Excluding cases of normal forgetting or deliberate non-recall, only three instances – slightly less than 1 percent – remained that could be attributed to unconscious repression (interestingly, 2.6 percent of subjects also reported forgetting a positive experience for an extended period of time).

Any of these figures – 3.5 percent, 1.5 percent, less than 1 percent – is far below the figures given, suggested, or implied by proponents of the trauma-memory argument. For all we know, this level of co-occurrence of trauma and amnesia might be nothing more than sheer coincidence. In any event, the estimate is so low as to refute the claim, or implication, that trauma causes amnesia with anything like the regularity claimed by advocates of the trauma-memory argument and recovered-memory therapy.

What about recovered memories?

Sometimes, recovered memories of abuse and other trauma are offered as evidence of repression or dissociation (Brown, Scheflin, & Hammond, 1998; Gleaves et al., 2004; Kihlstrom, 2004; Sivers, Schooler, & Freyd, 2002). It is a telling point that, more than a century after the emergence of the trauma-memory argument, the most convincing evidence that its promulgators can offer are individual cases of doubtful generality. And even these are precious few in number, far between – and often of doubtful validity. For example, Karon and Widener (1997, 1998) offered, as an example of repression in battlefield neurosis, the case of a World War II veteran who had apparently repressed an airplane crash in which he rescued the pilot and earned a medal for his bravery. But it is not at all clear whether the episode actually represented the lifting of amnesia, as opposed to the patient's more causal report that he had once received a medal (for detailed critiques, see Lilienfeld, 1998; Pendergrast, 1998; Piper, 1998). Although there are serious questions about whether this recovered memory is accurate (Giglio, 1998; for a reply, see Karon & Widener, 1998), the fact remains that Karon and Widener did not even corroborate the one absolutely confirmable detail – that the patient in question did, in fact, receive a medal for bravery.

Other reported cases of recovered memory suffer from similar problems. For example, Cheit (1998) claimed to have validated 35 cases of recovered memory of child sexual abuse, only to have the claim systematically disman-tled by Piper (for a reply, see Cheit, 1999; Piper, 1999). Corwin and Olafson (1997) presented the case of Jane Doe, whose recovery of a memory of child-hood sexual abuse was actually captured on videotape. Although this case study was compelling to many (if not all) researchers who were asked to comment on it, closer scrutiny raises the question of whether the subject in question recov-ered a memory of *abuse*, or only a memory of her previous *testimony about* abuse. The difference is critical – especially since the victim in question was the object of a vigorous custody dispute between divorcing parents, and there are seri-ous questions about whether any abuse actually took place at all (Loftus & Guyer, 2002a, 2002b).

With respect to trauma and memory, the argument seems to be that because repression and dissociation can be reversed *in theory*, the recovery of memories shows that they were repressed or dissociated in the first place. At first blush, this would seem to be a textbook example of the logical fallacy of *affirming the consequent*: if repressed memories can be recovered, then recovered memories were repressed. But the recovery of a traumatic memory, even one that is independently corroborated (Schooler, 2001), does not by itself imply that the event was forgotten due to repression or dissociation. Researchers must be careful to distinguish between recoveries mediated by the lifting of repres-sion or breaching of dissociation from other causes of remembering, includ-ing the normal effects of shifting retrieval cues, reminiscence effects, and hypermnesia. The recovery of a forgotten trauma may be no different in kind than the recovery of one's memory for where one put the car keys, or the name of one's third-grade teacher. Remembering a forgotten event may be traumatic, even if the trauma did not cause the forgetting.

Of course, self-reported amnesia requires confirmation, just as self-reported trauma does. Two of the seven instances of "discovered" memories corrobo-rated by Schooler (2001) are problematic in this respect: both TW and MB (also referred to as "WB") discussed the events with their spouses during the time they supposedly had forgotten them. It is also important to distinguish between the recovery of a forgotten memory of trauma and a reinterpretation of an event that had always been remembered. As Schooler notes, "Rather than discovering the existence of the memory itself, these individuals may be discovering the emotionally disturbing understanding of the experience. Nevertheless, because of the profound sense of discovery, individuals may conclude that they must have just remembered a long inaccessible memory" (p. 113). In any event, it should surprise no one if traumatic events are occasionally forgotten, and if recovered memories of trauma are occasionally corroborated. Neither empirical fact demands interpretation in terms of trauma-induced repression or dissociation.

What about dissociative amnesia?

Sometimes, proponents of the trauma-memory argument point to the existence of the dissociative disorders as evidence that trauma can be repressed, or dissociated, and thus lost to conscious recollection. As was the case with recovered memories, the argument verges on the circular: dissociative disorders exist, dissociative disorders are instigated by trauma, therefore trauma causes dissociative amnesia. Moreover, the argument seems to confuse the two meanings of the term *dissociation* discussed earlier: the dissociative disorders are "dissociative" in the descriptive sense of entailing a loss of the integrative functions of consciousness, and not because they are *caused* by stress-induced "dissociation." It is in this descriptive sense that the conversion disorders can also be described as dissociative in nature, although the dissociations in question affect sensory-perceptual and motor functioning, rather than memory (Kihlstrom, 1992b, 1994).

In fact, dissociative disorder is a valid diagnostic category (Kihlstrom, 2005) and functional amnesia a genuine phenomenon (Kihlstrom et al., 2000; see also Kopelman, 2002; Markowitsch, 2000) – although genuine cases appear to be vanishingly rare. Thigpen and Cleckley (1954, 1957), who treated and reported the famous *Three Faces of Eve*, never saw another valid case despite repeated referrals over the next 30 years – even at the height of the multiple personality "epidemic" (Thigpen & Cleckley, 1984). Given the apparent incidence of child sexual abuse, if the trauma-memory argument – and particularly arguments about betrayal trauma (Freyd & Gleaves, 1996) – were correct, we should see more cases of dissociative amnesia than we do.

Although there are undoubtedly some cases of dissociative disorder which present histories of trauma, including incestuous child abuse, apparently this is not always, or even often, the case. For example, the eponymous Eve denied ever having been abused, and complained that people who attended her speaking engagements insisted that she was in denial about having been abused (Ganaway, 1995). Even when a patient with dissociative disorder presents a documented history of child sexual abuse, inferring a causal link between abuse and dissociation is fraught with difficulty (Pope & Hudson, 1995b; Rind, 2003; Sbraga & O'Donohue, 2003). For example, the most widely cited evidence for an association between child sexual abuse and dissociative amnesia is retrospective in nature, and retrospective studies by their very nature necessarily overestimate the relation between antecedent and consequent variables (Dawes, 1993; Swets, Dawes, & Monahan, 2000). Moreover, such studies often rely on excessively liberal definitions of abuse and trauma to begin with.

In point of fact, there is actually no good evidence that trauma plays a particular role in the etiology of these disorders – that is, evidence based on random or prospective samples (Kihlstrom et al., 2000). In such studies, the fact is that examples of multiple personality disorder and other dissociative disorders simply do not figure prominently among the sequelae of documented child sexual abuse (see also Bailey & Shriver, 1999; Beitchman et al., 1991, 1992; Kendall-Tackett & Marshall, 1998; Kendall-Tackett, Williams, & Finkelhor, 1993; Lange et al., 1999; Rind, 1998). The dissociative disorders cannot be cited as evidence that trauma impairs memory unless and until there is convincing evidence that such traumas as child sexual abuse actually cause dissociative disorder. Occasional cases of dissociative disorder who also have a history of trauma have helped keep the trauma-memory argument alive. But even then they are the exceptions that test, one might even go so far as to say *prove*, the rule that emotion – even negative emotion, even at extremely high levels – generally enhances memory, such that trauma is typically remembered particularly well by those who have actually experienced it.

"Organic" and "functional," "somatogenic" and "psychogenic"

A word is in order about the distinction between "organic" and "functional" (or "somatogenic" and "psychogenic") amnesia and other mental disorders. In medicine, the term "functional" often means that the biological basis of a disorder is not yet known, and there is no necessary implication that the disorder has no organic basis. For example, general paresis, a form of dementia, was considered functional until the discovery of the syphilis spirochete, at which point the illness was reclassified from functional to organic. On the other hand, the term "psychogenic" implies that the underlying etiology is psychological rather than biological in nature. Some forms of depression may reflect anomalies of neurotransmitter function, and thus be properly classified as somatogenic in nature. On the other hand, other forms of depression may be considered psychogenic because they are caused by certain beliefs held by the patient – the "depressogenic" schemata of Beck (1967), perhaps, or the pessimistic attributional style that lies at the core of the reformulated hopelessness theory (Abramson, Metalsky, & Alloy, 1989).

The memory disorder envisioned by the trauma-memory argument is, in theory, both functional and psychogenic. Traumatic amnesia is "functional" in that it "is attributable to an instigating event or process that does not result in damage to brain structures, and produces more forgetting than would normally occur in the absence of the instigating event or process" – in this case, trauma (Kihlstrom & Schacter, 2000, p. 409). And it is "psychogenic" in that it is caused by a mental state, namely mental trauma, or mental processes of repression or dissociation.

The fact that dissociative amnesia might have biological correlates (Markowitsch, 1999) does not mean it is really "organic" in nature after all: it is axiomatic in contemporary psychology and cognitive science that all mental states have their neural correlates, and this is no less true for dissociative amnesia than it is for conscious recollection. What makes dissociative amnesia functional, at least in principle, is the absence of demonstrable brain insult, injury, or disease as an instigating factor. There are many other disorders of memory that are functional in just the same way (Kihlstrom & Evans, 1979a). These include posthypnotic amnesia, which is also psychogenic because it only occurs in response to suggestion (Kihlstrom, 1979, 1985, 2005; Kihlstrom & Evans, 1979b). But the category also includes infantile and childhood amnesia, which is not psychogenic.

By contrast, the memory dysfunction commonly associated with PTSD is "organic" because it is (ostensibly) caused by a stress-induced "glucocorticoid cascade" (Bremner, 2002; O'Brien, 1997) that damages the hippocampus; but it is also "psychogenic" because stress is defined psychologically by the experience of unpredictable and/or uncontrollable events (Mineka & Kihlstrom, 1978). To be clear: a functional amnesia is one that is not associated with brain insult, injury, or disease; a psychogenic amnesia has a mental, as opposed to an organic cause. The two categories overlap, but they are different.

 # A WILL-O'-THE-WISP, A MYTH, AN URBAN LEGEND

The trauma-memory argument and recovered-memory therapy have been with us for more than 100 years, and have embedded themselves deeply into both our professional practices and our wider culture. But there was never any good evidence for either, and there still is none. Maybe such evidence will be forthcoming in the future. There are occasional cases in which traumatic stress and amnesia *seem* to go together, inviting interpretations in terms of repression or dissociation. But nothing in the case literature justifies assertions that trauma impairs memory as a matter of course, or in the majority of cases, or often – even *sometimes* seems too extreme. In view of the paucity of evidence that trauma causes amnesia, discussion of implicit memories of trauma seems pointless. Laboratory analogs of traumatic amnesia are models in search of a phenomenon; theories of traumatic amnesia are explanations in search of facts.

AUTHOR NOTE

Correspondence concerning this chapter should be addressed to John Kihlstrom, Department of Psychology, MC 1650, University of California, Berkeley, 3210 Tolman Hall, Berkeley, California 94720-1650, USA. Email: jfkihlstrom@berkeley.edu; URL: www.socrates.berkeley.edu/~kihlstrm.

NOTES

1 In a sense, Nadel and Jacobs revived an even earlier concept of dissociation, one that arose in nineteenth-century chemistry, referring to the separation by heat of compounds into their constituent elements. Traumatic stress, in this view, impairs some aspects of memory, while simultaneously enhancing others: applying the psychological heat of mental stress, the various elements of an integrated memory become separated from each other.

2 Nadel and Jacobs attempt to bolster their position further by citing an earlier paper as supporting the notion that "even in the presence of extensive autobiographical amnesia, intrusive emotions or images associated with the trauma (and related events) may appear" (Jacobs et al., 1996, p. 156; see also Thomas et al., 1995). Unfortunately, the paper cited presents no empirical data to support this or any other notion about traumatic memory. Instead, these authors offer yet another hypothesis about "the conditions under which a memory for a traumatic event has a high, medium, or low probability of accurately reflecting the target event," as well as a series of fictional (*sic*) cases illustrating the basic points of the proposed model. This hypothesis was not tested in the Jacobs et al. (1996) paper, and as such remains highly speculative.

REFERENCES

Abramson, L. Y., Metalsky, G. I., & Alloy, L. B. (1989). Hopelessness depression: A theory-based subtype of depression. *Psychological Review, 96*, 358–372.

American Psychiatric Association (1994). *Diagnostic and statistical manual of mental disorders* (3rd ed.). Washington, DC: Author.

Anderson, M. C. & Green, C. (2001). Suppressing unwanted memories by executive control. *Nature, 410* (15 March), 366–369.

Anderson, M. C. & Levy, B. (2002). Repression can (and should) be studied empirically. *Trends in Cognitive Sciences, 6,* 502–503.

Arrigo, J. M. & Pezdek, K. (1997). Lessons from the study of psychogenic amnesia. *Current Directions in Psychological Science, 6,* 148–152.

Bailey, J. M. & Shriver, A. (1999). Does childhood sexual abuse cause borderline personality disorder. *Journal of Sex and Marital Therapy, 25,* 45–57.

Bass, E. & Davis, L. W. (1988). *The courage to heal: A guide for women survivors of child sexual abuse.* New York: Harper & Row.

Beck, A. T. (1967). *Depression: Causes and treatment.* Philadelphia: University of Pennsylvania Press.

Beitchman, J. H., Zucker, K. J., Hood, J. E., & DaCosta, G. A. (1991). A review of the short-term effects of child sexual abuse. *Child Abuse & Neglect, 15,* 537–556.

Beitchman, J. H., Zucker, K. J., Hood, J. E., & DaCosta, G. A. (1992). A review of the long-term effects of child sexual abuse. *Child Abuse & Neglect, 16,* 101–118.

Berntsen, D. (2001). Involuntary memories of emotional events: Do memories of traumas and extremely happy events differ? *Applied Cognitive Psychology, 15,* S135–S158.

Berntsen, D., Willert, M., & Rubin, D. C. (2003). Splintered memories or vivid landmarks? Qualities and organization of traumatic memories with and without PTSD. *Applied Cognitive Psychology, 17,* 675–694.

Bjork, R. A. (1972). Theoretical implications of directed forgetting. In A. W. Melton & E. Martin (Eds.), *Coding processes in human memory* (pp. 217–235). New York: Halsted.

Bjork, R. A. (1978). The updating of human memory. In G. H. Bower (Ed.), *The psychology of learning and motivation* (pp. 235–259). New York: Academic.

Bliss, E. L. (1986). *Multiple personality, allied disorders, and hypnosis.* New York: Oxford University Press.

Blume, E. S. (1990). *Secret survivors: Uncovering incest and its aftereffects on women.* New York: Wiley.

Bohanek, J. G., Fivush, R., & Walker, E. (2005). Memories of positive and negative emotional events. *Applied Cognitive Psychology, 19,* 51–66.

Boor, M. (1982). The multiple personality epidemic: Additional cases and inferences regarding diagnosis, etiology, dynamics, and treatment. *Journal of Nervous and Mental Disease, 170,* 302–304.

Bremner, J. D. (2002). *Does stress damage the brain? Understanding trauma-related disorders from a mind-body perspective.* New York: Norton.

Breuer, J. & Freud, S. (1893–5/1953). *Studies on hysteria* (Vol. 2). London: Hogarth.

Brown, D., Scheflin, A. W., & Hammond, D. C. (1998). *Memory, trauma treatment, and the law.* New York: Norton.

Brown, D., Scheflin, A. W., & Whitfield, C. L. (1999). Recovered memories: The current weight of the evidence in science and in the courts. *Journal of Psychiatry & Law, 27,* 5–156.

Butler, S. (1880/1910). *Unconscious memory.* London: A. C. Fifield.

Byrne, C. A., Hyman, I. E., & Scott, K. L. (2001). Comparisons of memories for traumatic events and other experiences. *Applied Cognitive Psychology, 15,* S119–S134.

Cahill, L. & McGaugh, J. L. (1996). Modulation of memory storage. *Current Opinion in Neurobiology, 6,* 237–242.

Cahill, L. & McGaugh, J. L. (1998). Mechanisms of emotional arousal and lasting declarative memory. *Trends in Neurosciences, 21*, 294–299.

Cahill, L., Prins, B., Weber, M., & McGaugh, J. L. (1994). Beta-adrenergic activation and memory for emotional events. *Nature, 371*, 702–704.

Cheit, R. E. (1998). Consider this, skeptics of recovered memory. *Ethics & Behavior, 8*, 141–160.

Cheit, R. E. (1999). Junk skepticism and recovered memory: A reply to Piper. *Ethics & Behavior, 9*, 295–318.

Christianson, S.-Å. (1992). *Handbook of emotion and memory: Research and theory*. Hillsdale, NJ: Erlbaum.

Conway, M. A. (2001). Repression revisited. *Nature, 410*, 319–320.

Corwin, D. L. & Olafson, E. (1997). Videotapes discovery of a reportedly unrecallable memory of child sexual abuse: Comparison with a childhood interview videotapes 11 years before. *Child Maltreatment, 2*, 91–112.

Crews, F. (1995). *The memory wars: Freud's legacy in dispute*. New York: New York Review of Books.

Crews, F. (2004). The trauma trap. *New York Review of Books, 51*, 37–40.

Dawes, R. M. (1993). Prediction of the future versus an understanding of the past: A basic asymmetry. *American Journal of Psychology, 106*, 1–24.

Easterbrook, J. A. (1959). The effect of emotion on cue utilization and the organization of behavior. *Psychological Review, 66*, 183–201.

Eich, E., Macaulay, D., Lowewenstein, R. J., & Dihle, P. H. (1996). Memory, amnesia, and dissociative identity disorder. *Psychological Science, 8*, 417–422.

Ellenberger, H. F. (1970). *The discovery of the unconscious: The history and evolution of dynamic psychiatry*. New York: Basic Books.

Erdelyi, M. H. (1990). Repression, reconstruction, and defense: History and integration of the psychoanalytic and experimental frameworks. In J. L. Singer (Ed.), *Repression and dissociation: Implications for personality, psychopathology, and health* (pp. 1–31). Chicago: University of Chicago Press.

Erdelyi, M. H. & Goldberg, B. (1979). Let's not sweep repression under the rug: Toward a cognitive psychology of repression. In J. F. Kihlstrom & F. J. Evans (Eds.), *Functional disorders of memory*. Hillsdale, NJ: Erlbaum.

Fisher, C. (1945). Amnesic states in war neuroses: The psychogenesis of fugues. *Psychoanalytic Quarterly, 14*, 437–468.

Fredrickson, R. (1992). *Repressed memories: A journey to recovery from sexual abuse*. New York: Simon & Schuster.

Freud, S. (1891/1953). *On aphasia: A critical study*. London: International Universities Press.

Freud, S. (1896/1962). Further remarks on the neuro-psychoses of defence. In J. Strachey (Ed.), *The standard edition of the complete psychological works of Sigmund Freud* (Vol. 3, pp. 159–185). London: Hogarth.

Freud, S. (1914/1957). The history of the psychoanalytic movement. In J. Strachey (Ed.), *The standard edition of the complete psychological works of Sigmund Freud* (Vol. 14, pp. 7–66). London: Hogarth.

Freud, S. (1915/1957). Repression. In J. Strachey (Ed.), *The standard edition of the complete psychological works of Sigmund Freud* (Vol. 14, pp. 146–158). London: Hogarth.

Freyd, J. (1996). *Betrayal trauma: The logic of forgetting childhood abuse.* Cambridge, MA: Harvard University Press.

Freyd, J. J. & Gleaves, D. H. (1996). "Remembering" words not presented in lists: Relevance to the current recovered/false memory controversy. *Journal of Experimental Psychology: Learning, Memory, & Cognition, 22,* 811–813.

Freyd, J. J., Putnam, F. W., Lyon, T. D., Becker-Blease, K. A., Cheit, R. E., Siegel, N. B., et al. (2005). The science of child sexual abuse. *Science, 308,* 501.

Ganaway, G. K. (1995). Hypnosis, childhood trauma, and dissociative identity disorder: Toward an integrative theory. *International Journal of Clinical & Experimental Hypnosis, 43,* 127–144.

Giglio, J. C. (1998). A comment on World War II repression. *Professional Psychology: Research & practice, 29,* 470.

Gleaves, D. H., Smith, S. M., Butler, L. D., & Spiegel, D. (2004). False and recovered memories in the laboratory and clinic: A review of experimental and clinical evidence. *Clinical Psychology: Science & Practice, 11,* 3–28.

Goodman, G. S., Ghetti, S., Quas, J. A., Edelstein, R. S., Alexander, K. W., Redlich, A. D., et al. (2003). A prospective study of memory for child sexual abuse: New findings relevant to the repressed-memory controversy. *Psychological Science, 14,* 113–118.

Grinker, R. R. & Spiegel, J. P. (1943/1945). *Men under stress.* New York: McGraw-Hill.

Harvey, M. R. & Herman, J. L. (1994). Amnesia, partial amnesia, and delayed recall among adult survivors of childhood trauma. *Consciousness & Cognition, 3,* 374–387.

Herbart, J. F. (1816/1881). *A textbook in psychology: An attempt to found the science of psychology on experience, metaphysics, and mathematics.* New York: Appleton.

Herman, J. L. (1981). *Father–daughter incest.* Cambridge, MA: Harvard University Press.

Herman, J. S. & Schatzow, E. (1987). Recovery and verification of memories of childhood sexual trauma. *Psychoanalytic Psychology, 4,* 1–14.

Hilgard, E. R. (1977). *Divided consciousness: Multiple controls in human thought and action.* New York: Wiley.

Holmes, D. S. (1974). Investigations of repression: Differential recall of material experimentally or naturally associated with ego threat. *Psychological Bulletin, 81,* 632–653.

Holmes, D. S. (1990). The evidence for repression: An examination of sixty years of research. In J. L. Singer (Ed.), *Repression and dissociation: Implications for personality, psychopathology, and health* (pp. 85–102). Chicago: University of Chicago Press.

Jacobs, W. J., Laurance, H. E., Thomas, K. G. F., Luzcak, S. E., & Nadel, L. (1996). On the veracity and variability of traumatic memory. *Traumatology, 2,* Article 3.

James, W. (1890/1980). *Principles of psychology.* Cambridge, MA: Harvard University Press.

Janet, P. (1889). *L'Automatisme psychologique; essai de psychologie expérimentale sur les formes inférieures de l'activité humaine [Psychological automatisms].* Paris: Alcan.

Janet, P. (1907). *The major symptoms of hysteria.* New York: Macmillan.

Kardiner, A. & Spiegel, H. (1941/1947). *War stress and neurotic illness* (2nd ed.). New York: Hoeber.

Karon, B. P. & Widener, A. J. (1997). Repressed memories and World War II: Lest we forget! *Professional Psychology: Research & Practice, 28,* 338–340.

Karon, B. P. & Widener, A. J. (1998). Repressed memories: The real story. *Professional Psychology: Research & Practice, 29,* 482–487.

Kendall-Tackett, K. & Marshall, R. (1998). Sexual victimization of children: Incest and child sexual abuse. In R. K. Bergen (Ed.), *Issues in intimate violence* (pp. 47–63). Thousand Oaks, CA: Sage.

Kendall-Tackett, K. A., Williams, L. M., & Finkelhor, D. (1993). Impact of sexual abuse on children: A review and synthesis of recent empirical studies. *Psychological Bulletin, 113*, 164–180.

Kihlstrom, J. F. (1979). Hypnosis and psychopathology: Retrospect and prospect. *Journal of Abnormal Psychology, 88*, 459–473.

Kihlstrom, J. F. (1983). Instructed forgetting: Hypnotic and nonhypnotic. *Journal of Experimental Psychology: General, 112*, 73–79.

Kihlstrom, J. F. (1985). Posthypnotic amnesia and the dissociation of memory. In G. H. Bower (Ed.), *Psychology of learning and motivation* (Vol. 19, pp. 131–178). New York: Academic.

Kihlstrom, J. F. (1992a). Dissociation and dissociations: A comment on consciousness and cognition. *Consciousness & Cognition, 1*, 47–53.

Kihlstrom, J. F. (1992b). Dissociative and conversion disorders. In D. J. Stein & J. Young (Eds.), *Cognitive science and clinical disorders* (pp. 247–270). San Diego: Academic.

Kihlstrom, J. F. (1994). One hundred years of hysteria. In S. J. Lynn & J. W. Rhue (Eds.), *Dissociation: Clinical and theoretical perspectives* (pp. 365–394). New York: Guilford Press.

Kihlstrom, J. F. (1996). The trauma-memory argument and recovered memory therapy. In K. Pezdek & W. P. Banks (Eds.), *The recovered memory/false memory debate* (pp. 297–311). San Diego: Academic.

Kihlstrom, J. F. (1997). Suffering from reminiscences: Exhumed memory, implicit memory, and the return of the repressed. In M. A. Conway (Ed.), *Recovered memories and false memories* (pp. 100–117). Oxford: Oxford University Press.

Kihlstrom, J. F. (1998). Exhumed memory. In S. J. Lynn & K. M. McConkey (Eds.), *Truth in memory* (pp. 3–31). New York: Guilford Press.

Kihlstrom, J. F. (2001). Dissociative disorders. In P. B. Sutker & H. E. Adams (Eds.), *Comprehensive handbook of psychopathology* (3rd ed., pp. 259–276). New York: Plenum.

Kihlstrom, J. F. (2002). No need for repression. *Trends in Cognitive Sciences, 6*, 502.

Kihlstrom, J. F. (2004). An unbalanced balancing act: Blocked, recovered, and false memories in the laboratory and the clinic. *Clinical Psychology: Science & Practice, 11*, 34–41.

Kihlstrom, J. F. (2005). Consciousness in hypnosis. In P. D. Zelazo, M. Moscovich, & E. Thompson (Eds.), *Cambridge handbook of consciousness* (pp. in press). New York: Cambridge University Press.

Kihlstrom, J. F., Eich, E., Sandbrand, D., & Tobias, B. A. (2000). Emotion and memory: Implications for self-report. In A. A. Stone, J. S. Turkkan, C. A. Bachrach, J. B. Jobe, H. S. Kurtzman, & V. S. Cain (Eds.), *The science of self-report: Implications for research and practice* (pp. 81–99). Mahwah, NJ: Erlbaum.

Kihlstrom, J. F. & Evans, F. J. (1979a). *Functional disorders of memory.* Hillsdale, NJ: Erlbaum.

Kihlstrom, J. F. & Evans, F. J. (1979b). Memory retrieval processes in posthypnotic amnesia. In J. F. Kihlstrom & F. J. Evans (Eds.), *Functional disorders of memory* (pp. 179–218). Hillsdale, NJ: Erlbaum.

Kihlstrom, J. F. & McGlynn, S. M. (1991). Experimental research in clinical psychology. In M. Hersen, A. E. Kazdin, & A. S. Bellack (Eds.), *Clinical psychology handbook* (2nd ed., pp. 239–257). New York: Pergamon.

Kihlstrom, J. F. & Schacter, D. L. (2000). Functional amnesia. In F. Boller & J. Grafman (Eds.), *Handbook of neuropsychology* (2nd ed., Vol. 2, pp. 409–427). Amsterdam: Elsevier.

Kihlstrom, J. F., Tataryn, D. J., & Hoyt, I. P. (1993). Dissociative disorders. In P. J. Sutker & H. E. Adams (Eds.), *Comprehensive handbook of psychopathology* (2nd ed., pp. 203–234). New York: Plenum.

Kopelman, M. D. (2002). Psychogenic amnesia. In A. D. Baddeley, M. D. Kopelman, & B. A. Wilson (Eds.), *Handbook of memory disorders* (2nd ed., pp. 451–471). Chichester: Wiley.

Lange, A., DeBeurs, E., Dolan, C., Lchnit, T., Sjollema, S., & Hanewald, G. (1999). Long-term effects of childhood sexual abuse: Objective and subjective characteristics of the abuse and psychopathology in later life. *Journal of Nervous & Mental Disease, 187*, 150–158.

Levy, B. L. & Anderson, M. C. (2002). Inhibitory processes and the control of memory retrieval. *Trends in Cognitive Sciences, 6*, 299–305.

Lilienfeld, S. O. (1998). Repressed memories and World War II: Some cautionary notes. *Professional Psychology: Research & Practice, 29*, 471–475.

Loftus, E. F., Garry, M., & Feldman, J. (1994). Forgetting sexual trauma: What does it mean when 38% forget? *Journal of Consulting & Clinical Psychology, 62*, 1177–1181.

Loftus, E. F. & Guyer, M. J. (2002a). Who abused Jane Doe? Part 1. *Skeptical Inquirer, 26*, 24–32.

Loftus, E. F. & Guyer, M. J. (2002b). Who abused Jane Doe? Part 2. *Skeptical Inquirer, 26*, 37–40.

Lyon, L. S. (1985). Facilitating telephone number recall in a case of psychogenic amnesia. *Journal of Behavior Therapy & Experimental Psychiatry, 16*, 147–149.

McGaugh, J. L. (2004). The amygdala modulates the consolidation of memories of emotionally arousing experiences. *Annual Review of Neuroscience, 27*, 1–28.

Mackinnon, D. W. & Dukes, W. F. (1964). Repression. In L. Postman (Ed.), *Psychology in the making* (pp. 662–744). New York: Knopf.

Macmillan, M. (1991/1997). *Freud evaluated: The completed arc.* Cambridge, MA: MIT Press.

McNally, R. J. (2003). *Remembering trauma.* Cambridge, MA: Harvard University Press.

Markowitsch, H. J. (1999). Functional neuroimaging correlates of functional amnesia. *Memory, 7*, 561–583.

Markowitsch, H. J. (2000). Functional amnesia: The mnestic block syndrome. *Revue de Neuropsychologie, 10*, 175–198.

Masson, J. M. (1984). *The assault on truth: Freud's suppression of the seduction theory.* New York: Farrar, Straus, & Giroux.

Metcalfe, J. & Jacobs, W. J. (1996). A "hot-system/cool-system" view of memory under stress. *PTSD Research Quarterly, 7*, 1–3.

Metcalfe, J. & Jacobs, W. J. (1998). Emotional memory: The effects of stress on "cool" and "hot" memory systems. In D. Medin (Ed.), *The psychology of learning and motivation: Advances in theory and research* (Vol. 38, pp. 187–222). San Diego: Academic.

Metcalfe, J. & Jacobs, W. J. (2000). Can "hot" emotions be captured by "cool" mathematical models? In E. Tulving (Ed.), *Memory, consciousness, and the brain: The Tallinn Conference* (pp. 228–242). Philadelphia: Psychology Press.

Mineka, S. & Kihlstrom, J. F. (1978). Unpredictable and uncontrollable events: A new perspective on experimental neurosis. *Journal of Abnormal Psychology, 87*, 256–271.

Morris, C. D., Bransford, J. P., & Franks, J. J. (1977). Levels of processing versus transfer appropriate processing. *Journal of Verbal Learning & Verbal Behavior, 16*, 519–533.

Nadel, L. & Jacobs, W. J. (1998). Traumatic memory is special. *Current Directions in Psychological Science, 7*, 154–157.

O'Brien, J. T. (1997). The "glucocorticoid cascade" hypothesis in man: Prolonged stress may cause permanent brain damage. *British Journal of Psychiatry, 170*, 199–201.

Payne, J. D., Nadel, L., Britton, W. B., & Jacobs, W. J. (2004). The biopsychology of trauma and memory. In D. Reisberg & P. Hertel (Eds.), *Memory and emotion* (pp. 76–128). New York: Oxford University Press.

Peace, K. A. & Porter, S. (2004). A longitudinal investigation of the reliability of memories for trauma and other emotional experiences. *Applied Cognitive Psychology, 18*, 1143–1159.

Pendergrast, M. (1996). *Victims of memory: Sex abuse accusations and shattered lives* (2nd ed.). Hinesburg, VT: Upper Access.

Pendergrast, M. (1998). Response to Karon and Widener (1997). *Professional Psychology: Research & Practice, 29*, 479–481.

Piper, A. (1998). Repressed memories from World War II: Nothing to forget. Examining Karon and Widener's (1997) claim to have discovered evidence for repression. *Professional Psychology: Research & Practice, 29*, 476–478.

Piper, A. (1999). A skeptic considers, then responds to Cheit. *Ethics & Behavior, 9*, 277–293.

Piper, A., Pope, H. G., & Borowiecki, B. S. (2000). Custer's last stand: Brown, Scheflin, and Whitfield's latest attempt to salvage "dissociative amnesia." *Journal of Psychiatry & Law, 28*, 149–213.

Pope, H. G. & Hudson, J. I. (1995a). Can individuals "repress" memories of childhood sexual abuse? An examination of the evidence. *Psychiatric Annals, 25*, 715–719.

Pope, H. G. & Hudson, J. I. (1995b). Does childhood sexual abuse cause adult psychiatric disorders? Essentials of methodology. *Journal of Psychiatry & Law, 23*, 363–381.

Pope, H. G., Jr., Hudson, J. I., Bodkin, J. A., & Oliva, P. (1998). Questionable validity of "dissociative amnesia" in trauma victims: Evidence from prospective studies. *British Journal of Psychiatry, 172*, 210–215.

Pope, H. G., Oliva, P. S., & Hudson, J. I. (2000). Repressed memories: B. Scientific status. In D. L. Faigman, D. H. Kaye, M. J. Saks, & J. Sanders (Eds.), *Modern scientific evidence: The law and science of expert testimony* (Vol. 1, 2000 Pocket Part, pp. 154–195). St. Paul, MN: West.

Porter, S. & Birt, A. R. (2001). Is traumatic memory special? A comparison of traumatic memory characteristics with memory for other emotional life experiences. *Applied Cognitive Psychology, 15*, S101–S118.

Rapaport, D. (1942). *Emotions and memory*. Baltimore, MD: Williams & Wilkins.

Rind, B. (1998). A meta-analytic examination of assumed properties of child sexual abuse using college samples. *Psychological Bulletin, 124*, 22–53.

Rind, B. (2003). An elaboration on causation and positive cases in child sexual abuse. *Clinical Psychology: Science & Practice, 10*, 352–357.

Ross, C. A. (1986). *Multiple personality disorder: Diagnosis, clinical features, and treatment.* New York: Wiley.

Ryle, G. (1949). *The concept of mind.* London: Hutchinson.

Sapolsky, R. M. (1996). Why stress is bad for your brain. *Science, 273*, 749–750.

Sbraga, T. P. & O'Donohue, W. (2003). Post-hoc reasoning in possible cases of child sexual abuse: Symptoms of inconclusive origins. *Clinical Psychology: Science & Practice, 10*, 320–334.

Scarf, M. (2004). *Secrets, lies, betrayals: The body/mind connection.* New York: Random House.

Schacter, D. L. (1987). Implicit memory: History and current status. *Journal of Experimental Psychology: Learning, Memory, and Cognition, 13*, 501–518.

Schacter, D. L. (2001). Suppression of unwanted memories: Repression revisited? *Lancet, 357*, 1724–1725.

Scheflin, A. W. & Brown, D. (1996). Repressed memory or dissociative amnesia: What the science says. *Journal of Psychiatry & Law, 24*, 143–188.

Schooler, J. W. (2001). Discovering memories of abuse in the light of meta-awareness. *Journal of Aggression, Maltreatment, & Trauma, 4*, 105–136.

Schreiber, F. R. (1973). *Sybil: The true story of a woman possessed by 16 separate personalities.* Chicago: Regnery.

Sears, R. R. (1936). Functional abnormalities of memory with special reference to amnesia. *Psychological Bulletin, 33*, 229–274.

Shobe, K. K. & Kihlstrom, J. F. (1997). Is traumatic memory special? *Current Directions in Psychological Science, 6*, 70–74.

Singer, J. L. (Ed.). (1990). *Repression and dissociation: Implications for personality theory, psychopathology, and health.* Chicago: University of Chicago Press.

Sivers, H., Schooler, J., & Freyd, J. J. (2002). Recovered memories. In V. S. Ramachandran (Ed.), *Encyclopedia of the human brain* (Vol. 4, pp. 169–184). San Diego: Elsevier.

Swets, J. A., Dawes, R. M., & Monahan, J. (2000). Psychological science can improve diagnostic decisions. *Psychological Science in the Public Interest, 1*, 1–26.

Taylor, E. (1999). William James and Sigmund Freud: "The future of psychology belongs to your work." *Psychological Science, 10*, 465–469.

Thigpen, C. H. & Cleckley, H. (1954). A case of multiple personality. *Journal of Abnormal & Social Psychology, 49*, 135–151.

Thigpen, C. H. & Cleckley, H. (1957). *The three faces of Eve* (Vol. 49). New York: Popular Library.

Thigpen, C. H. & Cleckley, H. (1984). On the incidence of multiple personality disorder. *International Journal of Clinical & Experimental Hypnosis, 32*, 63–66.

Thomas, K. G. F., Laurance, H. E., Jacobs, W. J., & Nadel, L. (1995). Traumatic memory and its recovery: Formulating hypotheses and critical experiments. *Traumatology, 1*, Article 3.

Tulving, E. & Thomson, D. M. (1973). Encoding specificity and retrieval processes in episodic memory. *Psychological Review, 80*, 359–380.

van der Kolk, B. A. (1994). The body keeps the score: Memory and the evolving psychobiology of posttraumatic stress. *Harvard Review of Psychiatry, 1*, 253–265.

van der Kolk, B. A. & Fisler, R. E. (1993). The biologic basis of posttraumatic stress. *Family Violence & Abusive Relationships, 20,* 417–432.

van der Kolk, B. A. & Fisler, R. (1995). Dissociation and the fragmentary nature of traumatic memories: Overview and exploratory study. *Journal of Traumatic Stress, 8,* 505–525.

Walker, L. E. (1994). *Abused women and survivor therapy: A practical guide for the psychotherapist.* Washington, DC: American Psychological Association.

Wegner, D. M. (1989). *White bears and other unwanted thoughts: Suppression, obsession, and the psychology of mental control.* New York: Penguin.

Wegner, D. M., Schneider, D. J., Carter, S. R., & White, T. L. (1987). Paradoxical effects of thought suppression. *Journal of Personality and Social Psychology, 53,* 5–13.

Widom, C. S. & Morris, S. (1997). Accuracy of adult recollections of childhood victimization. Part 2: Childhood sexual abuse. *Psychological Assessment, 9,* 34–46.

Williams, L. M. (1994). Recall of childhood trauma: A prospective study of women's memories of child sexual abuse. *Journal of Consulting & Clinical Psychology, 62,* 1167–1178.

Yerkes, R. M. & Dodson, J. D. (1908). The relation of strength of stimulus to rapidity of habit-formation. *Journal of Comparative & Neurological Psychology, 18,* 459–482.

Zeller, A. (1950). An experimental analogue of repression: I. Historical summary. *Psychological Bulletin, 47,* 39–51.

AUTHOR INDEX

SUBJECT INDEX